THE CAMBRIDGE COMPANION TO
JOHN CALVIN

John Calvin (1509–1564) stands with Martin Luther (1483–1546) as the premier theologian of the sixteenth-century Protestant Reformation. Calvin's thought spread throughout Europe to the New World and later throughout the whole world. His insights and influence continue to endure today, presenting a model of theological scholarship grounded in Scripture as well as providing nurture for Christian believers within churches across the globe. Dr Donald K. McKim gathers together an international array of major Calvin scholars to consider phases of Calvin's theological thought and influence. Historians and theologians meet to present a full picture of Calvin's contexts, the major themes in Calvin's writings, and the ways in which his thought spread and has increasing importance. Chapters serve as guide to their topics and provide further readings for additional study. This is an accessible introduction to this significant Protestant reformer and will appeal to the specialist and non-specialist alike.

DONALD K. MCKIM has served as Academic Dean and Professor of Theology at Memphis Theological Seminary and Professor of Theology at the University of Dubuque Theological Seminary, in addition to being a pastor in Presbyterian Church (USA) churches. He is the author and editor of over twenty-five books and currently works as Academic and Reference editor for Westminster John Knox Press.

CAMBRIDGE COMPANIONS TO RELIGION

A series of companions to major topics and key figures in theology and religious studies. Each volume contains specially commissioned chapters by international scholars which provide an accessible and stimulating introduction to the subject for new readers and non-specialists.

*Other titles in the series*

THE CAMBRIDGE COMPANION TO CHRISTIAN DOCTRINE
edited by Colin Gunton (1997)
ISBN 0 521 47118 4 hardback      ISBN 0 521 47695 8 paperback

THE CAMBRIDGE COMPANION TO BIBLICAL INTERPRETATION
edited by John Barton (1998)
ISBN 0 521 48144 9 hardback      ISBN 0 521 48593 2 paperback

THE CAMBRIDGE COMPANION TO DIETRICH BONHOEFFER
edited by John de Gruchy (1999)
ISBN 0 521 58258 x hardback      ISBN 0 521 58751 6 paperback

THE CAMBRIDGE COMPANION TO LIBERATION THEOLOGY
edited by Chris Rowland (1999)
ISBN 0 521 46144 8 hardback      ISBN 0 521 46707 1 paperback

THE CAMBRIDGE COMPANION TO KARL BARTH
edited by John Webster (2000)
ISBN 0 521 58476 0 hardback      ISBN 0 521 58560 0 paperback

THE CAMBRIDGE COMPANION TO CHRISTIAN ETHICS
edited by Robin Gill (2001)
ISBN 0 521 77070 x hardback      ISBN 0 521 77918 9 paperback

THE CAMBRIDGE COMPANION TO JESUS
edited by Markus Bockmuehl (2001)
ISBN 0 521 79261 4 hardback      ISBN 0 521 79678 4 paperback

THE CAMBRIDGE COMPANION TO FEMINIST THEOLOGY
edited by Susan Frank Parsons (2002)
ISBN 0 521 66327 x hardback      ISBN 0 521 66380 6 paperback

THE CAMBRIDGE COMPANION TO MARTIN LUTHER
edited by Donald K. McKim (2003)
ISBN 0 521 81648 3 hardback      ISBN 0 521 01673 8 paperback

THE CAMBRIDGE COMPANION TO ST PAUL
edited by James D. G. Dunn (2003)
ISBN 0 521 78155 8 hardback      ISBN 0 521 78694 0 paperback

THE CAMBRIDGE COMPANION TO POSTMODERN THEOLOGY
edited by Kevin J. Vanhoozer (2003)
ISBN 0 521 79062 x hardback      ISBN 0 521 79395 5 paperback

THE CAMBRIDGE COMPANION TO MEDIEVAL JEWISH PHILOSOPHY
edited by Daniel H. Frank and Oliver Leaman (2003)
ISBN 0 521 65207 3 hardback      ISBN 0 521 65574 9 paperback

THE CAMBRIDGE COMPANION TO JOHN CALVIN
edited by Donald K. McKim (2004)
ISBN 0 521 81647 5 hardback     ISBN 0 521 01672 X paperback

THE CAMBRIDGE COMPANION TO URS VON BALTHASAR
edited by Edward T. Oakes, SJ and David Moss (2004)
ISBN 0 521 81467 7 hardback     ISBN 0 521 89147 7 paperback

THE CAMBRIDGE COMPANION TO REFORMATION THEOLOGY
edited by David Bagchi and David Steinmetz (2004)
ISBN 0 521 77224 9 hardback     ISBN 0 521 77662 7 paperback

THE CAMBRIDGE COMPANION TO AMERICAN JUDAISM
edited by Dana Evan Kaplan (2005)
ISBN 0 521 82204 1 hardback     ISBN 0 521 52951 4 paperback

THE CAMBRIDGE COMPANION TO FRIEDRICH SCHLEIERMACHER
edited by Jacqueline Mariña (2005)

*Forthcoming*

THE CAMBRIDGE COMPANION TO THE GOSPELS
edited by Stephen C. Barton

THE CAMBRIDGE COMPANION TO ISLAMIC THEOLOGY
edited by Tim Winter

THE CAMBRIDGE COMPANION TO EVANGELICAL THEOLOGY
edited by Timothy Larsen and Daniel J. Treier

THE CAMBRIDGE COMPANION TO THE QUR'AN
edited by Jane Dammen McAuliffe

THE CAMBRIDGE COMPANION TO
# JOHN CALVIN

Edited by Donald K. McKim

CAMBRIDGE
UNIVERSITY PRESS

CAMBRIDGE UNIVERSITY PRESS
Cambridge, New York, Melbourne, Madrid, Cape Town, Singapore, São Paulo,
Delhi, Dubai, Tokyo, Mexico City

Cambridge University Press
The Edinburgh Building, Cambridge CB2 8RU, UK

Published in the United States of America by Cambridge University Press, New York

www.cambridge.org
Information on this title: www.cambridge.org/9780521016728

First published 2004
4th printing 2010

Printed in the United Kingdom at the University Press, Cambridge

*A catalogue record for this publication is available from the British Library*

*Library of Congress Cataloguing in Publication data*
The Cambridge companion to John Calvin / edited by Donald K. McKim.
    p.   cm. – (Cambridge companions to religion)
Includes bibliographical references and index.
ISBN 0 521 81647 5 – ISBN 0 521 01672 X
1. Calvin, John, 1509–1564.   I. McKim, Donald K.   II. Series.
BX9418.C386   2004
230′.42′092 – dc22   2003063362

ISBN 978 0 521 81647 2 Hardback
ISBN 978 0 521 01672 8 Paperback

# Contents

# Notes on contributors

**Joel R. Beeke** is President and Professor of Systematic Theology and Homiletics at Puritan Reformed Theological Seminary, pastor of the Heritage Netherlands Reformed Congregation in Grand Rapids, Michigan, and editor of *Banner of Sovereign Grace Truth*. He is the author of *Assurance of Faith: Calvin, English Puritanism, and the Dutch Second Reformation*.

**Wulfert de Greef** heads an organization promoting Reformation studies in the Netherlands. He is the author of *The Writings of John Calvin: An Introductory Guide*.

**Dawn DeVries** is John Newton Thomas Professor of Systematic Theology at Union Theological Seminary and the Presbyterian School of Christian Education in Richmond, Virginia. She is the author of *Jesus Christ in the Preaching of Calvin and Schleiermacher*.

**Jane Dempsey Douglass** is Hazel Thompson McCord Professor of Historical Theology, Emerita at Princeton Theological Seminary. She is author of *Women, Freedom and Calvin*.

**Paul Fields** is Librarian at Calvin College and Seminary, Grand Rapids, Michigan and a member of the International Congress for Calvin Research.

**Richard C. Gamble** is Professor of Systematic Theology at the Reformed Theological Seminary, Oviedo, Florida. He is the editor of *Articles on Calvin and Calvinism*.

**Alexandre Ganoczy** is Professor Emeritus at the University of Würzburg, Germany. Among his writings is *The Young Calvin*.

**B. A. Gerrish** is John Nuveen Professor, Emeritus at the University of Chicago. Among his many books is *Grace and Gratitude: The Eucharistic Theology of John Calvin*.

**Guenther H. Haas** is Associate Professor in the Religion and Theology Department at Redeemer College, Ancaster, Ontario, Canada. He has written *The Concept of Equity in Calvin's Ethics*.

**I. John Hesselink** is Albertus C. Van Raalte Professor of Systematic Theology, Emeritus at Western Theological Seminary. Among his books is *Calvin's First Catechism: A Commentary*.

**R. Ward Holder** is Assistant Professor of Theology at St. Anselm College, Manchester, New Hampshire and a member of the International Congress for Calvin Research.

**Karin Maag** is Director of the H. Henry Meeter Center for Calvin Studies at Calvin College and Seminary. Among her books is *Seminary or University?: The Genevan Academy and Higher Reformed Education 1560–1620*.

**William G. Naphy** is Head of the Department of History/Director of Teaching, School of History and History of Art, King's College, the University of Aberdeen, Scotland. He has written *Calvin and the Consolidation of the Genevan Reformation*.

**Jeannine E. Olson** is Professor of History at Rhode Island College, Providence, Rhode Island. Among her books is *Calvin and Social Welfare: Deacons and the Bourse française*.

**Andrew Pettegree** is Professor of Modern History at the University of St Andrews, Scotland. Among his many books is *Europe in the Sixteenth Century*.

**William R. Stevenson, Jr.** is Professor of Political Science at Calvin College, Grand Rapids, Michigan. He has written *Sovereign Grace: The Place and Significance of Christian Freedom in John Calvin's Political Thought*.

**John L. Thompson** is Professor of Historical Theology at Fuller Theological Seminary. He is the author of *Writing the Wrongs: Women of the Old Testament among Biblical Commentators from Philo through the Reformation*.

**Carl R. Trueman** is Associate Professor of Church History and Historical Theological Theology at Westminster Theological Seminary, Chestnut Hill, Pennsylvania. He is the author of *The Claims of Truth: John Owen's Trinitarian Theology*.

**David F. Wright** is Professor of Patristic and Reformed Christianity at New College of the University of Edinburgh, Scotland. He is the editor of *Martin Bucer: Reforming Church and Community*.

# Preface

John Calvin (1509–1564) stands with Martin Luther (1483–1546) as the premier theologian of the sixteenth-century Protestant Reformation. Like his older contemporary, Calvin was concerned with the reform of the Christian church and with understanding the message of the Holy Scriptures as the Word of God. Calvin's thought spread throughout Europe to the New World and later throughout the whole world. His followers, in various ways, have allied themselves with his theological understandings or developed and modified them according to the needs of their times and places. Today, Calvin's insights and influence continue to endure, presenting a model of theological scholarship grounded in Scripture as well as providing nurture for Christian believers within churches across the globe. The reach of Calvin's thought has been extensive, pervading not only Christian theology, but also such arenas as biblical interpretation, Christian spirituality, and social ethics. Historically and intellectually, Calvin's labors have had lasting significance.

This *Companion* introduces the life and work of John Calvin. The writers here are Calvin specialists who are eminently suited to discuss their topics. Their essays are oriented toward students and those with little or no background in Calvin studies. But scholars will also find their pieces eminently suggestive and helpful. Together they constitute an introduction and an overview of the significant Genevan reformer.

Calvin's life and context are considered in the Part I of this book. The two opening essays survey Calvin's experiences and the city of Geneva where most of his work was carried out. These perspectives are important for understanding who Calvin was and the environment in which he lived and ministered. They orient us with insights on the formative influences that shaped his life journey.

Part II considers Calvin's wide-ranging work. Here the scope of his writings is examined as well as his practice as a biblical interpreter, an aspect of Calvin's activities which continues to bring insights today. Calvin's theology is explored here as it developed, consideration being given to its main themes and to the theological topics to which it contributed. Since Calvin's theological thought is tightly linked to his ethical insights these are also discussed as an important dimension for understanding Calvin. One of Calvin's primary duties was preaching which he did numerous times per week, so Calvin's work in this dimension of his ministry is also considered, both in terms of his theological understanding of the nature of preaching and his preaching practices as well.

Despite the rigors of his theology, Calvin's writings also provide a rich sense of devotion to God and personal appropriation of the Christian gospel. So Calvin's piety is presented here to highlight this aspect of the reformer's writings. Yet Calvin's was not an "inward-looking spirituality." Instead, his theology and his faith catapulted him into the midst of social-ethical issues as he played an important role in the public life of the city of Geneva. His views on the nature of church and state took on a key place in his work with the city government and as a pastor and teacher. His developing theological views also propelled him into prominent roles in dealing with controversies of his day which for him and his contemporaries were often life and death matters. Essays emphasizing these elements are found in this section as well.

Part III of this volume is entitled "After Calvin." The essays here relate to how Calvin's thought spread, initially through Europe, and then beyond. This is the focus of the first piece in the section. Theologically, followers of Calvin became known as Calvinists. An essay in this section considers the theological developments fostered by those who looked to Calvin for essential directions but then modified and developed his thought in light of the contexts and controversies they faced as "Calvinism" grew in prominence. The worldwide spread of Calvin's heritage is considered here as well. This essay demonstrates the wide reach and expanse of Calvin's influence among theologians and churches throughout the world.

It should not be thought that Calvin's emphases and thought spread and then disappeared. In "Calvin Today," Part IV, scholars consider Calvin's role in church history, his place in Christian theology, and Calvin in today's ecumenical context. Here we see how churches who look to Calvin as one who set basic trajectories for theology (often called "Reformed" theology – and churches, often called "Reformed" churches) continue to find nourishment in his work and how these churches have worked in the ecumenical settings of Christian churches worldwide. The final essay in the volume acquaints readers with the numerous significant resources for studying Calvin's thought today. These tools will provide appropriate next steps for those who have found the preceding essays springboards toward further Calvin study.

This volume was aided immensely by the support and kind advice of Kevin Taylor of Cambridge University Press. Kevin's help has been very important and our friendship is much valued. His fine assistant, Gillian Dadd, also provided splendid support and good humor along the way. Kate Brett, Senior Commissioning Editor for Religious Studies at the Press, who took over Kevin's duties, has been patient and kind in the final stages of the work, a delightful person with whom to work. I would also like to thank Joanne Hill for her splendid copy-editing work on this volume.

This book, as all other of my writings, is presented with deepest gratitude for my family, LindaJo, Stephen, and Karl McKim. Their love and support means everything to me. Through this work, I give back to them in a small way a measure of the joy they have given me through the years and continue to provide.

It is appropriate to dedicate this book to three persons who have helped my own studies of Calvin through the years. My former pastor, John E. Karnes, secured my first copy of Calvin's *Institutes* thirty-five years ago and introduced me to Calvin's theology. At Westminster College I studied Calvin with Jack Rogers, a delightful experience with a master teacher and wonderful friend. My teacher at Pittsburgh Seminary was Ford Lewis Battles, a Calvin scholar without peer, and for whose support of my work I'll always be deeply grateful.

DONALD K. MCKIM
*July 10, 2003*
*494th anniversary of the birth of John Calvin*

# Chronology of John Calvin

| 1509 | Born in Noyon, Picardy, France |
| 1521 | Receives first benefice |
| 1523–1527 | University of Paris |
| 1528–1529 | University of Orléans |
| 1529–1531 | University of Bourges |
| 1531–1533 | In Paris and Orléans |
| 1532 | Publishes *Commentary on Seneca's* De Clementia |
| 1533 | Nicholas Cop's Address |
| 1534 | In Paris, Angoulême, and Noyon; resigns benefices |
| 1534 | To Basle |
| 1535 | First edition of the *Institutes* published in Latin (6 chapters) |
| 1536–1538 | Pastor in Geneva until expelled |
| 1538–1541 | Pastor of French refugees in Strasbourg |
| 1539 | Second edition of the *Institutes* published in Latin (17 chapters) |
| 1541–1564 | Return and ministry in Geneva |
| 1541 | Edition of the *Institutes* in French |
| 1543 | Edition of the *Institutes* in Latin (21 chapters) |
| 1545 | Sabastian Castellio banished from Geneva |
| 1551 | Bolsec Controversy |
| 1555 | Michael Servetus executed |
| 1559 | Final Latin edition of the *Institutes* published (80 chapters) |
| 1560 | Final French edition of the *Institutes* published |
| 1564 | Dies in Geneva and buried in unmarked grave |

# Selected English language sources

## CALVIN'S WRITINGS

*The Bondage of and Liberation of the Will: A Defence of the Orthodox Doctrine of Human Choice against Pighius*. Ed. A. N. S. Lane, trans. G. I. Davies. Texts and Studies in Reformation and Post-Reformation Thought, 2. Grand Rapids: Baker, 1996.

*Calvin: Institutes of the Christian Religion*. Ed. John T. McNeill, trans. Ford Lewis Battles. Library of Christian Classics. vols. XX and XXI. Philadelphia: Westminster Press, 1960. (This is the 1559 edition of Calvin's *Institutes*.)

*Calvin's Commentaries*. 47 vols., rpt. of the Edinburgh edition (various editors and translators). Grand Rapids: Eerdmans, 1948–50.

*Calvin's Commentary on Seneca's De Clementia*. Ed. and trans. Ford Lewis Battles and André Malan Hugo. Leiden: E. J. Brill, 1969.

*Calvin's Ecclesiastical Advice*. Trans. Mary Beaty and Benjamin W. Farley. Louisville: Westminster John Knox Press, 1991.

*Calvin's New Testament Commentaries*, 12 vols. Ed. David W. Torrance and Thomas T. Torrance (various translators). Edinburgh: Saint Andrew Press; Grand Rapids: Eerdmans, 1959–72.

*Concerning the Eternal Predestination of God*. Trans. J. K. S. Reid. Rpt. Louisville: Westminster John Knox Press, 1997.

*Daniel I: Chapters 1–6*. Trans. T. H. L. Parker. Calvin's Old Testament Commentaries. The Rutherford House Translation. Ed. D. F. Wright. Grand Rapids: Eerdmans, 1993.

*Ezekiel I: Chapters 1–12*. Trans. David Foxgrover and Donald Martin. The Rutherford House Translation. Ed. D. F. Wright. Grand Rapids: Eerdmans, 1994.

*Institution of the Christian Religion Embracing almost the whole sum of piety, & whatever is necessary to know of the doctrine of salvation: A work most worthy to be read by all persons zealous for piety, and recently published*. Trans. Ford Lewis Battles. Atlanta: John Knox Press, 1975.

Revised edition published as *Institutes of the Christian Religion 1536 Edition*. Grand Rapids: Eerdmans, 1986. (This is the 1536 edition of Calvin's *Institutes*.)

*Instruction in Faith (1537)*. Ed. and trans. Paul T. Fuhrmann. Philadelphia: Westminster Press, 1949; Louisville: Westminster John Knox Press, 1992.

*John Calvin's Sermons on the Ten Commandments*. Ed. and trans. Benjamin W. Farley, Grand Rapids: Baker, 1980.

*A Reformation Debate: Sadoleto's Letter to the Genevans and Calvin's Reply*. Ed. John C. Olin. New York, 1966; rpt., Grand Rapids: Baker, 1976.

*Selected Works of John Calvin: Tracts and Letters*. 7 vols. Ed. Henry Beveridge and Jules Bonnet, trans. Henry Beveridge, David Constable, and M. R. Gilchrist, 1849; rpt., Grand Rapids: Baker, 1983.

*Sermons on the Book of Micah*. Ed. and trans. Benjamin W. Farley. Phillipsburg, NJ: P&R Publishing, 2003.

*Treatises Against the Anabaptists and Against the Libertines*. Ed. and trans. Benjamin Wirt Farley. Grand Rapids: Baker, 1982.

## OTHER RESOURCES

Battles, Ford Lewis assisted by John R. Walchenbach, *Analysis of the Institutes of the Christian Religion of John Calvin*. Rpt. Phillipsburg, NJ: P&R Publishing, 2001.

McKim, Donald K., ed., *Calvin's Institutes: Abridged Edition*. Louisville: Westminster John Knox Press, 2001.

# Abbreviations

BC      *Bibliotheca Calviniana: les oeuvres de Jean Calvin publiés au xvie siècle.* Ed. Rodolphe Peter and Jean-François Gilmont. 3 vols. Travaux d'humanisme et Renaissance, no. 255, etc. Geneva: Librairie Droz, 1991–.

CO      *Ioannis Calvini opera quae supersunt omnia.* Ed. G. [Wilhelm] Baum, E. Cunitz, and E. Reuss. 59 vols. bound in 31. *Corpus Reformatorum,* vols. 29–87. Brunswick: C. A. Schwetschke and Son, 1863–1900.

Inst.      *Institutes of the Christian Religion.*

OC      *Ioannis Calvini opera omnia.* Series 2: *Opera exegetica.* Geneva: Droz, 1998–. Series 3: *Scripta ecclesiastica.* Geneva: Droz, 1991–.

OS      *Ioannis Calvini opera selecta.* Ed. Peter Barth, Wilhelm Niesel, and Dora Scheuner. 5 vols. Munich: C. Kaiser, 1926–52.

SC      *Supplementa Calviniana. Sermons inédits.* Ed. Erwin Mülhaupt et al. Neukirchen: Neukirchener Verlag, 1936–61.

T&T      *Tracts and Treatises.* Trans. Henry Beveridge. 3 vols. Grand Rapids: Eerdmans, 1959.

TT      *Calvin: Theological Treatises.* Trans. with Introduction and notes by John K. S. Reid. Library of Christian Classics. Philadelphia: Westminster Press, 1954.

# Part I

*Calvin's Life and Context*

# 1  Calvin's life

ALEXANDRE GANOCZY

TRANSLATED BY DAVID L. FOXGROVER

AND JAMES SCHMITT

Calvin was born on July 10, 1509, in Picardy in northern France, farm country marked by strong religious and ecclesiastical ties. His birthplace, Noyon, along with Amiens, Beauvais, Laon, and Senlis, belonged to the cathedral cities of this province, rich in tradition, which also possessed important abbeys such as Corbie and Péronne. The Picards made up one of the four recognized "nations" among the students of the University of Paris, and Calvin was proud throughout his life to belong to this elite. Even his character largely matched the "Picardian": intelligent, logical, sensibly diligent, morally serious, and devoted to freedom and order – as well as overly sensitive, self-confident, and irritable. At the time of his birth, both a religiosity bordering on mysticism and a growing openness to humanist ideas were determining the spiritual climate of the land. *"spiritual"*

Calvin's father was a financial administrator of the cathedral chapter of Noyon. His mother, who died early, was a truly humble woman about *religious influence* whom little is known other than her zeal for pilgrimages. Calvin had four brothers and two sisters, most of whom are later found in the reform camp. Calvin admired his somewhat authoritarian father and profited from this aspiring man who tried to raise himself from a humble background to moving in educated circles, even that of the elegant family of de Hangest-Genlis. According to his father's wishes, John was intended to become a priest. His studies were financed by generous ecclesiastical benefices that soon made it possible for him to enjoy instruction in famous Parisian schools.

The spiritual atmosphere of the capital city was largely determined by the wavering political course of the king, Francis I. In 1515, Francis had attained from Pope Leo X the right of nominating all bishops. That brought, at least in principle, a close interaction between the ruler and the Catholic Church. On the other hand, this *roi très catholique* ("most Catholic King") supported the Protestant forces in Germany in order to weaken the power of Emperor Charles V. At home, Francis vacillated between supporting conservative representatives of the church, such as the teachers of the Faculty of Theology, and humanists eager for reform, such as Erasmus, Lefèvre

*conservative vs. liberal*

d'Etaples, the "circle of Meaux" around Bishop Briçonnet, his own sister Marguerite of Navarre, as well as the teachers of the *Collège Royal*. The *Collège*, which had been founded by Francis, represented a strong counterbalance to the inquisitorial authority of the Sorbonne and even showed an appreciation of Luther. Despite the subsequent condemnation in 1521 by the Faculty of Theology (or more precisely the Sorbonne) of 104 Lutheran teachings, the Catholic reform party for years did not retract in any way its sympathy for the German reformer.

In 1513, in accordance with his father's decision, the fourteen-year-old Calvin went to Paris: first, to the *Collège de la Marche* where he was educated under the direction of the great and deeply religious pedagogue Marthurin Cordier; then, after a few months, to the *Collège Montaigu* where he studied the liberal arts for four years in preparation for a priestly vocation. Cordier conveyed to Calvin a piety centered on the person of Christ in the spirit of the *devotio moderna* and on the foundation of a contemporary teaching method. In 1550 Calvin dedicated a biblical commentary to Cordier and in 1562 obtained a position at the Genevan Latin School for him. By contrast, Calvin had few good memories of the *Collège Montaigu*.

At Montaigu not only did an overly strict discipline hold sway under the direction of Noël Bédier and Pierre Tempête, but there was also a narrow-minded and hair-splitting orthodoxy. This was consistent with the attitude responsible for several death penalties against alleged or real supporters of Luther, for example, against the Augustinian monk Jean Vallière, who was burned alive in 1523, the year Calvin came to Paris. This inquisitorial activity originated in the theological faculty of the Sorbonne and exerted great influence on other anti-reformers besides Bédier. In 1525 even the Scottish philosopher and theologian John Major, who was formerly conciliatory about criticizing the pope, emerged as an opponent of Luther. At the same time, a heresy trial against Bishop Briçonnet of Meaux was initiated, and a biblical commentary by Lefèvre d'Etaples, who subsequently moved to Strasbourg, was banned. The year 1526 saw an intense battle unleashed between Erasmus and Bédier – and more funeral pyres flared up.

Under these circumstances, Calvin studied the liberal arts (but probably not scholastic theology) behind the protective walls of Montaigu. No document allows the historian to conjecture about any reactions from the fourteen- to eighteen-year-old to these events. We are much better informed about what happened after 1528, when Calvin moved to Orléans. He moved at the behest of his father who, after a falling out with the cathedral chapter of Noyon, decided John would pursue the career of a lawyer instead of a cleric. The son obeyed. He became a zealous student of the famous jurist Pierre de l'Estoile who was also the Vicar General of the diocese of Orléans.

In this capacity de l'Estoile played a significant role in 1528 in the provincial synod of Sens, where measures were inititated in both internal church reform and in opposition to Luther.

How did Calvin react to the activities of de l'Estoile? Most likely he responded with great discernment. On one hand, the documents clearly point out Calvin's openness to the renewal movement in the church initiated by Luther and, in particular, by the humanists in France, where Calvin sided with his relative Pierre Robert Olivétan, with whom he had already made contact in Paris. We can surmise that both Calvin and Olivétan watched closely the reform represented by Erasmus and Lefèvre, and they were sympathetic to the basic intentions and even the individual theses of the German reformer. Olivétan pursued his biblical studies, we assume, even more intensely than his legal subjects with the result that he was able to produce his own independent translation of the Bible into French in 1535. Calvin wrote two forewords to this translation in which explicit anti-Roman emphases are readily found.

But in 1528, matters had not yet gone that far. Calvin was still searching and struggling to reconcile humanist reform with loyalty to his teachers who were very faithful to the church. In these circumstances, probably in the year 1529, Calvin wrote a foreword to the *Antapologia* that one of his friends, Nicolas Duchemin, was to publish in 1531 in defense of Pierre de l'Estoile against the attacks of the Italian professor of law, Andrea Alciati. In this writing of Calvin, one searches in vain for any polemical utterances against the Roman Church. Furthermore, Calvin maintained friendly relationships with men such as François Daniel and François de Connan, who would become no more Lutheran than Duchemin. Regarding the influence of Melchior Wolmar, the teacher of Greek in Wuertemberg who worked in Orléans and apparently was a supporter of Luther, he appears to be similar to Olivétan. Calvin exchanged ideas with him and enjoyed listening to him. But for years Calvin's statements divulge nothing about accepting their reform views as his own. It is not until his writings of 1535 that there is clear evidence of a turning-point.

In 1530, the Faculty of Theology began a general offensive against several suspected teachers of Lutheranism, such as the Hellenists Guillaume Budé and Pierre Danes, as well as the Hebraist François Vatable – all of them teachers at the *Collège Royal*. They were "guilty" of being convinced that a deeper scientific knowledge of the original biblical languages was essential for a correct interpretation of Scripture. The Vulgate, the Latin translation, was inadequate. Moreover, Bédier attacked "secret Lutherans" – he meant Erasmus among others. But a welcome counter-balance for the accused was the equally influential sister of the king, Marguerite of Navarre. Academic freedom at the University of Bourges, where Calvin moved in 1530, was due to her protection.

But Calvin did not remain in Bourges for long. In March 1531 he set out on a dangerous journey to Paris to take care of the printing of Duchemin's *Antapologia*. There he learned that his father was seriously ill. He went to Noyon as quickly as possible to be at his father's side during his last days. Gérard Calvin died in the state of excommunication imposed on him by the cathedral chapter two years earlier because of a questionable financial matter. The family was forced to carry out humiliating negotiations with the cathedral officials to make a church burial for the deceased possible. Once more Calvin experienced the inflexible conduct of clergy who were scarcely able to differentiate between worldly and spiritual power.

At that time Calvin himself defended the notions of freedom of conscience for the Christian and of tolerance as a special virtue of rulers. The first view is evident in his letter, dated June 23, 1531, to Daniel; the second in 1532, in his first published work, a commentary on Seneca's treatise *De Clementia (On Clemency)*. In the letter just mentioned Calvin relates that he had visited Daniel's young sister in her convent shortly before she took her vows and respectfully admonished her that the fulfillment of her commitment was to be attained more by God's grace than by her own willpower. Inner freedom and joy are mentioned here, not a fundamental rejection of vows or life in a cloister. In the Seneca commentary, which Calvin dedicated to Claude de Hangest, abbot of St-Eloi in Noyon, the young jurist unfolded a theory of moderation and tolerance that every ruler – the Stoic as well as the Christian – should exercise in fulfilling his office. He is indeed the servant of the merciful God to assure order and general welfare in society. It is also interesting that there is no direct allusion in this writing to the persecution of the "Lutheran sects" which the French king permitted or even incited.

The conviction that both state and church need a ruling authority deserving of respect is clearly discernible from time to time in all the ecclesiastical and political statements of Calvin's life. This also explains why Calvin detected very early in the so-called "free church" movement of the Anabaptists a deadly danger to the unity of the church and the authenticity of Christianity. A person who, like these "sectarians" or "fanatics" (as Luther called them), gives preference to individual spiritual experience or enlightenment over the church's interpretation of the Bible will also give free rein to arbitrary theologies. An example is the teaching of "soul sleep" after death instead of believing that the deceased are with Christ and that the faithful will rise again. In his work *Psychopannychia (On Soul Sleep)*, written in 1534, Calvin argues against such a misunderstanding of the Christ-centeredness of our religion and in favor of the traditional belief in the resurrection. Calvin offers not only extensive knowledge of the Old and New Testaments (277 quotes in a booklet of only fifty-one pages!), but also arguments from the great expositors of the Bible such as Irenaeus, Tertullian, and Augustine. The learned jurist shows himself to be a confident theologian and controversialist, which he had become not by attending schools of higher learning, but by private study and reading the sources.

In the meantime, the "Sorbonnists'" harsh war of attrition against the remaining fortresses of humanist reform continued, clearly with growing success. The reform party had seemed to gain the upper hand in 1533. Gérard Roussel was permitted to preach in the king's court. Bédier called Roussel's religious orthodoxy into doubt, but he had to leave at the behest of the bishop of Paris, Jean du Bellay. The new rector of the University, Nicholas Cop, successfully defended the Queen of Navarre when her booklet, *Miroir de l'âme pécheresse* (*Mirror of a Sinful Soul*), was censored by conservative theologians and her character ridiculed by rebellious students. The letters of Calvin stemming from this time show solidarity with Marguerite, Roussel, and Cop – and also with Guillaume Petit, bishop of Senlis, who likewise affirmed the religious orthodoxy of the queen's group of humanists.

A significant incident occurred after the events following a speech the rector, Cop, made on the Feast of All Saints in 1533 at the opening of the academic year. Cop was a physician; however, his speech had a spiritual and theological character. It contained Erasmian thoughts on a Christian philosophy of life, Luther's theme of law and gospel, and, finally, the teaching of the justification of the sinner "through faith without works of the law." The speech began with praise of Mary, the Mother of the Lord and the most perfect of all creatures. Then followed an explanation of the Beatitudes of the Sermon on the Mount according to Matthew, with special emphasis on the lines: "Blessed are you when you are cursed and persecuted because of me . . ." Cop included an explicit rejection of the accusation that those fellow Christians who sincerely want to obey the gospel are heretics.

Who was behind this speech? Scholarly opinions differ. Some attribute to Calvin merely an advisory role; others think that Calvin wrote the speech himself; and others attribute to Cop, the Erasmian physician, a time of private study and a competence in theology similar to the young jurist. One thing is certain: Calvin felt solidarity with Cop and was able to affirm his statements. At any rate, the reaction of the opposition affected Calvin exactly as it did the university rector: both found themselves in that constantly shifting middle ground of loyalty to the church and a desire for reform. In the eyes of the Sorbonne occupying middle ground still meant schism and heresy. This radically conservative group was successful in regaining the confidence of the king by December, 1533. He ordered the extermination of the "damned Lutheran sects."

Calvin found shelter with the well-to-do Louis du Tillet, canon of Angoulême and rector of Claix. Thanks to this friend's hospitality and his extensive theological library, the future reformer enjoyed the leisure needed to continue his private studies for about five months. He read the church fathers along with the Bible. He gladly accepted material help from a churchman like du Tillet, while denouncing the income he had drawn since childhood for a completely fictitious Noyon pastorate. Presumably, Calvin saw in the canon of the Cathedral of Angoulême a kind of patron or benefactor for the studies that he carried out in the service of evangelical renewal.

Soon, however, Calvin left Claix – this "quiet nest" as he put it – and set out, according to his earliest biographers, for Paris and Orléans, apparently to become more familiar with the teachings of the Anabaptists. This allowed him to test the correctness of the faith of a young man – Calvin referred to him as "brother" – who was suspected of Anabaptism, and then to re- commend him as an irreproachable Christian in a letter to Martin Bucer, the "bishop" of the already evangelical Strasbourg. This letter testifies not only that our self-taught theologian already considered himself capable of passing judgment on matters of orthodoxy and heterodoxy, but also that he harbored no sense of inferiority towards such a famous man as the reformer of Strasbourg.

In October, 1534, a crisis affecting church and state erupted. When Antoine Marcourt, a preacher from Neuchâtel who sympathized with Luther, initiated blatant attacks against the sacrifice of the Mass and publi- cized them in the form of placards, the men of the Sorbonne and Parliament urged the king to take up the harshest measures of punishment. Even such an upright reformer as Guillaume Budé decidedly rejected Marcourt's dog- matic aggression. Thus there came a new wave of persecution, with impris- onments and executions. Calvin found himself forced to leave France. In January, 1535, he met with du Tillet and Cop in evangelical Basle.

There existed in Basle at that time a healthy pluralism in matters of faith regarding reform. Erasmus lived there in seclusion. Oswald Myconius, a former colleague of Zwingli, led the community that between 1523 and 1531 received a well-structured and balanced reform of its church order under the direction of the monk Johannes Oeclampadius, who had become a Lutheran. Myconius wrote a corresponding profession of faith in 1534, but sought to gain its acceptance in an ecumenical spirit. He intended to mediate between the positions of Lutherans and Zwinglians – and Erasmians, too. Calvin preferred the theology of Luther during his stay in Basle. It was Luther's theology, more than all other sources (Melanchthon, Zwingli, Bucer) that inspired the first edition of his *Christianae Religionis Institutio* (*Institutes of the Christian Religion*), which came off the press in Basle in 1536.

One can only marvel at how quickly this theological compendium – a kind of expanded catechism for educated adults – was written. Even more admirable is the biblical, patristic, and reformed theological documentation, as well as the treatment of sources chosen according to a specific viewpoint. Among these sources are, above all, both of Luther's catechisms and his treatises on *The Freedom of the Christian* and *The Babylonian Captivity*. The *Institutes* was immediately a bestseller. It went through numerous, expanded editions in Latin (1539, 1543, 1550, 1553, 1559) and French (1541, 1545, 1551, 1560). The final Latin edition was five times larger than the first.

For the Foreword to the 1536 *Institutes*, Calvin wrote an open letter to the French king, which was a definite testimony to his reform faith and likewise a defense of the "party of the gospel" against the accusations of being Anabaptist, heretical, schismatic, and politically rebellious. Thus the entire work had a clearly anti-Roman emphasis and contained pronouncements critical of the papacy. Along with Calvin's contemporaneous Forewords to Olivétan's translation of the Bible and his own commentary on the letter to the Romans, this open letter may be considered the first indisputable proof of Calvin's complete turn to reform.

People everywhere like to label this turn a "conversion," mostly in the modern, confessional, sense of the word. Nevertheless, as the documents of the time clearly show, Calvin himself did not understand "conversion" in this modern sense, but rather in the biblical sense of "repentance," i.e., the fundamental penitential act of the believer. In the texts mentioned above, everything indicates that the young Calvin by no means intended to join a new church community opposed to the Catholic Church, but rather to "re-form" the one church of Christ in the spirit of the gospel. Inasmuch as the truth of the gospel had been "de-formed" – distorted – under the very exacting rule of the papacy, the entire demoralized church community should be "converted" itself, repent, and, in the footsteps of the church of the first five centuries, return to the God of Jesus Christ. That is quite different than an individual going from one "denomination" to another.

It is true that in 1557 the mature Calvin designated his turn to reform as a *subita conversio*, a "sudden conversion." However, the wider context of this statement shows that Calvin understood his life story as analogous to that of the Apostle Paul, who on his way to Damascus suddenly turned from the sin of opposing Christ to unconditionally serving Christ. In reality, a comparable turn for Calvin took place gradually over several years. However, this view is not incompatible with Calvin's statement of 1557, which, because of its literary context, is much more theological and confessional in meaning than autobiographical.

Furthermore, nothing in Calvin's writings allows us to recognize the concern for dating one's personal "conversion" that was so characteristic of later Pietists. Clearly, the young Calvin was more concerned about his gradually discovered "calling" (*vocatio*) to reform the church than about a confessional change in the individual in the modern sense of the concept.

The successful formulation of reform theology soon led to a corresponding praxis. Guillaume Farel, who had led the reform in Geneva with the help of the city council and in part through the use of force as well, felt overwhelmed by the emerging chaos. He pleaded with the now famous Calvin to stand at his side in the difficult work of leading the community. Farel pressured him with really overwhelming arguments: if Calvin did not accept Farel's summons, he would be cursed by God. After some hesitation, Calvin agreed and took the office in Geneva of "reader" (*lector*) of Holy Scripture. Calvin began his activity with lectures on the letters of Paul. He also participated in the Lausanne Disputation in October, 1536, between reform theologians and those faithful to Rome. The latter must have felt defeated when Calvin, quoting patristic texts from memory, refuted the allegation that the "evangelicals" disregarded the teaching of the church fathers about the Last Supper.

The reputation of the young man from Noyon, whose theological and legal knowledge – as well as his gift for controversy – had proven highly useful to the reform camp, continued to grow. Bucer wrote in a friendly way that he wanted to meet him and would leave it to him to choose the proper place. Calvin did not react with false modesty, even less with the subservience that many laymen tended to show priests and bishops even after they turned to the "gospel." To be sure, the author of the *Institutes* esteemed the episcopacy as an important ministry for leading the church. This is the sense in which he addressed Bucer himself as "Bishop of Strasbourg" and congratulated Gerard Roussel for his ordination as bishop of Oléron, even though his old friend remained in the Roman camp.

On the other hand, Calvin was able to see that the sacrament of ordination – especially as it was connected at the time one-sidedly to the priestly function of sacrifice – was not an indispensable requirement for serving God's Word and leading the community. Calvin himself never wanted to be an ordained pastor, even though he knew he was called to the pastoral office through the Word and sacrament as the content of his reform activities. This interpretation is also consistent with the theological viewpoint that distinguishes all the writings of Calvin: the exact determination of the ontological status of a person or a thing is not crucial, but rather its function under the working of God's Spirit is key. The reformer's position regarding priestly ordination as well as "transubstantiation" in the Eucharist can be cited as an example of this viewpoint.

To "function" and act according to God's will a church community needs a clear confession of faith and a church order to rule everyday life. Therefore, in 1536 Calvin composed a "confession of faith" (*confessio fidei*) and a series of "articles" (*articuli*). The articles provided for the community the frequent – at least monthly – celebration of the Lord's Supper, which should be an occasion of preaching, professing (the creed), and praising God. This requirement met with resistance from the city council, especially regarding the frequency of the Lord's Supper, as well as the public and obligatory character of a personal profession of faith. This resistance prepared the way for the crisis in Geneva in 1538 that would lead to an open break between the council and Calvin.

However, before this break occurred, a dogmatic dispute with Pierre Caroli, a former co-worker of Bishop Briçonnet in Meaux, caused our theologian considerable worry. Caroli had become a pastor in Lausanne without agreeing with his reform colleagues on all questions of religious faith and practice. Caroli allowed prayer for the deceased and criticized the doctrine of the Trinity advocated by Viret, the reformer of Lausanne, as well as by Farel and Calvin. Caroli considered their doctrine of the Trinity to be inconsistent with the Athanasian Creed (the *Quicumque* Symbol), and in reality to be Arian. Calvin suggested a synod be called, a response that fit the tenet he advocated his entire life that dogmatic disputes be decided by gatherings of pastors. The religious colloquies held in 1537 in Berne should be seen in this connection as successfully leading to the unification of the Swiss and Alsace Reformed churches concerning the Lord's Supper and the Trinity. Thus, Calvin's "Confession of Faith" was affirmed.

Other events caused Calvin pain. His good friend and patron, Louis du Tillet, left him because it was impossible for him to approve the manner in which Calvin took on priestly and even episcopal duties. Calvin, however, saw the reason for the separation, which was very painful for him, to be due more to his being outspoken and impolite to du Tillet. The correspondence in this matter shows how capable Calvin was of self-criticism.

Calvin also displayed inflexibility toward the Genevan council when it meddled in church affairs and wanted to give preference to the ritual for church services imported from Berne rather than that prepared by the Genvan pastors. Since Calvin and Farel did not give in, a public conflict resulted and both church leaders were expelled from the city. They left for Basle in the spring of 1538. During these events Calvin showed a mixture of guilt and confidence which was characteristic of him at that time. On the one hand he definitely recognized deficiencies in his ability to communicate; on the other hand, he identified his own views with the cause of God.

One can detect in Calvin's reaction a variation of the Lutheran theme *simul iustus et peccator* ("at once a justified person and a sinner"), or, more precisely, the insight that the servants of God are objectively justified, insofar as they seek to make people accept God's will. But this does not at all preclude their subjective behavior being burdened by grave errors. Calvin was so aware of such errors after his expulsion from Geneva that he even doubted the genuineness of his calling to pastoral ministry. Of course, he did not allow this doubt to be expressed by anyone else, such as du Tillet.

Once again, help came from Strasbourg. Bucer played the "divine will card" in order to confirm the pastoral calling of his young colleague against any doubt. His calling was undeniably real, as well as the extraordinary talent that accompanied it. This calling must be followed, but not necessarily in Geneva; it could also be in Strasbourg. Calvin agreed and accepted the charge of the French-speaking pastorate in the Alsatian capital city. This allowed Calvin to practice in a small way what had been unsuccessful for him in Geneva. Moreover, he had sufficient time to steep himself in his private theological studies. From this followed, of course, as in Basle, the unusually fast transition from reading to writing, from learning to teaching. An eloquent example of this is the writing of a second, expanded edition of the *Institutes* in Latin.

In an amazingly brief amount of time, there also appeared, in 1539, Calvin's answer to Cardinal Sadolet's letter to the Genevans, in which the bishop of Carpentras, an irreproachable reformer, invited his addressees to return to the bosom of the church, i.e., to the community faithful to Rome. He was writing at a time of widespread confusion and perplexity that had arisen a few months after Calvin and Farel's expulsion. Many in Geneva had lost the certainty they needed to carry out the reform. Would it not have been better and more beneficial for the saving of souls to maintain unity with the pope and the bishops? Did not heretics and schismatics also oppose the church in Rome?

Sadolet was clever enough to know how to take advantage of his addressees' problems of conscience. His over-zealousness caused him to accept the rumors that the expelled pastors had proven to be "enemies of Christian unity and peace" because they advocated the separation of the people from the traditions of their fathers. If this rumor were true, these people were irresponsible "innovators," schismatics, and enemies of the true church of Christ which lives essentially by "consensus" about what was believed always, everywhere, and by all, and whose hierarchical leaders give laws and regulations dictated by the Holy Spirit. Thus these pastors were mangling the body and bride of Christ.

Sadolet's letter was sent from the Genevans to Basle and from there to Strasbourg with the urgent request that Calvin answer it. Calvin did so quickly and with theological mastery. Not only did he reject the accusation of schism with Luther's argument that the evangelicals did not separate themselves from Rome, but he further asserted that Rome had expelled the evangelicals. As a result it is the Romans who are the schismatics. It is interesting, however, that Calvin took care not to use Luther's term for the church remaining true to Rome: "die nichtige Kirche" (the nonexistent church). Calvin prefers to see the group faithful to Rome as a corrupting and corrupted faction among other parts of the church. He had spoken this way in his letter to Francis of a "devilish faction within the church." This faction may well make the one church of Christ unrecognizable. But this faction still contains remnants or "traces" (*vestigia*) of the one church.

Therefore, the evangelicals do not seek a break in the church, but a correction of the "catholic church" from within. She is also their "Mother" and remains so even if she, in her visible behavior, has become a "false" church. The "false church" is therefore not allowed to be separated from the "true" church. The dispute about ecclesiastical authenticity and falsehood is occurring within an indivisible community. One must therefore maintain community with the "catholic church" (*ecclesia catholica*) as the "church of Christ" (*ecclesia Christi*). Even under the papacy the church possesses baptism, the Word of the gospel, the texts of Scripture, and the offices. These are all elements that remain basically "holy," since they are constitutents of the holy church.

But how should the "church" (*ecclesia*) be defined? The notion of a consensus holding sway everywhere and forever, as adopted by Sadolet, is inadequate. On the contrary, the qualitative concepts of "the Word," the "teaching of Christ," and the "community of the saints" gathered world-wide by the Holy Spirit must provide the starting point. Do the evangelicals spread new teachings? That is what the Romans do, by whom the traditions of the "ancient church" of the biblical and patristic ages have been falsified or replaced. The pope should not be allowed to boast of the heathen title *pontifex*, introduced much later; rather, he must confess and teach an unadorned faith in Christ as Peter did. If the pope were to do that, the evangelicals would not refuse to offer obedience.

Later, one also finds similar considerations in the *Institutes*. Hypothetically speaking, if the faith and ministry of Peter were re-established, the primacy of the Roman bishop could be recognized as "first among equals" (*primus inter pares*). This would be an essential component of an evangelical reform carried out in Rome itself. Unfortunately, nothing of the kind can be found at present; the *pontifex maximus* exercises a tyrannical rule and further distorts the true identity of the church. Therein lies the schism that can only be regretted by all true Christians. What Calvin (and Luther before him) demands is a return to church unity based on the truth.

Calvin's letter to Sadolet testifies to Calvin's self-understanding as a pastor directly chosen by God and commissioned to the task of reform. Calvin saw his calling willed by God as much as that of Luther or Bucer who, unlike Calvin, were ordained priests. The young author of the *Institutes* considered himself "ordained" directly by God and likewise spiritually wedded to the Genevan community. This thought calls to mind the fundamental experience of the Old Testament prophets and their extraordinary commission for the renewal of the people according to the word and will of Yahweh. In his letter Calvin actually proposes a comparison between his own destiny and that of the prophets who often had to accuse the priests and then were persecuted by them as a result. The prophets were indeed the reformers of the church before Christ.

Calvin's reply was not without results. The bishop of Carpentras had to admit defeat. Calvin was recalled by the Genevans. Before he returned, however, two important events occurred: Calvin married and made a closer acquaintance with the German reformers through several colloquies. As far as the thirty-year-old Calvin was concerned, he would – according to his own admission – rather have remained unmarried. But Bucer insisted on marriage. Calvin's state of mind when he finally gave in is revealed in his explanation: "If I do it, then it is to be able to devote more time to the Lord and less to daily duties." After careful deliberation, in 1540 he chose Idelette de Bure from Liège, the young widow of a former Anabaptist at Fattin. The marriage was blessed by Guillaume Farel. Idelette brought with her two children from her first marriage. The family had very limited living space at their disposal, since Calvin had arranged student living quarters in his Strasbourg house to increase somewhat his meager income.

The marriage was to last nine years. After Calvin's return to Geneva, a son was born to the couple. However, the child died while still an infant. The reformer, who had grown fond of his wife and welcomed the birth of his child with great joy, felt despondent. When Idelette herself was torn from him in 1549, Calvin wrote: "The best companion of my life is taken from me. If anything serious had happened to me, she would not only have been ready to accompany me into exile and poverty, but even death. As long as she lived, she was a true helper in my office."

As pastor of the Strasbourg French community, Calvin was invited to participate in various religious colloquies in Germany. These came about at the insistence of the emperor who sought by every means possible to establish confessional unity in his empire. The primary participants on the Roman side were the papal nuncio and theologians like Eck and Gropper. On the evangelical side, Melanchthon and Bucer played a considerable role. The colloquies took place in Frankfurt in 1539, in Hagenau in 1540, and in Worms and Regensburg in 1541. In Regensburg the theologians succeeded in achieving accord on the themes of original sin, freedom of the will, and justification. Unfortunately, Luther and the pope rejected the doctrinal formulation of "double justification," and the doctrine of transubstantiation remained in dispute. A great ecumenical opportunity was missed. From the very beginning Calvin was skeptical about these attempts and considered the proposed formulas of compromise to be questionable. According to Calvin, they represented a misleading and fictitious consensus. Therefore, Calvin left the Regensburg colloquy early.

It appears the real benefit of these colloquies for Calvin was that he became better acquainted with Melanchthon. Both theologians remained bound to each other in mutual esteem for years. Without reservation Calvin approved of the *Augsburg Confession* (*Confessio augustana variata*) which originated from the pen of his German colleague. Calvin might also have been able to meet Luther, but he did not participate in the doctrinal discussions mentioned above. Calvin understood no German and Luther no French, so correspondence between them was possible only in Latin. Indeed, the only letter the Frenchman, younger by twenty-six years, wrote to the German never arrived. Melanchthon refrained from delivering it since, in part, he feared a negative reaction from the recipient because of its theologically controversial content. That was unfortunate. Calvin showed great respect for the person of Luther, whom he called not only "brother," but also "father"; and he expressed the wish to exchange ideas with Luther "face to face" (*viva voce*). According to a contemporary witness, someone not easily identified, the German reformer, shortly before his death, is supposed to have praised Calvin's treatise on the Lord's Supper as the work of a learned man, pious and trustworthy in matters of faith.

The great impact of Calvin's response to Sadolet certainly contributed to the fact that the Genevans attached high expectations to the return of the expelled reformer. Accordingly they showed themselves to be generous. They offered Calvin and his wife an entire house and a good salary as well as benefits "in kind." Calvin's attitude may be described as sober and without illusions, but also without rancor or revenge. He made it clear to the council that he wanted only to serve the common good, but to do that it was necessary to achieve unity about a clearly formulated church order. Characteristic of his personal approach, Calvin continued his preaching at the place in the

Bible where he had stopped three years before, as if nothing unusual had happened in the meantime. His quickly written *Ecclesiastical Ordinances* exhibits a successful synthesis of the positions of the first Genevan church order and elements of the Strasbourg and Basle patterns, especially in the structure of the four offices: pastor, teacher, elder, and deacon.

Pastors are appointed for the ministry of preaching the Word of God and administering the sacraments. They exercise their responsibility for teaching and discipline in a collegial manner, in the form of the Company of Pastors (*Compagnie des pasteurs*). In this group, those who hold the teaching office are to "continue to learn" in a weekly common Bible study. Along with the Bible study, there is also consultation over matters of pastoral care as well as a brotherly examination every three months, i.e., a self-critical examination of each one's personal conduct. The Company chose its new members from those who were nominated by the city council and recommended by agreement of the entire community. Certainly that cannot be called a democratic procedure of voting in the modern sense of the term. This structure corresponds more to Calvin's preference for oligarchic structures of leadership. The newly nominated pastors were not ordained by the laying on of hands – though Calvin's doctrine of the church considered this desirable, following the model of the ancient church. Instead, pastors took an oath before the council.

Academic instruction and theological training of future pastors is the task of teachers. Holders of this office also require nomination by the council. Of course, it hardly agreed with the reformer's aspirations to give preference in the realm of education to political considerations over competency in a subject and ecclesiastical concerns. Later, Calvin expanded the educational program by establishing an academy, entrusted to the teachers, which was structured like a university in which theology no longer stood alone.

The supervision of the moral life of community members was entrusted to the elders or presbyters. They were twelve in number and were chosen from the members of the various civil councils and then elected by them. Along with the pastors they formed the Consistory, to which both the secular and ecclesiastical leadership of the city-state were obligated. At the beginning the Consistory recognized no clear separation between the two areas of control. Only from 1555 on was Calvin successful in opening the group of elders to people other than members of the councils. However, the chairmanship of the Consistory fell to one of the syndics. The Consistory met every Thursday to examine moral misconduct and to impose penalties.

The fourth office was that of deacon. Their duty was to administer community resources on the one hand, and to care for the sick, the poor, and the elderly on the other. This office attests to the strong social concern of the reformer, and it soon served as a model followed worldwide. Thus Calvin built on the ministry of charity of the ancient church and reformed an office that had shrunk to a mere liturgical function in the Roman community.

When evaluating this church order, today's historians point out its questionable aspects – not least its "state church" character and its mixing of the civil and ecclesiastical realms in practical matters. That of course does not go back to the model of the original church or even the "ancient church" – at least not to a pre-Constantine model that tried to promote Christianity by proclaiming the good news rather than by means of massive institutional power. When Romans 13:1 says every Christian should offer "obedience to those empowered by the state" since the state originates from God, Paul does not have in mind church authority at all. Therefore, this text is certainly not valid in a social context in which worldly power lies in Christian hands.

Even more problematic is the conclusion drawn from such a theory of powers that the honor of the one ruling and commanding coincides with the honor of God, and that ascribes the rank of "God's Word" to human judgments. Thus, in extreme cases, every death penalty can be theologically justified. Examples of this are the tortures and executions during the 1540s in Geneva of those who slandered the government and even Calvin himself, as in the case of Jacques Gruet in 1547, as well as witches, "plague mongerers," heretics, conspirators, murderers, and hardened criminals. This of course corresponded to the penal authority of Emperor Charles V, which was carried out even more radically in areas faithful to Rome. In any case, one must doubt whether this authority, in any objective sense, deserves to be called "Christian."

In this connection, two opponents of Calvin must be mentioned: Sebastian Castellio and Michael Servetus. Servetus in particular is the focus of events that weigh heavily on the reputation of the Genevan reformer even in the eyes of Reformed people today. An example of changed attitudes is the inscription on the monument that was erected in 1903 in Geneva and which proclaims the "error" of the great reformer in thinking that "freedom of conscience" is incompatible with the "true foundations of reform and the gospel."

The case of Castellio should be discussed first. In his treatise, *Whether Heretics Should Be Persecuted* (*De haereticis, an sint persequendi*), published in 1554, one year after Servetus was burned at the stake, Castellio proved even at that time that a theory of toleration could be developed on the foundation of the Christian gospel. This fact is more important in the view of the non-partisan historian than the removal of Castellio from his position as rector of the Latin School of Geneva because of his criticism of Calvin's theses about predestination, the Trinity, and Christ's descent into hell.

Castellio was merely reprimanded by the Genevan council and forbidden to speak – a much more lenient penalty than Servetus who had been burned in public. It is pointless here to go into the chain of events that led to this. All the biographies of the reformer report it in detail. Only a few facts need to be considered. The dispute was initiated by the teaching of Servetus on the Trinity. This physician who taught himself theology supported the opinion that three persons do not exist in God, but rather three "modes of acting," with the result that Christ cannot be considered the eternal "Son" and "second person of the Trinity." A similar thesis is connected with the name of Sabellius from the fourth century. It was rejected by the church fathers as a *de facto* denial of Christ's divinity, and then unanimously by the Roman and evangelical church communities as well.

Calvin saw in this opinion a deadly threat to faith in Christ. Since this was also the position of the Inquisition based in Lyon, still faithful to Rome, the result was cooperation between the Inquisition and the Genevan church leadership. The death penalty for the "heresy" of Servetus was, indeed, pronounced and carried out in 1553 in the city of Calvin and at his urging. The reformer did not want to bear alone the responsibility for this act. He requested verdicts from the sister communities of Zurich, Berne, Basle, and Schaffhausen: all supported the sentence. Bullinger and Haller emphatically sanctioned the death penalty. Melanchthon subsequently agreed as well.

For all these great leaders of the reform camp there existed no freedom of conscience to affirm a doctrine that deviated from theirs. The confession of faith was understood very "dogmatically" and as such was considered holy and untouchable. Its value stood higher than a person's life. Nevertheless, the historian must realize that at that time the concept of tolerance and a purely spiritual expression and defense of the faith had several advocates, forerunners of a humanism that was both "enlightened" and true to the gospel.

The question of freedom was raised in Geneva at this time in a more collective way. It concerned the right of the ecclesiastical structure, narrowly defined, i.e., independent of the civil and political authorities, to validate its own laws and commands. Thus Calvin never tired of demanding a specifically ecclesiastical moral discipline – especially of excommunication, i.e., exclusion of specific sinners of the Genevan community from the Lord's Supper. Moreover, Calvin was concerned about the self-determination of the Genevan community in relation to the more powerful Bernese which tried again and again to force its own laws onto other sister communities, including the regulation of the order of church services.

Not many Genevans supported these endeavors. So it was understandable that Calvin sought allies among numerous French brothers in the faith who fled from their country and found refuge in Geneva. Among them were the destitute, as well as the well-to-do and the highly educated, who included people such as the publishers Robert and Henri Estienne, the Hellenist Guillaume, the physician Léo Colladon, and the officer Laurent de Normandie, originally from Noyon. Thanks to such partisans, the internal political balance switched in favor of the reformer, away from the native Genevans and their patriotic groups, the so-called "Libertines." Under the direction of the influential Perrin family, these "Libertines" appealed to the people and led a demonstration in May, 1555, under the motto: "For God and Geneva!" It came to blows. The city guards had to intervene. Bloodshed was avoided; but after a short trial, four of the instigators had to pay for the deed with their lives. Perrin and his friends fled.

Calvin's victory brought great progress in the implementation of the moral discipline he conceived. For example, every luxury in goods and clothing had to be repressed and public theaters closed their doors. On the other hand, there was a successful advance in social conditions and the economy. Practical results occurred from the combination of three values characteristic of the reformer: vocation as a divine calling, work, and welfare. In addition, Calvin allowed the charging of interest in moderation in order to form capital. The textile industry was promoted and many unemployed found work.

All this is certainly not enough to make Calvin the "father of capitalism"; nevertheless, the Puritan work ethic, which later would wed predestination and economic success, is found on the course set by Calvin. He did not make a distinction between a concern about a dignified standard of living and its promotion through planned financial commerce. This makes it apparent that the determination of this goal did not have anything to do with "capitalism"; the concern was not profit for the sake of profit, but making possible the use of acquired goods for the welfare of all. The Genevan council was grateful to the reformer: in 1559, it finally offered him citizenship.

In the field of education, Calvin achieved just as much success. He planned very carefully. In 1556, he traveled to Strasbourg to obtain the advice of Johannes Sturm who directed the famous complex of gymnasium and academy. Calvin also intended to combine a school of higher learning with the six or seven grades of the comprehensive "Latin school." He wanted an academy with two departments: a "private school" (*schola privata*), where children would first learn to read and write and then receive instruction in Latin, Greek, and philosophy; and a "public school" (*schola publica*) where the pupils, after successfully completing the "private school," could continue their studies at university level in theology (including the "liberal arts") or in law or medicine.

The Academy was opened with great festivity on June 5, 1559. Calvin, a city secretary, and the founding rector, the noted theologian Theodore Beza, took the opportunity to speak. Enrollment began with 600 students. The number would grow sharply in the coming years, not least through the influx of many foreigners. When Calvin died in 1564, the "private school" had about 1200 pupils and the "public school," 300. The Academy was very illustrious from the beginning. French, Germans, Dutch, and East Europeans enjoyed its high-quality instruction, which of course was inseparably linked with evangelical spirituality. This is how an educated reformed elite who would strongly influence the confessional destiny of Europe arose.

The library of Geneva deserves special attention. Its catalog, originating in the year 1572, shows the library contained books that formerly belonged to Calvin himself and the Italian academic Peter Martyr Vermigli, along with other acquisitions and many gifts from publishers. One is struck by the surprising spiritual breadth to the collection. The writings of the great Scholastics, the humanists faithful to Rome, and the theological controversialists are strongly represented to a surprising degree, along with biblical commentaries, the church fathers, and the reform theologians. For those responsible for this library there apparently was no list of "forbidden books," no "Index."

The Academy drew many talented young people from all over Europe. The founder was very interested in the church–state issues of all European countries – especially France, of course. Calvin carried on an active correspondence with pastors persecuted for their religious convictions, but also with politically influential personalities (in Poland and England, for example). He showed he was very aware that an armed insurrection is most often an unacceptable response to established power. He disapproved of the conspiracy of reformed nobles in Amboise in 1560. He rejected even more energetically the thought that pastors themselves are supposed to participate in armed revolt. For example, Calvin made his views clearly known to the leaders of the Lyon community in 1562.

Calvin supported an oligarchic view of church and state, according to which only a small group of the community's upper class and nobility have the divine call to bring about radical changes in the existing order to the extent of using force. On the basis of this theory, Calvin approved the action of Louis de Condé and Gaspard de Coligny who sought to gain religious freedom for the evangelicals through open revolt. Calvin also supported collecting money for the Huguenot army. Through the Genevan council Calvin attempted to arrange assistance for Swiss cities and German princes with Lutheran sympathies. A high point of Calvin's involvement was certainly his *Humble Exhortation to the Invincible Emperor* on the occasion of the Imperial Diet in Speyer, in which he called upon Charles V to support the reform movement immediately. This writing was probably not without some success inasmuch as the Emperor seriously considered calling a national council to remedy the confessional divisions.

It was the religious leaders of the evangelical camp, of course, who were the reformer's preferred partners in correspondence. We name only John Knox in Scotland, whom he admonished about his rigor in formulating the order of church services; and Heinrich Bullinger, Zwingli's successor in Zurich, with whom Calvin prepared the 1549 *Consensus Tigurinus*, a statement of doctrinal unity on the Lord's Supper. For his compatriots remaining in France, Calvin produced in 1539 a draft confession whose content became an extensive part of the *Confessio Gallica* and served as a model for other national confessions.

The restoration of unity in issues of doctrine and faith in the European arena was among Calvin's most favored goals. It is not without reason that people today see Calvin as a forerunner of the ecumenical movement. However, unity of belief among the different Christian groups, which were already consolidated as "confessions" in the second half of the sixteenth century, remained a utopia. The groups began to change only very laboriously, and negotiated consensus in doctrine produced hardly any practical results. Part of the tragedy of the Reformation is that the sacrament of fraternal unity, the Lord's Supper, became precisely the main point of contention among the confessional groups.

The Catholic reform movement, which was connected with the Council of Trent, was and is judged in various ways from the reform viewpoint. Today an unprejudiced examination of important Tridentine decrees, especially those on justification, the Eucharist, and practical church reform, shows that Trent quietly integrated important concerns of the reformers. That is true to an even greater extent for Vatican II (for example, the principles of collegiality, christocentrism, the priority of God's Word – a kind of *sola scriptura*, etc.). The biographer of Calvin who is interested in ecumenism must admit that the reformer did not react to the Tridentine decrees mentioned above and dealt in detail only with the decree about the "sacraments in general"; this decree merely contained anathemas and developed no arguments, and therefore it easily gave rise to misunderstandings.

In his *Antidote* written in 1547, Calvin argues very sharply against the sacramental principle *ex opere operato* ("according to the work worked"), according to which grace in the sacrament becomes effective by "the doing of the act itself" and not by the subjective disposition of the officiant or the recipient. This viewpoint is open to charges of a blasphemous over-valuation of a material event and a human act, and consequently a corresponding devaluation of divine action. It is impossible to say whether this objection rests on a misunderstanding of the formulation intended by Thomas Aquinas and, indeed, intended in one sense by the concerns of the reformers themselves. The historian can only hold fast to one fact: at that time the representatives of evangelical theology and the advocates of Roman Catholic reform did not speak the same language, and mutual distrust was too great to guarantee an objective dialogue between the two parties.

Regarding the unification of the reform groups among themselves, Thomas Cranmer, the Anglican Archbishop of Canterbury, suggested in 1552 the holding of a great inter-confessional consultation – almost a "Council." Calvin joyfully agreed. He wrote:

> If only we could succeed in getting serious-minded men from the most important churches to come together and discuss the individual points of faith in order to reveal the solid teaching of the Bible to our progeny in regard to everything that is common among us! But the great misunderstandings of our time have caused the individual churches to be separated from one another so that there could hardly be unity among us as men, much less as a community of saints who confess with their mouth, but only a few practice in deed.

Cranmer's plan was bound to fail, not least because Melanchthon and Bullinger reacted very hesitantly.

The last decade of Calvin's life demonstrates in an impressive way his extraordinary powers of work that could not be halted by his many illnesses. He continued to write a great deal, drawing less from reading new sources than from the treasure of his memory. We are indebted to Calvin for commentaries on almost all the works of the Old and New Testaments, which still today are gladly quoted by critical exegetes. When Calvin could no longer write himself, he dictated his works to a secretary. He also preached without interruption. In the period between 1549 and 1564 alone, his stenographers copied over two thousand of the sermons which he delivered extemporaneously. In addition, there was the burden of an extensive correspondence that Calvin willingly undertook. Calvin's writings were collected from 1863 to 1900 in the *Corpus Reformatorum*, comprising fifty-nine volumes. There are also various *supplementa*.

In his fifties, this author and man of the church was increasingly plagued by physical ailments: headaches, insomnia, shortness of breath (probably due to advanced tuberculosis), coughing fits, hemorrhages, fevers, colitis, kidney stones, hemorrhoids . . . In the spring of 1564, Calvin sensed his last hour was coming. He prepared for his death with great calmness, as a man who always tried to be available to others. His final will was written in April. It contains a humble confession of guilt and expressions of unconditional trust in God, as well as directions about his modest estate. In addition to Calvin's relatives, the Bourse for refugees and the Academy were to inherit a few florins.

On April 27, the terminally ill Calvin offered a long farewell speech to the members of the Small Council. Words of thanks, a request for forgiveness and an admonition were expressed. On the next day he spoke to the pastors; he asked them as well for forgiveness and had them swear to change nothing of what he had done. He then commended to them Theodore Beza, who shortly before had been elected his successor. In the four weeks that remained to Calvin, many of his friends and colleagues came to visit him, among them the eighty-year-old Guillaume Farel. The dying man had something personal to say to everyone, mostly in regard to the welfare of the community and the continuation of the reform. What was happening there reminds one of dying biblical figures, like Moses, who as leader of a community by divine mandate spoke, taught, and admonished, spending his last hours in humble awareness of his authority. Calvin died on May 27, 1564. His last words were "*Quousque, Domine?*" (How long, O Lord?). At his own wish, Calvin was buried without services in a place still unknown today.

The biographer of a Christian reformer would accomplish only half of his task if he were content to offer a value-free chronological treatment, for we are dealing with a "person of universal history" (Hegel) whose life is inseparable from his effect on history that carries meaning and value. It would be inadequate to present such persons without any evaluation, all the more since they themselves saw the meaning of their existence in the battle for social values. They expose themselves to the verdict of future generations, a verdict that necessarily contains positive as well as negative judgments. Weighing these judgments with as much objectivity and fairness as possible is the biographer's duty. One may not idealize one-sidedly or condemn in a biased manner, but should neither harmonize nor exaggerate contradictions.

From this viewpoint, the following can be said in conclusion. Calvin was a Christian of his time, who took his faith very seriously and wanted to give it unconditional meaning in his own life, as well as in society and the church. Under the influence of Luther, he considered a radical *re-formation* to be essential, that is, a *re-newal* of Christianity which at that time was *de-formed* in many ways and places. For that he lived and fought. Calvin knew he was called to do that. The unprejudiced historian must make conclusions based on the extant documents to produce an endeavor of integrity. This man worked unselfishly to re-establish the values of the gospel in the church, which he could conceptualize only as one, holy, apostolic, and catholic.

Many of Calvin's deeds certainly correspond to the gospel, but only in intention not in actuality. It is tragic that Calvin lacked, as did many of his opponents, several basic Christian traits that he himself sought: patience, tolerance, love for enemies, an awareness of the inviolable worth of the individual, a readiness to dialogue, a desire for the highest possible objectivity. On the other hand, he was aware, for the most part, of his mistakes. That followed logically from the principle fully affirmed by Calvin that the believer is at once justified and sinful, and that his justification comes to him from Christ alone by grace. One can say that Calvin was so radically fixed on the grace of God that his own mistakes never gave him occasion to despair.

In the course of the history of the western world and the church, there are several measurements of significance. One relates to the question of whether a particular life story did or did not effectively produce universal historical results. In Calvin's case the answer is definitely affirmative. He formed an especially dynamic type of western Christianity in which faith in the efficacy of divine grace in no way limits the intensity of human striving, but powerfully stimulates it, and in which a strong consciousness of sin is connected with a no less tenacious struggle to be virtuous.

From this resulted, not least of all, an ethos of work and vocation as a divine calling. Puritanism with its Calvinistic roots contributed, as is well known, to the origin of what we characterize as North American civilization; and the Reformed churches of Europe produced social, cultural, and economic elites everywhere. Thus a much more independent humanism was able to develop than was possible during the lifetime of the reformer. Finally, the important role that individuals and groups play today in the ecumenical movement goes back in large part to Calvinistic roots. In brief: only those who consider Calvin's impact on world history can judge his life and work properly.

## 2  Calvin's Geneva

WILLIAM G. NAPHY

To most visitors today, Geneva is a respectable, prosperous, staid city resting at the end of Lake Geneva where the Rhône River pours forth to begin its rush to the sea. The city is Swiss, neutral, and a center for international diplomacy. In the mind it is associated with peace conferences and conventions designed to protect the weak and vulnerable. However, this was not the city in which Calvin ministered. More than just the passing years have moved across the face of Geneva. In Calvin's day the city was smaller, less secure, and decidedly isolated. It was a locale facing the constant threat of armed assault. It was over-crowded and stuffed with refugees. And it was poor. Most surprising of all for most people today to realize is that Geneva was not Swiss. Indeed, Geneva did not enter the Helvetic Confederation until the end of the Napoleonic Wars. For most of the years between its independence in 1535 and its entry into the Swiss state, Geneva did not even share a border with Switzerland. Thus, any real appreciation of Calvin's ministry in Geneva must begin with a realistic understanding of the environment in which he labored. What was his parish like? What was Geneva like?

Throughout most of the fifteenth century, Geneva had been a relatively prosperous market town. Its fairs attracted important business and its location at the confluence of the Rhône and the Lake made it a major transit point for goods. In addition, it lay along the trade route between Italy and the Low Countries that would later gain fame and infamy as the "Flanders Road." However, at the end of the fifteenth century, the French Crown had decided to grant significant concessions to establish rival fairs in Lyon. These quickly eclipsed Geneva and the city began to sink into economic decline. Its physical location would insure that it remained an important weigh-station and crossroads for trade but it was no longer a center for banking and exchange. The Genevan economy had become "collateral damage" in France's increasing involvement in Italy.

If Geneva was being economically crippled by France's actions then it risked being obliterated by the kingdom's territorial ambitions. As an important crossroads, Geneva's location was coveted. To the east of the city, the armies of Berne (and, to a lesser extent, Fribourg) were on the move. To the west, France was moving to secure the passes across the Alps to allow greater access to the plains of Northern Italy. In the middle lay the ancient duchy of Savoy. In an effort to secure its position and to better guard its exposed northern frontier, the Savoyard dukes proposed to relocate their capital to Geneva, the duchy's largest city. Strategically, this made perfect sense. Politically, it was a catastrophic mistake.

For Geneva was not simply a large city under ducal control. It was, in fact, an Imperial free city under the suzerainty of a prince-bishop. Personally, he was a vassal of the dukes of Savoy and, in most cases, a scion of a cadet branch of the ducal family. While his extensive personal possession might technically be under the dukes' control, the city itself was not. The Savoyards had limited control over the city except in the area of criminal justice where the duke's representative, the *vidomme*, played a key role. However, the prince-bishop and, more importantly, the cathedral canons also had political and economic power. Finally, the citizenry also had an elected senate, led by four syndics, whose job was to protect the rights and privileges granted to the citizenry and, in particular, those of the late fourteenth-century *Franchises* (in effect, a constitution *cum* bill of rights).

In practice, this triangular political arrangement meant that the city was primarily governed by the senate. However, in the key areas of criminal justice and final executive power, the roles of the *vidomme*, the canons, and the prince-bishop were crucial. As the city began to experience economic decline, tensions began to appear in this complex political settlement. Increasingly threatened both by foreign powers and by ducal aggrandisement, the citizenry looked enviously to the Swiss city-states. Many began to think that the city's brightest and safest future lay in "turning Swiss."[1] For them, security lay in the protective might of the Swiss Confederation. Not only did these Genevan patriots (the so-called *Enfants de Genève*) fear the advance of France but, more immediately, they feared the loss of their ancestral liberties to the machinations of the Duke of Savoy.

Thus in 1519, leading local merchant-politicians called upon the Swiss (Berne and Fribourg) to help the city free itself from the duchy. However, Savoy's skilful diplomacy was able to convince Berne and Fribourg to accept a negotiated settlement. The treaty averted a war but left Geneva's leaders exposed. In violation of the clauses meant to protect them, a number were executed. The result was disastrous for Savoy. Its opponents became convinced the duke could not be trusted and that a rupture between the duchy and Geneva was essential. Nevertheless, from a pragmatic point of view, the duke had successfully crushed the nascent revolt. He made his triumph and pre-eminence explicit in 1523–24 when he took up residence in the city. This astute move allowed him to stamp his authority upon the city (for example, by holding council meetings under the gun). However, he also made his ambitions apparent not only to the citizenry but also to the prince-bishop, the canons, and the neighbouring states. They all realized that if the duke were to make Geneva his capital, then clerical power would be undermined and the territorial ambitions of the French and Swiss would be damaged.

The second phase of Geneva's revolt against Savoy flared up in the late 1520s. The body politic split into three distinct groups. This fracturing of Genevan society into political factions replete with party symbols, slogans, and labels set the pattern for the city politics of the next quarter century. The smallest party was called *Seigneuristes* or *Mamelus* and they supported the duke. A slightly larger faction favoured the bishop (*Peneysans*). The final and largest group (*Enfants de Genève* or *Eidguenots*) sought independence and membership of the Swiss Confederation.[2] The reliance of the latter party on the Swiss in general and Berne in particular forced religion into the equation. In the 1520s Berne had adopted Protestantism and this meant that the price of Bernese military support was, at least, toleration and, at worst, adoption of its confessional stance. The Savoyard nobles who lived in Geneva and were the core of the *Seigneuristes* quickly fled while the prince-bishop attempted to mediate between Savoy and the *Enfants*. Clearly he hoped to avoid Swiss intervention and thus save the city for Catholicism as well as securing his lands, titles, and position. The house of cards that was Genevan politics collapsed before the onrushing armies of Berne and the abandoning of the city by the prince-bishop and the canons. Thus, the most important result of the revolt, after the political independence of Geneva, was that the city unanimously adopted Protestantism. Henceforth, Catholicism would be inextricably linked to Savoyard (or French) domination and Protestantism to Genevan patriotism (and liberty).[3]

However, no sooner had Geneva gained its freedom than its citizens faced a greater threat – occupation by Berne. Following the absorption of its neighbouring bishopric, Lausanne, in Berne's expanding lands, the prospect was frighteningly real. The city was saved by the threat of French intervention. France, too, feared an expansive Berne and wished to maintain a "buffer state" between its territories and those of the Swiss state. Faced with this French threat, Berne withdrew and Geneva's centuries as a small city-state mutually protected and threatened by its greater, aggressive neighbours began.

## THE RELATIONSHIP WITH BERNE: APPEASEMENT *VERSUS* RECALCITRANCE (1536–38)

Calvin entered this revolutionary republic in 1536. In retrospect, he would consider his first years in Geneva as a period of conflict against forces in the city opposed to his idea of a truly reformed society. Scholars have seen this opposition as an expression of latent Catholicism or nascent Anabaptism. The truth is more complex and yet surprisingly banal. Calvin and Guillaume Farel (the city's chief reformer) were caught in the cross-fire of another factional fight. This time, the debate was over the best way to guarantee continued Bernese support. Moreover, *ille gallus* hired by the city was but a minor player in the conflict. Calvin's "fame" in 1536 was clearly confined to a select band. It was based on a limited *œuvre*: a commentary on Seneca's *De Clementia* and two prefaces to Olivétan's French Bible. He had also written his attack on the Anabaptist belief in "soul sleep" (*Psychopannychia*) but left it unpublished. More importantly for his future renown, in March, 1536 Calvin published (in Basle) the first (Latin) edition of his *magnum opus, Institution* (or *Institutes*) *of the Christian Religion*.

The city's leaders, however, had more on their minds than the theology of their newest ministerial employee. The city was completely dependent on Berne in a very fluid and dangerous situation. Berne, Fribourg, and France had, in effect, successfully dismembered and occupied the ancient duchy. Geneva alone, with the lands previously controlled by the prince-bishop and the canons, had retained some semblance of independence. By 1538, Geneva's rulers were forced to decide how best to maintain the alliance with Berne that underpinned (and, to some extent, undermined) the city's freedom.[4] The party that gained power in 1538 favored appeasement of all Bernese demands short of outright annexation.[5]

In 1538, Calvin became a victim of this foreign policy. Geneva's ecclesiastical system was conformed to Berne's by senatorial fiat. Even Calvin admitted that the changes were *adiaphora* (unimportant) but he and Farel vehemently opposed the means. They denied that the state had competence in religious affairs without regard to the ministers. The senate was unwilling to be lectured on a foreign policy decision and, a lesson not lost on Calvin, had no need to be as the ministers were not united on the matter. Calvin and Farel remained opposed and were expelled. Among those hired to replace them was Antoine Marcourt, the man credited with the *Affaires des Placards*, the "Affairs of the Placards," which was the 1534 incident in Paris where Protestants posted placards denouncing the Catholic doctrine of the Mass and which led to persecution becoming the official policy of the French monarchy. Calvin left, and after journeying through Switzerland settled in Strasbourg.

## APPEASING BERNE (1538–41)

As one might expect, the immediate aftermath of the new policy was turmoil in the church. However, Marcourt and Morand, the new ministers, quickly restored some equilibrium. In fact, any objective reading of the ministers' attitude towards immorality, religious instruction, or stabilization of the ecclesiastical structure implies that the personnel changes had little impact. On two levels, though, there were shifts in the ecclesiastical situation. First, the ministers accepted the primacy of the state in Geneva's religious life. This (Zwinglian) model gave the city's magistrates the power their fellows enjoyed throughout Protestant Switzerland. More dangerously, the church became a focus for political protest. Political protest was closed to the opponents of appeasement as it could be seen as treasonable and might damage the very alliance the new policy was striving to strengthen. However, Calvin and Farel were ready-made martyrs for these politicians and their political goals. Calvin rejected the use of the church as a political tool from his exile in Strasbourg; he strongly advised the Genevans to accept the new ministers.

Surprisingly, Calvin was eventually asked to return to the city. More surprsingly, he agreed. In the course of 1540–41 another political upheaval had occurred in the city and had brought to power the opponents of the *Articulants*. The surrender of Genevan territorial rights and jurisdiction in most of its rural possessions (in the Articles signed with Berne) had been too much for the citizenry. The anti-appeasement party (which became known as *Guillermins* or *Farets* after Guillaume Farel) was able to capitalize on the popular fury and rout the *Articulants*.[6] The treaty was repudiated and the alliance allowed to lapse. The new party traded populism and power for security. To survive alone, Geneva desperately needed internal stability. The newly elected government proved unable to work with the ministers (who quickly resigned) hired by their political opponents. Lacking ecclesiastical leadership and facing the aftermath of a failed *coup d'état* the magistrates recalled Calvin. In exile, Calvin had been supportive yet conciliatory, he knew the local situation and he was an extremely gifted preacher, administrator, and lawyer; unlike 1538, he was needed in the right place at the right time.

## CONSOLIDATING A PROTESTANT SETTLEMENT (1541–46)

Calvin was given two crucial tasks: first, to draft regulations for Geneva's church; second, to draft a secular constitution for the republic.[7] Very quickly, the committee's members updated the city's fourteenth-century charter. They replaced ducal, episcopal, and cathedral powers and personnel with elected and appointed magistrates. The new constitution validated and confirmed the city's transformation from a prince-bishopric into an independent republic. Likewise, the *Ecclesiastical Ordinances* were radical and conservative. The initial draft made the church free in its own sphere; this was watered down to imply magisterial overlordship. The establishment of a Consistory was radical but not novel. Berne had Consistories and Geneva had discussed setting one up during Calvin's exile. The most obvious example of the conservative nature of the *Ordinances* is apparent in the "adoption" of the pre-existing social welfare system as the city's deaconate structure.[8] Thus, the *Ordinances* placed Geneva's church on a clear, stable, legal footing.

Calvin, learning from the experience of 1538, realized that this new structure needed a unified ministerial cadre. In the period 1541–46, he undertook two major tasks. First, he collected an impressive array of ministers (Company of Pastors). Secondly, he sought councillors to work with the Company in an effective and efficient Consistory. By 1546, Calvin had gathered round himself a group of extremely gifted, well-educated, socially prominent and financially secure French religious refugee ministers. Also, Calvin managed to gather a group of elders who would serve on the Consistory for nearly a decade. Thus, by 1546, Calvin was in a very secure position supported by the entirety of the *Company* and buttressed by the elders.[9]

More importantly, by 1546, Calvin's theories of ecclesiology were nearly complete in practice. The Company of Pastors met every week for discussion, improvement, admonition, and support as a Genevan national synod. The Consistory was an ecclesiastical court which, on its own, could become the local governing body of the church. The local school system remained under state control but the ministers were involved in the hiring of teachers (doctors). Despite their best efforts, however, it was not until 1559 that they succeeded in establishing a forum for higher education, the Academy. Although always under secular control the provision of poor relief by the state-controlled *Hôpital* provided a model for other Calvinist communities and governments.[10]

The components of this system were not unique to Geneva or Calvin. During Calvin's exile the church and state had discussed consistories and deacons in keeping with the situation in other Swiss Protestant cities. The emphasis on education was not new: the public school system was pre-Reformation and a vital part of Geneva's civic structure.[11] Moreover, social welfare had been centralized and rationalized by the new Republic from its inception. However, interplay of these components in the system and the close interrelationship between church and state made the resulting whole, novel. The ministers were on a level footing with the magistrates and, in the secular realm, they claimed full competence and responsibility. Thus, the Consistory asserted its absolute right to excommunicate; a view resisted by most of the magistracy. In effect, Calvin was successful in freeing the ministers from magisterial control in most "religious" areas.[12]

Nevertheless, serious reservations abound. First, the "Calvinist system" never really matured in Geneva; a ministerially controlled deaconate remained unknown. In fact, the system of session, presbyteries, and synods seen in other Calvinist polities only developed in larger states. It is crucial to recall that Geneva assumed that all its ministers would – and could – meet and gather every week. The Consistory also had ministers and elders in, more or less, equal number. Being called before the Consistory meant facing a dozen politicians and a dozen ministers. This system was urban, confined, politically responsive, and, in its ethos, republican.

## CHAFING UNDER THE CALVINIST YOKE (1546–50)

However, no system, no matter how well crafted, could guarantee Genevan stability in the immediate aftermath of a revolution, reformation, and failed *coup d'état*. The first sign of trouble was when a number of leading politicians and their wives were accused of dancing at a wedding. Their conspiracy of silence only collapsed when the newly elected syndic, Amblard Corne, confessed. In an unrelated development, the Consistory asserted its supremacy in the area of excommunication; a matter the final version of the *Ordinances* had left vague. Despite this, both the ministers [*religious control*] (and their political allies on the Consistory) and the senators were convinced that each held supreme power in excommunication. Indeed, until 1555, the Senate consistently ruled that the Consistory could only admonish sinners and recommend their excommunication. Calvin (a foreign employee of the state) and the other ministers were as firm in asserting their absolute right to excommunicate.

Baptismal names also proved problematic. The ministers demanded that names be stripped of superstition and latent Catholicism. Thus, traditional names for the Magi (Balthasar, Gaspard, and Melchior) and names associated with the Deity (e.g., Emmanuel) were banned. Unfortunately, they [*legalistic(?)*] also decided to ban Claude; their logic was faultless. The shrine of St. Claude was nearby and, thus, the ministers concluded the name's popularity (almost unknown in France) implied a vestigial form of cult-worship. Genevans viewed the name as traditional and local. The methodology employed by the ministers made the situation worse. A father presented his son at the font. When the minister was given the name "Claude" for the child, he baptized it "Abraham." A riot then erupted. The magistrates asked for a list of forbidden names and the ministers complied. However, they continued to make *ad hoc* decisions at the font when they deemed it necessary.[13]

Just as Calvin finally (by 1546) succeeded in gaining a loyal and high-quality group of fellow ministers as well as a working Consistory, it seemed that the brief period of stability inaugurated in 1541 was going to end in disaster. However, despite the numerous opportunities for a rupture between the church and state, the threat of invasion in the midst of the various confessional wars swirling around Geneva managed to impose an uneasy consensus on Geneva's rulers both secular and sacred. Factionalism, for the first time in nearly a half-century, appeared to have disappeared. External pressures made Genevans lay aside their internal squabbles and maintain a united front as the only means of securing the city's liberty.

## GENEVAN LIBERTIES *VERSUS* CALVINIST DISCIPLINE (1551–54)

By 1551, the threat of invasion was receding and factionalism again reared its ugly and divisive head. While the wars in Germany had concentrated Genevan minds on unity and stability, the new influx of refugees from France's religious wars threatened the city's threadbare social fabric. The pressure of nearly 5,000 refugees into a city of about 10,000 was intolerable. In response, xenophobia and confessional solidarity grew as one. The refugees' skills and wealth upset Geneva's economy. Prices, rents, and property values increased. The arrival of noble refugees with their prejudices and societal expectations exacerbated the situation. Geneva's merchant society resented the pretensions of refugee nobles. All these issues paled into insignificance before the greater questions: how many refugees would stay and how was the city to limit their impact on Geneva's factional politics?

Two particular outsiders nearly rent the city apart: Bolsec and Servetus. In 1551, Bolsec challenged Calvin on predestination. The Protestant Swiss cities also disliked Calvin's views, and Geneva's leaders were unclear how best to appease their co-religionist and their ministers. Both ministers and magistrates canvassed (and lobbied) the Swiss Protestants for advice (and support).[14] The Swiss were unwilling to support Calvin's theology but also were profoundly conservative in supporting the *status quo*. Thus, they sided with the established ministers over Bolsec who was then expelled by Geneva's Senate. Paradoxically, though, this left both magistrates and ministers dependent on Swiss support in matters of "domestic" theology.

The case against Servetus followed a similar course. In 1553, Servetus appeared in Geneva having been sentenced to death for heresy in Catholic Vienne. The ministers then instigated his arrest. However, from that point onwards the case (as with Bolsec) was prosecuted by the state. Calvin, as an "expert witness," was asked to evaluate Servetus' theology; he declared Servetus an anti-trinitarian (an "atheist"). This perplexed Geneva's leaders. Hitherto, the religiously heterodox (such as Anabaptists) had been banished for "heresy." Catholics had already used this leniency (by sixteenth-century standards) to suggest that Geneva was a haven for all heresies. Since they did not wish to appear lenient to an atheist already sentenced to death by the Catholics, the city became convinced that banishment would not suffice.[15] Still, the magistrates hesitated. Servetus, told he could return to Vienne, declined the offer. This forced the magistrates to seek moral support from the Swiss. This was more an attempt "to share the blame" with the Swiss than to prevaricate and "save Servetus." Put simply, the city did not want to kill people for religious beliefs. As many Genevans did business in French Catholic cities one can understand their reluctance.[16] Diplomatically, Geneva's appeals for leniency in French heresy trials would become meaningless once the city killed its first "heretic." Once the Swiss concurred with the death penalty, however, the city acted. Servetus was convicted and sentenced to death the very next day.

While Servetus' "atheism" was more shocking, Bolsec's attacks on Calvin's predestinarian theology were more dangerous. Although Calvin's views were not radically out of step with other reformers (compare Luther's *De servo arbitrio* or much of Augustine) the problem for the Swiss was the place Calvin gave to this belief in his preaching ministry. They preferred Luther's approach which was to present his views in Latin and not the vernacular. What the Swiss and many Genevans clearly could not understand was why Calvin considered this (to them) troubling and troublesome belief so important.

Of course, they were not refugees from religious persecution. To Protestants being persecuted for their faith, these doctrines were of great comfort. Calvin, ever-conscious of the plight of his fellow French Protestants, knew the power of this doctrine. It insured that sufferings, persecution, exile, deprivation, and even death were not meaningless but, ultimately, were part of God's plan for believers. If God's will moved in all things, then all things were bearable, all things endurable. Punishment was part of God's sanctifying work. However, in Protestant societies it was much more difficult to discern God's will, plan, or election for the individual and, thus, predestinarian preaching left many troubled. This dichotomy explains the unease this doctrine produced in the magistrates and ministers of settled Protestant polities.

## CONSOLIDATING A CALVINIST SETTLEMENT (1555–59)

The tensions that had appeared in 1546 and simmered for nearly a decade finally exploded in late 1554. Anti-French xenophobia produced attacks on refugees and rioting. Calvin turned to locals who saw the refugees as martyrs and deplored the unsettled situation in Geneva. Many more

Genevans saw the wealthier refugees as sources of much-needed cash. In addition, as in 1538, Calvin became part of a factional struggle in the city. His supporters hoped to use the city's turmoil to oust the supporters of Ami Perrin. These so-called *Perrinistes*, part of the *Guillermin* faction of 1538–42, were the largest single faction in Genevan politics, commanding a plurality in the Senate. Their major goal was admission to the Swiss Confederation. In part, this explains their enthusiasm for a more Zwinglian ecclesiastical settlement, thereby "conforming" their ecclesiastical settlement to the Swiss model. In the early 1550s, the *Perrinistes* had been the dominant party but had been unable to bring stability to the city. They faced two insuperable problems. First, the Company of Pastors and the Consistory were united and this prevented the Senate from bringing them to heel. Also, refugees increasingly involved Geneva in French affairs and complicated the efforts to join the Confederacy.

In 1555, the *Perrinistes* suffered a slight electoral setback. The pro-French, anti-*Perrinistes* gained a majority of one in the Senate. The new government moved to secure its narrow electoral base with haste and determination. Despite legal and extra-legal protests by the *Perrinistes*, a large number of French refugees were made *bourgeois*.[17] Since they were, thus, immediately able to vote, they consolidated the anti-*Perriniste* position. Also, since *bourgeois* could not be Senators, the new *bourgeois* would remain loyal voters and could never become political opponents. By May, the *Perrinistes* accepted that they could not regain political power by democratic means. They rioted on May 16; reaction was swift and decisive. The rioters were traitors just like the *Articulants* with their attempted *coup d'état* of 1540. Perrin and his followers were arrested or fled and their estates were confiscated. Within six months, a third of Geneva's ruling elite had disappeared. The Swiss were horrified and furious.[18] Despite the drama, the reality was that after twenty years Geneva had stability, a secure ecclesiastical settlement, and had abandoned its goal of membership in the Confederacy.

Inevitably, one tries to explain Calvin's triumph. In reality there is no simplistic answer. However, the single most important element of Calvin's success was probably his pulpit ministry. By 1549 there was a sermon every day (and three times on Sunday). Every week saw catechism classes, theological debates and Bible studies (*congrégations*), meetings of the ministers, and Consistory sessions. Calvin was the visible face – and audible voice – of authority in the city. He interpreted the Scriptures, declared God's Word, admonished, cajoled, and threatened the people of Geneva. Clearly, Calvin was, first and foremost, a (good) minister. He devoted himself to his charges in Geneva and to the French Protestant cause. Any attempt to overlook Calvin the Genevan minister and politician in favor of Calvin the theologian and "celebrity" is problematic. Not only was the ecclesiastical model he devised in Geneva a local creation but the place of ministerial freedom and the role of excommunication were settled in the Republic. Clearly, Calvin was influenced by and interacted with events and people outside Geneva, but there is a very real sense in which one should never cease to view Calvin, his work, his writing, and his beliefs as the product of a minister living in Geneva. It is certainly true that Calvin had more than one flock but it is essential to realize that much of the advice and counsel he gave to his distant and persecuted flock in France arose from the experiences he had working in Geneva.

The final segment of Calvin's ecclesiastical model did not appear immediately in 1555. It was not until 1559 that the Senate agreed to use the *Perrinistes'* property to found the Academy. Thereafter, the city had a functioning Consistory, a high-quality Company of Pastors, a ministerially dominated public school system, and a seminary for training (foreign) ministers. However, Calvin had not transformed Geneva into a theocracy. The introduction of draconian legislation on morals in 1557 was rejected by the *Conseil Générale* as "too severe." Also, the secular authorities retained control of poor relief.[19] Despite these local yet important aberrations, the "Calvinist" system was in place and functioning by 1559.

## THE REVOLUTION AND REFORMATION CONSOLIDATED (1560–68)

After 1559, although Calvin's health began to fail, the arrival of Beza provided him with a supporter and obvious successor. Although ill, Calvin was still asked to head the committee to re-draft (his) 1542 Constitution. Calvin died before the constitution was complete but he clearly had a major impact on the resulting 1568 Constitution. Geneva had been a difficult "parish" for Calvin and yet, by 1555–59, it had become a model for Calvinists across Europe. Why would others want to visit the same traumas upon their homeland? It is important to remember that many of the non-French refugees (especially the English and Scots) arrived after the worst of the 1555 crisis. Thus, they saw a Geneva purged of opposition, full of zealous refugees. It was a place of enthusiasm, learning, devotion, and determination – truly a godly, reformed city.

*Notes*
1 The appeal of the Swiss model, especially for urban areas, has been excellently detailed in Thomas A. Brady, *Turning Swiss: Cities and Empire, 1450–1550* (Cambridge: Cambridge University Press, 1985); see also William G. Naphy, "Genevan Diplomacy and Foreign Policy, c. 1535–1560: Balancing on the edge

of the Confederacy," in W. Kaiser, C. Sieber-Lehmann, and C. Windler, eds., *Eidgenössische ≪Grenfälle≫ : Mülhausen und Genf* (Basle: Schwabe & Co., 2001), 189–220.

2 *Seigneuristes* meant, essentially, loyalist/royalist while their opponents named them *Mamelus* for the slaves who had come to dominate Egypt. The bishop's party was named for their base of operations in the village of Peney, while the "patriots" called themselves "the Sons of Geneva" or *Eidguenots* (from *Eidgenossen*, Swiss for confederates), a reference to the *Enfants'* desire to join the Confederacy. Some suggest this may be the source for *Huguenot*. One presumes their opponents simply called them traitors.

3 For more on Geneva's military situation see William G. Naphy, "The Price of Liberty: Genevan Security and Defence Spending, 1535–1555," *War in History* 5 (1998), 379–99. The development of nationalism and Protestantism in Geneva is discussed in William G. Naphy, "'No history can satisfy everyone': Geneva's Chroniclers and Emerging Religious Identities," in Bruce Gordon, ed., *Protestant History and Identity in Sixteenth-Century Europe* (Aldershot: Scolar Press, 1996), II (of 2), 23–38.

4 The Genevan political system needs some explanation. There were four categories of civic status: *citoyen* (the native-born child of a *citoyen* or *bourgeois*), *bourgeois* (a person naturalised *gratis* or upon payment of a fee), *habitant* (a legal, resident alien), or *natif* (a local with no civic status). An adult *citoyen* and *bourgeois* could attend and vote in the annual meeting of the *Conseil Générale*, which met in February to validate rulings made by the higher councils the previous year and elected magistrates for the coming year. It elected the *Conseil des Deux Cents* which set wine and grain prices and elected the city's investigating magistrates in November. From this large council came the *Conseil des Soixante* (which met primarily to consider foreign affairs). This smaller body contained the *Petit Conseil* (Senate) comprising the four ruling syndics, a treasurer, secretary, factor (*saultier*), and other senators to a total of (around) 25. Only *citoyens* could serve in the Senate.

5 They became known as *Articulants* (for the Articles they signed with Berne) or, derogatorily, *Artichaux* (artichokes).

6 The *Guillermins*, after Guillaume Farel, or, pejoratively, the *Farets* (burnt-out candles).

7 Calvin's first training had been in the law.

8 The Senate-nominated, council-elected *procureur* for this *Hôpital générale* and his assistants remained as they were.

9 For more on this process see William G. Naphy, "The Renovation of the ministry in Calvin's Geneva," in Andrew Pettegree, ed., *The Reformation of the Parishes* (Manchester: Manchester University Press, 1993), 113–32.

10 The system operated by the private fund to support poor French refugees (*Bourse française*) existed as an additional but non-competitive model with officials called "deacons." Unfortunately, these two patterns, the former controlled by the ministers, the latter by the state, allowed for debate and argument over the best method of providing for the needy. Magistrates wanting to control this powerful tool of social discipline were quick to use Geneva, the "Calvinist" model, as an example in discussions with their "Calvinist" ministers (who, unsurprisingly, favored ministerial control).

11 For more information on schooling in Geneva see William G. Naphy, "The Reformation and the Evolution of Geneva's Schools," in B. Kümin, ed., *Reformations Old and New: Essays on the Socio-Economic Impact of Religious Change, c. 1470–1630* (Aldershot: Scolar, 1996), 185–202.

12 Clearly, which affairs pertained to the church and which to the state was a matter susceptible to endless debate.

13 This issue is discussed in greater detail in William G. Naphy, "Baptisms, Church Riots and Social Unrest in Calvin's Geneva," *Sixteenth Century Journal* 26 (1995), 87–97.

14 For more on these letters and a wider discussion of Calvin's "lobbying" correspondence see William G. Naphy, "Calvin's Letters: Reflections on their Usefulness in Studying Genevan History," *Archiv für Reformationsgeschichte* 86 (1995), 67–90.

15 The Vienne sentence served as a marker laid down for the Genevan officials. They could hardly allow themselves to appear less trinitarian than the Catholics. It might also be that Calvin was sensitive to the charge of tolerating such views since his own trinitarianism had been called into question in the 1530s.

16 The dangers inherent in visiting French cities can be seen in William G. Naphy, "Catholic Perceptions of Early French Protestantism: The Heresy Trial of Baudichon de la Maisonneuve in Lyon, 1534," *French History* 9 (1995), 451–77.

17 In 1555, 127 were admitted and another 144 the following year. This total of 271 compares with 269 for the entire period 1543–54.

18 In protest, Berne allowed their defensive alliance to lapse.

19 There remained voices in Geneva arguing for a more "humanistic" and tolerant form of Protestantism: see William G. Naphy, "François Bonivard and his *Difformes Reformateurs*," *Renaissance et Réforme* 20 (1996), 57–80.

**Part II**

*Calvin's Work*

# 3  Calvin's writings

WULFERT DE GREEF

It is not easy to do justice to Calvin's writings in a short article. Most of his writings deal with the Bible and the church, which is not surprising. As a reformer, Calvin devoted himself to the church's reformation. In this he let himself be guided by the Bible.[1] The Bible and then the church – that was the right order for Calvin, and that is the order that we will be following in this chapter.

Calvin thought that people needed to have at their disposal a good translation of the Bible and he did everything to make that possible. He also spent much of his energy in explaining the Bible. Most of his writings are a direct fruit of this effort. Other writings can be connected to his devotion to church reformation of which his fight against heresy, sects, and other abuses is also a part. Some of his writings about doctrinal subjects like free will, election, and the Trinity are also significant. However, my decision to focus on the Bible and church means that those subjects will only be mentioned at the end of the article.

## CALVIN AS A HUMANISTIC JURIST

Calvin's earliest writing has nothing to do with theology. On the advice of his father who in 1527 became involved in a conflict with the cathedral chapter of Noyon, Calvin studied law in Paris at the Collège de Montaigu. In 1532 he wrote a commentary on De Clementia, a work from the beginning of the Christian era by the Roman philosopher Seneca.[2] Seneca appealed to the Emperor Nero to show clemency to the heretics in Rome. It is not clear whether Calvin tried with his publication to move King Francis I to take a more benevolent position toward the evangelicals but that was surely not the primary intent of his study. Calvin wanted to make a name as a humanistic jurist by making available and correcting the editions of De Clementia which Erasmus had published. Calvin's commentary brought to light his philological skills which were a great help in writing his biblical commentaries.

## CALVIN AND THE BIBLE

In his address *Concio academica*[3] delivered on November 1, 1533, Nicolas Cop, rector of the University of Paris, talked about Christian philosophy and drew attention to the distinction between law and gospel. Calvin was involved in drawing up Cop's address. Like Cop, he fled from Paris. An important change had taken place in Calvin's life.

In 1535 the French Bible translation by Olivetanus, a cousin of Calvin, was published in Serrières. According to Theodore Beza, Olivetanus instructed Calvin in the true religion when both were studying in Paris. The Bible translation of Olivetanus starts with a letter from the hand of Calvin to "emperors, kings, princes and all people who are subjected to the rule of Christ" (*Ioannis Calvinus caesaribus, regibus, principibus, gentibusque omnibus Christi imperio subdita salutera*).[4] In this letter Calvin makes a powerful plea for the Bible and its authority. He also pleas for good Bible translations for ordinary people.

Preceding the text of the New Testament, a letter is published which Calvin wrote "to all who love Jesus Christ and his gospel" (*A tous amateurs de Iesus Christ, et de son S. Evangile, salut*).[5] This letter is Calvin's first theological writing. It summarizes the Christian faith. Since 1551 it has been given the title *Letter to the Believers Demonstrating How Jesus Christ is the End of the Law*, corresponding to the title of a booklet that was published in 1543 in Geneva. This booklet contains two letters of which the first is this letter of Calvin.[6] According to the title Calvin wants to show how Jesus Christ is the end of law and the sum of all that it is necessary to look for in Scripture.

Calvin was closely involved in publishing the revised editions of Olivetanus' Bible translation.[7] In the edition of 1546 Calvin emphasizes in his letter to the reader (*Jean Calvin au lecteur*)[8] the special meaning of the Bible that is given by God and intended for everybody. We need the guidance of the Holy Spirit to understand God's teaching. The Bible teaches us to trust in God and to live our lives in acknowledgment of him. Because the Old Testament points to Jesus Christ who is the center of the gospel, our only aim must be the knowledge of Jesus Christ.

The Bible played a crucial role in Calvin's own life. He tried his very best to provide good Bible translations for people. He also went out of his way to help people to understand the Bible. With these aims in view, he published many writings.

## THE *INSTITUTES*

The *Institutes* of 1536 is a guidebook made up of six chapters.[9] More extensive editions followed later. In 1559 the *Institutes* numbered four books and eighty chapters. Calvin's intent with the book changed over the course of the years. The first edition begins with a letter addressed to King Francis I. This letter says that many people in the country are hungering and thirsting for Jesus Christ, but that until now only a few have a right knowledge of him. That is why Calvin wishes to provide instruction in the Christian faith. His book is also a confessional defence. He wants to inform the king about the motives of the evangelicals who were persecuted by him as though they were Anabaptist rebels. Calvin distances himself from the Anabaptists and refutes the accusations of sectarianism brought against the evangelicals. His concern is the one holy catholic church.

Calvin mentions the catechetic intention of the *Institutes* (1536) in the full title. He wants to provide a summary of what true piety is (*summa pietatis*) and of what it is necessary to know about the doctrine of salvation. The *Institutes* resemble a catechism. In the first chapters Calvin gives an explanation of the law, the Apostles' Creed, the Lord's Prayer, and the sacraments of baptism and the Lord's Supper.

The apologetic character of the book can be seen in the following chapters. These deal successively with the remaining five sacraments which, according to Calvin, are false sacraments. They also deal with Christian freedom and with the Christian doctrine of church and state.

The second edition of the *Institutes*, published in 1539 in Strasbourg, was three times as long as the 1536 edition.[10] In this edition Calvin follows the same catechetic scheme, but the title no longer mentions the "sum of piety." The word *institutio* is now connected to the contents of the book. Calvin's intention is to familiarize the theological students with the main points of biblical doctrine. He keeps the chapters from the first edition but also adds chapters in which he treats new subjects that also appear in Melanchthon's *Loci Communes* from 1535. Calvin was influenced by Melanchthon who, in his choice and arrangement of his *Loci*, was guided by Paul's epistle to the Romans.

The larger size of the 1543 and 1550 editions of the *Institutes* has to do with Calvin's increased exegetical knowledge and also several theological debates that had taken place in the years between these editions and the previous ones.

The last Latin edition of the *Institutes* appeared in 1559.[11] The full title shows that Calvin now offers instruction in the Christian faith in four books. The material has increased to such an extent that it can almost be spoken of as a new work. The division of chapters is inspired by the Apostles' Creed. The first book deals with the knowledge of God the Creator, and the second with the knowledge of God the Redeemer in Christ, first disclosed to the Fathers under the law and then also to us in the gospel. The third book treats the way in which the grace of Christ is received, the benefits that come to us from it, and the effects that follow. The fourth book is about the external means or aids by which God invites us into the community of Christ and keeps us in it. Calvin employed the original catechetical scheme and the topics which, under Melanchthon's influence, he derived from Paul's epistle to the Romans. The Pauline model remains an important principle for the way in which Calvin orders his material.[12] As far as the expansion of the material is concerned, we can detect the influence of doctrinal debates in which Calvin had been engaged. These included the debate with Joachim Westphal over the Lord's Supper, the debate with Andreas Osiander about the image of God, the work of Christ, and justification, and the debate with Lelio Sozzini about the merits of Christ and the bodily resurrection from the dead.

## DISTINCTION BETWEEN THE *INSTITUTES* AND THE COMMENTARIES

From 1539 onwards, Calvin's purpose with the *Institutes* was different from what it was in 1536. This difference in purpose has to do with the distinction he made between the *Institutes* and a commentary.[13] Calvin is of the opinion that an exegete should give a continuous commentary on all the texts, and that his commentary should be clear and brief (*perspicua brevitas*). In the letter preceding the *Institutes* of 1539, Calvin says that in a commentary he limits himself to the exposition of Scripture without giving a lengthy discussion of doctrinal matters. In the *Institutes*, however, he does go into doctrinal topics by discussing the *loci communes* as does Melanchthon.

Calvin's method of working implies that the *Institutes* as well as his commentaries are of interest for the knowledge of his theology. The *Institutes* expound the main points of the Christian faith. At the same time, the *Institutes* are important for understanding the Scriptures. In the letter preceding the French edition of the *Institutes* (1541), Calvin writes that one should read the quoted texts in the Bible itself. This remark emphasizes that Calvin, in his *Institutes* as well as in his commentaries, is concerned with the understanding of Scripture itself.

## COMMENTARIES AND LECTURES (*PRAELECTIONES*)[14]

Calvin's commentary on the epistle to the Romans came off the press in 1540. It was followed by commentaries on 1 and 2 Corinthians (1546), Galatians, Ephesians, Philippians, and Colossians (1548), 1 and 2 Timothy (1548), Hebrews (1549), Titus (1550), 1 and 2 Thessalonians and Philemon

(1550), James, 1 and 2 Peter, 1 John, and Jude (1551), Acts (1552), John (1553), and Matthew, Mark, and Luke (1555). As far as the Old Testament is concerned, Calvin wrote commentaries on Isaiah (1551, and a much more extensive one in 1559), Genesis (1554), the Psalms (1557), Exodus through Deuteronomy (1563), and Joshua (published in 1564, just after Calvin's death). Each of the commentaries was published both in Latin and French. They were all written by Calvin himself. He had often dealt with the material in his commentaries first during his lectures for students, ministers, and other interested persons. From 1557 onwards other people made notes during these lectures that were published in Latin as well as in French. *Praelectiones* were published as follows: Hosea (1557), Minor Prophets (1559 and 1560), Daniel (1561 and 1562), Jeremiah and Lamentations (1563 and 1565), Ezekiel 1–20:44 (1565). Calvin only gave permission for the publication of his lectures with great difficulty. He thought he had spent too little time preparing them. Finally he surrendered because he could not find the time to re-work the lectures into a commentary. The *Praelectiones* are more extensive than his commentaries, but his desire is still simply, with a few exceptions, to engage in actual exposition of Scripture.

## SERMONS[15]

Although Calvin's first task in Geneva was to lecture, he also began his work as a minister some time before 1537. From 1541 he began to conduct services practically every day. On Sunday mornings he preached from the New Testament in *lectio continua*, while on Sunday afternoons he would choose a psalm. During the week he gave attention to the Old Testament. In 1549 the deacons appointed Denis Raguenier as stenographer so that Calvin's sermons could be printed. Calvin left the publishing of his sermons to others with the exception of four sermons which he revised and published himself along with a brief exposition of Psalm 87.[16] Some sermons were published during Calvin's lifetime; others appeared later. The editors of the *Opera Calvini* did not place a lot of value on the sermons, but still included 872 of them. This attitude to Calvin's sermons has since changed. Almost all remaining sermons preserved in manuscript are published today in the *Supplementa Calviniana*. Occasionally new manuscripts of sermons are found and printed.[17]

## WEEKLY BIBLE STUDIES (*CONGRÉGATIONS*)

In 1536, Guillaume Farel and Calvin began to hold so-called *congrégations* in Geneva every Friday morning. In doing so, they were following the example of Zurich where since 1535 the so-called "prophesyings" had been held. The *congrégations* were meetings in which ministers from Geneva and its vicinity participated. Others were also allowed to come and listen to these Bible studies, which were held in French. The usual practice was to discuss books of the Bible in *lectio continua*. Worth mentioning is a particular *congrégation* which was held on December 18, 1551 and which was devoted to the subject of election (*Congrégation sur l'élection eternelle de Dieu*, 1562).[18] This meeting was held in response to Jérôme Bolsec. During a *congrégation* held by one of the ministers, Bolsec had protested against the predestinarian interpretation of John 8:37.

## WRITINGS ON THE CHURCH

### Reformation of the church

Reformation is above all reformation of the church. In this regard, an important piece by Calvin is *Responsio ad Sadoletum*.[19] Following the banishment of Calvin, Farel, and Courault from Geneva in April 1538, Sadoleto, bishop of Carpentras, wrote in March 1539 an open letter to the Council and citizens of Geneva with the challenge to return to "obedience to the bishop of Rome." According to Sadoleto, the Roman Catholic Church has always and everywhere been one in Christ and guided by the one Spirit of Christ. Disunity is impossible. A Christian ought to be guided by the decrees, norms, and sacraments of this church and not by people like the banished ministers from Geneva who only wanted division. The Council of Geneva asked the Council of Berne how to respond to Sadoleto's letter. The Bernese ministers then called for Calvin's help. The ministers in Strasbourg also urged him to answer Sadoleto.

Calvin wrote his *Responsio ad Sadoletum* in six days. It was published with Sadoleto's letter in 1539 in Strasbourg. In 1540 a French edition was printed so that the common people might become acquainted with the contents. In his response Calvin points out that the whole discussion is about the true service of God. Sadoleto misunderstands him if he thinks that Calvin and his followers are trying to take people away from the worship of God as it has always been done in the Roman Catholic Church. Regarding the church, however, more needs to be said than that she is one in Christ and guided by the one Spirit of Christ. The most important feature of the church is that she is founded upon the Word. Christ promised that the church would be guided by the Spirit, but that guidance must be understood in connection with the Word. Calvin appeals for the renewal of the old church. He mentions the doctrine, discipline, and the sacraments and also the forms of worship.

In his letter, Sadoleto does mention justification by faith, but it is with the meaning of this term that Calvin takes issue. If the knowledge of justification by faith disappears, the honor of Christ will be extinguished, religion abolished, the church destroyed, and the hope of salvation will disappear. Justification by faith is according to Calvin the heart (*summum*) of the religion.

Concerning the relation between faith and works, we must look upon Christ who is given for our justification and sanctification. Other matters which are mentioned are the penances (*poenitentiae et satisfactiones*), the Lord's Supper, the confession, the intercessions of the saints (*intercessio sanctorum*), and purgatory. Sadoleto bases his argument on the authority of the church. Calvin, however, in a few examples, makes it clear how remote he is from the old church. The church, says Calvin, must humbly acknowledge the Word and submit to it.

The reformation of the church is also the subject of an open letter Calvin wrote in 1543 to Charles V who wanted to discuss the matter of the reformation during a diet in Speyer. Calvin wrote the open letter (*Supplex exhortatio ad Caesarem*)[20] at the request of Bucer who had asked him in 1543 to write a defense of the faith for the evangelicals. In this way, the emperor would get an understanding of the problem.

In the name of all who long for Christ to reign, Calvin urges the emperor to work for the restoration of the church. He defends the changes which some have brought following in the footsteps of Luther and others. He exposes the infirmities of the church, indicates the remedies, and says why help is urgently needed. Calvin also reacts to the accusation that the correction of the church's defects has produced only discord. He opposes the accusation of separation by referring to the apostles and the prophets. The unity of the true church has everything to do with Christ who as the Head of the church is due the highest authority.[21] Finally Calvin calls upon the emperor and the princes to make an end to the miserable condition of the church. He acknowledges that if it pleases Christ to do so, he is able miraculously to preserve his church even apart from the actions of people. He goes on, however: "But I tell you, if you hesitate any longer, very soon we will find the visible church in Germany no more."

At the diet in Speyer (1544) Charles V promised the Protestants that he would do his best to convene a Council. Pope Paul III responded to that with a "fatherly admonition" in which he reproaches the emperor for reaching a temporary settlement with the Protestants, and planning a Council without consulting him about it. It benefits an emperor to listen and not to instruct, writes the pope. Calvin published the admonition of the pope along with his own comments (*Admonitio paterna Pauli III. Romani pontificis ad invectissimum Caesarem Carolum V. Cum scholiis*).[22] In his comments Calvin sharply criticizes the pope, who in his "fatherly admonition" has deprived the Protestants of any prospect for rapprochement. Calvin argues that Christian princes have an obligation with respect to the church when the ecclesiastical hierarchy is deficient in its task. At a Council the matter should be decided according to the Word of God. Finally, he makes an indirect appeal to the emperor to keep the promise that he made at the diet in Speyer.

In December, 1544 Pope Paul III opened a Council in Trent which in March, 1547 was adjourned until 1551. Farel, Viret, and others urged Calvin to refute the decrees of Trent. His *Acta Synodi Tridentinae cum Antidoto* (1547)[23] provides the text of the decrees, of the canons, and of a speech delivered at Trent, followed by his own commentary. With his antidote he wants to assist his fellow believers in disputing the ideas of Trent.

Because the Council of Trent was rejected by the Protestants, and because Emperor Charles V was not satisfied with the way things were going at the Council, he tried at the diet in Augsburg (1548) to find a solution to these problems in his empire. Awaiting a general Council, he established in the *Interim* in twenty-six articles the most important matters regarding the faith and the church for Roman Catholics and Protestants. The only permission he gave to the Protestants was to pass the cup during the celebration of the Lord's Supper and for priests to get married. Both Heinrich Bullinger and Martin Bucer urged Calvin to respond to the *Interim*. He did so with his *Interim adultero-germanum, cui adiecta est: Vera christianae pacificationis et Ecclesiae reformandae ratio* (1549).[24] The treatise also appeared in a French translation. It comprises the text of the *Interim* along with Calvin's view on the Christian peace and the reformation of the church. In his criticism of the *Interim* he expounds in depth the "doctrines on which not the least bit of ground may be yielded." He treats the subjects of justification by faith, confession of guilt and penance, the service of God, the church, the sacraments, intercession of the saints and angels, prayers for the dead, fasting, celibacy, and ceremonies. The gap between him and Rome seems impossible to bridge.

### A necessary choice

The struggle for the Reformation has personal and practical consequences for believers, a matter which comes to the fore in two letters Calvin wrote to friends.

The first letter is written to Nicolas Duchemin, who had studied with him in Orléans and secured an ecclesiastical position in the diocese of Le Mans. Duchemin had asked Calvin's opinion about participating in Roman Catholic worship services. Calvin wrote that he disapproves of those who do not publicly reveal their decision to become an evangelical and who go on participating in the Roman Catholic worship services.

The second letter is addressed to Gérard Roussel, "an old friend" from the time when Calvin stayed in Nérac. When Calvin heard that Roussel had received an appointment as bishop in Orolon, he wrote him a letter in which he gives his view of the office of bishop and calls upon Roussel to take a radical step. Compromise and wavering are options that are not in line with Scripture. Calvin published these letters as an encouragement for others to publicly reveal their evangelical faith (*Epistolae duae*, 1537).[25]

Some more publications followed dealing with the same matter. In a "short treatise" (*Petit traicté*)[26] Calvin deals with the question: How should one of the faithful who knows the truth of the gospel act among Roman Catholics? It is Calvin's opinion that Protestants in France should declare their faith openly. His advice is to emigrate. If that is not possible, he advises them to stay away entirely from Roman Catholic church services. Those who do participate in church services should continually confess their guilt before God, so that their consciences do not fall asleep. Moreover, they should pray to God for deliverance and then look for a means to get out of their situation.

When several believers complained about his being too rigorous, Calvin offered his apology in his *Excuse à Messieurs les Nicodémites*, 1544.[27] Calvin thinks that these believers refer unjustly to Nicodemus who went to Jesus by night to be educated by him. Later Nicodemus openly displayed his faith as a disciple at Jesus' burial. In the title of the Latin translation of *Petit traicté* and *Excuse à Messieurs les Nicodémites* (1549),[28] Calvin calls these believers pseudo-Nicodemites.

The evangelicals in France were upset by Calvin's view. Antoine Fumée, a member of the Parliament of Paris, asked Calvin to find out the opinions of Luther, Philip Melanchthon, and Bucer concerning Calvin's disapproval of the so-called Nicodemites. The letters in response written by Melanchthon, Bucer, and Peter Martyr Vermigli (*Conseils*) were included in a little book containing reprints of Calvin's *Petit traicté* and *Excuse* (1545). All three supported Calvin's position. In 1550, a letter by Heinrich Bullinger was included in a reprint of the Latin 1549 edition. Calvin's position that the French Protestants had the choice of either dying as martyrs in France or confessing their faith elsewhere became known far and wide in Europe through the translation of his *Petit Traicté* and *Excuse* into various languages. It contributed to the fact that many people, French and others, sought refuge in Geneva.

The Dutch Theodore Coornhert stood up for the Nicodemites in his little book *Verschooninghe van de Roomsche afgoderye* (1560). He argued that what matters is what is internal, not external. Calvin responded with his *Response à un certain Holandois* (1562)[29] because Coornhert's view could harm the advance of the Reformation in the Netherlands.

### Building up the church

Under Guillaume Farel's leadership, the entire citizenry of Geneva had decided for the Reformation in May, 1536. Shortly afterwards, Farel persuaded Calvin to stay in Geneva in order to shape the Reformation. After that time, Calvin devoted his energy to this cause. Together with Farel and Courault he wrote a series of articles (*Articles concernant l'organisation de l'église et du culte à Genève*, 1537)[30] in which they state the points that they consider of primary importance for a church of law and order. In particular, they mention four issues: the celebration of the Lord's Supper and matters related to it, the singing of psalms, the instruction of the youth, and marriage laws. The *Articles* indicate the directions that we find in a few of Calvin's other publications.

### Confession of faith

Calvin wrote a short and simple confession of faith for the instruction of children with respect to the celebration of the Lord's Supper (*Instruction et confession de foy don't on use en l'église de Genève*, 1537).[31] This work closely parallels the treatment of this subject in the *Institutes*. The part about the five false sacraments was not included because of its polemic nature. Later Calvin wrote a catechism for the youth in which he employed the question-and-answer form (*Le Catechisme de l'église de Genève*, 1542 with a Latin translation in 1545). This catechism was translated into various languages and served as the forerunner of the Heidelberg Catechism. Calvin's *L'ABC François* (1551) contains an explanation of what children who want to participate in the Lord's Supper need to know. He provides twenty-one questions and answers which were included in the editions of the catechism from 1553 (*La Manière d'interroguer les enfans*).[32]

With his *Instruction et confession de foy don't on use en l'église de Genève*, Calvin intended to instruct the youth, but this work was also meant as a confession which the inhabitants of the city should endorse. The Council of Geneva, however, thought that the document was too extensive for this purpose. In the Latin translation, Calvin indicates in the title and the foreword that he sees this work (*Catechismus, sive christiana religionis institutio*, Basle, 1538)[33] as a confession of faith in which the unity of the church in Geneva with other churches is put into words. From 1545 onwards the Latin translation of the Catechism of Geneva did not serve just as a norm for the teaching of the church in Geneva but also as an expression of solidarity with other churches.

Calvin was also involved in the drafting of the French Confession of Faith (*Confessio Gallicana*, 1559).[34] He wrote the draft for the first national synod that was secretly held in Paris. The synod approved this first draft of the Gallican Confession with a few insignificant changes. A synod in La Rochelle then decided upon the official text in 1571. The Dutch Confession of Faith (1561) is a revision of the *Confessio Gallicana*.

### The Lord's Supper

This section on the building up of the church should also include Calvin's writing about the celebration of the Lord's Supper. At the insistence of others, Calvin wrote a treatise in which he explained for the people in the pew the basic meaning of the Lord's Supper (*Petit traicté de la saincte cène*, 1541).[35] Jesus Christ established the sacrament in order to signify and seal the promises of the gospel, to train us to recognize his exceeding goodness towards us, and to urge us to lead a Christian life (Calvin mentions particularly unity and brotherly love). He rejects the conception of the Lord's Supper as a sacrifice and the doctrine of transubstantiation.

Calvin takes up the debate about the Lord's Supper that Protestants had been involved in prior to his writing. Concerning the religious colloquy in Marburg (1529) he mentions the positive contributions of Luther on the one hand, and Zwingli and Oecolampadius on the other; he also indicates the weaknesses in their ideas. Calvin expresses the hope that before long all those involved will draw up a generally accepted formula that is so greatly needed. Calvin ends with the confession that in the celebration of the Lord's Supper believers partake of the body and blood of Christ. This may be described better by one person than another. This much, however, is certain: Christ is in heaven and not enclosed in the elements of bread and wine. It is the Holy Spirit who effects our partaking of Christ; that is why we use the term *spiritual*.

In the 1540s Luther and the followers of Ulrich Zwingli had an ongoing conflict about the Lord's Supper. Calvin got involved in the discussion when in 1547 by order of the Council of Geneva he began a journey through a number of Swiss cities to encourage those who felt threatened by Charles V, who had been successful in his struggle with the German Protestant princes. In Berne Calvin ascertained that there were large differences between the Zwinglian and Lutheran ministers. He tried his best to help them bridge their differences. After he was presented with Bullinger's treatise on the Lord's Supper (*Absoluta de Christi Domini et catholicae eius ecclesiae sacramentis tractatio*, printed in London in 1551) he began a correspondence about this matter with Bullinger. In May, 1549 he went with Farel to Zurich. The discussion about the Lord's Supper on the basis of the Confession of

Geneva led to an agreement that was recorded in the twenty-six articles of the *Consensus Tigurinus*.[36] The official text was published after the Swiss churches adopted the agreement. Calvin took care of a French translation while Bullinger published a German edition.

Calvin did not manage to reach an agreement with the Lutherans about the Lord's Supper. Joachim Westphal, a Lutheran minister in Hamburg, began from 1552 to write against the *Consensus Tigurinus*. He considered Calvin's view of the Lord's Supper a serious threat. At the urgent request of Bullinger, Calvin responded when he saw that Westphal's attacks were having an adverse influence on Lutheran–Reformed relations in various places, such as in Frankfurt and Wesel. In 1555 in Geneva and Zurich a work was published in which Calvin defended the *Consensus Tigurinus* (*Defensio sanae et ortodoxae doctrinae de sacramentis*).[37] Nevertheless the written discussion continued. In the foreword to his reaction to Westphal's second treatise, however, Calvin clearly shows that he does not want a conflict (*Secundo defensio fidei contra Westphali calumnias*).[38] With reference to the unity in Christ, he calls upon the Lutheran ministers to fight against any threatening division. This war of words, however, continued in an even more intensive way.

### Liturgy

Calvin's concern for the liturgy was part of his concern for the building up of the church. In the *Institutes* of 1536 he pleaded for a weekly celebration of the Lord's Supper. He advocated the singing of psalms in his *Articles* (1537). He set some psalms to verse as well as the Song of Simeon, the Ten Commandments and the Apostles' Creed. He published these along with thirteen psalm versifications by Clément Marot (*Aulcuns pseaulmes et cantiques mys en chant*, 1539).[39] In 1543 another publication followed in which more psalm versifications, mainly by Marot, were included. After Marot's death, Beza set the 101 remaining psalms to verse and these were published in 1562 in a large impression. About 27,000 copies were sent to France.

In his *La Forme des prières et chantz ecclésiatiques* (1542),[40] Calvin devoted considerable attention to the structure of public worship. He says that there are three important elements in a worship service: preaching, prayers (including singing), and the administration of the sacraments.

### Church order

The new church order appeared in 1541 (*Les ordonnances ecclésiastiques*) and was revised in 1561.[41] Not everything that Calvin had in mind could be implemented. In each of the city's three churches a quarterly celebration of the Lord's Supper was instituted in place of monthly communion. There is no mention of the complete independence of the Consistory. The laying on of hands at the ordination of a minister was not accepted. It is significant that the new church order under the influence of Bucer speaks of four offices: minister, doctor or teacher, elder, and deacon. The task of the "doctor" is concerned with the instruction of believers in sound doctrine, but he is also involved in training ordinands.

## DISPUTES AGAINST HERESIES, SECTS, AND ABUSES

The doctrine of soul sleep had been condemned already at the Fifth Lateran Council in 1513. Urged by his friends, Calvin opposed this doctrine in his *Psychopannychia*. In 1536 he wrote in a letter to the readers that the pastoral goal he has in mind is to reclaim those who have erred. The writing was published in 1542 in Strasbourg.[42] According to the title, *Vivere apud Christum non dormire animis sanctos, qui in fide Christi decedunt*, Calvin wants to demonstrate that the saints who die in faith in Christ, live with him, and their souls do not fall asleep. Calvin is of the opinion that there are adherents of soul sleep among the Anabaptists. That is the reason why he provides a summary of his *Psychopannychia* at the end of his *Brève instruction* (1544).[43] He wrote this latter work at the instigation of Farel who had grown concerned about the Anabaptist influence in Neuchâtel and its vicinity. Along with his request, Farel had sent a French translation of the *Confessio Schlattensis*. This confession contains seven articles that the Anabaptists had adopted in 1527 at their synodical meeting in Schleitheim. The articles which Calvin refutes in his writing concern baptism, discipline, the Lord's Supper, separation from the world, pacifism, the offices, the state, and oaths. Calvin distinguishes between the Anabaptists and others who accept Scripture, and the Libertines who consider themselves so spiritual that they do not need Scripture. He wrote his *Contre la secte phantastique et furieuse des libertins, qui se nomment spirituelz* (1545)[44] at the request of Poullain and Farel who called for his help in the battle against the Libertines. This group included followers not just in France but also in Holland and Germany. Calvin analyses the hermeneutics which the Libertines employ, refutes their pantheistic fatalism, and writes about the relation between God's reign and our responsibility.[45]

Calvin wrote his *Traité des reliques* (1543)[46] to reach and influence the common people. He attacks the abuses that are caused by the veneration of relics. This practice denies the unique position of Jesus Christ as Mediator. It also deprives God of the honor that is due to him. Calvin gives a detailed summary of what has been happening in the area of relics. He gives examples of fraud in order to bring people to their senses. He hopes that Christian monarchs will protect their subjects from this fraud.

In the sixteenth century the new focus on the classics had led to a growing interest in astrology. In his *Advertissement contre l'astrologie* (1549)[47] Calvin speaks out against the superstitious belief that the course of one's life can be determined from the stars. He attempts, therefore, to get the Council of Geneva to do away with the old almanacs. Our course of life depends above all on God who operates in our lives according to his wisdom, justice, and goodness.

In 1550 Calvin published his *De scandalis*[48] in which he writes against those who slander the gospel under the pretext that it creates stumbling blocks. He has people from humanist circles in mind who disdained the gospel and believed they were not really learned if they did not mock God. People from Roman Catholic circles also wished to do the Reformation harm. Above all Calvin intended to fortify the faith of those who had to contend with various arguments that were being brought against the gospel.

## SOME DOCTRINAL MATTERS

### Free will and election

In 1542 Albertus Pighius published his treatise about free will and God's grace (*De libero hominis arbitrio et divina gratia*). This work contains ten books in which Pighius disputes Calvin. Calvin responded with a defense of the orthodox doctrine about bondage and liberation of the will (*Defensio sanae at orthodoxae de servitute et liberatione humani arbitrii*, 1543).[49] He refutes the first six books of Pighius' work. The following four books he refutes in his *De aeterna Dei praedestinatione* (1552)[50] which he wrote as a joint statement on behalf of all the Genevan ministers. The treatise that in the name of the Council was offered to all pious people has a pastoral aim. For our assurance of faith we should not look to the hidden decree of God, but fix our gaze upon Christ. Through faith in Christ we gain access to God's kingdom. Whoever is content with the clear promises of the gospel must also recognize that it is God who has opened our eyes, because he elected us to be faithful before we were conceived in the womb.

### The Trinity

Whoever disputes the Trinity, according to Calvin, departs from the Christian faith. The discussion about the Trinity had begun already in 1537 when Pierre Caroli charged Calvin and Farel with Arianism. Calvin published two treatises, his *Confessio de trinitate propter calumnias*

*P. Caroli* (1537)[51] and his *Pro Farello et collegis eius adversus Petri Caroli calumnias defensio Nicolai Gallasii* (1545).[52] A strong opponent of the Trinity was Michael Servetus. Calvin defends the orthodox doctrine of the Trinity against the errors of Servetus in particular in his *Defensio ortho- doxae fidei de sacra Trinitate, contra prodigiosos errores Michaelis Serveti Hispani* . . . (1554).[53] In this connection we also mention Calvin's discussion with the Italians Gribaldi, Gentile, and Biandrata, and the Polish Unitarian Stancaro.[54]

### Notes

1  In his will, Calvin thanks God for his grace. He declares that he has exerted himself to the extent of that grace to proclaim the Word purely and to explain the Scriptures faithfully. See *CO* XX, 298–302.

2  *Calvin's Commentary on Seneca's De Clementia*, ed. and trans. F. L. Battles and A. M. Hugo (Leiden: E. J. Brill, 1969).

3  *CO* IX, 873–76; *CO* Xb, 30–36; *OS* I, 4–10. English translation in *Institutes of the Christian Religion 1536 Edition*, ed., F. L. Battles (revised edition rpt., Grand Rapids: Eerdmans, 1986), 363–72.

4  *CO* IX, 787–90. "John Calvin. To Emperors, Kings, Princes and To All Peoples Subject to Christ's Rule, Greeting," in *Institutes of the Christian Religion 1536 edition*, 373–77.

5  *CO* IX, 791–822; J. Calvin, *Epitre a tous amateurs de Jésus Christ*, avec intro- duction sur une édition française de l'Institution dès 1537 par J. Pannier (Paris: Fischbacher, 1929).

6  See for the text of this letter *Calvin. Oeuvres choisies. Edition d' Olivier Millet* (Paris: Gallimard, 1995), 29–50.

7  See J. F. Gilmont, *Jean Calvin et le livre imprimé* (Geneva: Librairie Droz, 1997), 199–200.

8  *CO* IX, 823–26.

9  *CO* I, 1–252; *OS* I, 11–283.

10  *CO* I, 253–1152 (with additions of *Institutes* 1543–54).

11  *CO* II; *OS* III–V. *Institutes of the Christian Religion*, ed. J. T. McNeill, trans. F. L. Battles, Libarary of Christian Classics, 2 vols. (Philadelphia: Westminster Press, 1960).

12  See Richard A. Muller, *The Unaccommodated Calvin: Studies in the Foundation of a Theological Tradition* (New York: Oxford University Press, 2000), 132–39.

13  See the letter to Grynaeus which he wrote at the time of the appearance of his commentary on Paul's epistle to the Romans (*CO* X, 402).

14  See for the references to the commentaries and the *praelectiones* in the *Cor- pus Reformatorum* W. de Greef, *The Writings of John Calvin. An Introductory Guide*, trans. L. D. Bierma (Grand Rapids: Baker, 1989). *Calvin's Commentaries* (Edinburgh: Calvin Translation Society, 1844–56; rpt., Grand Rapids: Eerdmans, 1948–50. *Calvin's New Testament Commentaries*, ed. D. W. Torrance and Thomas F. Torrance, 12 vols. (Edinburgh: Saint Andrew Press; Grand Rapids: Eerdmans, 1959–72).

15  For an overview of Calvin's sermons see de Greef, *Writings of John Calvin*, 110–17.

16  *CO* VIII, 369–452.

17  See Max Engammare, "Des sermons de Calvin sur Esaïe découverts à Londres," in Olivier Millet, ed., *Calvin et ses contemporains. Actes du Colloque de Paris 1995* (Geneva: Librairie Droz, 1998), 69–81.

18  *CO* VIII, 8:85–140. P. C. Holtrop, *The Bolsec Controversy on Predestination from 1551 to 1555*, I (Lewiston, NY: Edwin Mellen Press, 1993), 695–720.

19  *CO* V, 365–416; *OS* I, 457–89. John Calvin and Jacopo Sadoleto, *A Reformation Debate*, ed. J. C. Olin (New York, 1966; rpt., Grand Rapids: Baker, 1976).

20  *CO* VI, 453–534. *T&T*, I, 121–234.

21  Compare Calvin's discussion with the Sorbonne in his *Articuli a facultate sacrae theologiae parisiensi determinati super materiis fidei nostrae hodie controversis. Cum antidoto*, [Geneva] 1544 (*CO* VII, 1–44).

22  *CO* VI, 453–534. *T&T* I, 121–234.

23  *CO* VII, 365–506. *T&T* III, 17–188.

24  *CO* VII, 545–674. *T&T* III, 189–358.

25  *CO* V, 233–312; *OS* I, 289–362. English translation of the letter to Duchemin in *T&T* III, 359–411.

26  *CO* VI, 537–88. The treatise, which is a translated version of the letter to Duchemin, contains as a postscript a letter that Calvin wrote on September 12, 1540 to an anonymous person and in which the same matters are discussed.

27  *CO* VI, 589–614. Eric Kayayan gives an English translation in *Calvin Theological Journal* 29 (1994), 346–66.

28  *CO* VI, 617–44 (*De vitandis superstitionibus* . . . , Geneva, 1549).

29  *CO* IX, 581–628. English translation by R. R. MacGregor in *Calvin Theological Journal* 34 (1999), 291–326.

30  *CO* Xa, 5–14; *OS* I, 369–77. *TT*, 48–55.

31  *CO* XXII, 25–74; *OS* I, 378–417. *Instruction in Faith (1537)*, ed. and trans. P. T. Fuhrmann (Philadelphia: Westminster Press, 1949; rpt. Louisville: Westminster John Knox Press, 1992).

32  See *CO* VI, 147–60.

33  *CO* V, 313–62.

34  *OS* II, 297–324.

35  *CO* V, 429–60; *OS* I, 503–30. *TT* II, 163–98.

36  *CO* VII, 733–44; *OS* II, 246–53. *TT* II, 212–20. An English translation by I. D. Bunting is in the *Journal of Presbyterian History* 44 (1966), 45–61.

37  The defense itself: *CO* IX, 15–36; *OS* II, 263–87. *T&T* II, 221–44.

38  *CO* IX, 41–120. *T&T* II, 245–345.

39  *Calvin's first psalter, with critical notes and modal harmonies to the melodies*, ed. R. R. Terry (London: Benn, 1932).

40  *CO* VI, 161–210; *OS* II, 11–58. *T&T* II, 99–128.

41  *CO* Xa, 15–30; *OS* II, 328–61. *TT*, 6–72. See for 1561 edition, *CO* Xa, 91–124.

42  *CO* Xa, 15–30; *OS* II, 328–61. *TT*, 6–72. See for 1561 edition, *CO* Xa, 91–124. Cf. George H. Tavard, *The Starting Point of Calvin's Theology* (Grand Rapids: Eerdmans, 2000).

43  *CO* VII, 45–142. "Brief Instruction for Arming All the Good Faithful Against the Errors of the Coming Sect of the Anabaptists," in *John Calvin. Treatises Against the Anabaptists and Against the Libertines*, translation, Introduction, and notes by B. W. Farley, ed. and trans. (Grand Rapids: Baker, 1982), 11–158.

44 *CO* VII, 145–252. *Against the Fantastic and Furious Sect of the Libertines Who Are Called "Spirituals",* in *John Calvin. Treatises Against the Anabaptists and Against the Libertines,* 161–326. A. Verhey and R. G. Wilkie, "Calvin's Treatise 'Against the Libertines'," *Calvin Theological Journal* 15 (1980), 190–219.

45 In the reprint of 1547 Calvin adds a letter to the believers of Rouen in which he warns them about a Franciscan monk whose ideas bear a strong resemblance to those of the Libertines (*Epistre contre un certain cordelier, suppost de la secte des Libertins, lequel est prisonnier a Roan*).

46 *CO* VI, 405–52. *T&T* I, 287–341.

47 *CO* VII, 509–42. *A Warning Against Judiciary Astrology and Other Prevalent Curiosities,* trans. Mary Potter, *Calvin Theological Journal* 18 (1983), 157–89.

48 *CO* VIII, 1–84; *OS* II, 162–240. *Concerning Scandals,* trans. J. W. Fraser (Grand Rapids: Eerdmans, 1978).

49 *CO* VI, 225–404. *The Bondage and Liberation of the Will. A Defense of the Orthodox Doctrine of Human Choice Against Pighius,* ed. A. N. S. Lane, trans. G. I. Davies (Grand Rapids: Baker, 1996).

50 *CO* VIII, 249–366. *John Calvin, Concerning the Eternal Predestination of God,* trans. J. K. S. Reid (Cambridge: Clarke, 1961).

51 *CO* IX, 703–10.

52 *CO* VII, 289–340.

53 *CO* VIII, 453–644.

54 See for Calvin's writing concerning this de Greef, *Writings of John Calvin,* 178–81.

# 4 Calvin as a biblical interpreter

## JOHN L. THOMPSON

Well in advance of Calvin's entry into his vocation as a reformer of the church in Geneva and Strasbourg, the sixteenth century had already displayed a remarkable preoccupation with biblical interpretation and, as a consequence, an unprecedented eruption of exegetical publications. Factors contributing to this eruption are not difficult to identify, and Calvin's career and character as a biblical interpreter would recapitulate most of them.

To begin with, the medium of intellectual exchange was forever altered by the dissemination of the printing press throughout Europe. As the costs of printing fell, books ceased to be a luxury item. Coupled to the growth of printing was a rising tide of scholarship that both consumed and produced those books. The humanist cry: *Ad fontes* – "back to the sources" – fueled scholars' appetites for these same sources as they emerged from the presses. Scholarship itself, along with scholarly standards, kept pace. A mastery of Latin alone was no longer enough to make one a respectable scholar: Greek and Hebrew were also required, and the growing competence of sixteenth-century scholars nourished, in turn, keener critical skills. For example, if these burgeoning sources, editions, and tools reminded scholars and preachers that there were new discoveries to be made in their old Bibles, Erasmus' early textual criticism of the New Testament undermined the *magisterium* of the Latin Vulgate and warned his readers they could not take even the wording of the Bible for granted, much less its theological content.

To these technological developments and philological discoveries, one should add other factors more unsettling still. Most notable of these was the climate of discontent within medieval Catholicism. Here was abundant tinder, for which Martin Luther was but a spark. The religious mood in Europe ranged between cynicism and anxiety, and ran not infrequently to the occult or the apocalyptic. Most European Christians would have claimed to take seriously the instructions of the Catholic Church regarding the way to salvation, but traditional Catholic teachings – along with the bulk of medieval exegesis and exegetical methods – were increasingly challenged by the rival views of Protestants and radicals, who typically appealed to Scripture as the only sufficient final authority. All in all, it is easy to see why the early reformers (and, in response, their Catholic opponents) found biblical interpretation easier but also more urgent than ever. Expository preaching and writing was not a diversion from the cares of the world, nor a mere antiquarianism. It instead served the defense of the gospel, the salvation of souls, and it was a matter of life and death. Virtually every aspect of daily life – not just preaching and sacraments, but also marriage and divorce, family life, commerce and consumption, as well as politics on every scale – was charged with theological and thus exegetical implications. For preachers and biblical scholars, the sixteenth century was unquestionably invigorating. It was also dangerous.

Calvin entered this context not in the first wave but in the second, and even somewhat accidentally. His desire was not to be a reformer or even to be much in the public eye, but rather to live the quiet and secluded life of a humanist scholar – or so he tells us in the 1557 preface to his commentary on the Psalms. Calvin would have been exposed to humanist teachings and values throughout his years of academic preparation, beginning with his studies in the early 1520s at the Collège de la Marche with Mathurin Cordier and continuing until he fled Paris in 1533, during which time he studied, by turns, theology and law in Paris, Orléans, and Bourges. His varied course of study would in every case have driven him to a firsthand examination of the Bible as well as classical and patristic sources, and all his early writings display his instincts as a humanist scholar. Calvin's self-published commentary on Seneca's *De Clementia* (1532) is a case in point, showcasing his mastery of ancient writers; his interest in history, philology, and textual criticism; his careful scrutiny of the text for the author's intended meaning; and his concern that eloquence be marshaled in the service of what could fairly be called an Erasmian moralism. These are many of the characteristics that would mark his later work as a biblical scholar.

Our inquiry will begin by probing Calvin's most important pronouncements about his own interpretative aims and method, then turn to examine some aspects of his actual practice as an interpreter of Scripture. As we will see, Calvin is in some ways a prism of his age, embodying in his approach to Scripture much that was traditional but doing so with new tools and perspectives. In other ways, he is marked by a strong streak of independence, sometimes crafted deliberately or defiantly, but sometimes, one may find, more idiosyncratically derived.

## CALVIN'S STATEMENTS ON THE THEORY AND PRACTICE OF BIBLICAL INTERPRETATION

Calvin's prescriptive or "theoretical" pronouncements about biblical interpretation are somewhat scattered. Unlike several of his contemporaries, he wrote no specific treatise on method. But there are two places in his early writings where he makes known his preferences for the interpretation of Scripture. The better known of the two is the 1539 preface to his commentary on Romans, which appeared the following year as the first of his commentaries and, in a way, Calvin's flagship commentary, insofar as his opening remarks (addressed to his friend Simon Gyrnaeus) are filled with programmatic intent.

> Three years ago, when we conferred together about the best sort of scripture exposition, I remember that the approach that pleased you most was also acceptable to me beyond all others. We both thought that the chief virtue of an interpreter consists in lucid brevity (*perspicua brevitate*). And truly, since almost his only responsibility is to lay open the mind of the writer (*mentem scriptoris*) whom he has undertaken to explain, to the degree that he leads his readers away from it, he goes astray from his own purpose (*a scopo suo*) . . .

*author's intent* [handwritten marginal note]

Interpreters of Calvin have traditionally seized upon these lines as a golden key to the mind of Calvin, and not without reason. While it might be too much to claim that "lucid brevity" constitutes a hermeneutical theory, the phrase hints at more than just Calvin's aspiration to write readable prose. Along with his stress on the writer's "mind" or intention and his evident deliberations upon the aim or "scope" of the biblical commentary, Calvin's allusion to *perspicua brevitas* testifies to the role that would be played in his own biblical exposition by the values and methods of Renaissance rhetoric – a legacy he obtained not only from his years of academic preparation but also from his most important Protestant forebears, as the balance of his preface makes evident.

As Calvin's letter to Gyrnaeus proceeds, he briefly salutes the "piety and erudition" of the many ancient commentators, then considers at some length how his own work compares with the Protestant commentaries on Romans that have preceded his own, and why he thinks he has something to add. While the reference to these living contemporaries might be taken as merely politic, the details speak of much more than Calvin's tact. Thus, when Calvin demurs over Philip Melanchthon's commentary for addressing only the main points of the epistle and wonders, on the other hand, at Martin Bucer's verbosity, his remarks are not really about style or aesthetics. Both

Melanchthon and Bucer were working out, in diverse ways, their own com-
mitments to a rhetorically informed methodology, a method of reading and
commenting – proposed by Rudolf Agricola in the late fifteenth century and
disseminated more recently by Erasmus – that sought to analyze a text in
terms of the writer's central arguments and concerns.[1] (Melanchthon himself was an influential advocate through his several textbooks on rhetoric,
including the 1531 *Elementa rhetorices*.) While Melanchthon's Romans
commentary deliberately restricted itself solely to these main "topics" or
"common places" (*topica* or *loci communes*), Bucer's was a detailed, verse-
by-verse commentary regularly interrupted by digressions on more or less
the same theological topics as they were raised by the biblical text. Calvin
carefully distanced himself from both precedents, but he by no means contested the rhetorical theory or method at work in them. To the contrary,
he embraced the theory but worked it out differently, so that the letter to
Gyrnaeus exactly confirms what Calvin had written just two months earlier,
in the preface to his 1539 revision of the *Institutes*, namely, that he had now
recast the *Institutes* as a repository for the "dogmatic digressions" and "common places" that naturally arise from the course of exegesis, enabling him
to preserve the brevity of the biblical commentaries he planned to write.

Taken as a whole, then, the letter to Gyrnaeus forecasts four things
about Calvin's biblical interpretation, all of which could be correlated to
one degree or another with the leading values of Renaissance humanism.

First, the goal of all interpretation is to understand the mind or intention of the writer, and Calvin typically employed the best tools of his day –
establishing historical contexts and background, searching for the precise
meaning of terms in the original Hebrew or Greek, worrying over geography
and chronology, and so on – to make his case for what the biblical authors
intended. To be sure, in the case of the Bible, "authorship" could be a bit
ambiguous, insofar as the texts attributed to human writers were understood to be also the inspired Word of God and thus superintended, if not
dictated, by the Holy Spirit. In the commentary on Romans, Calvin typically
sorts out the meaning of sentences and paragraphs by appealing to what
the apostle intended. However, Calvin often stresses less what the apostle
intended to *say* than what Paul intended his words to *effect* in the life of the
church at Rome. And though the epistle to the Romans is explained mostly
in terms of what Paul the writer intended, there are places where Calvin
recognizes that Paul, called and commissioned to be Christ's apostle, is also
guided by a higher, divine intentionality. (In Calvin's later commentaries
on other biblical genres, particularly those that feature direct divine commands or prophecy, Scripture's duality of intention or authorship is even
more prominent, but Calvin is little bothered by the ambiguity and can

commonly be found to make dual references, alluding almost interchangeably to the intention of, say, Moses *or* the Holy Spirit.)

Second, Calvin was committed to effective communication, that is, to an exposition of Scripture that would be useful in serving the cause of gospel and church. "Lucid brevity" was, for him, not merely the pursuit of eloquence that was so prized by some rhetoricians. It was also, and predominantly, the way for speech to teach and persuade effectively or "usefully" – a point made long before Calvin by Agricola and Melanchthon, among others. As Calvin twice states in the Preface, his sole motive for writing a new commentary on Romans was to seek "the common good of the church." Both accents – lucid brevity and utility – fall into orbit with yet another principle, that of accommodation, in that effective communication must be suited to the capacity and circumstances of one's hearers. A principle at once rhetorical and theological and complex, accommodation is regularly cited in Calvin's first commentary as not only Paul's teaching method or strategy, but also as the pattern followed by God in his revelatory activity and by Jesus Christ in the incarnation itself. Accommodation is further commended as a path of discipleship, whereby Christians gauge their own behavior to the profit of their brothers and sisters.[2] Much as was the case also for Melanchthon, Calvin saw Scripture as ultimately the perfect instrument of a rhetor truly divine.

Third, despite the widespread misconception that by the motto *sola scriptura* Protestants wished to dispense with all post-apostolic traditions and writings, Calvin laconically indicates here that he highly values the biblical work of his ancient predecessors. The inference is borne out not only by what we suspect of Calvin's earlier training but also by his widespread reading and copious use of the church fathers throughout his later career. In fact, right about the time Calvin wrapped up both the 1539 edition of the *Institutes* and his commentary on Romans, he was apparently also planning a rather ambitious patristic project (see below).

Fourth, as argued by his critique of Melanchthon and Bucer, Calvin's labors in biblical interpretation were by no means a reaction against a rhetorical approach to the analysis and exposition of texts, nor were Calvin's exegetical efforts at odds with his work as a writer of dogmatic or systematic theology, that is, of the *loci communes* found in his *Institutes*. The two labors were by design intertwined and interdependent, and if they appeared in print as two quite diverse genres, they nonetheless mutually reinforced Calvin's commitment to discerning and expounding the *scopus* of the biblical text and the mind of its author – which, in twain, pointed to and proclaimed the good news about God's redeeming work as promised and fulfilled in Jesus Christ.

Within a year or so of his commentary on Romans, Calvin penned a second set of reflections on the best way to interpret Scripture. These thoughts are found in his *Preface to the Homilies of Chrysostom*, a document less well known than the Preface to his Romans commentary, mostly because Calvin's project – to translate the homilies of John Chrysostom into French – was never carried beyond his rough draft of the introduction.[3] The *Preface to Chrysostom* deserves notice for adding or amplifying three points.

First, lest one read his concise praise of the ancient commentators (in his remarks to Gyrnaeus) as cloaking an actual indifference, Calvin here crafts a sustained apology for reading the church fathers. They offer substantial benefits, including guidance in the meaning of Scripture, examples of and exhortation to moral uprightness and discipline, and insight into the life and practices of the early church, which was better ordered and purer than the church of later centuries. One must not overlook the implications here for Calvin's view of the authority of Scripture versus tradition: the writings of the church fathers are aids for the reading of Scripture, indeed, resources *provided by the Lord* (he says) to serve in tandem with the inward, illuminating work of the Holy Spirit. Such writings are not to be accepted uncritically, to be sure, but to spurn them would be an act of gross ingratitude. Once again, whatever *sola scriptura* may have meant for Calvin and whatever constituted good exegesis for him, he was naturally inclined to draw the Fathers into the conversation rather than push them away.

Second, the *Preface to Chrysostom* highlights Calvin's dedication to a biblical interpretation that would serve the uneducated – in other words, the laity, though Calvin also acknowledged that some ministers of his day were less than fluent in Greek and Latin. Given that it was barely a quarter of a century since Erasmus' controversial call for vernacular translation of the Bible, Calvin's plan to translate Chrysostom's sermons into the vernacular would be a still greater novelty.[4] Even here, Calvin's vision for an educated laity was not an end in itself but was framed as part of his larger agenda for the general reform and renewal of the church.

Third, Calvin's recommendation of Chrysostom above all other patristic writers points directly to one of his hallmarks as an exegete, namely, his avowed commitment to the "literal" or "historical" sense of the text. While Calvin admits that Chrysostom's theology has its flaws, he lauds him above all for sticking in his interpretation with the plain meaning of Scripture and the simple meaning of its words (*simplici verborum sensu*). Calvin's position here is hardly new or unique, of course, for he was preceded by many other reformers who felt that the church had been badly misled by fanciful and capricious exegesis, particularly the so-called "spiritual" or allegorical exegesis of many patristic and medieval writers. No one came in for a drubbing on this score more than Origen, the third-century Alexandrian exegete, whose "constant allegories" Calvin faulted for obscuring the Bible's plain meaning (*scripturae sinceritatem*). Here, too, Calvin was saying nothing new, for – with the notable exception of Erasmus, who praised Origen and commended allegory – most of Calvin's colleagues leveled similar criticisms, making Origen a whipping boy for the abuses of "spiritual" interpretation in general. But in the *Preface to Chrysostom*, Calvin is not merely parroting a Protestant party line, for he had already discountenanced Origen's specific assertion that Romans 7:14 ("For we know that the law is spiritual") warranted the dismissal of the literal sense of Scripture. In his later commentaries, Calvin would replay his condemnation of Origen whenever he found texts that offered what he felt were spurious encouragement for unwarranted allegory or "spiritual" exegesis. Nevertheless, as we turn to examine Calvin's actual exegetical practice, we will see how his seemingly absolute dismissal of allegory was heavily modified in the field.

## CALVIN'S EXEGETICAL PRACTICE

To this point we have deliberately focused on Calvin's earliest reflections or pronouncements about biblical interpretation. These two prefaces, drafted more or less in the course of writing his first biblical commentary, provide an open window into Calvin's study and intentions, but they do not tell the whole story. Did Calvin do what he said he would do? To what extent did he, in fact, interact with the work of others? How did he address certain traditional and unavoidable problems of Christian exegesis, including the role of figurative exegesis, the relationship of the Old Testament to the New, biblical prophecy and its fulfillment, and so on? How did he approach the more workmanlike tasks of exegesis, and how was his work received and appreciated?

We may begin by focusing on Calvin's interaction with other writers and sources – a line of inquiry that brings before us several questions, including the possible influence exerted by earlier interpreters as well as by his contemporaries, Calvin's attitude toward traditional exegesis and exegetical tradition, and his exegetical method. The prefaces examined above speak explicitly of Calvin's enthusiasm for the church fathers, so that one would expect patristic sources to play a prominent role in his own exegetical work – and they do. However, Calvin's signals here are rather mixed, for if he labored in the *Preface to Chrysostom* to exonerate the virtues of Chrysostom's non-allegorical exegesis from the faults of his theology, his commentaries routinely dissented also from Chrysostom's exegesis, suggesting that Calvin was more enamored with Chrysostom's moral seriousness than with his actual exegetical findings.[5] Calvin's ambiguous relationship to Chrysostom prods us to remember that use and influence are distinct issues: while the former can at times be documented, the latter case is vastly more difficult to prove.[6] Nonetheless, Calvin does follow a general pattern in citing his sources: it is the church fathers above all whom he will name in his writings, as a mark of respect for their authority (second, of course, to Scripture), whereas scholastic and contemporary writers will normally not be mentioned by name because they are not seen as authorities. In Calvin's commentaries, though, patristic citations are of two sorts: when discussing dogmatic issues raised in the course of exegesis, the Fathers will often be cited as authorities, usually in the service of Calvin's theological polemic; when the issues are more purely exegetical, Calvin will cite the arguments of the Fathers there, too, but they are treated more as debating partners with whom he is just as likely to disagree.[7]

Calvin is thus only moderately helpful in informing the reader about his sources and method, for he appears to name his sources only when it serves his rhetorical purpose, that is, to buttress his argument. But there are other factors making Calvin's sources harder to trace. For instance, even where he names a patristic source, he may be quoting or paraphrasing the source from his own impressive memory, or he might have derived the reference from an intermediate source, such as a handbook of quotations or another commentator. Calvin's contemporary sources are more hidden still, as indicated by his 1555 letter to Francis Burkhard. Defending his right to disagree with Luther, Calvin asserts that he prefers to "bury errors in silence" – assuredly a testimony that his tacit dissent from Luther was not accidental but deliberate, and a clue that Calvin's absorption of Luther might well lie behind his common objections to what "some" or "others" say. Accordingly, studies of late have attempted to track Calvin's sources and patterns of usage not by assuming that named references represent books that lay open on his desk, but by searching throughout the literature available to Calvin and by examining even unnamed citations or generic references (what "the Jews" or "the ancients" say) with an eye to establishing the most immediate and plausible sources on which Calvin might have drawn.

Proceeding in this painstaking manner, one can verify that Calvin's knowledge of rabbinic writings was not obtained directly but derived most often from the annotations in Sebastian Münster's *Biblia Hebraica,* which  summarized rabbinic arguments in Latin, and occasionally from other secondary sources, such as Martin Bucer's commentary on the Psalms.[8] Another recent study has scrutinized every named reference in Calvin's commentary on Genesis (and every specific but unnamed reference in Genesis 1–11) in an attempt to ascertain the sources that Calvin the pastor actually used. It proves to be a modest collection. Virtually all Calvin's citations in this commentary can be accounted for by consulting fewer than ten books, including five Bibles or translations, mostly with annotations; the "questions" on Genesis written by both Jerome and Augustine; the first half of Luther's commentary on Genesis; and – of surprising importance – a more or less philological study of the Vulgate text of Genesis written by the late Vatican librarian, Agostino Steucho.[9] What is impressive about this list is not just its brevity, but also that it consists mostly of reference tools and translation aids. Only Luther offers anything like a theological commentary, but Calvin assuredly mined Luther for his other data, including additional secondhand reports of rabbinic exegesis. Conspicuously absent are two standard repositories of exegetical opinion, the *Ordinary Gloss* and its frequent companion, the *Postils* of Nicholas of Lyra. These findings suggest at least two things: first, that Calvin was far too busy to root his lectures or sermons in any fresh or extensive polling of his exegetical forebears; second, if Calvin is to be credited with an independence of mind in his biblical interpretation, it would be too generous to credit his independence as always forged in awareness of the full sweep of patristic or medieval exegesis.

In other cases, however, the independence of Calvin's positions may actually mask a great deal of thought and an unheralded dialogue with his peers. Moreover, from the standpoint of exegetical method, his treatment of high doctrine is often less revealing than seemingly mundane issues of morals or polity. For example, it was customary for Christian preachers and teachers to invoke the patriarchs and other Old Testament figures as moral exemplars – a problematic practice, at least in those instances where the patriarchs acted scandalously, by lying or committing polygamy, then went on their way, utterly uncensured by the biblical narrator. Invariably, interpreters filled the scriptural silences with excuses for these misdeeds, usually by appealing to some hidden divine permission or by crediting the patriarchs' behavior as the lesser of two evils. Though he knows these traditional excuses, Calvin stands alone in repudiating them all. True, Scripture supplies neither excuse nor condemnation, but Calvin thinks it safer to presume the sinfulness of the patriarchs than to fabricate a miracle of which the text knows nothing. In other words, Calvin's moral conservatism and exegetical caution are reflexes of one another. By contrast, in the case of the New Testament prohibitions against women speaking in church, Calvin's exegesis is a striking mixture of the traditional and the progressive: like most of his theological predecessors, he believes that men were created to lead in church, home, and society, yet he can also voice the opinion of a very few of his contemporaries who would allow women to exercise public ministry in emergency circumstances – a view almost certainly informed not only by Calvin's nuanced reading of the Pauline injunctions, but also by events in Geneva and elsewhere in the early days of the Reformation.[10]

Calvin's interpretative practice, with its ambiguous debt to tradition and traditional exegesis, is further exposed by examining his exegesis in light of his advocacy for "literal" or non-allegorical exposition. Though Calvin sometimes rails against the rabbis for their invention of allegories, Origen is far more often his target, as noted earlier. But it remains to see what exactly impelled Calvin's rejection of allegorical exegesis as well as what he meant by the literal or plain meaning of Scripture. Unlike Calvin, who was schooled decades later, Martin Luther could reminisce about his mastery of the "fourfold" pattern of medieval exegesis that expounded not only the Bible's "letter" or historical meaning but also its three spiritual senses – allegory, tropology, and anagogy, which discovered extra lessons in Scripture about Christ and the church, morality and discipleship, and the eternal life to come. Calvin admits of no such expertise and would seem never to have known anything but an instinctive contempt for allegory, but the point should not be overdrawn: it would be absurd to expect Calvin, the pastor of an often wayward flock, to be hostile to the lessons sought by these "spiritual" approaches, as if he could possibly be reluctant to teach his readers and hearers about Christ or the church or eternal life, much less Christian morality!

The complexity of Calvin's use and rejection of figurative exegesis is captured in depth in his comments on Galatians 4 – arguably, the Bible's interpretative crux with respect to allegory. There, in verse 24, St. Paul presents the conflict between Sarah and Hagar (and their sons Isaac and Ishmael) as an *allegoria* of the contrast between faith and works and between the gospel and the law. Not surprisingly, Calvin begins by railing against "Origen and many others" who have twisted Scripture from its "true" sense, which is the literal meaning, simple and straightforward. The "mysteries" and "multiple meanings" invented over the centuries are a trick of Satan intended to corrupt the authority of Scripture. Calvin despises allegories of this sort as arbitrary and fictive. But what of the apostle's own discovery of an allegory here, strung between Genesis 21 and Galatians 4? In this instance, Calvin does follow Chrysostom: Paul uses "allegory" loosely, to indicate what is more properly called *typology*. In discussions among biblical scholars of the later twentieth century, typology was often distinguished as more legitimate or more respectable than allegory, on the grounds that whereas allegory is an arbitrary metaphor often constructed from the words of a text without regard for the context or narrative, typology is generally constructed or inferred with deliberate attention paid to the larger historical narrative. In fact, the boundary between allegory and typology is not always so nicely marked, but Calvin's instincts do run in this direction. Paul's "allegory" is legitimate, Calvin explains, precisely because it is not really a departure from the literal sense: Paul can compare the fracture in Abraham's family to the birth of the church in the New Testament because in Abraham's own day his household *was* the church, literally and historically.

Calvin's exposition of Galatians 4 is a dense microcosm of much of his biblical work. Without a doubt, he wants to leaves room for "figurative" readings of Scripture, yet he always strains to find a direct tie to the literal or historical sense, even if he has to read the historical narrative and the "mind of the writer" somewhat generously. Thus, he generally shies away from "allegory" but will happily embrace plausible analogies, types, metaphors, and so on – as a rhetorically trained critic, his technical vocabulary is rich and precise – so long as he sees a warrant in the context of the narrative that serves as the source of the type or analogy or application. Accordingly, Calvin will dismiss out of hand any allegory that he finds utterly off the subject of the scriptural text or that wrenches words out of context while ignoring the plot. On the other hand, as we will see, he finds embedded in both the New Testament and the Old many other instances of "allegory"[11] – defined, to be sure, as a rhetorical device or metaphor rather than as a theological discovery.

We can conclude our examination of Calvin's practice as a biblical interpreter by exploring the two crucial dimensions of his own "figurative" exegesis. One pertains to his understanding of how the Old Testament relates to the New; another to how the church of his own day is addressed by the whole witness of Scripture.

Though critically aware of the hermeneutical patterns the New Testament seems to follow in its use of the Old, Calvin's biblical interpretation is also shaped by convictions drawn largely from Pauline and Augustinian theology. Most importantly, Calvin knows of but one people of God, one salvation history, and one covenant; the two Testaments represent but different administrations. He gets this especially from Paul. If Abraham is the father of those who are justified by faith, and if the standing of the Christian church is identical with that of Isaac, the freeborn son of promise, then the Old Testament has just as much to teach Christians about God and faith and salvation as does the New. Every biblical text, then, has as its larger context the divine plan – the "scope" of Scripture and the "mind" of the Spirit that guided the biblical writers – to save a fallen race of sinners through the death of Jesus, who was the promised Messiah of the Old Testament people of God and the full revelation of God for those in the New. The material continuity of the Bible vastly upstages the more formal disjuncture between the two Testaments. In the New Testament, the life of the Christian church is deliberately patterned on the main features of the Old Testament, so that institutions such as circumcision, sacrifice, and the priesthood are types or even (Calvin says) allegories for us. To be sure, the New Testament offers a clearer view of the divine plan than was enjoyed by Israel, whereas the Old Testament represents the childhood of the church: a state of relative immaturity necessarily addressed with the sort of condescension (or better, "accommodation") appropriate for children.

One might expect, then, that Calvin would be prone to go about finding Christ or Christian doctrines throughout the Old Testament, but he was actually criticized in his own day for being overly restrained in this respect. For instance, Calvin was a staunch defender of a trinitarian doctrine of God, but he saw no reason to suppose that the word for "God" in Genesis 1:1 (*elohim*, plural) was meant to prove the plurality of divine persons in the godhead (though he does find the Trinity in the plural verb at Gen. 1:26). While many Christian scholars were eager to use Jewish sources and informants to learn the interpretive secrets locked within the Hebrew Scriptures, others were deeply suspicious of the rabbis and of any reading of the Bible that countenanced "the Jews and their fables." Just so, Calvin's own countryman, Faber Stapulensis, urged Christian readers to take the "literal" sense of the Psalms to refer not to David but to Christ, of whom David wrote; a "fleshly" literal reading would miss the sweetness of Scripture by focusing only on the historical context, as the Jews do who deny Christ. In contrast to Faber, and even to Luther, Calvin attempted to respect both the "Jewish" and the "Christian" reading of the Old Testament, but his results did not please every Christian reader. Calvin does read some psalms for their messianic content, just as the New Testament does, but even the psalms he regards as genuinely messianic do not lose their character as psalms also genuinely about David, whose kingdom foreshadowed a grander kingdom to come without losing its own historical integrity. Calvin's treatment of biblical prophecy thus recalls the "double" literal sense proposed two centuries earlier by Nicholas of Lyra, who distinguished in the Psalms between their "literal-historical" referent (David) and their "literal-prophetic" referent (Christ). Indeed, with his penchant for drawing also the church of his own day into the biblical frame of reference, Calvin may well register a third and more eschatological "literal" sense, one that looks to "our" participation in the kingdom of Christ.[12]

Calvin's exegetical restraint appears in other ways, too. Many aspects of Christian worship were articulated in the Pauline epistles as types of Old Testament practices, as at 1 Corinthians 10:1–5, where the events of Exodus 13–17 – crossing the Red Sea, being fed in the wilderness – correspond to baptism and the Lord's Supper. Calvin wrote commentaries on both books, but while he is happy to elaborate on these Old Testament "sacraments" in his commentary on 1 Corinthians, his treatment of the same stories in his Exodus commentary sticks closely to the historical context and to the intention of Moses; the apostle's typological expositions are mentioned but remain distinctly in the background. The subdued character of Calvin's Old Testament exegesis has quite fairly been attributed to his respect for the original historical context and for the intention of the Old Testament writer: Calvin interprets these texts on their own terms, sharing their authors' historical limitations rather than imposing a Christian triumphalism.[13] Calvin can exercise such seeming restraint, however, largely because he is so thoroughly convinced of the continuity of salvation history. Not only does the Old Testament lead to its fulfillment in the New Testament, the two together lead also "to us," to the church of today.

The bridge from biblical history to Calvin's own day can take various forms. Often he appeals to analogy, to the "similarity of the times" between, say, the circumstances of Daniel and those of today. Sometimes he argues that the Old Testament prophecies of an earthly restoration of Israel, or of a great cataclysm, or a new earth, were not intended for literal fulfillment. They were instead originally meant as hyperbolic, as figurative, as *allegories* of the wholly spiritual kingdom of Christ that was yet to come. Fulfilled by the advent of Christ's kingdom, these texts now apply to the church of today. Of course, the immediacy of that application brings into the present not only biblical promises but also biblical threats and enemies. Calvin addressed his readers and hearers as the heirs of Abraham by faith, but the blessing was a mixed one. Every day, the children of the patriarch were threatened by the descendants of Hagar and Ishmael, whose hostility and arrogance Calvin saw reborn in the "papists" and their allies. Truly, if pastoral application is a hallmark of Calvin's biblical interpretation, polemical outbursts against the vicious character of papal religion and Jewish obtuseness are inscribed immediately below it.

## CALVIN'S EXEGETICAL LEGACY

Did Calvin's practice conform to the expectations raised by his more theoretical statements? The answer must be a mixture of yes and no. Calvin's fierce commitment to the literal sense of Scripture and to expounding the mind or intention of the author was diligently pursued through all his commentaries, as well as in his sermons, and the doctrinal fruits of his exegesis were faithfully laid before his readers and hearers as useful for their edification. But even as it is misleading to think Calvin's rejection of allegorical interpretation distances him definitively from his patristic or medieval forebears, so too it would be mistaken to think that the object of his literal exegesis was the same as what historical-critical scholarship seeks today. Calvin was driven by a passion for application. It would be truer to say that he did not discard the three "spiritual" senses, but pruned their excesses[14] and, in many cases, used rhetorical analysis and an extended sense of what constitutes the "context" of the Bible to root a text's spiritual applications in the author's intention rather than in the reader's invention. His motive was far more to reassert and defend the priority of the literal sense of Scripture than to deny the complex of figurative relationships that bind the New Testament to the Old, and both Testaments to the church of his day.

Though in his own day and in the centuries to follow, Calvin has been regularly lionized for his brilliance as a biblical interpreter, a longer and more comparative study could demonstrate in detail just how unoriginal the elements of his exegesis often are. There is little he says by way of methodology or the theory of interpretation that cannot be traced to others before him, whether Melanchthon, Bullinger, Bucer, or the various contributors to the humanist revival of the sixteenth century. Moreover, in his own day and in the centuries to follow, Calvin's exegesis has also been regularly targeted: for excessive polemic, for too close a tie to his theology or theological agenda, or for prizing practical application and theological exegesis over critical and technical insights. Writing at a century's remove from Calvin, that great compiler of exegesis Matthew Poole could bear witness to both views, and to Calvin's pervasive presence: while some saw Calvin as "a great man," to others he was "worse than a dog or snake." Nonetheless, Poole claimed, "almost everyone has Calvin in their hands and libraries" – even his foes.

If not to his originality, then, to what might one attribute Calvin's longevity? Probably his importance and influence have been conveyed as much by what he intended in his work as a biblical interpreter as by what he actually achieved. That is to say, no one has ever faulted Calvin for attempting to tether his exposition to the literary and historical context and to the mind and intention of the author, and to do so with clear, concise, effective prose. While most of his contemporaries would have agreed with this agenda, they often stumbled or temporized where Calvin succeeded, even by the standards of commentators today. If some fault his exposition for failing to meet these goals, the blame often stems from Calvin's other presuppositions about the Bible, which he saw as a unified book with a unified plot, inspired in its wording by the same Spirit that was needed to guide its reading, its interpretation, and its application. Calvin was not a detached critic and would not have wanted to be one. Neither was he uncritical in his judgments. Not surprisingly, his legacy burns brightest in churches and communities wherein is treasured, if also variously updated, Calvin's ideal: to discern throughout one's reading of Scripture a union of Word and Spirit, criticism and faith, text and practice, hearing and obedience.

### Notes

1 See Richard A. Muller, *The Unaccommodated Calvin: Studies in the Foundation of a Theological Tradition* (New York: Oxford University Press, 2000), 108–17; and Olivier Millet, *Calvin et la dynamique de la parole: étude de rhétorique réformée*, Bibliothéque littéraire de la renaissance, série 3, tome 28 (Geneva: Editions Slatkine, 1992), 125–35.

.2 The concept of accommodation, of course, is not restricted to instances where Calvin uses *accommodare*. See David F. Wright, "Calvin's 'Accommodation' Revisited," in Peter De Klerk, ed., *Calvin as Exegete: Papers and Responses Presented at the Ninth Colloquium on Calvin and Calvin Studies, 1993* (Grand Rapids: CRC, 1995), 171–90.

3 W. Ian P. Hazlett, "Calvin's Latin Preface to His Proposed French Edition of Chrysostom's Homilies: Translation and Commentary," in James Kirk, ed., *Humanism and Reform: The Church in Europe, England, and Scotland* (Oxford: Blackwell, 1991), 129–50. Cf. Millet, *Calvin et la dynamique de la parole*, 171–5.

4 Hazlett, "Calvin's Latin Preface", 140 n. 6.

5 Alexandre Ganoczy and Klaus Müller, *Calvins handschriftliche Annotationen zu Chrysostomus: Ein Beitrag zur Hermeneutik Calvins* (Wiesbaden: Franz Steiner, 1981); cf. John Robert Walchenbach, "John Calvin as Biblical Commentator: An Investigation into Calvin's Use of John Chrysostom as an Exegetical Tutor," Ph.D. dissertation, University of Pittsburgh (1974).

6 A distinction trenchantly argued by A. N. S. Lane, *John Calvin: Student of the Church Fathers* (London: T.&T. Clark; Grand Rapids: Baker, 1999), 15.

7 These are the conclusions of ibid., 28–32.

8 Max Engammare, "*Johannes Calvinus trium linguarum peritus?* La question de l'Hébreu," *Bibliothèque d'Humanisme et Renaissance* 58 (1996), 35–60. Engammare also concludes that Calvin's translations of biblical Hebrew were relatively faithful but not without occasional flaws.

9 Lane, *Student of the Church Fathers*, 233. The Bibles include Stephanus' 1545 Bible, Münster's *Hebraica Biblia Latina*, Fagius' *Thargum*, Servetus' marginal notes, and the translation of Santi Pagnini. Steucho's work was entitled *Veteris testamenti ad Hebraicam veritatem recognitio, sive in Pentateuchum, Annotationes*.

10 John L. Thompson, "The Immoralities of the Patriarchs in the History of Exegesis: A Reassessment of Calvin's Position," *Calvin Theological Journal* 26 (1991), 9–46; John L. Thompson, *John Calvin and the Daughters of Sarah: Women in Regular and Exceptional Roles in the Exegesis of Calvin, His Predecessors, and His Contemporaries* (Geneva: Librairie Droz, 1992).

11 Substantial examples are furnished by David L. Puckett, *John Calvin's Exegesis of the Old Testament* (Louisville: Westminster John Knox Press, 1995), 105–32.

12 See Richard A. Muller, "The Hermeneutic of Promise and Fulfillment in Calvin's Exegesis of the Old Testament Promises of the Kingdom," in David C. Steinmetz,

ed., *The Bible in the Sixteenth Century* (Durham: Duke University Press, 1990), esp. p. 78.

13 T. H. L. Parker, *Calvin's Old Testament Commentaries* (Edinburgh: T.&T. Clark, 1986), 77–82.

14 David C. Steinmetz, "Calvin and the Irrepressible Spirit," *Ex Auditu* 12 (1996), 94–107; see also John L. Thompson, "Calvin's Exegetical Legacy: His Reception and Transmission of Text and Tradition," in David L. Foxgrover, ed., *The Legacy of John Calvin: Calvin Studies Society Papers 1999* (Grand Rapids: CRC, 2000), 31–56.

# 5 Calvin's theology

## I. JOHN HESSELINK

## THE THEOLOGIAN

Philip Melanchthon, Luther's close friend and colleague and himself no mean theologian, reportedly dubbed Calvin "the theologian." Other Reformation leaders, including Luther, published theological treatises of significance. On the Reformed side, Zwingli, Bullinger, Bucer, Beza, and Peter Martyr made theological contributions. Yet it was only Melanchthon who wrote something like a systematic theology with his *Loci Communes* (1521 and later editions). Even so, Melanchthon was quite willing to acknowledge that Calvin was without peer when it came to theology.

### The *Institutes*

That reputation originally resulted from the favorable reception of Calvin's *magnum opus*, the *Institutes of the Christian Religion*, which has been hailed as one of the books "that has changed the world." A more modest assessment, and one generally recognized, is that it is a classic of Protestant theology. It should be kept in mind, however, that the first edition of the *Institutes* (1536) takes up only 243 pages in volume I of the *opera selecta*, whereas the second edition (1539), in which Calvin really comes into his own, is three times as large; and the final edition of 1559 is almost five times as large as the first edition.

Before proceeding to analyze the structure and nature of the *Institutes* and its distinctive theological characteristics, a common error must be corrected. That is, that Calvin is basically a man of one book, the *Institutes*, and further, that one can grasp Calvin's theology by simply studying this classic. As Calvin himself points out in his preface to the final edition of the *Institutes* ("John Calvin to the Reader"), the eventual purpose of this work was not only to provide a summary of Christian doctrine, but also to be a guide to the Scriptures, and it should be read in conjunction with his commentaries on the Scriptures.[1] Of particular significance is Calvin's commentary on Romans which was written at the same time as he produced the second edition (1539) of the *Institutes*. The subsequent editions of the *Institutes* often incorporate and reflect insights gained from his work on recent commentaries. In addition to the commentaries, one must be familiar with Calvin's sermons, treatises, and catechisms in order to appreciate the breadth and depth of his theology. For the pastoral dimensions of his theology, his voluminous correspondence is an invaluable resource.

Thus, there is more to Calvin's theology than the *Institutes*. Nevertheless, it is here that we find the reformer's thought expressed in its most comprehensive and ordered manner. This was a lifetime project, for the various editions span almost his whole career as a reformer. He died only four years after publishing the final French edition of 1560.

In the past – and unfortunately occasionally still today – Calvin has been caricatured as the dictator of Geneva, who was ruthless and cold, without feeling and devoid of any sense of the love of God, a "Gesetzlehrer," a man of law, who had little appreciation for the gospel revealed in Jesus Christ.[2] However, a careful reading of the reformer's works, including the *Institutes*, reveals a man with a pastoral heart, whose theology reflects his piety, and is intended to edify, inspire, and challenge as much as to instruct and inform.

### Editions of the *Institutes*

The various editions of the *Institutes* reflect different purposes, but from the outset the pastoral, evangelical purpose is apparent. The first edition of 1536, a slight volume of only six chapters, was designed as a manual or handbook for religious inquirers. A second purpose was to provide a summary of and apology for the evangelical faith. In his Prefatory Address to King Francis I of France who was persecuting Protestants, Calvin writes:

> My purpose was solely to transmit certain rudiments by which those who are touched with any zeal for religion might be shaped to true godliness (*formentur ad veram pietatem*) and I undertook the labor especially for our French countrymen, very many of whom I knew to be hungering and thirsting for Christ; but I say very few who had been duly imbued with even a slight knowledge of him.

He adds that in this book there is only "an elementary form of teaching" and that it is his confession and defense of the new faith that is now undergoing frightful persecution.[3] In terms of content, the first edition is often considered the "Lutheran edition" because of Calvin's indebtedness to Luther for both form and content. It has even been called "a false start" as a specifically Reformed treatise, but such a charge overlooks the fact that much of the first edition remains in the final edition, including numerous passages which were taken over verbatim.

Even so, it is true that Calvin comes into his own in the second (1539) edition which represents a major breakthrough. It is not only three times the size of the first edition, but is also completely re-ordered. Moreover, Calvin now has in mind students of theology. Here we have a more properly theological introduction to the reading of Holy Scripture. The wider scope of this edition is also indicated by a slight change in the wording of the title. In the first edition, it reads in part, *"The Institute of the Christian Religion, containing almost the whole sum of piety and whatever it is necessary to know in the doctrine of salvation."* In the 1539 edition the "sum of piety" is changed to "a sum of our wisdom." However, we shall see later that a constant concern of Calvin's theology was always the promotion of piety or godliness and the "usefulness" (*utilitas*) of true doctrine.

In successive editions of 1543 f. and 1550 f. the scope and purpose of the *Institutes* remained the same, but the growth is significant. Calvin not only amplifies certain doctrines such as the person of Christ, predestination, and the church for polemical reasons, but he also reveals a growing knowledge of the church fathers[4] and an enriched understanding of Scripture. However, the preface to the 1539 edition is virtually repeated in the final 1559 edition. After stating that his purpose is "to prepare and instruct candidates in sacred theology," he adds, "I believe I have so embraced the sum of religion in all its parts, and have arranged it in such an order that if anyone rightly grasps it, it will not be difficult for him to determine what he ought to seek especially in Scripture, and to what he ought to relate its contents."[5]

However, Calvin never forgot ordinary believers who were not trained in theology. This is why he continually published French translations of the various editions, with the exception of the first one. As he states in his preface to the French edition of 1560: "It [the *Institutes*] can be a key to open the way for all the children of God into a good and right understanding of Holy Scripture."[6]

These are some of the factors that made the *Institutes* not only an immediate success in its first edition, but an enduring classic with a wide appeal to readers lay and learned. It is not a dogmatics or systematic theology in the modern sense. Calvin is noted for his systematic genius, often linked with his legal training, but it is not as systematic or logical as Thomas Aquinas' *Summa Theologica*, Schleiermacher's *Der Christliche Glaube* (*Christian Faith*), or Paul Tillich's *Systematic Theology*. It also differs in style and form from the first Protestant approach to a "systematic theology," Melanchthon's *Loci Communes* (*Common Places/Topics*). As Jean-Daniel Benoit points out, in the *Institutes* we have a book of profound learning which has a definite appeal to the intellect. Then he asks,

But what does this work have to do with the heart, the needs of souls, with that holy service which consists of the tact and concern (*sollicitude*) required for spiritual guidance? And yet, the *Institutes* is a religious book, in a certain respect, a book of piety perhaps more than a dogmatic treatise. It has nourished the spiritual life of many generations whose taste has not been dulled by daintiness (*faussé par des mièvreries*) and who were not afraid of strong nurture ... The *Institutes* is not only the book of a theologian; it is the book of a man who even before he became a pastor was haunted by a concern for souls.[7]

The *Institutes* is not a speculative system of theology deduced from some overruling principle such as the sovereignty of God. To the contrary, it contains so many surprises and seeming logical inconsistencies that Herman Bauke described Calvin's theology as a *complexio oppositorum*.[8] But this is going too far, for Calvin was largely successful in his goal of relating doctrinal topics according to "the right order of teaching." He spent a lifetime rearranging the various topics covered in his classic and was finally satisfied with the result in the 1559 *Institutes*. Hence, there is an impressive order and symmetry in this work. However, as John T. McNeill pointed out,

One who takes up Calvin's masterpiece with the preconception that its author's mind is a kind of efficient factory turning out and assembling parts of a neatly jointed structure of dogmatic logic will quickly find this assumption challenged and shattered. The discerning reader soon realizes that not the author's intellect alone but his whole spiritual and emotional being is enlisted in his work ... He was not, we may say, a theologian by profession, but a deeply religious man who possessed a genius for orderly thinking and obeyed the impulse to write out the implications of his faith. He calls his book not a *summa theologiae* but a *summa pietatis*. The secret of his mental energy lies in his piety; its product is his theology, which is his piety described at length.[9]

### The knowledge of God

The last statement could be misunderstood, however, for the *Institutes*, though expressive of Calvin's faith and piety, is not about piety, as such, despite frequent references to it.[10] The theme of the *Institutes* is the knowledge of God and of ourselves. This was stated in the first sentence of the first edition: "Nearly the whole of sacred doctrine consists in these two parts: the knowledge of God and of ourselves."[11] In the final edition this statement is repeated in amplified form: "Nearly all the wisdom we possess, that is to say, true and sound wisdom, consists of two parts: the knowledge of God and of ourselves. But, while joined by many bonds, which one precedes and brings forth the other is not easy to discern" (*Inst.* I.1.1).

Initially, Calvin gives the impression that the knowledge of self comes first, for as we look upon ourselves we inevitably turn our thought to God. In particular, it is our sinfulness that "compels us to look upward" (ibid.). However, we will never attain a clear knowledge of ourselves until we first "look upon God's face, and then descend from contemplating him to scrutinize [ourselves]" (*Inst.* I.1.2; modified). So although this mutual knowledge is reciprocal, logically and experientially it is only the knowledge of God's majesty that will sufficiently impress on us our "lowly state" (ibid.). Moreover, Calvin concludes that the order of right teaching requires that we discuss "the knowledge of God first" (ibid.).

Calvin proceeds to discuss the knowledge of God under two headings, the knowledge of God the Creator in Book I and the knowledge of God the Redeemer in Books II–IV. According to Edward A. Dowey, it is this *duplex cognitio Dei* which is the ordering principle of the *Institutes*.[12] In Calvin's words: "Since the Lord first appears in the creation of the world as in the general doctrine of Scripture, simply as a Creator, and afterwards as a Redeemer in Christ, a twofold knowledge (*duplex cognitio*) of him hence arises: of these the former is now to be considered, the latter will afterwards follow in order" (I.2.1, Beveridge translation).

T. H. L. Parker recognizes that the knowledge of God is a prominent theme in the *Institutes* but is critical of Dowey's thesis that the twofold knowledge of God is the governing ordering principle of the *Institutes*.[13] Parker maintains, rather, that the four books of the *Institutes* are based on the Apostles' Creed. This is really a misplaced debate, for obviously both are true, although the credal model is modified at several points. As Richard Muller has demonstrated, the structure or ordering of the *Institutes* is also influenced by the catechetical model (law, faith, prayer, and the sacraments) that was followed in the first edition of the *Institutes*, as well as by the Pauline model found in Romans. In the latter regard, Muller believes that from the second edition on, Calvin was influenced by Melanchthon's *Loci Communes* of 1536.[14]

### A central dogma?

Acknowledging that the knowledge of God is a major motif in Calvin's theology, the question has been raised repeatedly whether there is some fundamental doctrine from which Calvin's "system" is deduced. Reference has already been made to Bauke's thesis that Calvin's theological method is not a deduction from one or more central doctrines but a *complexio oppositorum*. Wilhelm Niesel rejected this thesis and the assumption that the nature of Calvin's theology can be settled by the study of its form. He agrees that no one special doctrine is the key to Calvin's theology. However, he is convinced that one must grasp the kernel or peculiar character of Calvin's theology in order to understand his thought. Niesel finds the golden thread that runs through all Calvin's theology in how Calvin seeks to relate his readers to the end and goal, the *scopus* of the Scriptures, viz., Jesus Christ. "The aim of all our attention to the Bible should be the recognition of Jesus Christ . . . In every aspect of doctrine, Calvin is concerned about only one thing, the God revealed in the flesh."[15]

Niesel here reflects the influence of his mentor and friend Karl Barth, who is noted for his radical christocentrism. However, to say that Calvin is christocentric is to say nothing special about his theology. For the same could be said with even greater force of Luther's theology. However, this emphasis was salutary in balancing the older traditional view of Calvin's theology as centering in his doctrine of God, particularly his sovereignty. A key passage in this connection is found in Calvin's commentary on Romans 10:4: "For Christ is the end (*telos*) of the law." Calvin interprets "end" here as completion or fulfillment and comments: "This remarkable passage declares that the law in all its parts has reference to Christ, and therefore no one will be able to understand it correctly who does not constantly strive to attain this mark."

Earlier, B. B. Warfield, an influential professor at Princeton Theological Seminary for many years, submitted that Calvin was above all the theologian of the Holy Spirit.[16] Subsequently, there have been several significant studies of the role of the Holy Spirit in Calvin's theology that confirm Warfield's thesis, the most significant being the magisterial work by Werner Krusche, *Das Wirken des Heiligen Geistes nach Calvin* (1957). Much can be said in favor of this view. Calvin's understanding of the relation of Word and Spirit, the inner witness of the Spirit in relation to the authority of Scripture, the role of the Spirit in faith and the Lord's Supper – these are all areas where Calvin more than any other reformer made significant contributions to theology.

However, it is not very helpful to single out one of these emphases as being "the" distinctive characteristic of Calvin's theology. He was indeed theocentric, christocentric, and pneumacentric, but all this says is that Calvin was thoroughly trinitarian. Whereas Calvin scholars have often described his view of the Trinity as traditional and not particularly significant, Philip Butin maintains that it is precisely his treatment of the

Trinity that is "the basis, pattern, and dynamic of the divine–human relationship . . . This understanding gives a particular contextuality, comprehensiveness, and coherence to his larger Christian vision."[17]

Rather than trying to find the hermeneutical key to Calvin's theology in one doctrine or motif or a general theme such as christocentrism, it is probably wiser to do as several German theologians have done, i.e., try to find several characteristic features of Calvin's theology that distinguish him from other theologians. One of the most helpful contributions has been that of Walter Kreck, for many years professor of theology at Bonn University. In an essay, "Die Eigenart der Theologie Calvins" ("The Distinctiveness of Calvin's Theology"),[18] he begins with the proposition that some of the distinctive features of Calvin's theology are to be found in his understanding of the Word of God. He points to several motifs in Calvin's theology, all of which hinge on his understanding of the Word of God and his approach to it.

1. _The first motif is the unity and inseparability of Word and Spirit._ Here Calvin differs from Luther, who emphasized the objective external Word in his conflict with the spiritual radicals. The result was the danger of uniting Word and Spirit so completely as to run the risk of identifying them. Calvin, in contrast to Luther, maintains that the Word and Spirit are intimately related but that they must also remain distinct and not be identified. The Spirit can, and sometimes does, work without the Word.[19] Calvin has occasionally been accused of being a spiritualist, but he does not speak of an inner light or Word of God that comes to people directly. Rather, it is the Holy Spirit who illumines the Word.

In response to those who charged that religion seems to be grounded in human opinion or that rational proof is required to confirm that the biblical writers spoke with divine authority, Calvin's response was his classic appeal to the internal and secret witness of the Holy Spirit:

> The testimony of the Spirit is more excellent than all reason. For as God alone is a fit witness of himself in his Word, so also the Word will not find acceptance in men's hearts before it is sealed by the inward testimony of the Spirit (_interiore Spiritus testimonio_). The same Spirit, therefore, who spoke through the mouth of the prophets must penetrate into our hearts to persuade us that they faithfully proclaimed what had been divinely commanded.   (_Inst._ I.7.4)

This emphasis on the unity and inseparability of Word and Spirit also has consequences for Calvin's concept of the church. In terms of this conviction he developed a relation between the historical church as the body of Christ and the kingdom of Christ in Book IV of the _Institutes_. "Through the Word and the Spirit, the church on earth is given continuous participation in the *regnum Christi* and is shaped and reformed in continuity with the christological pattern of the kingdom."[20] Thus Calvin explains the petition in the Lord's Prayer, "Thy kingdom come," in the following way:

> This is done partly by the preaching of the Word, partly by the secret power of the Spirit. He would govern us by his Word, but as the voice alone, without the inward influence of the Spirit, does not reach down into the heart, the two must be brought together for the establishment of God's kingdom.   (*Comm. Matt. 6:10*)[21]

2. *The second distinctive motif is the importance of the incarnate eternal Word.* For Calvin, it was crucial that God's Word in the flesh, Jesus Christ, does not remain high above us but exists in solidarity with us. In the opening section of his discussion of the person of Jesus Christ, Calvin quotes 1 Timothy 2:5: "For there is one God and there is one mediator between God and man, the man Jesus Christ." Calvin is sure that there is a special reason why Paul here distinctly reminds us that God's eternal Son is a real man. This could have been omitted, but Calvin feels that the Holy Spirit, knowing our weakness, therefore portrays "the Son of God familiarly among us as one of ourselves." Calvin then adds that if anyone wants to know where to find the mediator and how we must come to him, the answer is here: "The Spirit calls him [that is, Jesus Christ] man, thus teaching us that he is near us, indeed touches us, since he is our flesh" (*Inst.* II.12.1).

Again, to contrast Luther and Calvin on this point, it could be said that Luther lays more emphasis on Christ for us, Calvin on Christ in us. Therefore, another distinctive doctrine of Calvin is often held to be his notion of the mystical union of the believer with Christ (*Inst.* III.11.10), not mystical in the usual sense but in terms of the intimate relationship which believers have by faith in their Lord.[22] Characteristic are Calvin's words: "Our common nature with Christ is the pledge of our fellowship with the Son of God; and clothed with our flesh he vanquished death and sin together that the victory and triumph might be ours" (*Inst.* II.12.3).

At the same time Calvin emphasizes the majesty and eternal sovereign freedom of Christ. The true manhood of Jesus Christ is the presupposition for our communion with him, but it would be fatal to think of his humanity apart from his divinity. No one less than God himself could conquer sin and death. This, of course, has always been the orthodox doctrine of the church. In contrast to Luther, however, Calvin insisted that just as God is free in regard to the efficacy of the Word, so also God remains sovereign and free in the incarnation:

Even if the Word in his immeasurable essence united with the nature of man into one person, we do not imagine that he is confined therein. Here is something marvelous – the Son of God descended from heaven in such a way that without leaving heaven he willed to be born in a virgin's womb, to go about earth and to hang upon the cross; yet he continuously filled the world, even as he had done from the beginning.  (*Inst.* II.13.4)

This and similar passages (e.g. *Inst.* IV.17.30) prompted the Lutherans to label this view the *extra Calvinisticum*, that "Calvinistic beyond." Where Calvin stressed that the ascended Christ's divinity could not be contained in his humanity, Lutherans stressed the unity of the person of Christ.[23]

3. *The Word both gives and commands*. Luther, in his conflict with the Roman Catholic Church, emphasized the distinction between law and gospel. For him, human effort, good works, and the curse and wrath of God are represented in the law. The law is a hammer that beats us down and drives us to Christ. The gospel, on the contrary, is sheer grace, a freely offered gift, to be accepted by trust and faith. Calvin, no less that Luther, stressed that faith is grounded exclusively in God's gracious promises in the gospel. But Calvin was equally emphatic in his insistence that the Word of God that frees us by his promises at the same time makes a total claim upon us through his commands.

Calvin characteristically emphasizes the work of the Holy Spirit in this regard. We are not only saved by Christ, but by faith we live in him. He is not only our justification but also our sanctification. We are saved from sin, death, and the demands of the law and the devil, as Luther loved to repeat. But Calvin is eager to add that we are saved for something, namely, to serve and glorify our Creator and Redeemer. We are called to be holy. Christ is not only the high priest who made the unique and eternal sacrifice for sin; he is also the King and Lord who claims us for his service. Hence, Calvin stressed also "the obedience of faith," a good Pauline term. He rejoices in the law of God, which now for Christians no longer threatens and curses but which in faith is the means by which they express their gratitude.

For the redeemed, the law, no less than the gospel, is a gift; the God who delivered his people Israel from the bondage of Egypt also gave them a law as a means by which they might know his will and live out their calling. It was not intended as a new form of bondage but rather as the means to true freedom – the freedom that is possible when one is subject to his rightful Lord. The law is the law of the covenant and the covenant is a covenant of grace. It is therefore not a burden, but a joy; not a restriction but an aid; not a means for attaining righteousness, but rather a guide for people already redeemed. This is the so-called third use of the law which for Calvin was the "principal" and "proper" use. For Luther, the first use of the law, the accusing and killing function, was the principal use. Calvin emphasized rather that the law rests on the bedrock of God's grace: "It was an inestimable favor that God condescended to deposit his law with the children of Israel" (*Comm. Deut. 30:15*).[24]

Calvin, therefore, sees great significance in the preface to the Decalogue or Ten Commandments. Before the first commandment is given, before the imperative – is the indicative: "I am the Lord your God, who brought you out of the land of Egypt, out of the house of bondage" (Exod. 20:2). By this, Calvin says,

> The Lord means that Israel has been freed from miserable bondage that they, in obedience and readiness to serve, worship him as the author of their freedom . . . Deliverance is mentioned in order that the Jews may give themselves over more eagerly to their Lord, who by right claims them for himself. But in order that it may not seem that this has nothing to do with us, we must regard the Egyptian bondage of Israel as a type of the spiritual captivity in which all of us are bound until our heavenly Vindicator, having freed us by the power of his arm, leads us into the Kingdom of his freedom . . . There is no one, therefore, who ought not to be captivated or to embrace the Lawgiver, in the observance of whose commandments he is taught to take especial delight; from whose kindness he expects both an abundance of all things and the glory of immortal life; by whose marvelous power and mercy he knows himself freed from the jaws of death. (*Inst.* II.8.15)

4. *The Word of God is an electing and rejecting word.* It is erroneous to claim that the doctrine of predestination is the center and foundation of Calvin's thought. It was Augustine, not Calvin, who first taught this doctrine. It is important to see that his original concern in taking up this doctrine was practical, not speculative. The question that troubled him was, how is it possible that when people hear the gospel, one accepts it and another rejects it? The answer, as he saw it, was that for some the Word remains external and thereby ineffectual. For others, the outer call to repentance and faith is accompanied by the inner call and witness of the Holy Spirit. Calvin then concluded that from eternity God elects some to salvation and rejects others to damnation. This is the so-called doctrine of double predestination, which appears already in Calvin's first catechism of 1538.[25] In his later extended discussion in the *Institutes* of 1559, Calvin referred to God's decree

of rejection as a "dreadful decree" (*decretum horribile, Inst.* III.23.7). But he was convinced that this was the Apostle Paul's teaching in Romans 9:6–24.

Calvin does not, however, teach that there is a symmetry or parallel between election and reprobation as taught by some later Calvinists. Nor does he speculate concerning who is elect and non-elect. "Let us not," he warns, "seek to penetrate into heaven itself, and to fathom what God from eternity decreed for us. Such thinking can only vex us with miserable anxiety and trouble" (1538 Catechism, article 13).

Rather, urges Calvin, let us shun such fruitless speculation and look to Jesus Christ, the pledge of our election in whom we were chosen before the foundation of the world (Eph. 1:4). Appealing to this text, he uses one of his favorite metaphors – the mirror – and like Augustine applies it to Christ in regard to our election: "If we have been chosen in him [Christ], we shall not find assurance of our election in ourselves; and not even in God the Father, if we conceive him as severed from his Son. Christ, then, is the mirror wherein we must, and without self-deception may, contemplate our own election (*Inst.* III.24.5).

Kreck rejects Calvin's doctrine of double predestination but not his whole doctrine of election. In the first place, he says, we must acknowledge that the phenomenon of unbelief remains an incomprehensible mystery. Second, for Calvin and his followers this doctrine did not mean fatalism. In no way did it weaken Calvin's zeal for preaching or lead to indifference or complacency. On the contrary, as Paul Jacobs has pointed out in his book on Calvin's doctrine of predestination, *Prädestination und Verantworklichkeit bei Calvin* (*Predestination and Responsibility in Calvin*),[26] this doctrine has ethical consequences, both personal and corporate. For Calvin, and particularly the later French Huguenots, this doctrine gave the will and the courage to endure persecution and resist all kinds of tyranny. It was also the certainty that their salvation and their cause were grounded in God's eternal election and not their own faith that gave them the courage to witness so courageously.

### Other distinctive contributions

The four motifs of Walter Kreck provide a framework for noting some major themes in Calvin's theology, but they have by no means exhausted the reformer's many contributions to theology. These contributions are in a sense not novel or unique. One of the things that gives Calvin's theology its enduring character is the catholicity of his thought. His goal was to recover the faith of the early church and submit all his thinking and efforts in submission to the Word of God. He used all the skills available to him: his brilliant intellect, his humanistic training, his knowledge of the Scriptures and the Fathers, and his use of rhetoric to complement his goal of brevity and lucidity. All this, mediated through his personal piety and zeal for the glory of God, combined to give his treatment of various doctrines or topics (*loci*) their distinctive character. There are at least ten such topics and they can only be listed very briefly.

1. *An appreciation for the created order.* One has only to read the first five chapters of the *Institutes* to see how Calvin marvels at the intricacies and beauties of the creation. He is "completely overwhelmed by the boundless force of its brightness" (*Inst.* I.5.1), this "dazzling theater" of God's glory (*Inst.* I.5.8; I.6.2).[27] The revelation of God's glory in Jesus Christ and the church should not draw us away from reveling in the mirror of God's glory in creation, which, with the eyes of faith, is like a garment in which God makes himself known to us. We are to find "delight and enjoyment" in the grasses, trees and fruit, and the beauty and pleasant odors of the flowers, quite apart from their usefulness (*Inst.* III.10.2).

2. *God's providential care for this universe and its inhabitants.* Calvin opposes Aristotle and the Stoics who do not recognize God's involvement in the world. Rather, not only does God "sustain the universe by his boundless might, regulate it by his wisdom, preserve it by his goodness, and especially rule mankind by his righteousness and judgment, bear with it in his mercy, and watch over it by his protection," but he is also the source of all wisdom and light, righteousness and truth (*Inst.* I.2.1). The sustenance and governing of the creation extends to God's providential care and guidance in the life of believers. "Nothing is more profitable than the knowledge of this doctrine" (*Inst.* I.17.3).[28]

3. *The polemic against idolatry.* One scholar has noted that "John Calvin's protest against idolatry is one of the dominating themes of his theology and churchmanship . . . Calvin does not contemplate the possibility of no-faith. Faith in the living God and idolatry exhaust the possibilities of human existence."[29] Idolatry for Calvin involved more than the making of images. It implies all forms of superstition and attempts to control and domesticate God. This insidious temptation lurks in the hearts of everyone, for "man"s nature, so to speak, is a perpetual factory of idols" (*Inst.* I.11.8).

4. *One covenant of grace.* Reformed theology has often been described as covenantal theology, and rightly so. However, it is Heinrich Bullinger, not Calvin, who first emphasized the role of the covenant. Nevertheless, Calvin gave classic form to the doctrine of the one covenant of grace, in contrast to the later Reformed notion of the covenant of works and the covenant of grace. The covenant takes several forms: Noahic, Abrahamic, Mosaic, the new covenant, etc., but the basic covenant promise is one: "I will be your God and you shall be my people" – and the substance of all the

covenants is Jesus Christ. The covenant is "settled (*constitisse*) in the free mercy of God and confirmed by the mediation of Christ" (*Inst.* II.10.4). This has hermeneutical implications for Calvin's emphasis on the unity of the Testaments, their diversity notwithstanding (*Inst.* II.10–11), and also the Reformed basis for infant baptism.[30]

5. *The significance of the humanity of Christ.* Calvin was Chalcedonian in his christology, maintaining that Jesus Christ was true God and true man. He affirmed the deity of Christ unequivocally, but gave a special place to the humanity of Christ in effecting our salvation. Calvin regarded the whole life of Jesus as redemptive and placed special emphasis on his obedience: "From the time when he took on the form of a servant, he began to pay the price of liberation in order to redeem us" (*Inst.* II.16.5).[31]

In contrast to Luther and his view of the ubiquity of Christ's body after the ascension, Calvin emphasized the ascended humanity of Christ at the right hand of God. This has direct consequences for Calvin's understanding of the nature of Christ's presence in the Lord's Supper.

6. *The threefold office of Christ (triplex munus Christi).* This doctrine did not originate with Calvin, but he gave it classic form. It continues to be followed not only in treatments of the works of Christ by theologians, but also by biblical scholars and ethicists. Calvin originally taught only two offices of Christ – as priest and king – but in the Geneva Catechism of 1541, in response to question 34, "What is meant by the name of Christ?" The teacher answers, "By this title his office is still better expressed – for it signifies that he was anointed by the Father to be ordained king, priest, and prophet."

Some Calvin scholars maintain that no real prominence is given to the prophetic office in Calvin's theology, despite his treatment in the catechism and two sections in the 1559 *Institutes* (II.15.1–2).[32] However, it is apparent that this office was close to his heart, for it includes both the preaching and teaching ministry. For Christ "received anointing, not only for himself that he might carry out the office of teaching, but for his whole body that the power of the Spirit might be present in the continuing preaching of the gospel" (*Inst.* II.15.2).

7. *The knowledge of faith.* Earlier it was stated that the twofold knowledge of God is a major theme in Calvin's theology. The nature of our knowledge of God has been variously described as intuitional, relational, and existential. In short, it is experiential, not theoretical. One statement bears this out: "We are not to conceive the Christian faith as a bare knowledge of God which rattles around the brain and affects the heart not at all . . . But it is a firm and solid confidence of the heart by which we securely repose in God's mercy promised us through the gospel" (1538 Catechism, article 14; cf. *Inst.* III.2.36).

When Calvin defines faith in the *Institutes*, the emphasis is the same. Faith is "a firm and certain knowledge of God's benevolence toward us, founded upon the truth of the freely given promise in Christ, both revealed to our minds and sealed upon our hearts through the Holy Spirit" (*Inst.* III.2.7). This emphasis on the heart will come as a surprise to those who think of Calvin as a cold rationalist. But this knowledge of faith "is more a matter of the heart than the brain, and more of the disposition (*affectus*) than of the understanding (*intelligentiae*)" (*Inst.* III.2.8). The "heart," however, does not signify the emotions, but "a serious and sincere affection" (*Comm. Rom. 10:10*). Moreover, the object of faith is Christ and, more particularly, the promises of God's mercy in Christ.

8. *The Lord's Supper.* Although Calvin agreed with Luther on all essentials of the faith, a difference, which was exacerbated by some of Luther's followers after his death, revolved around the nature of Christ's presence in the Lord's Supper. Whereas Zwingli held that the Supper was a mere memorial and Luther believed that Christ was in a sense physically present – in, with, and under the elements – Calvin maintained that Christ was truly present through the Holy Spirit. The focus is not so much on Christ's presence in the elements as on the total act of the Lord's Supper whereby we have communion with the flesh and blood of the ascended Christ – *sursum corda!* – through the Holy Spirit. Since "Christ's body is in heaven and we are still pilgrims on earth," this gap is bridged "by the miraculous and secret virtue of Christ's Spirit for whom it is not difficult to associate things that are otherwise separated by an interval of space" (*Geneva Catechism,* Qs. 353–55).

Hence Calvin's doctrine of the Lord's Supper can be described as "christocentric-pneumatological,"[33] for it is concerned with the real presence of Christ through the Holy Spirit.

9. *The unity and catholicity of the church.* Calvin has been hailed as "the churchman" of the Reformation, for none of the reformers had a higher view of the church and a larger vision of its catholicity. Also, no one in the sixteenth century worked so tirelessly towards achieving its unity. He has been dubbed the "Cyprian of the Reformation," because he follows him in speaking of the church as "the mother of all the godly with which we must keep unity." Further, "there is no other way to enter life unless this mother conceive us in her womb, give us birth, and nourish us at her breast . . ." (*Inst.* IV.1.4). Related to this is Calvin's exalted view of the ministry, but that ministry was to be shared with elders and deacons, the foundation for what became the Presbyterian system of church government. However, the ultimate authority and power rest not in the church or its ministry but in Jesus Christ, the head of the church, whose "authority should be exercised by his Word alone" (*Inst.* IV.3.1).

Calvin, like Luther, left the Roman Catholic Church because he felt he was forced out of it in his desire to be faithful to the gospel. Hence, he could still call schism "the worst and most harmful evil in the church of God" (*Comm. John 9:16*). He allowed that representatives of the churches could disagree on many issues as long as they believed in common a few essential doctrines such as "God is one, Christ is God, the Son of God, and our salvation rests on God's mercy, and the like" (*Inst.* IV.1.12). Where such agreement exists, "it is for us to work hard and strive in every way to bring if possible the whole world to agree in the unity of the faith" (*Comm. John 10:8*).

This goal was expressed most eloquently in Calvin's famous letter to Archbishop Cranmer in which he proposed that representatives of the various churches share their confessions and then try to "hand down to posterity some certain rule of faith." Toward that end, he offered, if necessary, "to cross ten seas for such a purpose."[34]

10. *Civil government as an instrument of God.* That Calvin's theological classic, the *Institutes*, concludes with a chapter on civil government is unusual, though not unique. It may be that this reflects the structure of Romans where Paul discusses the state (chapter 13), after discussing election (chapters 9–11). In any case, Calvin here eschews any kind of sectarian spirituality that would consider the political realm an activity unworthy of a Christian. He considers the state a positive blessing and speaks in the most laudatory terms of the magistrates as having a sacred calling. Echoing the Apostle Paul he writes, "We hold the supremacy and dominion of kings and princes, as also of other magistrates and officers, to be a holy thing and a good ordinance of God" (*Inst.* IV.20.4). Not that Calvin had any illusion about kings! In 1536, he had appealed to Francis I of France for tolerance, but if Francis ever received the letter (prefixed to the *Institutes*), he did not heed it, for brutal persecutions followed.

For Calvin, the spheres of church and state must not be confused, yet ultimately both of them serve the same end, viz., the rule of Christ. Calvin could not have imagined a secular state (nor a theocratic one), for to countenance such a state is to deny the lordship of Christ. Calvin, more than Luther or Zwingli, sought to free the church from the dominance of the state in Geneva. He was never completely successful, and in practice these intersecting circles sometimes were confused. But his goal was a revolutionary one for the time: a church and a state, separate, and with distinct functions, but both in the service of God. As the Roman Catholic theologian Alexandre Ganoczy concludes, "By joining his political theology to his pneumatic ecclesiology, Calvin helped the Reformation to survive and spread."[35]

## CONCLUSION

Wherein lies the perduring appeal and influence of Calvin's theology? Several answers can be given: the blending of intellect and piety, his concern for the usefulness of Christian doctrine and his abhorrence of empty and frigid speculation, his goal of brevity and simplicity, his knowledge of Scripture and the church fathers, the catholicity of his thought, and his passion for the glory of God. All these combine to produce a synthesis, more than a system, which is expressed in eloquent and lucid Latin and French.

One of the secrets of Calvin's success in communicating the gospel was his effective use of rhetoric, which aims to persuade as well as to inform.[36] A well-known illustration is found in his chapter, "The Sum of the Christian Life: The Denial of Ourselves" (*Inst.* III.7.1):

> Now the great thing is this: we are consecrated and dedicated to God in order that we may thereafter think, speak, meditate, and do, nothing except to his glory. For a sacred thing may not be applied to profane uses without marked injury to him.
>
> If we, then, are not our own [cf. 1 Cor. 6:19] but the Lord's, it is clear what error we must flee, and whither we must direct all the acts of our life.
>
> We are not our own: let not our reason nor our will, therefore, sway our plans and deeds. We are not our own: let us therefore not set it as our goal to seek what is expedient for us according to the flesh. We are not our own: in so far as we can, let us therefore forget ourselves and all that is ours.
>
> Conversely, we are God's: let us therefore live for him and die for him. We are God's: let his wisdom and will therefore rule all our actions. We are God's: let all the parts of our life accordingly strive toward him as our only lawful goal [Rom. 14:8, cf. 1 Cor. 6:19]. O, how much has that man profited who, having been taught that he is not his own, has taken away dominion and rule from his own reason that he may yield it to God!

This is not only an impressive illustration of rhetoric; it also has an autobiographical ring. This is even more self-evident in a passage that follows shortly after the above:

> Let this therefore be the first step, that a man depart from himself in order that he may apply the whole force of his ability in the service of the Lord. I call 'service' not only what lies in obedience to God's Word but what turns the mind of man, empty of its own carnal sense, wholly to the bidding of God's Spirit.

This was Calvin's goal, and to a remarkable degree he achieved it. Its fruit is in his theology – not only the *Institutes*, but his whole corpus – a singular legacy to the whole Christian church.

The words do not occur in the passage cited above, but Calvin, who was constantly overwhelmed by the majesty of God, consecrated himself and his theology to the glory of God. As a modern writer says so well, "His theology is compelled and enthralled by an overwhelming awareness of the grandeur of God, and this is the source of the distinctive aesthetic coherency of his religious vision, which is neither mysticism nor metaphysics, but mysticism as a method of rigorous inquiry, and metaphysics as an impassioned flight of the soul."[37]

## Notes

1 John Calvin, *Institutes of the Christian Religion*, ed. John T. McNeill, trans. Ford Lewis Battles. Library of Christian Classics, vols. XX and XXI (Philadelphia: Westminster, 1960). Further references to the *Institutes* will be incorporated into the text and abbreviated as *Inst.*

2 A modern caricature, widely propagated through the popular series "The Story of Civilization," is by Will Durant, *The Reformation* (New York: Simon and Schuster, 1957), VI, 490. For a corrective, see Richard Stauffer, *The Humanness of John Calvin* (Nashville: Abingdon, 1971).

3 McNeill–Battles edition of the *Institutes*, 9.

4 Cf. Anthony N. S. Lane, *John Calvin: Student of the Church Fathers* (Edinburgh: T.&T. Clark; Grand Rapids: Baker, 1999).

5 McNeill–Battles edition of the *Institutes*, 4.

6 Ibid., 7.

7 J.-D. Benoit, *Calvin directeur d'Ames* (Strasbourg: Oberlin, 1947), 14.

8 H. Bauke, *Die Probleme der Theologie Calvins* (Leipzig: J. C. Hinrichs Buchhandlung, 1922), 16. On the precise nature of the "system" in the *Institutes* see Richard Muller, *The Unaccommodated Calvin: Studies in the Foundation of a Theological Tradition* (New York: Oxford University Press, 2000), 177 ff.

9 Foreword to McNeill–Battles edition of the *Institutes*, 8.

10 Cf. Ford Lewis Battles, *The Piety of John Calvin. An Anthology Illustrative of the Spirituality of the Reformer* (Grand Rapids: Baker, 1978); and Lucien Joseph Richard, *The Spirituality of John Calvin* (Atlanta: John Knox Press, 1974) and *John Calvin: Writings on Pastoral Piety*, ed. and trans. Elsie Anne McKee, The Classics of Western Spirituality (New York: Paulist Press, 2001).

11 *Institutes of the Christian Religion. 1536 Edition*, translated and annotated by Ford Lewis Battles (revised edition rpt., Grand Rapids: Eerdmans, 1986), 15.

12 Edward A. Dowey, Jr., *The Knowledge of God in Calvin's Theology* (Columbia University Press, 1952; 3rd expanded edition, Grand Rapids: Eerdmans, 1994).

13 T. H. L. Parker, *Calvin's Doctrine of the Knowledge of God* (Grand Rapids: Eerdmans, rev. edition 1959). The first edition of 1952 appeared at the same time as Dowey's book on the knowledge of God. The only difference in this edition is the addition of an appendix that is sharply critical of Dowey's approach. Parker acknowledges that the *duplex cognitio* is a theme of the *Institutes* but of

the knowledge of God and ourselves, not that of God the Creator and God the Redeemer, p. 119.

14 Muller, *The Unaccommodated Calvin*, 132 ff.

15 Wilhelm Niesel, *The Theology of Calvin*, trans. Harold Knight (Philadelphia: Westminster, 1956; rpt. 1980), 27, 246.

16 B. B. Warfield, "Calvin the Theologian," in *Calvin and Augustine*, ed. Samuel G. Craig (Philadelphia: Presbyterian and Reformed Publishing Co., 1956), 484–85.

17 Philip Walker Butin, *Revelation, Redemption and Response: Calvin's Trinitarian Understanding of the Divine–Human Relationship* (New York: Oxford University Press, 1995), 132.

18 This essay is in the symposium *Calvin Studien 1959* (Neukirchen: Neukirchener Verlag, 1960). Although I use Kreck's outline, I will be inserting material not found in his essay.

19 For illustrations of this, see my essay, "Governed and Guided by the Spirit – a Key Issue in Calvin's Doctrine of the Holy Spirit," in H. A. Oberman, Ernst Saxer et al., eds., *Das Reformierte Erbe. Festschrift für Gottfried W. Locher zu seinem 80. Geburtstag* (Zurich: Theologischer Verlag, 1992), 161–71.

20 T. F. Torrance, *Kingdom and Church* (Edinburgh: Oliver & Boyd, 1956), 98.

21 This and other references to Calvin's New Testament Commentaries use the translations in *Calvin's New Testament Commentaries*, 12 vols., ed. David W. Torrance and Thomas T. Torrance (various translators) (Edinburgh: Saint Andrew Press; Grand Rapids: Eerdmans, 1959–72).

22 In Dennis E. Tamburello, *Union with Christ: John Calvin and the Mysticism of St. Bernard* (Louisville: Westminster John Knox Press, 1994).

23 E. David Willis has shown that the view attributed to Calvin by the Lutherans has precedence in several church fathers. See his *Calvin's Catholic Christology* (Leiden: E. J. Brill, 1966).

24 Translation taken from *Calvin's Commentaries*, 47 vols., rpt. of the Edinburgh edition (various editors and translators) (Grand Rapids: Eerdmans, 1948–50).

25 This catechism forms the preface for I. John Hesselink's *Calvin's First Catechism*: *A Commentary* (Louisville: Westminster John Knox Press, 1997). Article 13 is on predestination, p. 17. This volume features Ford Lewis Battles' translation of Calvin's 1538 Catechism.

26 Paul Jacobs, *Prädestination und Verantworklichkeit bei Calvin* (Neukirchen: Neukirchener Verlag, 1937; rpt. Darmstadt: Wissenschaftliche Buchgesellschaft, 1968).

27 Cf. Susan E. Schreiner, *The Theater of His Glory. Nature and its Natural Order in the Thought of John Calvin* (Durham, NC: Labyrinth Press, 1991).

28 Cf. Charles B. Partee, "Calvin on Universal and Particular Providence," in Donald K. McKim, ed., *Readings in Calvin's Theology* (rpt. Eugene, Oregon: Wipf and Stock Publishers, 1998, 69–88; reprinted from Partee's *Calvin and Classical Philosophy* [Leiden: E. J. Brill, 1977]).

29 John H. Leith, "John Calvin's Polemic Against Idolatry," in J. McDowell Richards, ed., *Soli Deo Gloria. Studies in Honor of William Childs Robinson* (Richmond, VA: John Knox Press, 1968), 111. Cf. Carlos Eire, *War Against Idols. The Reformation of Worship from Erasmus to Calvin* (New York: Cambridge University Press, 1986).

30 Cf. M. Eugene Osterhaven, "Calvin on the Covenant," in McKim, ed., *Readings in Calvin's Theology*, 89–106; reprinted from *Reformed Review* 33 (1979–80).

31 Cf. David L. Foxgrover, "The Humanity of Christ: Within Proper Limits," in Robert V. Schnucker, ed., *Calviniana*, Sixteenth Century Essays and Studies, vol. 10 (Kirksville, MO: Sixteenth Century Journal Publishers, 1988), 93–105.

32 See, e.g., John F. Jansen, *Calvin's Doctrine of the Work of Christ* (London: James Clarke, 1956), ch. 2.

33 Paul Jacobs, in Oskar Thulin, ed., *Illustrated History of the Reformation* (St. Louis: Concordia, n.d.), 78. Cf. B. A. Gerrish, *Grace and Gratitude: The Eucharistic Theology of John Calvin* (Minneapolis: Fortress, 1993).

34 Letter of April 1552, cited in John T. McNeill, *Unitive Protestantism. The Ecumenical Spirit in its Persistent Expression*, rev. edition (Richmond, VA: John Knox Press, 1964), 247.

35 Alexandre Ganoczy, "Calvin," in Pierre Chaunu, ed., *The Reformation* (Goucester: Alan Sutton Publishing, 1989), 136. Cf. John T. McNeill, "Calvin and Civil Government," in McKim, ed., *Readings in Calvin's Theology*, 260–74; reprinted from John T. McNeill, ed., *John Calvin, On God and Political Duty*, The Library of Liberal Arts (Indianapolis: Bobbs-Merrill, 1956).

36 The importance of rhetoric in Calvin's theology has received much attention in recent years. See especially the magisterial work of Olivier Millet, *Calvin et la dynamique de la parole* (Geneva: Slatkins, 1992). For a brief study in English, see E. David Willis, "Rhetoric and Responsibility in Calvin's Theology," in Alexander J. McKelway and E. David Willis, eds., *The Context of Contemporary Theology* (Atlanta: John Knox Press, 1974).

37 Marilynne Robinson, *The Death of Adam. Essays on Modern Thought* (Boston: Houghton Mifflin Co., 1998), 188.

# 6 Calvin's ethics

GUENTHER H. HAAS

The foundational theological doctrine for understanding Calvin's view of Christian ethics is creation. In the act of creation God brings into existence, not only all creatures, but also "the very order of things" directing them. This ordering is the means by which God governs all of his creation. Creatures in their diversity obey God by submitting to the "order of nature" that he has determined for them. This is also the case for human beings. Though they are distinct from all other creatures in that they are made in the image of God, their lives are still governed by the order of nature. It prescribes their relations to God, to one another, and to the rest of creation. The entry of sin and evil into the world has not changed that. Calvin appeals to Romans 2:14–15 to argue that all people, including the Gentiles who have no knowledge of the Mosaic law, are still subject to the divinely established order of nature as the ethical law for human life.[1]

The fall of humanity described in Genesis 3 has radically affected human ethical life. Calvin's view is that the whole of human nature and its faculties are corrupted by the effects of sin. He makes a sharp break with classical philosophers and medieval scholastic theologians who view reason as a sufficient guide for human conduct, both in its ability to discern good and evil, and in its power to direct the human will and affections into virtuous action.[2] Sin corrupts the mind, the will, and the affections with the result that humans cannot know moral truth, are not drawn to it, and do not choose to practice it. Reason is so blinded by the effects of sin that only the renewing work of the grace of God in the human heart, and the ongoing guidance of the Holy Spirit, enable the heart to accept, the mind to understand, and the will to pursue the ethical life that God requires. This renewal is accomplished through the redemptive work of Jesus Christ. Sinful humans can only gain a knowledge of God and of what he requires of them in the divine revelation given in the Scriptures. There, the law of God is revealed as "one everlasting and unchangeable rule to live by," and "a perfect pattern of righteousness."[3]

Even though sin has wreaked such havoc on human nature, sinful humans continue to have some understanding of the moral order of creation. Here one finds in Calvin a concept of natural law, though not a natural theology or ethic. Because of his mercy and grace, God grants to fallen humanity some apprehension of right and wrong, justice and injustice. Appealing to Romans 2:14–15 Calvin notes that God imprints upon human hearts some understanding of his moral law, and God sustains the conscience as the faculty that judges between good and evil, justice and injustice. This knowledge and judgment is always defective and imperfect. But the laws of the nations provide abundant evidence of the "seeds of justice" that remain among the pagans.[4]

Calvin attributes this understanding of the moral law in sinful humans apart from Christ, not to their innate goodness and insight into ethical truth, but to the continuing grace of God. God's benevolence is manifested in his maintenance of creational and moral law as an enduring order for creation. God restrains human corruption inwardly by the power of the Spirit, though he does not purge it from those who do not know Christ. He maintains his law in their hearts so that they seek for truth and justice, and cultivate social and civil well-being. For, without the working of God, humans rebel against his law when confronted by it, and turn to superstitions and evil.[5]

The insight that sinful humans have into the moral law of God is restricted to the second table of the Decalogue, the final six commandments. Concerning the first table, Calvin believes that natural reason and conscience are not able to grasp its principal points, such as trusting and worshiping God. Humans are so hostile to God and his righteousness that their reason and conscience corrupt any insight into idolatry and superstitions. They have a better understanding of the second table because of their natural instinct to foster and preserve civil society. They realize that principles of justice and equity, summarized in the second table, must be embodied in social laws to maintain order. These insights certainly fall short of God's requirements and are inconsistently applied. Nevertheless, the civil laws of the pagans manifest the grace of God that grants them some insight into his moral law.[6]

The radical transformation of the human heart that enables sinners to understand and embrace God's moral order for their lives is the result of union with Christ. This doctrine lies at the heart of Calvin's teaching on salvation and the Christian life. It is accomplished by faith and the regenerating work of the Holy Spirit. When people are engrafted into Christ's body, Christ communicates his life to them by the power of the Spirit. He dwells in them so that they are progressively able to live the life that is pleasing to God.[7] Thus, Christians have communion with Christ in both the grace of justification and sanctification.

The goal of the Christian life, for Calvin, is the restoration of the image of God which sin has distorted and defaced. The righteous nature of this restored image is evident in the person of Jesus Christ. His life is set before Christians "as an example, whose pattern" they ought to express in their lives. He is the image or universal rule to guide the godly in living a righteous life that is pleasing to God.[8]

Following the example of Christ does not mean slavishly copying all his activities. Many of his actions are unique to his calling as the Redeemer of the elect, and are intended to reveal his divine nature. Christians are called, rather, to be conformed "*to the image of Christ*," which means for Calvin "conformity to the humility of Christ." Imitation follows the pattern of Christ's own life: death and resurrection. Believers have died with Christ to sin and the sinful nature, and they have been raised with Christ to a new life of the Spirit in fellowship with God. Calvin stresses that these are decisive events that result from our union with Christ. But they also are the ongoing processes of the mortification of the flesh and the vivification of the Spirit.[9]

Imitation of Christ encompasses not merely outward behavior, but the inmost affections of the heart. The pattern of imitation of the death of Christ has both an inward and an outward aspect. The inward aspect of this pattern is self-denial. If, like Christ, believers are to present themselves as living sacrifices, holy and acceptable to God (Rom. 12:1), they must accept that they are not their own but belong completely to God. All self-concern must be subordinated to the will and glory of God, and to the good of one's neighbor. Self-denial is the necessary remedy for the inordinate love of self. Only by dying to self-will and to the sinful nature are believers able to imitate Christ's life of service to God and neighbor.[10]

The outward aspect of the imitation of the death of Christ is bearing the cross. This involves accepting the hardships and difficulties that God brings into the lives of Christians, both the afflictions they share with all humans, but especially those undergone for the sake of the gospel and the cause of righteousness. Bearing the cross leads to patience, obedience, a greater trust in God, and resting in the spiritual consolation of God.[11]

Participation in the resurrection of Christ should direct believers to view their lives as fulfilled and perfected in the glorified Christ. This is achieved through meditation on the future life with him. Such participation is never experienced apart from participation in Christ's death. His own life on earth is the pattern for Christians. Christ gave his disciples an example by enduring the shameful death on the cross through his joyful anticipation of exaltation at the right hand of God. Similarly, the longing for the blessings of eternal life should spur believers to endure the troubles and miseries of this life, and to persevere in the light of the life to come. They ought to believe that, no matter what sufferings they experience in this life, Christ will triumph over the devil, sin, and evil, he will raise them from the dead, and he will grant them their blessed inheritance in glory.[12]

This life of self-denial, bearing the cross, and hope does not entail a withdrawal from earthly things. The Christian life supports the use of and participation in the good gifts of God in creation. Calvin recognizes that sinful humans tend to misuse and abuse earthly goods, especially in licentious indulgence and idolatry. But believers must not react to this by forgoing all creational goods except those necessary for life. God has given humans these gifts, not merely for their good, but also for their delight, enjoyment, and comfort. This takes Calvin's understanding of these gifts beyond the bare notion of necessary use, to the sense of loveliness, beauty, and goodness.[13]

Calvin views the use of the creation by Christians in the context of two key themes of God's calling to men and women. The first is the restoration of humanity's calling of dominion and lordship over creation as described in Genesis 1:26–28. Though this was disrupted by the Fall, it has been restored in Jesus Christ. Through union with Christ believers participate in his lordship over creation. Their dominion over creation is limited by sin, but must be characterized by devotion to him and service of his kingdom. (This sense of calling is usually designated by Reformed theologians and ethicists as the creational or cultural mandate.) The second theme is the notion of the specific calling or vocation that each one receives from God. God grants grace and gifts appropriate to the diversity of callings in life so that each one can carry out his or her appointed duties. These gifts are to be exercised in faithful service to Christ so that the restoration of his kingdom is promoted. All will have to give an account before God for the way they have carried out their God-given vocation.[14]

For Calvin moderation is an important virtue in the moral life. It serves to guide believers in the proper use of creational gifts; but it is also vital for other areas of the Christian life. Sin produces unrestrained passions and excessive desires of the sinful nature. This leads to the misuse and distortion of those gifts and creational goods given by God. Calvin considers moderation as the necessary virtue to restrain such sinful tendencies and to guide the faithful use of creation. It prevents luxurious display in rulers and the wealthy. It leads to contentment with one's position in life and the limitations of one's calling. It results in patience in adversity. The fruit of moderation is a humble spirit that enables one to love one's neighbor from the heart.[15] Christ himself sets the example for his people of what a life of moderation should embody. He bestows this gift of the Spirit upon his people to equip them for discipleship.[16]

Calvin gives the concept of law a major role in his ethics. This is evident in the prominence he gives to the Decalogue and its exposition in a number of his writings. His catechism for the church in Geneva (1545) contains a major section of questions and answers in which the requirements and prohibitions enjoined in the commandments are explained. He devotes two chapters in the *Institutes* to the law, one of which contains a lengthy exposition of the Ten Commandments. His sermons on Deuteronomy contain sixteen sermons on the Decalogue, as well as on the introductory and concluding texts. His commentary on the last four books of Moses organizes most of the material from Exodus to Deuteronomy, except for the historical accounts, according to the topics covered in the Ten Commandments. The law has this importance because it is the "perfect rule of righteousness" that God has given to his people.[17]

Because the law reveals the eternal will of God, it is, for Calvin, the ultimate moral norm. God alone has the authority to establish the rules and laws which govern people's lives. They cannot depart from the law without abandoning God himself. It presents his character and reveals his perfect righteousness to them. If they would be holy as God is holy, then they must submit to the law as the perfect rule for a godly life.[18]

The origin and foundation of the law is the will of God. His will is neither arbitrary nor capricious. Calvin rejects the view that drives a wedge between God's power to enact the law and God's character behind the law. The law is the authority because God wills it to be so, but he wills it to be so because it expresses his righteous and holy character. The law is as firm and constant as God's own character. It "has been established to be permanent, to endure from age to age." It contains the truth of God that never perishes, and is his permanent moral guide for humanity. For this reason, the law must be preached and taught until the end of the world.[19]

God clearly reveals his will for human life in the Scriptures, and summarizes it in the Ten Commandments. As noted above, even after the Fall God continues to reveal his moral law to all through the law written on their hearts, to which their consciences bear witness (Rom. 2:14–15). This is the same law that God reveals in the Bible. Because sin has so clouded human understanding of the law in their hearts, people have little understanding of the first table of the law, and a defective understanding, subject to vanity and error, of the second table. This is why all people, even believers, need the written law in Scripture as a clear witness of the will of God.[20]

Those committed to lives of obedience to God must submit to biblical law. They must not forge any new laws for themselves, nor have different laws for different times. In fact, God forbids adding to his law or taking anything away from it. He has spoken once for all in the law, and his will is that all embrace his law as setting forth "one everlasting and unchangeable rule to live by," as a "perfect pattern of righteousness."[21]

The meaning of the moral law which God has revealed in Scripture is not obscure and hidden, but clear and obvious. Its meaning is that intended by the Holy Spirit, the divine author of Scripture. However, sinners cannot grasp its clear and plain meaning. The work of the Spirit is necessary, not merely in regenerating people's hearts so that they submit to Scripture's authority, but also in illuminating their minds to understand what it reveals. This is one of the important purposes for which Christ gives the gift of the Spirit to his disciples – that they may understand his teaching in Scripture.[22]

For Calvin the work of the Spirit in instructing believers must never be separated from the teaching of Scripture. The Spirit neither corrects nor adds to biblical teachings. The law revealed therein is sufficient for human life, omitting nothing that is necessary and useful. Besides, the Spirit who produced the Scripture is the same Spirit who leads believers into a proper understanding of it. As the Spirit of discernment he is the faithful interpreter who expounds what he himself speaks in Scripture. In addition to exposition of Scripture, the Spirit has an important ongoing role to guide believers in applying the teachings of Scripture to contemporary situations. But for both interpretation and application, the Spirit must never be set in opposition to the written Word or the law of God revealed in it.[23]

For Calvin the law is misunderstood if one attempts to comprehend it apart from the covenant of grace, and from Christ, the heart of this covenant. The law was revealed through Moses, not to lead the chosen people away from Christ, but to prepare them for Christ's coming. The fact that the Mosaic law was given after the covenant promise to Abraham means that the former must be understood in the context of the latter. The law is a gift of the covenant because it prepares people to seek after Christ. It does this, first, in the ceremonies and sacrificial system of the Old Testament. The priesthood, the physical rituals of cleanness and uncleanness, the sacrifices, and all the other ceremonies were shadows and types that found their fulfillment in Christ. Second, the moral law, summarized in the Decalogue, also points to Christ. Appealing to Romans 10:4, Calvin describes Christ as the fulfillment or end of the law, for he is the one who fulfills the righteous demands of the law. When the law is separated from the promises fulfilled in Christ, it becomes "bare law" or "law as letter," whereby people attempt to merit righteousness through works of obedience. Such a misuse of the law must be condemned as "vanity." The law requires perfect righteousness before God, although this is impossible for sinful humans to accomplish. When they realize their failure to achieve this, it should cause them to abandon their own attempts at righteousness, and to embrace the grace and righteousness of God in Christ.[24] Thus, a proper understanding of the law always views it as being "graced with the covenant of free adoption."[25]

Christ is also the "best interpreter" of the law for Calvin in several other important senses. First, in his teaching on the law, notably in the Sermon on the Mount (Matt. 5–7), Christ expounds the depth and extent of the righteousness that God requires of his people. This is important because of the misinterpretations and distortions that the Pharisees in Jesus' day (and those, since then, who follow in their approach) applied to God's law. Christ's teaching restores the law to its original integrity.[26]

Second, Christ deepens the understanding of the law by manifesting in his own ministry the nature of the love of the triune God for humanity. Many passages in the New Testament testify to this. But "the chief example (*exemplar*)" of divine love, which transcends everything else, is God's sending his only begotten Son to die for his people. Believers are called to reflect this love in their obedience to the law, especially to the second table.[27] The third way in which Christ interprets the law is by providing in his own life the perfect example of what conformity to the law entails. He is "the perfect pattern (*exemplar*) of purity" and "the example (*exemplar*) of perfect obedience." The goal of the law – the restoration of the image of God in knowledge, righteousness, and holiness – is fully manifested in Christ. The law reveals the will of God for human life, and that will finds its fulfillment, and pattern, in Jesus Christ.[28]

Although Calvin understands the law of God as a unity, he distinguishes between three types of law in the Mosaic legislation: moral law, ceremonial law, and judicial law. The moral law, as summarized in the Decalogue, is foundational, and provides the basis for the other two. It is the "true and eternal rule of righteousness" which God has prescribed for all people of all nations and times who are committed to obeying his will. The ceremonial law refers to the various rituals of purity, worship, and sacrifice in the Old Testament era. It prescribed for the Jews the manner in which they fulfilled their obligations to God according to the first table of the Decalogue. These various laws are all shadows and types that find fulfillment in the Redeemer. When the fulfillment has come, the shadows and types are abrogated. The judicial law is the legislation that God gave to the Jews to maintain their civil life and government as a distinct nation devoted to God. It prescribed the manner of their obedience to the second table of the Decalogue, that is, the laws governing their social relationships. When Calvin considers the relevance of these judicial laws for nations other than Israel, he makes a distinction between the forms of these laws and the equity upon which they are based. The forms of these judicial laws in the Mosaic legislation have application only to the Jewish nation before Christ. They are not normative for all nations. However, the equity underlying these laws does have binding authority. In fact, Calvin contends that the principles of justice and equity upon which Israel's judicial laws were based are the same principles which God reveals to all nations in the natural law. Because these are necessary for the preservation of human society, they are embodied, to some extent, in the civil laws of all the nations. Of course, the laws of the nations do not always faithfully reflect the principles of equity; they may be unjust, and even barbarous. However, no nation can avoid having some elements of justice and equity in its laws. Thus, the continuing value and authority of the judicial law is found in the normative value of the principles of justice and equity embodied in it.[29]

Another important feature in Calvin's understanding of the law is his view of the threefold use or function of the law. The first use is the pedagogical use. The law reveals the righteousness which God demands of every person. In doing so, it functions like a mirror to all who would contemplate themselves in it. It unmasks the unrighteousness of every man and woman by highlighting how far short each one falls of the holiness of God. It confronts all humans with their weakness in attaining God's righteousness, with the iniquity that results from their weakness, and with the curse of the law that results from both. Their sins leave them in a state of condemnation before a holy God. This awareness has the ultimate goal of driving sinners to embrace the grace and mercy of God revealed in Christ. By abandoning any attempts at attaining righteousness by the works of the law, they can be clothed by faith with the righteousness of Christ. Thereby, they have the assurance that in Christ the righteous requirements of the law are satisfied.[30]

The second use of the law is the civil use. Here the law functions to restrain people in civil society from engaging in evil actions that violate public peace and justice. This restraint occurs, not because of any inner conviction or motivation of the heart, but because of the fear of punishment or of public shame. Calvin appeals to 1 Timothy 1:9–10 to argue that this use has primary application to the unregenerate, since believers have the inner motivation to submit to the law. This forced, external righteousness is necessary to maintain some measure of order and harmony for the maintenance of civil society. Even pagan rulers understand that the laws of society must require a measure of outward righteousness and justice from its citizens to retain civil order.[31]

Calvin describes the third use of the law as the "principal use," because this is the proper purpose for which the law was originally intended. It has application only to Christians. Here, the law functions as a positive instrument to enable believers to understand and embody the will of God in their lives. Only in this use does the law cease to be "bare law" or "letter." Rather, it functions as covenant law, "law graced with the covenant of free adoption."[32]

Calvin claims that the law guides believers in holy living in two ways. First, the law is the best instrument to provide thorough instruction for believers in the nature of the Lord's will, and to confirm their understanding of it. If people embody what it enjoins, they will express the image of God in their lives. Second, because believers still struggle with sin, the law has the power to exhort them to holiness, especially when they become weary, complacent, or apathetic. "The law is to the flesh like a whip to an idle and balky ass, to arouse it to work." It remains "a constant sting" that arouses believers to obedience, strengthens them to press on, and draws them back from sin.[33]

Calvin embraces three principles of interpretation that shape his exposition of the Ten Commandments. He presents these in his introductory comments to the Decalogue in the *Institutes*. The first principle is that the law is concerned, not merely with outward behaviour, but with "inward and spiritual righteousness." God desires obedience in the whole person – with the affections of the heart as well as with compliance in the body. Appealing to Romans 7:14 Calvin contends that the perfection of the law "requires a heavenly and angelic righteousness, in which no spot appears." This is supported by the teaching of Christ, who is the "best interpreter" of the law. In the Sermon on the Mount Christ reveals that the law is fulfilled, not simply by outward works, but by spiritual purity. This adds nothing to the Mosaic law, but merely restores it to its original integrity.[34]

The second principle of interpretation is that one must attend to the intention of God in the commandments. The reason for this is that the words of the commandments are quite specific and limited. They must be interpreted according to the principle of synecdoche, where a part stands for the whole. To understand the scope of each commandment one must go beyond the exact words to understand God's will and intention revealed in it. Calvin notes that God frequently uses strong language in the wording of the commandments. The reason for this is that God wants to shock his people to recognize the heinous nature of such sin, in the face of their tendency to tolerate and justify it. God's intent is that his people hold with the same abhorrence that he does all the sins forbidden by the commandments.[35]

Calvin presents three facets of this principle. First, one must determine the area of concern of each commandment. For example, the seventh commandment, prohibiting adultery, is concerned with human sexuality and all human relationships affected by it. Second, one must determine the purpose of the commandment so as to discern what is pleasing and displeasing to God. Again, using the seventh commandment as example, one notes that God's purpose in the seventh commandment is that there be modesty and purity in all human sexual relationships. Third, one must apply the rule of opposites to each commandment. If the commandment is expressed as a positive precept, then the opposite is forbidden. If it is expressed as a prohibition, then the opposite prescription – the positive command – is enjoined.

The third principle for interpreting the commandments concerns the division of the Decalogue into two tables and the relationship between them. Calvin places the first four commandments in the first table, and the last six in the second. The first table deals with those ethical duties that have reference to God, notably the duties of piety and worship; the second table deals with one's ethical responsibilities to one's fellow humans. These duties are summarized by Christ in the twofold commandment of love (Matt. 22:37–39): to love God with one's whole being, and to love one's neighbor as oneself.[36]

Calvin insists that an unbreakable bond exists between the two tables. The duties of both are required for the Christian life; one cannot devote oneself to one table and neglect the other. In fact, it is impossible to observe the duties of either table by neglecting those of the other. Put positively, one can only fulfill the duties of one table when one also observes the duties of the other. The first table has a primary status because "the worship of God [is] the beginning and foundation of righteousness." One cannot preserve equity and love among humans without the righteousness of the first table. However, service and devotion to God must result in the duties of the love of neighbor. In fact, the love of neighbor is the evidence and necessary result of the love of God. God's concern is for both tables – for obedience to him and for the good of men and women.[37]

The twofold commandment of love, spoken by Christ in Matthew 22:37–40, teaches believers that love alone fulfills the Decalogue. Any instruction in the law for leading a holy and upright life must be directed by the goal of love. Calvin understands the love of God as piety, which is essentially faith in God manifested by reverence and worship of God. The love of neighbor is understood by Calvin in terms of the concept of equity. He considers Matthew 7:12 to be the best summary statement of the second table. Here, Christ teaches the love of neighbour in the form of what is commonly designated the Golden Rule: "In everything, do to others what you would have them do to you, for this sums up the Law and the Prophets." This statement provides a rule of thumb to guide believers in implementing the love of neighbor. All that Scripture teaches on love and righteousness between humans is satisfied if their behavior toward each other is guided by this rule.[38] Equity, then, is the prime concept for Calvin's understanding of loving and just relations in human social life. God's intent in the commandments of the second table is that equity be realized among humans. Thus, equity can be used to harmonize all the laws of Scripture dealing with human social life. And it is the key concept to direct the implementation of love in human relations so that justice is enacted. Calvin makes extensive use of the concept of equity in his exposition of the commandments of the second table, of the nature and calling of the state, of the value for Israel's judicial law for subsequent civil societies, and of the Christian duty to help the poor and the oppressed.

Another element in Calvin's ethics is Christian freedom.[39] It consists of three parts. First, there is freedom of conscience that believers have from the requirements and curse of the law. Through union with Christ by faith, they have assurance of forgiveness before God. Second, there is freedom that believers have to obey God through obedience to the law. As children of God, Christians have the assurance that they may offer their imperfect and defective acts of obedience to God, who delights in them as a loving Father. He evaluates them, not by the standards of perfect righteousness, but by grace revealed in Christ. Third, there is freedom in "things indifferent," that is, things which are neither prohibited nor prescribed by the law of God. This freedom enables believers to make use of the gifts of God for their enjoyment and edification. Such freedom must not be used for selfish indulgence and luxury. And it must not be a cause of stumbling for weaker Christian brothers or sisters who are led to sin against their weak consciences. In the latter case, more mature Christians must abstain from the practice of this freedom so that the weaker ones may be built up in love.

Another important theme in Calvin's ethics is the place of the church in shaping the ethical life of believers. While this theme is noted by many scholars, in this author's view, it has not received recognition as a significant feature of his moral teaching. Union with Christ always entails union with his disciples in the church. The imitation of Christ that flows from union with him is realized in the pattern of self-denial, mutual subjection, and love in relations with others in the body of Christ. Through the preaching of the Word and the exercise of discipline, believers are guided on the right path, restrained from departing from it, and chastised into returning to it should they depart. In the body of Christ they learn to be concerned for the welfare of each other, to use their gifts to serve others, and to pray for each other.[40] Through full participation in the teaching, worship, communal life, and diaconal service of the church, the ethical character and life of believers is shaped by the church. Calvin has the moral life in mind when he states: "It is always disastrous to leave the church."[41]

Calvin's understanding of Christian ethics is not static, but rather dynamic. The laws revealed in Scripture must be interpreted according to the intention of the Lawgiver. They need not always be accepted in the form in which they are recorded. This is evident in the case of Israel's judicial laws. But it also applies to the moral laws of Scripture. The concept of equity has a crucial role here in guiding believers in implementing the justice demanded by love of neighbor. In addition, Christ is the living example for believers so that they might imitate his example, not slavishly, but by following his humility and devotion to God. Finally, Calvin gives a central place to the work of the Spirit in enlightening and guiding believers in the way of obedience. The Spirit provides the insight and wisdom necessary for embodying a life of righteousness in new and ever-changing contexts.

*Notes*

1  John Calvin, *Institutes of the Christian Religion*, ed. John T. McNeill, trans. Ford Lewis Battles, vols. XX and XXI of the Library of Christian Classics (Philadelphia: Westminster Press. 1960), II.14.2, 20; II.2.22; *Comm. Rom. 2:14–15*. Here and elsewhere Calvin's New Testament commentaries can be found in *Calvin's New Testament Commentaries*, 12 vols., ed. David W. Torrance and Thomas T. Torrance (various translators) (Edinburgh: Saint Andrew Press; Grand Rapids: Eerdmans, 1959–72).

2  *Inst.* II.1.8; II.2.2–3.

3  *Inst.* I.6.1–4; II.8.13.

4  *Comm. Rom. 2:14–15*; *Inst.* II.2.13.

5  *Inst.* II.3.3, 9.

6  *Inst.* II.8.1; II.2.15, 24; *Comm. 1 Pet. 2:14.*

7  *Comm. Eph. 5:31*; *John 17:21*; *Inst.* III.2.24.

8  *Inst.* III.6.1–3.

9  *Rom. 8:29–30; 6:5–11.*

10  *Inst.* III.6.4; III.7.1–10.

11  *Inst.* III.8.1–11.

12  *Comm. Heb.12:1–3*; *Inst.* III.9.1–6.

13  *Inst.* III.10.1–3; cf. *Comm. 1 Tim. 4:4.*

14  *Inst.* III.10.5–6; *Comm. 1 Tim. 4:5*; *Heb. 8:5–6; 1 Cor. 7:20.*

15  *Inst.* III.10.3–5; IV.20.13; *Comm. Ps. 104:15; 91:11*, in *Calvin's Commentaries*, 47 vols., rpt. of the Edinburgh edition (various editors and translators) (Grand Rapids: Eerdmans, 1948–50); *Comm. 1 Thess. 5:16*; *Rom. 14:10–11.*

16  *Comm. Ps. 141:4; 36:5.*

17  "Catechism of the Church of Geneva," in *Calvin: Theological Treatises*, ed. and trans. J. K. S. Reid, vol. XXII of Library of Christian Classics (Philadelphia: Westminster Press. 1954), 118.

18  *Comm. 2 Pet. 1:19*; *Inst.* II.8.59; *Serm.* Deut. 6:1–4, in *John Calvin's Sermons on the Ten Commandments*, ed. and trans. Benjamin W. Farley (Grand Rapids: Baker. 1980), 290.

19  *Inst.* III.23.2; *Serm.* Deut. 4:44–5:3, pp. 48–49.

20  *Inst.* II.6.1–2; II.8.1.

21 *Serm.* Deut. 5:22, pp. 238–42; *Inst.* II.7.13.
22 *Comm. 2 Tim. 3:16*; *Inst.* I.9.3.
23 *Comm. 1 John 4:6*; *Inst.* II.2.25; I.9.3.
24 *Inst.* II.9.4–6; II.7.3–9.
25 *Inst.* III.7.1–2.
26 *Inst.* II.8.7; *Comm. Matt. 5:19–21.*
27 *Comm. 1 John 4:9–11.*
28 *Comm. 1 John 3:3*; *Heb. 10:17*; *1 Pet. 1:14*; *Eph. 5:1.*
29 *Inst.* IV.20.15–16; *Comm. 1 Pet. 2:14.*
30 *Inst.* II.7.6–9; *Comm. Gal. 3:24*; *Rom. 10:4.*
31 *Inst.* II.7.10–11; *Comm. 1 Tim. 1:9–10.*
32 *Inst.* II.7.12–13; II.7.2.
33 *Inst.* II.7.12, 14; II.8.1, 51.
34 *Inst.* II.8.6–7; *Comm. Rom. 7:14.*
35 *Inst.* II.8.8–10.
36 *Inst.* II.8.11–12; II.8.51–54.
37 *Comm. 1 Cor. 10:32*; *Luke 22:39*; *Rom. 13:8.*
38 *Inst.* II.8.50, 53; *Comm. Matt. 22:37–40*; *Ps. 78:7*; *Matt. 7:12.*
39 *Inst.* III.19.1–16.
40 *Inst.* III.7.4; IV.1.2, 5; IV.11.3–5; *Comm. Rom. 15:4*; *1 Cor. 12:4, 7, 11*; *Ps. 14:7.*
41 *Inst.* IV.1.4.

# 7 Calvin's preaching

### DAWN DeVRIES

> Observe here that the minister of the word is said in some way to save
> those whom he leads to the obedience of faith . . . [P]reaching is an
> instrument for effecting the salvation of the faithful, and though it
> can do nothing without the Spirit of God, yet through his inward
> operation it produces the most powerful effects.
>
> Calvin, *Commentary on Romans 11.14*

It is not surprising that a theologian who argued consistently that preaching
was the ordinary means appointed by God for the salvation of the elect
understood the delivery of sermons as among his most important duties.
During his ministry in Geneva (1536–38, 1541–64), John Calvin preached
well over two thousand sermons. From 1549, his most characteristic pattern
of preaching was twice on Sunday and every weekday of every other week.
His sermons typically lasted for more than an hour, and they were delivered
without a manuscript or notes. Toward the end of his life, when poor health
prevented his free movement, he even asked to be carried to church in a chair
so that he could fulfill his responsibilities in the pulpit. The sheer volume
of his preaching endeavors demonstrates their importance to him. Needless
to say, it would be impossible within the scope of this essay to summarize
the rich content of his many extant sermons. In order to gain a better
understanding of Calvin the preacher, however, we first need to examine
his theology of preaching, for only when we ascertain the significance of the
act of preaching within the economy of faith as Calvin himself understood
it will we grasp his own urgent sense of commitment to the preaching
task.

## CALVIN'S THEOLOGY OF PREACHING

Calvin affirmed the doctrine of justification by faith as the "chief hinge"
on which true religion turns. Faith, he maintained, and not any human work,
was the vehicle through which God's saving grace grasped human beings

and delivered them from death to life. But what is this faith, and how do human beings come to possess it? These questions occupied Calvin as few others, and much of the final edition of his *Institutes of the Christian Religion* (1559) is devoted to answering them.

Faith is strictly the remedy for or opposite of unbelief, and already in his discussion of the sin of Adam and Eve in the Garden of Eden Calvin gives away much of his thinking about the genesis of faith. Eve was led away from God's Word by the serpent's deceit. Adam, "contemptuous of the truth . . . turned aside to falsehood." Calvin goes on, "[S]urely, once we hold God's Word in contempt, we shake off all reverence for him. For, unless we listen attentively to him, his majesty will not dwell among us, nor his worship remain perfect." In concluding his discussion of the Fall, Calvin states, "Bernard rightly teaches that the door of salvation is opened to us when we receive the gospel today with our ears, even as death was then admitted by those same windows when they were opened to Satan. For Adam would never have dared oppose God's authority unless he had disbelieved in God's Word."[1] Sin in its most basic form is disbelief in God's Word – a failure to attend to God's voice and take his Word to heart. And just as sin arises from what is *not* heard, so faith comes from what *is* heard (Rom. 10:17).

Calvin defines faith as "firm and certain knowledge of God's benevolence toward us, founded upon the truth of the freely given promise in Christ, both revealed to our minds and sealed upon our hearts through the Holy Spirit" (*Inst.* III.2.7). Because faith is a kind of knowledge, it rests upon God's disclosure of himself in the Word. Calvin argues that there is a permanent relationship between faith and the Word: one could not separate these two any more than one could separate the rays of the sun from the sun itself, or fruit from the living root of a tree (*Inst.* III.2.6, 31). Throughout the Scripture, both Old and New Testament, Calvin maintains, "to hear" is understood as meaning "to believe." God's Word is like a mirror in which we can gaze upon God himself, and once we see who God is we can confidently trust him. Take away the Word, and there can be no faith (*Inst.* III.2.6). But not every word of God arouses faith in the heart of the believer. God proclaims words of judgment and damnation that are "so far from being capable of establishing faith that they can of themselves do nothing but shake it" (*Inst.* III.2.7). What, then, does faith look for in the Word? It looks for the assurance of God's good will – God's grace – as attested in the gift of Christ. In Christ, the pledge of God's good pleasure, the believer is confronted with God's mercy and God's will to save in a way that draws her toward God in an attitude of confident trust. Faith itself, then, is the meaning of salvation understood as a reconciled relationship to God – a relationship characterized by trust and reverence rather than by servile fear, apprehension, and suspicion.

Faith rests on God's Word – the word about Christ. This Word comes to believers, Calvin argues, primarily through preaching, but also through the evangelical sacraments, which function as "appendages" to the Word. In both preached Word and sacraments, the Holy Spirit works through outward means to create faith, to justify, and to sanctify those who receive these means of grace. More than that, the Holy Spirit unites believers more and more with Christ himself so that they grow into one body with him (*Inst.* III.2.24, 35). Without being joined to Christ in an inner, mystical union, there can be no reconciliation with God, according to Calvin (*Inst.* III.1.1; III.2.30). And while in his omnipotence God could create faith and union with Christ in a person without any external means, that is not ordinarily the way God chooses to work. Instead, mindful of human weakness, God "accommodates" himself by approaching humans through finite means of grace. Primary among these is preaching.

Calvin argues that God uses human ministers to deliver his Word for several reasons. First, in this way he provides for our weakness in that he prefers "to address us in human fashion through interpreters in order to draw us to himself, rather than to thunder at us and drive us away" (*Inst.* IV.1.5). Second, God uses human ministers to exercise our humility "when he accustoms us to obey his Word, even though it be preached through men like us and sometimes even by those of lower worth than we. If he spoke from heaven, it would not be surprising if his sacred oracles were to be reverently received without delay by the ears and minds of all . . . But when a puny man risen from the dust speaks in God's name, at this point we best evidence our piety and obedience toward God if we show ourselves teachable toward his minister, although he excels us in nothing" (*Inst.* IV.3.1). Finally, the human ministry serves as a bond of union between believers, knitting the church together into a cohesive community. If each person were able to interpret the written Scripture for himself, each would go off on his own and despise the others. Instead, God joins all believers together to one who is appointed pastor to teach the rest, and the benefits of salvation are communicated to the many through the service of the one. The ministry of the Word, then, is like a sinew that holds tissue and bones together in one body (*Inst.* IV.3.2).

Calvin holds a high view of the office of preacher. When a preacher who is duly called and appointed by God speaks, it is as if God himself were speaking through him. The Word of God is not distinguished from the word of the prophet.[2] God wishes to be heard through the voice of his ministers.[3] For this reason, Christians should not lightly criticize ministers, nor too easily separate themselves from the outward ministry of the Word. Rather, it should be assumed that wherever sound preaching is taking place, God is present and wills to be heard in the voice of his ministers.

The real presence of Christ in the preaching of the Word is understood by Calvin analogously to the real presence of Christ in the sacrament of the Lord's Supper. In fact, just as the sacraments are "visible words," so the Word is an "audible sign" (*Inst.* IV.14.26).[4] The Word, Calvin maintains, is the instrument by which Jesus Christ and all his benefits are dispensed to us.[5] But how does this actually work?

Calvin understands the sacraments as exhibitive signs: that is, sacraments both represent and offer that which they signify. So in the Lord's Supper, when bread and wine are presented, they represent the crucified body and blood of Christ and at the same time actually present or offer Christ's flesh and blood as nourishment for the souls of believers. Christ is really present in the sacramental action, and the sacraments are more than a reminder of that fact. The sacramental elements are the vehicles through which, by the power of the Holy Spirit, the risen Christ is present to believers. In a similar way, preaching functions as a sacramental event in which Christ's presence is manifested to believers through the spoken words of the sermon.

Calvin is careful to define sacramental efficacy in such a way as to avoid what he took to be the errors of the Roman Catholic and the Zwinglian views of sacraments. The Roman Catholics, he argues, wrongly equate the efficacy of the sacrament with its performance, claiming that sacramental grace is available *ex opere operato*. This view infringes on the freedom of God to act where and when he will. No less in error, however, are the Zwinglians who understand the sacramental signs to be wholly separate from the grace that they symbolize. Calvin argues instead for an instrumental view: the signs are the tools that the Holy Spirit ordinarily uses to dispense grace. In the same way, human ministers, especially in the act of preaching, are the instruments of God's grace. In commenting on 2 Corinthians 3.6, Calvin states:

> We are, then, *Ministers of the Spirit*, not as if we held him [Christ] inclosed within us, or as it were captive – not as if we could at our pleasure confer his grace upon all, or upon whom we pleased – but because Christ, through our instrumentality, illuminates the minds of men, renews their hearts, and, in short, regenerates them wholly. It is in consequence of there being such a connection and bond of union between Christ's grace and man's effort, that in many cases *that* is ascribed to the minister which belongs exclusively to the Lord.[6]

While the efficacy of the preached Word rests wholly on the operation of the Holy Spirit through it, the sermon is the instrument employed by the Spirit to do the work of regeneration and reconciliation.

As in his sacramental teaching, Calvin is careful to define the "matter" (*res sacramenti*) of the sermon as Jesus Christ and his benefits. Though his natural body is ascended to heaven and therefore removed from the world, Christ is spiritually present to believers in the Word and sacraments in such a way that they can unite with him and receive his gifts and graces. While some might object, "Where is Christ now, the peacemaker between God and us? At what a distance he resides from us!" Calvin answers that "he daily presents to us the fruit of his suffering through means of the Gospel, which he designed, should be in the world, as a sure and authentic register of the reconciliation, that has once been effected. It is the part of ministers, therefore, to apply to us . . . the fruit of Christ's death."[7] And they do this by the preaching of the gospel. Further, not only the benefits of Christ's obedience, death, and resurrection are present in the proclamation of the gospel: Christ himself is there, as surely as he was bodily present to his first disciples. Christ acts in and through preachers in such a way that he wants "their mouth to be reckoned as his mouth, and their lips his lips."[8] Indeed, believers should regard the proclaimed word as no less certain than if Christ were visibly present.[9] The proclaimed word about Christ – the gospel – under the power of the Holy Spirit renders the real presence of Christ in the event of proclamation. The Word offers and presents Christ and with him all the benefits he has secured for the elect.

Calvin understands the event of preaching, then, in christological and sacramental terms. The pure preaching and hearing of the Word of God and the proper administration of the sacraments according to Christ's own institution are the marks of the true church (*Inst.* IV.1.9). This is because only as the Word is preached and the sacraments rightly celebrated are believers united with the present Christ in such a way as to constitute his body in the world. In this mystical union with the Savior, believers are clothed in Christ's righteousness and imbued with his life, and thus are delivered from sin to salvation, from death to eternal life. Calvin understood preaching to be about much more than education, edification, reproof, or prophetic critique of the world. The preaching event was the primary means of grace. The whole drama of salvation unfolded as the gathered people listened to the sermon.[10] It is hardly surprising, then, that Calvin himself rated preaching as among his most significant duties; nor that Calvin and the Geneva Consistory insisted that the citizens of Geneva attend preaching services as often as possible. More was at stake than educating the people of Geneva about the reforms their church was undergoing: the state of their souls was on the line. But now we must look more carefully at Calvin's own preaching practice. To what extent did he live up to his exalted theology of preaching?

## CALVIN'S HOMILETICAL PRACTICE

Though Calvin preached regularly before 1549, the evidence for documenting his preaching during that time is slim. Fortunately, beginning in 1549 and continuing until his death in 1564, his sermons were regularly transcribed by accomplished stenographers – especially the French refugee Denis Raguenier, who developed his own system of shorthand for recording each and every word of Calvin's sermons accurately. From Raguenier's manuscripts and catalogue, we know it was Calvin's practice to preach on Old Testament texts on weekdays and New Testament texts on Sundays. There were a few exceptions to this rule: for a time he preached on the Psalms on Sunday afternoons, and during festival seasons like Holy Week he would substitute appropriate New Testament texts for the weekday Old Testament sermons.

Calvin is lauded as a great expository preacher. He generally preached straight through a biblical book, usually in segments of several verses each, from beginning to end. In many cases this led to an extraordinary number of sermons on individual biblical books: 200 on Deuteronomy, 174 on Ezekiel, 189 on Acts. Between 1549 and 1564, he preached series of sermons on the following books: Psalms, Jeremiah, Lamentations, Micah, Zephaniah, Hosea, Joel, Amos, Obadiah, Jonah, Daniel, Ezekiel, 1 and 2 Thessalonians, 1 and 2 Timothy, Titus, 1 and 2 Corinthians, Job, Deuteronomy, Isaiah, Galatians, Ephesians, Harmony of the Gospels, Acts, Genesis, Judges, 1 and 2 Samuel, and 1 Kings.[11] It is interesting in view of his christological understanding of preaching that Calvin did not get around to preaching a series on the Synoptic Gospels until the last five years of his life. Though he preached straight through books of the Bible, it is unlikely many parishioners heard the entire series of sermons on any particular book. It was the practice of the pastors of Geneva to rotate among the three main pulpits in the city from week to week. The exposition of individual books in order seems to have been a pattern chosen more for the sake of the preacher than for any advantage it may have presented to the hearers of the sermons. But it is not inconceivable that Calvin had some admirers who followed him from pulpit to pulpit week by week.

The story of the transmission of the texts of Calvin's sermons is a long and complicated one, and we can only give the barest outline here.[12] In brief, Raguenier prepared the first catalogue of manuscript volumes of Calvin's sermons, including only the sermons that he himself had transcribed. His list included some thirty-six volumes containing over two thousand sermons. Of these, quite a few were published during Calvin's lifetime, and many more were published after his death, both in French and in translation (English, Latin, Italian, German, Dutch). Unfortunately, in the early nineteenth century, the manuscripts of Calvin's sermons held by the University of Geneva were sold along with duplicate books in order to create shelf space in the library. Some of these were discovered later in a junk shop and bought by weight and returned to the university library. Even after several more serendipitous finds were returned to the university library, however, only fourteen of the original manuscript volumes were recovered. The sermons included in the *Corpus Reformatorum* edition of Calvin's works had all been previously published, and the editors did not try to transcribe any of the manuscript volumes they had at hand. Only with the appearance of the *Supplementa Calviniana* are the manuscript volumes gradually being published.

In order to gain a clearer understanding of Calvin's preaching style, it will be useful to analyze briefly four of his sermons: two on Old Testament passages, and two on New Testament passages. Of course, it is nearly impossible to rationalize a selection of four from more than a thousand published sermons.[13] Those chosen for analysis here are from the series on Job, Deuteronomy, Galatians, and Ephesians. They were preached between 1554 and 1559. All of them were recorded by Raguenier, and all of them were circulated in sixteenth-century translations. They certainly may be regarded as representative of Calvin's mature preaching. The variation from earlier to later sermons is not significant: Calvin was a remarkably consistent preacher, and his style changed little over the years. We will consider the sermons in the order in which they were preached.

Calvin's series of sermons on Job was preached between late February of 1554 and mid-March of 1555. The sermon chosen for analysis here comes toward the end of that series and is based on the first four verses of the thirty-eighth chapter of Job – the beginning of God's answer to Job from the whirlwind.[14] Calvin often begins, as he does in this sermon, by reminding the congregation of where he had left off in the last sermon. The main point at the end of the previous sermon had been that God graciously condescended to approach Job through the ministry of Elihu – a mortal man. This was so that Job would not be overwhelmed but would receive God's Word in an approachable form. And God does the same thing for present-day believers by approaching them through the words of human ministers. Unfortunately, this approach did not work for Job: his questioning did not stop. So God reverted to the opposite method – overwhelming Job with a sense of his greatness and majesty. Calvin concludes this first thought with one of the customary formulas he uses to mark a transition in the sermon: "This is what we have to note in the first place from this passage."[15] The point is that believers have no excuse for not hearing and receiving God's Word since God accommodates himself in every way to human weakness – first by humbling himself and speaking through the ministry of human beings, second by revealing himself in all his majesty in a way that humbles human presumption.

Calvin then elaborates on the significance of the fact that God spoke "from a whirlwind." Scripture often mentions God's self-revelation through storms – thunder, lightning, earthquakes, whirlwinds. God's intention in manifesting his glory through frightening natural events is to get the attention of those he wishes to address, not to overwhelm or frighten them. If even such a holy man as Job needed God to check him with a display of power, it is certainly to be expected that we will occasionally need such manifestations of power as well. For present-day believers, though, they take a different form: "[O]ne will have some scruples, and some troubles in his conscience, another will be afflicted by illnesses, another will have other adversities."[16] But when this happens, Calvin argues, believers should pay attention because these problems are signs that God is saying something to them. Unfortunately, not everyone pays attention, even after repeated divine chastisements. It is as if God repeatedly hit these "ill-starred fellows" on the head with "great blows of the hammer." The point to take is that we should strive to be more pliant recipients of God's Word.

The following part of the text, the words spoken by God to Job, form the remainder of the sermon. With each phrase, Calvin attempts to say what the text means, both for Job and for his congregation. The question "Who art thou?" is explained as God's mocking of Job. God does this to remove all human pretension to greatness. This is further intensified by the words, "Gird thy loins like a valiant man." That, Calvin explains, is as if God were to say to Job, "Give it your best shot, arm yourself from head to foot, but at the end of the day you can never win in a battle against me." The general principle to be inferred from this part of the text is that "great and small . . . [should] learn to be ashamed of themselves" and to recognize that God sees nothing of worth in any human being.[17] The question "Who are you?" is in fact more spoken to us than to Job. Calvin connects God's question to Job with Paul's rhetorical question in Romans 9, "But who indeed are you, a human being, to argue with God?" Unconditional double predestination may seem unfair or repulsive to us as mortals, but we have no right to quarrel with God.

Next Calvin moves on to God's accusation against Job: he "wrapped counsel in propositions without knowledge." Because Job was not properly humble in his self-estimation, he exceeded the limits in quarreling about things he did not understand. Calvin draws the general principle that believers should be cautious and reverent in their approach to questions about God; they should be guided by God's self-revelation in Scripture, and they should willingly avoid subjects which God did not wish them to know about. "[W]hen we shall not find in the Word of God what we wish to know; let us know that we must remain ignorant; and then after that we must keep our mouths closed; for as soon as we may wish to say a word, there will be no knowledge; there will be only deception in us."[18]

The final point of the sermon revolves around the phrase, "Answer all my questions." This further intensifies God's mockery of Job, Calvin thinks, and it points to another general principle: that is, it is unnatural for humans to speak and for God to listen. If believers truly know the God with whom they are dealing, they will certainly not want to be put in the position of having to answer his questions to them. Calvin concludes that believers must learn to humble themselves to learn in the "school of God," and to develop such a sense of God's glory that they will find everything that proceeds from God to be good. The message of Job in general is that God's works in nature and history need no justification.

For anyone familiar with Calvin's *Institutes*, a number of important theological themes come through in this sermon: the concept of divine accommodation to human weakness as the general context of revelation; the correlative knowledge of God and self; the universality of sin; and the proscription of theological speculation. Calvin is certainly controlled by the words of his text, not only for the general explanation, but even for the more imaginative application to his congregation. It is worth noting, however, that this sermon, like many of the Old Testament sermons, contains no reference to Jesus Christ. But now we must turn to our other example of Calvin's Old Testament preaching.

Calvin preached his long series of sermons on Deuteronomy between March, 1555 and July, 1556. The sermon chosen for analysis here was preached in July of 1555.[19] The text is Deuteronomy 5:19. Calvin offers a comprehensive interpretation of the commandment against stealing. While no one would wish to be called a thief, he states, many people improperly imagine that they are not guilty of stealing simply because they have not been convicted of theft in a human court. But God's immutable law, which attaches blessings and curses to the commandments, is not at all based upon the opinion of the world. Calvin explicates the many different forms that stealing can take: unfair prices, taking advantage of illiterate and uneducated people's gullibility, selling damaged goods, loafing on the job, unjust lawsuits. In fact, "stealing is not simply committed with our hands, when . . . someone is able to steal another person's money or coins. But stealing occurs when a man possesses what isn't his, and when we don't attempt to protect what God has put in a person's hands."[20]

Having elaborated the many faces of thievery, Calvin turns to the question: How should we conduct ourselves to avoid falling under divine condemnation for stealing? In answer to this question, he offers several general principles. First, as Paul said in Romans 13, we should let our actions toward others be ruled by charity. Second, again appealing to Paul (Phil. 4:12), Calvin says we need to learn how to avoid the craving to be rich. This is difficult for everyone. The poor, for obvious reasons, would like some of the misery of their poverty relieved through greater wealth. It is those who are already relatively rich who have the most need to learn contentment. His remarks are pointed and provocative:

> [T]he majority of the rich would not even be satisfied had God given
> them the whole earth to possess. For . . . they are still jealous that the
> poor have a common ray of light, and that they drink water, and
> work . . . And although . . . [the rich man] draws their sweat and blood,
> it seems to him that when they eat at his expense they are wringing
> him of his very intestines and bowels. And unfortunately, this
> parsimony, or rather brutal cruelty on the part of the rich, is far too
> common.[21]

Beyond learning a kind of contentment that prevents exploitation of the poor, the rich also have to learn poverty of spirit. Here Calvin references the case of Job: it is possible that God will take away everything that he has given to a rich person. Unless the rich person has true poverty of spirit, he or she will not be able to say with Job, "The Lord gave and the Lord has taken away; blessed be the name of the Lord." So both those who are rich and those who are poor should pray to be enabled to keep the commandment. The poor should pray that God will deliver them from the temptation to steal when they are genuinely hungry, thirsty, cold, and in need. But the rich should pray to be released from the craving for wealth. "God's benediction constitutes true wealth. Therefore it is crucial to drink from that fountain and to be satisfied by it if we want to restrain ourselves from every form of stealing."[22]

Moreover, the commandment does not simply prohibit outright theft. It also calls for the promotion of justice and equity. "For when I see with my own eyes someone who has been oppressed and make no effort to help him, indeed, I am consenting to the thief."[23] Many of the rich, Calvin explains, have gained their goods at the expense of others. "[L]et us realize," he writes, "that they have cut the throats of the poor and have made many widows and orphans."[24] God tests the obedience of believers in this situation, because they should help the poor, even while they should be on guard against any wrongdoing while so helping them. The sermon concludes with another general principle:

> [L]et none of us think that it is only lawful for us to guard what we
> have, rather, as the principle of charity exhorts us, let us see that we
> preserve and procure our neighbor's property as much as our
> own . . . [and] that we should always aspire toward that celestial
> heritage, knowing that therein we shall possess the fullness of all
> goods in perfection.[25]

This sermon offers a far more expansive application of the text – a single verse – to the setting in sixteenth-century Geneva than did our first sermon. Class differences, violence, the plight of widows and orphans, and business ethics all appear in Calvin's interpretation of the commandment against stealing. Nonetheless, there is much that is consistent with our first example as well. Strikingly, once again there is no mention of Jesus Christ. Calvin does make a few more cross-references to New Testament texts in this sermon, and the rules of charity and contentment that function significantly in his argument come from Paul. But the sermon as a whole seems to be less a presentation of the gospel than an attempt thoroughly to explore the meaning of the commandment for right living before God – the third and primary use of the law according to Calvin. And even though this sermon is less strictly controlled by the actual words of the biblical text, Calvin still follows the somewhat haphazard organization that is customary of all his sermons. He never either begins or ends with a summary of the one, two, or three main things he wants his hearers to remember. Perhaps for Calvin such thematic organizing strategies were an unwarranted insertion of extra-biblical words between the text and the hearers. Or perhaps the style is a result of his extemporaneous preaching practice. One can read many of Calvin's sermons two or three times without being able to summarize concisely what he said. Apparently, it was true that at least some of his contemporaries had difficulty remembering the content of his sermons.[26] Still, it is hard to believe that a wealthy merchant in church that day would not have remembered at least some of the meaning Calvin drew from the eighth commandment!

We turn, now, to a consideration of two of Calvin's Sunday sermons on New Testament texts. He preached his series on Galatians from November, 1557 through May, 1558. The sermon chosen for analysis here comes approximately half-way through the series and is based on Galatians 3:26–29.[27] Calvin begins by noting that the gospel gives believers the dignity of being called children of God through faith. Faith in this case means much more than "crediting of some story when we hear it or read it." Rather, it implies receiving Jesus Christ inwardly with full assurance as he is offered to us by God the Father. The faith that receives Christ, however, is not in itself meritorious. No, God accepts believers as children by free adoption, and the source is purely God's goodness. Faith merely conveys God's adopting grace to those who believe. Only Christ is the Son of God by nature. Through faith, believers are united with Christ and "clothed" with Christ's righteousness. Specifically, it is in the sacrament of baptism that believers "put on" Christ. The notion of union with Christ is fundamental. Believers are so united with Christ that they "have not so much as one drop of the heavenly life, but of his inspiring or breathing into us."[28] And Paul says that we receive this new life in union with Christ through baptism.

Calvin continues with a discussion of sacramental efficacy. It is true that not everyone who receives the outward sign – the water – of baptism is perfectly united with Christ through faith. And how could so great a gift as union with Christ actually be conferred by a corruptible element like water? Those who insist that the water of baptism actually brings about regeneration "pervert all order." The sacraments, rather, are the outward means by which God chooses to effect what he wills in those who receive them. Just as God established the sun to serve as the source of light in the world, and wills that bread should provide nourishment to the body, so also God established baptism as the means through which we are clothed with Christ. The actual source of regeneration, however, as also the source of light and life, is God himself. What conveys true life is not the sacramental elements but the union with Christ that is symbolized by them. The sacramental elements should not be confused with the matter of the sacrament.

The next major point concerns the implications of believing that we need to be clothed with Christ's righteousness. Calvin argues that this should convince the believer even more of his or her unworthiness before God. We come to God either wrapped in Adam's sinful curse or clothed with Christ's righteousness. Just as Jacob came to receive Isaac's blessing, clothed as if he were his brother, so believers need to put on Christ in order to receive God's blessing. Baptism is the outward sign of our having been clothed with Christ; from baptism should flow assurance of one's acceptance by God in Christ. Calvin urges the congregation to remember their baptisms, and to remind themselves of the blessing of baptism whenever they see it performed in the church.

The final point has to do with the claim of Galatians 3:28 that in Christ the distinctions between Jew and Gentile, slave and free, and male and female are overcome. The point Paul intends to make in the verse, Calvin argues, is that with regard to our salvation, we all come before God as absolute equals. That is to say, the only thing that any human being can bring to God is an acknowledgment of his sinfulness, and the open hand of faith, waiting to receive what God wills to give through Jesus Christ. There is nothing else apart from repentance and faith – no human honor or status symbol – that matters in receiving God's grace. What Paul does not mean, however, is that there are no differences between people with regard to the worldly order.

> For we know there are masters and servants, magistrates and subjects: in a household there is the good man which is the head, and the good wife which ought to be subject. We know then that this order is inviolable, and our Lord Jesus Christ is not come into the world to make such confusion as to abolish that which was established by God his father.[29]

So Paul's point has to do with human status before God (Lat. *coram deo*) and not with the social order of this world. In this world, Christians should uphold the God-given order in which some rule and others are ruled over.

The last sermon chosen for analysis here is from the series of sermons that Calvin preached on Ephesians from May of 1558 through March of 1559. It is the twentieth-ninth sermon in the series, based on Ephesians 4:20–24.[30] Calvin's reflections begin with the meaning of the statement, "You have not so learned Christ." He draws several ideas from this. First, there is a difference between believers and unbelievers with regard to their knowledge of God. Since Christ the "sun of righteousness" has shone on believers, they have no excuse for not knowing what has been revealed to them. They should, therefore, conduct themselves like those who have knowledge, and not like unbelievers who wander aimlessly in darkness. Second, Paul means to cut off any excuses people offer for their lack of knowledge. They have been taught. In fact, it is God himself who fills the office of a good and faithful teacher. In the preaching of the gospel, believers can see Jesus Christ. And the presentation of this teaching does not happen once and for all but over and over again, since God ordained "that the gospel should be preached continually . . . [and] that we might be confirmed in it all the time of our life."[31] A third lesson Calvin draws is that believers who have been enlightened should be especially attendant to receiving what God gives them in the Word. God accommodates himself to human weakness and "brings himself down as much as possible to . . . [their] capacity, so that he even lisps . . . to tell . . . his secrets after a sweet and loving fashion, as if one wishing to feed a little babe should chew his meat for him."[32] When all that is left for the believer to do is to swallow, so to speak, she ought to make every effort to do that.

The next major point Calvin makes has to do with the aim or target of Scripture (the *scopus scripturae*). It is not an accident, he says, that Paul links Jesus Christ with the doctrine of the gospel, because he is the end and substance of it. Those who want to profit from God's Word need a definite mark at which to aim, and that mark is Jesus Christ. "For we see a number that have turned over the Scripture leaf by leaf and are able to give a good account of it, but, even so, they do not know what is its main thrust, for their aim is not directed at our Lord Jesus Christ."[33] Believers need to understand that "Jesus Christ is the goal to which God the Father calls"[34] them.

Calvin proceeds to a consideration of the clause "if you have learned him well." The first lesson he draws from it is that it is easy enough to say one is a Christian, but not all who claim to be Christian know what that means. Scarcely one in a hundred knows what is entailed.

> To say that men may lawfully eat flesh on a Friday, and to mock all the superstitions of popery, and to say that they are but empty and trivial things – that they can do with ease. But . . . if a man asks them what it is to be regenerate, what patience is, what newness of life is, and what it is to be fashioned again after the image of God – there the majority of them will show that they never tasted the truth of the gospel.[35]

Calvin warns his congregation to examine themselves and make sure that the gospel has taken root in their hearts.

Next comes a consideration of the statement, "You have put off the old man." Calvin says there are two fountainheads of the human race – Adam and Christ. Until we have put off the corrupt nature inherited from Adam we cannot be renewed in Jesus Christ and made new creatures. So the first general point is that we have to give up on ourselves before we can receive the help offered in Christ. The second point is that Christ has been given in order to restore us to the image of God. That is to say, it is not enough to be forgiven alone. Rather, human beings are to be sanctified by the Holy Spirit. This involves a constant "battle of offering force and violence to all our thoughts and affections in order to bring them into captivity to the obedience of God."[36] A third point has to do with self-examination. Calvin states that Paul is inviting the Ephesians to compare their current state to where they were before. Such self-examination is useful because it reveals where growth is needed. Finally, Calvin reflects on the word "old." Just as we associate old age with declining strength and vigor, so the "old man" of sinful existence is doomed to decline and death.

The concluding reflections of the sermon have to do with the renewal of mind. The devil is a master of deceit, and those who are bewitched by him do not see what is happening to themselves – their minds become very dull. But if we cast aside our own corrupt reason and rely upon the mind that is restored in us through God's Word, we will grow in new life. This requires patience, because the renewal does not happen all at once. But God's saving purpose is precisely about the renewal of the person. Calvin draws a metaphor from farming. If you want to harvest a good crop, first you have to clear the field of thorns and brambles, then the ground must be plowed and good seed planted. But all of this preparation of the field is in order that God may receive the fruit which he asks of us, namely "that he may be honoured at our hands, and that we may show in very truth that we know ourselves to be indebted to him for all good things."[37] The renewed human being who honors God as the fountain of every good thing is the goal of the process of reconciliation.

Clearly, Calvin's New Testament preaching sounds some different notes than his Old Testament sermons. There is enormous emphasis throughout the New Testament sermons on Jesus Christ as the sum and substance of the gospel, and on the necessity of union with Christ as the source of new life. Calvin tends to make more frequent reference to the sacraments in the New Testament sermons as well, and this is not surprising since many Sunday services would have included baptism or the Lord's Supper. Rather than emphasizing the majesty, inscrutability, or hiddenness of God, the New Testament sermons tend to emphasize God's fatherly goodwill, his gratuitous goodness, and his intimacy with believers through Christ. While continually reminding his hearers of their hopelessness apart from Christ, Calvin in his New Testament sermons also consistently reminds them that God's saving purpose is to restore them in his own image. The New Testament sermons, in short, emphasize the gospel over the law – even in its third use.

We are given no clues as to whether Calvin understood the purpose of the weekday Old Testament sermons to be different from the purpose of the Sunday sermons. They did, however, occur in the context of a different kind of liturgy, and that alone would have created a different impression for those attending. The Old Testament sermons correspond less well with Calvin's theology of preaching than the New Testament sermons. If the purpose of the preached Word is to "offer and present Christ," then it has not achieved its purpose if an entire sermon can make no mention of Jesus Christ, as both of our Old Testament examples do not.[38] And although in the Ephesians sermon analyzed above Calvin chastises unnamed opponents for searching the Scripture but missing its target, he himself seems to fall into the same trap when preaching on texts like Job. The humiliated human, reduced to silence by the overwhelming power of God, that we saw at the end of the Job sermon is a far cry from the believer who rests with assurance in the love of God poured out on his children that we saw in the Galatians sermon. Of course, Calvin is constrained by the topics and even by the religious moods of the texts on which he preaches. But that raises the question about the coherence of his theory and practice of preaching. Should every biblical book be treated by the preacher according to exactly the same theological principles? Apparently, Calvin thought the New Testament deserved a special place on Sundays. Ironically, that meant that six days out of seven, it was the Old Testament that he was preaching.

Calvin has surely been one of the most influential preachers in the history of Christian thought. His sermons were circulated widely during his lifetime and after his death, and they probably had more to do with the spread of his influence than any of his theological treatises. The sermons are always earnest attempts to explicate and apply the words of the biblical text. Calvin's style, however, leaves something to be desired. This was recognized even by his admiring successor and biographer, Theodore Beza. In commenting on the cooperative ministries of Calvin, Farel, and Viret, Beza notes that the three had very different preaching styles.

> Farel excelled in a certain sublimity of mind, so that nobody could either hear his thunders without trembling, or listen to his most fervent prayers without feeling almost as it were carried up into heaven. Viret possessed such winning eloquence, that his entranced audience hung upon his lips. Calvin never spoke without filling the mind of the hearer with the most weighty sentiments. I have often thought that a preacher compounded of the three would have been absolutely perfect.[39]

The preacher who performed his task well, Calvin believed, would "penetrate into the consciences of men, to make them see Christ crucified, and feel the shedding of his blood. When the Church has painters such as these, she no longer needs the dead images of wood and stone, she no longer requires pictures."[40] His own preaching style, however, was usually grave, sedate, and unfocused – perhaps even ponderous. Still, as an expository preacher, he has inspired generations of Reformed pastors. Karl Barth, in his *Göttingen Dogmatics*, well captures the spirit of Calvin's preaching:

> How this man is grasped and stilled and claimed – not too quickly must one suppose by his experience of conversion, or by the thought of predestination, or by Christ, or even, as is commonly said, by

passion for God's glory – no, but in the first instance simply by the authority of the biblical books, which year by year he never tired of expounding systematically down to the very last verse![41]

Calvin held a christological and sacramental theology of preaching. But in his own sermons he treated the words of the Bible simply as "oracles of God," worthy of being expounded down to the very last verse – without regard to the "target" at which (in his view) the Scriptures take aim. There is some tension, then, between Calvin's theology of preaching and his own preaching practice, just as there is a tension between his eucharistic theology and his efforts to construct a Reformed liturgy.

*Notes*

1 John Calvin, *Institutes of the Christian Religion*, English translation of the 1559 edition, ed. John T. McNeill, trans. Ford Lewis Battles, 2 vols., Library of Christian Classics, vols. XX–XXI (Philadelphia: Westminster Press, 1960), II.1.4. Hereafter cited as *Inst.* by book, chapter, and paragraph parenthetically within the body of the text. I have chosen throughout this essay to cite accessible English translations, even reprints of older translations. However, I have checked them for accuracy against the original Latin or French.

2 John Calvin, *Comm. Haggai* 1:12, in *Calvin's Commentaries*, Calvin Translation Society (Edinburgh, 1844–56), reprinted in 22 volumes (Grand Rapids: Baker, 1981), XV/1, 341. Hereafter cited by biblical text, volume, part volume, and page number and by the designation *Calvin's Commentaries*.

3 *Comm. John 10:4, Calvin's Commentaries*, XVII/2, 396.

4 Cf. *Comm. Gen. 9:12, Calvin's Commentaries*, I/1, 208.

5 John Calvin, *Short Treatise on the Holy Supper of Our Lord Jesus Christ*, in *Selected Works of John Calvin: Tracts and Letters*, ed. Henry Beveridge and Jules Bonnet, 7 vols. (Grand Rapids: Baker, 1983), II, 166.

6 *Comm. II Cor. 3:6, Calvin's Commentaries*, XX/2, 174.

7 *Comm. II Cor. 5:19, Calvin's Commentaries*, XX/2, 238.

8 *Comm. Isaiah 11:4, Calvin's Commentaries*, VII/1, 381.

9 *Comm. Rom. 10:8, Calvin's Commentaries*, XIX/2, 391.

10 So the epigraph to this chapter, *Comm. Rom. 11:14, Calvin's Commentaries*, XIX/2, 424.

11 See the discussion in T. H. L. Parker, *Calvin's Preaching* (Louisville: Westminster John Knox Press, 1992), 59–64, 150–52.

12 See the thorough discussion in ibid., 65–75, 153–62, 179–98.

13 For an analysis of Calvin's sermons on the Harmony of the Gospels, see Dawn DeVries, *Jesus Christ in the Preaching of Calvin and Schleiermacher* (Louisville: Westminster John Knox Press, 1996), 26–47. For Calvin's sermons on the Beatitudes, Micah, and the Passion narratives of the Gospel of Matthew, see Hughes Oliphant Old, *The Reading and Preaching of the Scriptures in the Worship of the Christian Church*, vol. IV: *The Age of the Reformation* (Grand Rapids: Eerdmans, 2002), 94–128; for his sermons on Acts, see Wilhelmus H. Th. Moehn, *God Calls*

*Us to His Service: The Relation Between God and His Audience in Calvin's Sermons on Acts* (Geneva: Librairie Droz, 2001); and for the sermons on Job, see Susan E. Schreiner, *Where Shall Wisdom Be Found? Calvin's Exegesis of Job from Medieval and Modern Perspectives* (Chicago: University of Chicago Press, 1994), 91–155, 228–50. T. H. L. Parker discusses many of Calvin's sermons, especially from the series on 1 and 2 Timothy, Job, Deuteronomy, and Isaiah 3–41 throughout *Calvin's Preaching*.

14 John Calvin, *Sermons from Job*, ed. and trans. Leroy Nixon (1952; rpt., Grand Rapids: Baker, 1980), 287–300.

15 Ibid., 288.

16 Ibid., 290–91.

17 Ibid., 294.

18 Ibid., 299.

19 *John Calvin's Sermons on the Ten Commandments*, ed. and trans. Benjamin W. Farley (Grand Rapids: Baker, 1980), 185–201.

20 Ibid., 190–91.

21 Ibid., 193–94.

22 Ibid., 197.

23 Ibid., 200.

24 Ibid., 196.

25 Ibid., 200–201.

26 Many of the cases brought before the Genevan Consistory had to do with attendance at the sermons, and many of those interrogated claimed that they could not understand or remember the ministers' preaching, including Calvin's. See *Registers of the Consistory of Geneva in the Time of Calvin*, vol. I: *1542–1544*, ed. Robert M. Kingdon, Thomas A. Lambert, and Isabella M. Watt, trans. M. Wallace McDonald (Grand Rapids: Eerdmans, 2000).

27 John Calvin, *Sermons on Galatians*, trans. Arthur Golding (London, 1574; rpt., Audubon, NJ: Old Paths Publications, 1995), 479–98.

28 Ibid., 484.

29 Ibid., 495.

30 John Calvin, *Sermons on the Epistle to the Ephesians*, revised version of translation by Arthur Golding (London, 1577; rpt., Edinburgh: Banner of Truth Trust, 1973), 420–32.

31 Ibid., 422.

32 Ibid., 423.

33 Ibid.

34 Ibid., 424.

35 Ibid.

36 Ibid., 428.

37 Ibid, 432.

38 Of course, many of Calvin's sermons on the prophets do contain references to Jesus Christ, whom Calvin takes to be the ultimate referent of all biblical prophecy. Nonetheless, even in his preaching on the prophets, Calvin did not consistently connect the Old Testament texts with the gospel. As a biblical commentator, he was accused of being a "Judaizer" because of his hesitation to interpret the Old Testament christologically. To what extent that is fair is a matter of

scholarly debate. See David L. Puckett, *John Calvin's Exegesis of the Old Testament* (Louisville: Westminster John Knox Press, 1995).

39  *The Life of John Calvin*, in *Selected Works of John Calvin: Tracts and Letters*, I, xxxix.

40  *Comm. Gal. 3:1, Calvin's Commentaries*, XXI/1, 80–81.

41  Karl Barth, *The Göttingen Dogmatics: Instruction in the Christian Religion*, vol. I, ed. Hannelotte Reiffen, trans. Geoffrey W. Bromiley (Grand Rapids: Eerdmans, 1990), 54.

# 8 Calvin on piety

JOEL R. BEEKE

John Calvin's *Institutes* have earned him the title of "the preeminent sys-
tematician of the Protestant Reformation." His reputation as an intellectual,
however, is often seen apart from the vital spiritual and pastoral context
in which he wrote his theology. For Calvin, theological understanding and
practical piety, truth, and usefulness are inseparable. Theology first of all
deals with knowledge – knowledge of God and of ourselves – but there is
no true knowledge where there is no true piety.

Calvin's concept of piety (Lat. *pietas*) is rooted in the knowledge of God
and includes attitudes and actions that are directed to the adoration and
service of God. In addition, his *pietas* includes a host of related themes,
such as filial piety in human relationships, and respect and love for the
image of God in human beings. Calvin's piety is evident in people who
recognize through experiential faith that they have been accepted in Christ
and engrafted into his body by the grace of God. In this "mystical union," the
Lord claims them as his own in life and in death. They become God's people
and members of Christ by the power of the Holy Spirit. This relationship
restores their joy of fellowship with God; it re-creates their lives.

The purpose of this chapter is to show that Calvin's piety is fundamentally biblical, with an emphasis on the heart more than the mind. Head and
heart must work together, but the heart is more important.[1] After an introductory look at the definition and goal of piety in Calvin's thinking, I will
show how his *pietas* affects the theological, ecclesiological, and practical
dimensions of his thought.

## THE DEFINITION AND IMPORTANCE OF PIETY

*Pietas* is one of the major themes of Calvin's theology. His theology is,
as John T. McNeill says, "his piety described at length."[2] He was determined
to confine theology within the limits of piety.[3] In his preface addressed to
King Francis I, Calvin says that the purpose of writing the *Institutes* was

"solely to transmit certain rudiments by which those who are touched with any zeal for religion might be shaped to true godliness (*pietas*)."[4]

For Calvin, *pietas* designates the right attitude of man toward God. It is an attitude that includes true knowledge, heartfelt worship, saving faith, filial fear, prayerful submission, and reverential love.[5] Knowing who and what God is (theology) embraces right attitudes toward him and doing what he wants (piety). In his first catechism, Calvin writes, "True piety consists in a sincere feeling which loves God as Father as much as it fears and reverences Him as Lord, embraces His righteousness, and dreads offending Him worse than death."[6] In the *Institutes*, Calvin is more succinct: "I call 'piety' that reverence joined with love of God which the knowledge of his benefits induces."[7] This love and reverence for God is a necessary concomitant to any knowledge of him and embraces all of life. As Calvin says, "The whole life of Christians ought to be a sort of practice of godliness."[8] Or, as the subtitle of the first edition of the *Institutes* states, "Embracing almost the whole sum of piety, & whatever is necessary to know of the doctrine of salvation: A work most worthy to be read by all persons zealous for piety."[9]

Calvin's commentaries also reflect the importance of *pietas*. For example, he writes on 1 Timothy 4:7–8: "You will do the thing of greatest value, if with all your zeal and ability you devote yourself to godliness (*pietas*) alone. Godliness is the beginning, middle and end of Christian living. Where it is complete, there is nothing lacking . . . Thus the conclusion is that we should concentrate exclusively on godliness, for when once we have attained to it, God requires no more of us."[10] Commenting on 2 Peter 1:3, he says, "As soon as he [Peter] has made mention of life he immediately adds godliness (*pietas*) as if it were the soul of life."[11]

### Piety's supreme goal: *soli Deo gloria*

The goal of piety, as well as the entire Christian life, is the glory of God – glory that shines in God's attributes, in the structure of the world, and in the death and resurrection of Jesus Christ.[12] Glorifying God supersedes personal salvation for every truly pious person.[13] So Calvin writes to Cardinal Sadolet:

> It is not very sound theology to confine a man's thought so much to himself, and not to set before him, as the prime motive for his existence, zeal to illustrate the glory of God . . . I am persuaded that there is no man imbued with true piety who will not consider as insipid that long and labored exhortation to zeal for heavenly life, a zeal which keeps a man entirely devoted to himself and does not, even by one expression, arouse him to sanctify the name of God.[14]

The goal of piety – that God may be glorified in us – is that for which we were created. It thus becomes the yearning of the regenerate to live out the purpose of their original creation.[15] The pious man, according to Calvin, confesses, "We are God's: let us therefore live for him and die for him. We are God's: let his wisdom and will therefore rule all our actions. We are God's: let all the parts of our life accordingly strive toward him as our only lawful goal."[16]

God redeems, adopts, and sanctifies his people that his glory might shine in them and deliver them from impious self-seeking.[17] The pious person's deepest concern therefore is God himself and the things of God – God's Word, God's authority, God's gospel, God's truth. He yearns to know more of God and to commune more with him.

But how do we glorify God? As Calvin writes, "God has prescribed for us a way in which he will be glorified by us, namely, piety, which consists in the obedience of his Word. He that exceeds these bounds does not go about to honor God, but rather to dishonor him."[18] Obedience to God's Word means taking refuge in Christ for forgiveness of our sins, knowing him through his Word, serving him with a loving heart, doing good works in gratitude for his goodness, and exercising self-denial to the point of loving our enemies.[19] This response involves total surrender to God himself, his Word, and his will.[20]

Calvin says, "I offer thee my heart, Lord, promptly and sincerely." That is the desire of all who are truly pious. However, that desire can only be realized through communion with Christ and participation in him, for outside of Christ even the most religious person lives for himself. Only in Christ can the pious live as willing servants of their Lord, faithful soldiers of their Commander, and obedient children of their Father.[21]

## THEOLOGICAL DIMENSIONS

### Piety's profound root: mystical union

"Calvin's doctrine of union with Christ is one of the most consistently influential features of his theology and ethics, if not the single most important teaching that animates the whole of his thought and his personal life," writes David Willis-Watkins.[22]

Calvin did not intend to present theology from the viewpoint of a single doctrine. Nonetheless, his sermons, commentaries, and theological works are so permeated with the union-with-Christ doctrine that it becomes the focus for Christian faith and practice.[23] Calvin says as much when he writes, "That joining together of Head and members, that indwelling of Christ in our hearts – in short, that mystical union – are accorded by us the highest degree of importance, so that Christ, having been made ours, makes us sharers with him in the gifts with which he has been endowed."[24]

For Calvin, piety is rooted in the believer's mystical union (*unio mystica*) with Christ; thus this union must be our starting point.[25] That union is possible because Christ took on our human nature, filling it with his virtue. Union with Christ in his humanity is historical, ethical, and personal, but not essential. There is no crass mixture (*crassa mixtura*) of human substances between Christ and us. Nonetheless, Calvin states, "Not only does he cleave to us by an indivisible bond of fellowship, but with a wonderful communion, day by day, he grows more and more into one body with us, until he becomes completely one with us."[26] This union is one of the gospel's greatest mysteries.[27] Because of the fountain of Christ's perfection in our nature, the pious may, by faith, draw whatever they need for their sanctification. The flesh of Christ is the source from which his people derive life and power.[28]

If Christ had died and risen but was not applying his salvation to believers for their regeneration and sanctification, his work would have been ineffectual. Piety shows the Spirit of Christ is working in us what has already been accomplished in Christ. Christ administers his sanctification to the church through his royal priesthood so that the church may live piously for him.[29]

### Piety's major theme: communion and participation

The heartbeat of Calvin's practical theology and piety is communion (*communio*) with Christ. This involves participation (*participatio*) in his benefits, which are inseparable from union with Christ.[30] That emphasis was already evident in the *Confessio Fidei de Eucharistia* (1537), signed by Calvin, Martin Bucer, and Wolfgang Capito.[31] However, Calvin's communion with Christ is not shaped by his doctrine of the Lord's Supper; rather, his emphasis on spiritual communion with Christ helped shape his concept of the sacrament.

Similarly, the concepts of *communio* and *participatio* helped shape Calvin's understanding of regeneration, faith, justification, sanctification, assurance, election, and the church. He could not speak of any doctrine apart from communion with Christ. That is the heart of Calvin's system of theology.

### Piety's double bond: the Spirit and faith

Communion with Christ is realized only through Spirit-worked faith, Calvin teaches. It is actual communion, not because believers participate in the essence of Christ's nature, but because the Spirit of Christ unites believers so intimately to Christ that they become flesh of his flesh and bone of his bone. From God's perspective, the Spirit is the bond between Christ and believers, whereas from our perspective, faith is the bond. These perspectives do not clash with each other, since one of the Spirit's principal operations is to work faith in a sinner.[32]

Only the Spirit can unite Christ in heaven with the believer on earth. Just as in the incarnation the Spirit united heaven and earth, so in regeneration the Spirit raises the elect from earth to commune with Christ in heaven and brings Christ into the hearts and lives of the elect on earth.[33] Communion with Christ is always the result of the Spirit's work – a work that is astonishing and experiential rather than comprehensible.[34] The Holy Spirit is thus the link that binds the believer to Christ and the channel through which Christ is communicated to the believer.[35] As Calvin wrote to Peter Martyr: "We grow up together with Christ into one body, and he shares his Spirit with us, through whose hidden operation he has become ours. Believers receive this communion with Christ at the same time as their calling. But they grow from day to day more and more in this communion, in proportion to the life of Christ growing within them."[36]

Calvin moves beyond Luther in this emphasis on communion with Christ. Calvin stresses that, by his Spirit, Christ empowers those who are united with him by faith. Being "engrafted into the death of Christ, we derive from it a secret energy, as the twig does from the root," Calvin writes. The believer "is animated by the secret power of Christ; so that Christ may be said to live and grow in him; for as the soul enlivens the body, so Christ imparts life to his members."[37]

Like Luther, Calvin believes that knowledge is fundamental to faith. Such knowledge includes the Word of God as well as the proclamation of the gospel.[38] Since the written Word is exemplified in the living Word, Jesus Christ, in whom all God's promises are fulfilled, faith cannot be separated from Christ.[39] The work of the Spirit does not supplement or supersede the revelation of Scripture, but authenticates it, Calvin teaches. "Take away the Word, and no faith will remain," Calvin says.[40]

Faith unites the believer to Christ by means of the Word, enabling the believer to receive Christ as he is clothed in the gospel and graciously offered by the Father.[41] By faith, God also dwells in the believer. Consequently, Calvin says, "We ought not to separate Christ from ourselves or ourselves from him," but participate in Christ by faith, for this "revives us from death to make us a new creature."[42]

By faith, the believer possesses Christ and grows in him. Furthermore, the degree of the believer's faith exercised through the Word determines one's degree of communion with Christ.[43] "Everything which faith should contemplate is exhibited to us in Christ," Calvin writes.[44] Though Christ remains in heaven, the believer who excels in piety learns to grasp Christ so firmly by faith that Christ dwells within the heart.[45] By faith the pious live by what they find in Christ rather than by what they find in themselves.[46]

For Calvin, communion with Christ flows out of union with Christ. Looking to Christ for assurance, therefore, means looking at ourselves in Christ. As David Willis-Watkins writes, "Assurance of salvation is a derivative self-knowledge, whose focus remains on Christ as united to his body, the Church, of which we are members."[47]

### Piety's double cleansing: justification and sanctification

According to Calvin, believers receive from Christ by faith the "double grace" of justification and sanctification, which, together, provide a twofold cleansing.[48] Justification offers imputed purity, and sanctification, actual purity.[49]

Calvin defines justification as "the acceptance with which God receives us into his favor as righteous men."[50] He goes on to say that "since God justifies us by the intercession of Christ, he absolves us not by the confirmation of our own innocence but by the imputation of righteousness, so that we who are not righteous in ourselves may be reckoned as such in Christ."[51] Justification includes the remission of sins and the right to eternal life.

Calvin regards justification as a central doctrine of the Christian faith. He calls it "the principal hinge by which religion is supported," the soil out of which the Christian life develops, and the substance of piety.[52] Justification not only serves God's honor by satisfying the conditions for salvation; it also offers the believer's conscience "peaceful rest and serene tranquility."[53] As Romans 5:1 says, "Therefore, being justified by faith, we have peace with God through our Lord Jesus Christ." This is the heart and soul of piety. Believers need not worry about their status with God because they are justified by faith. They can willingly renounce personal glory and daily accept their own life from the hand of their Creator and Redeemer. Daily skirmishes may be lost to the enemy, but Jesus Christ has won the war for them.

Sanctification refers to the process in which the believer increasingly becomes conformed to Christ in heart, conduct, and devotion to God. It is the continual re-making of the believer by the Holy Spirit, the increasing consecration of body and soul to God.[54] In sanctification, the believer offers himself to God as a sacrifice. This does not come without great struggle and slow progress. It requires cleansing the pollution of the flesh and renouncing the world.[55] It requires repentance, mortification, and daily conversion.

Justification and sanctification are inseparable, Calvin says. To separate one from the other is to tear Christ in pieces,[56] or like trying to separate the sun's light from the heat that light generates.[57] Believers are justified for the purpose of living piously in order to worship God in holiness of life.[58]

## ECCLESIOLOGICAL DIMENSIONS

### Piety through the church

Calvin's *pietas* does not stand apart from Scripture or from the church. Rather, it is rooted in the Word and nurtured in the church. While breaking with the clericalism and absolutism of Rome, Calvin nonetheless maintained a high view of the church. "If we do not prefer the church to all other objects of our interest, we are unworthy of being counted among her members," he writes.

Augustine once said, "He cannot have God for his Father who refuses to have the church for his mother." To that Calvin adds, "For there is no other way to enter into life unless this mother conceive us in her womb, give us birth, nourish us at her breast, and lastly, unless she keep us under her care and guidance until, putting off mortal flesh, we become like the angels." Apart from the church, there is little hope for forgiveness of sins or salvation, Calvin wrote. It is always disastrous to leave the church.[59]

For Calvin, believers are engrafted into Christ and his church, for spiritual growth happens within the church. The church is mother, educator, and nourisher of every believer, for the Holy Spirit acts in her. Believers cultivate piety by the Spirit through the church's teaching ministry, progressing from spiritual infancy to adolescence to full maturity in Christ. They do not graduate from the church until they die.[60] This lifelong education is offered within an atmosphere of genuine piety in which believers love and care for one another under the headship of Christ.[61] It encourages the growth of one another's gifts and love, as it is "constrained to borrow from others."[62]

Growth in piety is impossible apart from the church, for piety is fostered by the communion of saints. Within the church, believers "cleave to each other in the mutual distribution of gifts."[63] Each member has his own place and gifts to use within the body.[64] Ideally, the entire body uses these gifts in symmetry and proportion, ever reforming and growing toward perfection.[65]

### Piety of the Word

The Word of God is central to the development of Christian piety in the believer. Calvin's relational model explains how.

True religion is a dialogue between God and humanity. The part of the dialogue God initiates is revelation. In this, God comes down to meet us, addresses us, and makes himself known to us in the preaching of the Word. The other part of the dialogue is the human response to God's revelation. This response, which includes trust, adoration, and godly fear, is what Calvin calls *pietas*. The preaching of the Word saves us and preserves us as the Spirit enables us to appropriate the blood of Christ and respond to him with reverential love. By Spirit-empowered human preaching, "the renewal of the saints is accomplished and the body of Christ is edified," Calvin says.[66]

The preaching of the Word is our spiritual food and our medicine for spiritual health. With the Spirit's blessing, ministers are spiritual physicians who apply the Word to our souls as earthly physicians apply medicine to our bodies. With the Word these spiritual doctors diagnose, prescribe for, and cure spiritual disease in those plagued by sin and death. The preached Word is used as an instrument to heal, cleanse, and make fruitful our disease-prone souls.[67] The Spirit, or the "internal minister," promotes piety by using the "external minister" to preach the Word. As Calvin says, the external minister "holds forth the vocal word and it is received by the ears," but the internal minister "truly communicates the thing proclaimed . . . that is Christ."[68]

To promote piety, the Spirit not only uses the gospel to work faith deep within the souls of God's elect, as we have already seen, but the Spirit also uses the law. The law promotes piety in three ways:

1. It restrains sin and promotes righteousness in the church and society, preventing both from lapsing into chaos.
2. It disciplines, educates, convicts, and drives us outside of ourselves to Jesus Christ, the fulfiller and end of the law. The law cannot lead us to a saving knowledge of God in Christ. Rather, the Holy Spirit uses the law as a mirror to show us our guilt, to shut us off from hope, and to bring us to repentance. It drives us to the spiritual need out of which faith in Christ is born. This convicting use of the law is critical for the believer's piety, for it prevents the ungodly self-righteousness that is prone to reassert itself even in the holiest of saints.
3. It becomes the rule of life for the believer. "What is the rule of life which [God] has given us?" Calvin asks in the Genevan Catechism. The answer: "His law." Later, Calvin says the law "shows the mark at which we ought to aim, the goal towards which we ought to press, that each of us, according to the measure of grace bestowed upon him, may endeavor to frame his

life according to the highest rectitude, and, by constant study, continually advance more and more."[69]

Calvin writes about the third use of the law in the first edition of his *Institutes,* stating, Believers . . . profit by the law because from it they learn more thoroughly each day what the Lord's will is like . . . It is as if some servant, already prepared with complete earnestness of heart to commend himself to his master, must search out and oversee his master's ways in order to conform and accommodate himself to them. Moreover, however much they may be prompted by the Spirit and eager to obey God, they are still weak in the flesh, and would rather serve sin than God. The law is to this flesh like a whip to an idle and balky ass, to goad, stir, arouse it to work.[70]

In the last edition of the *Institutes* (1559), Calvin is more emphatic about how believers profit from the law. First, he says, "Here is the best instrument for them to learn more thoroughly each day the nature of the Lord's will to which they aspire, and to confirm them in the understanding of it." Second, it causes "frequent meditation upon it to be aroused to obedience, be strengthened in it, and be drawn back from the slippery path of transgression." In this way the saints must press on, Calvin concludes. "For what would be less lovable than the law if, with importuning and threatening alone, it troubled souls through fear, and distressed them through fright?"[71]

Viewing the law primarily as a guide that encourages the believer to cling to God and obey him is another instance where Calvin differs from Luther. For Luther, the law is primarily negative. It is closely linked with sin, death, or the devil. Luther's dominant interest is in the second use of the law, even when he considers the law's role in sanctification. By contrast, Calvin views the law primarily as a positive expression of the will of God. As Hesselink says, "Calvin's view could be called Deuteronomic, for to him law and love are not antithetical, but are correlates."[72] For Calvin, the believer follows God's law, not out of compulsory obedience, but out of grateful obedience. Under the tutelage of the Spirit, the law prompts gratitude in the believer, which leads to loving obedience and aversion to sin. In other words, for Luther, the primary purpose of the law is to help the believer recognize and confront sin. For Calvin, the primary purpose of the law is to direct the believer to serve God out of love.[73]

### Piety in the sacraments

Calvin defines the sacraments as testimonies "of divine grace toward us, confirmed by an outward sign, with mutual attestation of our piety toward him."[74] The sacraments are "exercises of piety." They foster our faith, strengthen it, and help us offer ourselves as a living sacrifice to God.

For Calvin, as for Augustine, the sacraments are the visible Word. The preached Word comes through our ears, the visible Word through our eyes. The sacraments hold forth the same Christ as the preached Word but communicate him through a different mode. We don't get a better Christ in the sacraments, but sometimes we get Christ better.

In the sacraments, God accommodates himself to our weakness, Calvin says. When we hear the Word indiscriminately proclaimed, we may wonder: "Is it truly for me? Does it really reach me?" However, in the sacraments God reaches out and touches us individually, and says, "Yes, it's for *you*. The promise extends to *you*." The sacraments thus minister to our weakness by personalizing the promises for those who trust Christ for salvation.

In the sacraments, God comes to his people, encourages them, enables them to know Christ better, builds them up, and nourishes them in him. Baptism promotes piety as a symbol of how believers are engrafted into Christ, renewed by the Spirit, and adopted into the family of the heavenly Father.[75] Likewise, the Lord's Supper shows how these adopted children are fed by their loving Father. Calvin loves to refer to the Supper as nourishment for the soul. "The signs are bread and wine which represent for us the invisible food that we receive from the flesh and blood of Christ," he says. "Christ is the only food of our soul, and therefore our heavenly Father invites us to Christ, that refreshed by partaking of him, we may repeatedly gather strength until we shall have reached heavenly immortality."[76]

As believers, we need constant nourishment. We never reach a point where we no longer need to hear the Word, to pray, or to be nurtured by the sacraments. We must constantly grow and develop. As we continue to sin because of our old nature, we are in constant need of forgiveness and grace. So the Supper, along with the preaching of the Word, repeatedly says to us: We need Christ, we need to be renewed in Christ and built up in him. The sacraments promise that Christ is present to receive us, bless us, and renew us.

For Calvin, the word *conversion* doesn't just mean the initial act of coming to faith; it also means daily renewal and growth in following Christ. The sacraments lead the way to this daily conversion, Calvin says. They tell us that we need the grace of Christ every day. We must draw strength from Christ, particularly through the body that he sacrificed for us on the cross.

As Calvin writes,

> For as the eternal Word of God is the fountain of life so his flesh is the channel to pour out to us the life which resides intrinsically in his

divinity. For in his flesh was accomplished man's redemption, in it a sacrifice was offered to atone for sin, and obedience yielded to God to reconcile him to us. It was also filled with the sanctification of the Holy Spirit. Finally having overcome death he was received into the heavenly glory.[77]

In other words, the Spirit sanctified Christ's body, which Christ offered on the cross to atone for sin. That body was raised from the dead and received up into heaven. At every stage of our redemption, Christ's body is the pathway to God. In the Supper, then, Christ comes to us and says: "My body is still given for you. By faith you may commune with me and my body and all of its saving benefits."

Calvin teaches that Christ gives himself to us in the Supper, not just his benefits, just as he gives us himself and his benefits in the preaching of the Word. Christ also makes us part of his body as he gives us himself. Calvin cannot precisely explain how that happens in the Supper, for it is better experienced than explained.[78] However, he does say that Christ does not leave heaven to enter the bread. Rather, in the Holy Supper, we are called to lift up our hearts on high to heaven, where Christ is, and not cling to the external bread and wine.

We are lifted up through the work of the Holy Spirit in our hearts. As Calvin writes, "Christ, then, is absent from us in respect of his body, but dwelling in us by his Spirit, he raises us to heaven to himself, transfusing into us the vivifying vigor of his flesh just as the rays of the sun invigorate us by his vital warmth."[79] Partaking the flesh of Christ is a spiritual act rather than a carnal act that involves a "transfusion of substance."[80]

The sacraments can be seen as ladders by which we climb to heaven. "Because we are unable to fly high enough to draw near to God, he has ordained sacraments for us, like ladders," Calvin says.

> If a man wishes to leap on high, he will break his neck in the attempt, but if he has steps, he will be able to proceed with confidence. So also, if we are to reach our God, we must use the means which he has instituted since he knows what is suitable for us. God has then given us this wonderful support and encouragement and strength in our weakness.[81]

We must never worship the bread because Christ is not *in* the bread, but we find Christ *through* the bread, Calvin says. Just as our mouths receive bread to nourish our physical bodies, so our souls, by faith, receive Christ's body and blood to nourish our spiritual lives.

When we meet Christ in the sacraments, we grow in grace. That's why they are called a means of grace. The sacraments encourage us in our progress toward heaven. They promote confidence in God's promises through Christ's "signified and sealed" redemptive death. Since the sacraments are covenants, they contain promises by which "consciences may be roused to an assurance of salvation," Calvin says.[82] The sacraments offer "peace of conscience" and "a special assurance" when the Spirit enables the believer to "see" the Word engraved upon the sacraments.[83]

Finally, the sacraments promote piety by prompting us to thank and praise God for his abundant grace. The sacraments also require us to "attest our piety toward him." As Calvin says, "The Lord recalls the great bounty of his goodness to our memory and stirs us up to acknowledge it; and at the same time he admonishes us not to be ungrateful for such lavish liberality, but rather to proclaim it with fitting praises and to celebrate [the Lord's Supper] by giving thanks."[84]

Two things happen in the Supper: the receiving of Christ and the surrender of the believer. The Lord's Supper is not eucharistic from God's perspective, Calvin says, for Christ is not offered afresh. Nor is it eucharistic in terms of any human merit, for we can offer God nothing by way of sacrifice. But it is eucharistic in terms of our thanksgiving.[85] That sacrifice is an indispensable part of the Lord's Supper which, Calvin says, includes "all the duties of love."[86] The Eucharist is an *agape* feast in which communicants cherish each other and testify to the bond that they enjoy with fellow believers in the unity of the body of Christ.[87]

We offer this sacrifice of gratitude in response to Christ's sacrifice for us. We surrender our lives in response to the heavenly banquet God spreads for us in the Supper. By the Spirit's grace, the Supper enables us as a royal priesthood to offer ourselves as a living sacrifice of praise and thanksgiving to God.[88]

The Lord's Supper thus prompts both piety of grace and piety of gratitude, as Brian Gerrish has shown.[89] The Father's liberality and his children's grateful response are a recurrent theme in Calvin's theology. "We should so revere such a father with grateful piety and burning love," Calvin admonishes us, "as to devote ourselves wholly to his obedience and honor him in everything."[90] The Supper is the liturgical enactment of Calvin's themes of grace and gratitude, which lie at the heart of his piety.[91]

In the Lord's Supper, the human and divine elements of Calvin's piety are held in dynamic tension. In that dynamic interchange, God moves toward the believer while his Spirit consummates the Word-based union. At the same time, the believer moves toward God by contemplating the Savior who refreshes and strengthens him. In this, God is glorified and the believer edified.[92]

### Piety in the Psalter

Calvin views the Psalms as the canonical manual of piety. In the preface to his five-volume commentary on the Psalms – his largest exposition of any Bible book – Calvin writes: "There is no other book in which we are more perfectly taught the right manner of praising God, or in which we are more powerfully stirred up to the performance of this exercise of piety."[93] Calvin's preoccupation with the Psalter was motivated by his belief that the Psalms teach and inspire genuine piety in the following ways:

- As the revelation from God, the Psalms teach us about God. Because they are theological as well as doxological, they are our sung creed.[94]
- They clearly teach our need for God. They tell us who we are and why we need God's help.[95]
- They offer the divine remedy for our needs. They present Christ in his person, offices, sufferings, death, resurrection, and ascension. They announce the way of salvation, proclaiming the blessedness of justification by faith alone and the necessity of sanctification by the Spirit with the Word.[96]
- They demonstrate God's amazing goodness and invite us to meditate on his grace and mercy. They lead us to repentance and to fear God, to trust in his Word, and to hope in his mercy.
- They teach us to flee to the God of salvation through prayer and show us how to bring our requests to God.[97] They show us how to pray confidently in the midst of adversity.[98]
- They show us the depth of communion we may enjoy with our covenant-keeping God. They show how the living church is God's bride, God's children, and God's flock (Ps. 100:4).
- They provide a vehicle for communal worship. Many use first-person plural pronouns ("we," "our") to indicate this communal aspect, but even those with first-person singular pronouns include all those who love the Lord and are committed to him. They move us to trust and praise God and to love our neighbors. They prompt reliance on God's promises, zeal for God and his house, and compassion for the suffering.
- They cover the full range of spiritual experience, including faith and unbelief, joy in God and sorrow over sin, divine presence and divine desertion. As Calvin says, they are "an anatomy of all parts of the soul."[99] We still see our affections and spiritual maladies in the words of the Psalmists. When we read about their experiences, we are drawn to self-examination and faith by the grace of the Spirit. The psalms of David, especially, are like a mirror in which we are led to praise God and find rest in his sovereign purposes.[100]

Calvin immersed himself in the Psalms for twenty-five years as a commentator, preacher, biblical scholar, and worship leader.[101] Early on, he began work on metrical versions of the Psalms to be used in public worship. On January 16, 1537, shortly after his arrival in Geneva, Calvin asked his council to introduce the singing of psalms into church worship. He recruited the talents of other men, such as Clement Marot, Louis Bourgeois, and Theodore Beza, to produce the Genevan Psalter. That work would take twenty-five years to complete. The first collection (1539) contained eighteen psalms, six of which Calvin put into verse. The rest were done by the French poet, Marot. An expanded version (1542) containing thirty-five psalms was next, followed by one of forty-nine psalms (1543). Calvin wrote the preface to both of those, commending the practice of congregational singing. After Marot's death in 1544, Calvin encouraged Beza to put the rest of the psalms into verse. Two years before his death in 1562, Calvin rejoiced to see the first complete edition of the Genevan Psalter.[102]

The Genevan Psalter is furnished with a remarkable collection of 125 melodies, written specifically for the Psalms by outstanding musicians, of whom Louis Bourgeois is the best known. The tunes are melodic, distinctive, and reverent.[103] They clearly express Calvin's convictions that piety is best promoted when priority is given to text over tune, while recognizing that psalms deserve their own music. Since music should help the reception of the Word, Calvin says, it should be "weighty, dignified, majestic, and modest" – fitting attitudes for a sinful creature in the presence of God.[104] This protects the sovereignty of God in worship and offers proper conformity between the believer's inward disposition and his outward confession.

Psalm-singing is one of the four principal acts of church worship, Calvin believed. It is an extension of prayer. It is also the most significant vocal contribution of people in the service. Psalms were sung in Sunday morning and Sunday afternoon services. Beginning in 1546, a printed table indicated which psalms were to be sung on each occasion. Psalters were assigned to each service according to the texts that were preached. By 1562, three psalms were sung at each service.[105]

Calvin believed corporate singing subdued the fallen heart and retrained wayward affections in the way of piety. Like preaching and the sacraments, psalm-singing disciplines the heart's affections in the school of faith and lifts the believer to God. Psalm-singing amplifies the effect of the Word upon the heart and multiplies the spiritual energy of the church. "The Psalms can stimulate us to raise our hearts to God and arouse us to an ardor in invoking as well as in exalting with praises the glory of his name," Calvin wrote.[106] With the Spirit's direction, psalm-singing tunes the hearts of believers for glory.

The Genevan Psalter was an integral part of Calvinist worship for centuries. It set the standard for succeeding French Reformed psalm books as well as those in English, Dutch, German, and Hungarian. As a devotional book, it warmed the hearts of thousands. The people who sang from it, though, understood that its power wasn't in the book or its words, but in the Spirit who impressed those words on their hearts.

The Genevan Psalter promoted piety by stimulating a spirituality of the Word that was corporate and liturgical, and that broke down the distinction between liturgy and life. The Calvinists freely sang the psalms not only in their churches, but also in homes and workplaces, on the streets and in the fields.[107] The singing of psalms became a "means of Huguenot self-identification" for those followers of Calvin.[108] This pious exercise became a cultural emblem. In short, as T. Hartley Hall writes, "In scriptural or metrical versions, the Psalms, together with the stately tunes to which they were early set, are clearly the heart and soul of Reformed piety."[109]

## PRACTICAL DIMENSIONS

Though Calvin viewed the church as the nursery of piety, he also emphasized the need for personal piety. Christians strive for piety because they love righteousness, long to live to God's glory, and delight to obey God's rule of righteousness set forth in Scripture.[110] God himself is the focal point of the Christian life[111] – a life that is therefore carried out essentially in self-denial, particularly expressed in Christlike cross-bearing.[112]

For Calvin, such piety "is the beginning, middle, and end of Christian living."[113] It involves numerous practical dimensions for daily Christian living, which are explained thoroughly in Calvin's *Institutes*, commentaries, sermons, letters, and treatises. Here is the gist of what Calvin says on prayer, repentance, and obedience as well as on pious Christian living in chapters 6–10 of Book III of the *Institutes* of 1559.[114]

### Prayer

Prayer is the principal and perpetual exercise of faith and the chief element of piety, Calvin says.[115] Prayer shows God's grace to the believer even as the believer offers praises to God and asks for his faithfulness. It communicates piety both privately and corporately.[116]

Calvin devoted the second longest chapter of the *Institutes* (III.20) to prayer. There are six purposes of prayer, according to Calvin: To fly to God with every need, to set all our petitions before God, to prepare us to receive God's benefits with humble gratitude, to meditate upon God's kindness, to instill the proper spirit of delight for God's answers in prayer, and to confirm his providence.[117]

Two problems are likely to surface with Calvin's doctrine of prayer. First, when believers obediently submit to God's will, they do not necessarily give up their own wills. Rather, through the act of submissive prayer, believers invoke God's providence to act on their behalf. Thus, our will, under the Spirit's guidance, and God's will work together in communion.

Second, to the objection that prayer seems superfluous in light of God's omniscience and omnipotence, Calvin responds that God ordained prayer more for humans as an exercise of piety than for himself. Providence must be understood in the sense that God ordains the means along with the ends. Prayer is thus a means to receive what God has planned to bestow.[118] Prayer is a way in which believers seek out and receive what God has determined to do for them from eternity.[119]

Calvin treats prayer as a given rather than a problem. Right prayer is governed by rules, he says. These include praying with:

• a heartfelt sense of reverence
• a sense of need and repentance
• a surrender of all confidence in self and a humble plea for pardon
• a confident hope.

All four rules are repeatedly violated by even the holiest of God's people. Nevertheless, for Christ's sake, God does not desert the pious but has mercy on them.[120]

Despite the shortcomings of believers, prayer is required for the increase of piety, for prayer diminishes self-love and multiplies dependence upon God. As the due exercise of piety, prayer unites God and humanity – not in substance but in will and purpose. Like the Lord's Supper, prayer lifts the believer to Christ and renders proper glory to God. That glory is the purpose of the first three petitions of the Lord's Prayer as well as other petitions dealing with his creation. Since creation looks to God's glory for its preservation, the entire Lord's Prayer is directed to God's glory.[121]

In the Lord's Prayer, Christ "supplies words to our lips," Calvin says.[122] It shows us how all our prayers must be controlled, formed, and inspired by the Word of God. That alone can provide holy boldness in prayer, "which rightly accords with fear, reverence, and solicitude."[123]

We must be disciplined and steadfast in prayer, for prayer keeps us in fellowship with Christ. We are also reassured in prayer of Christ's intercessions without which our prayers would be rejected.[124] Only Christ can turn God's throne of dreadful glory into a throne of grace, to which we can draw near in prayer.[125] Prayer is the channel between God and humans. It is the way in which Christians express their praise and adoration of God as well as asking for God's help in submissive piety.[126]

## Repentance

Repentance is the fruit of faith and prayer. Luther said in his *Ninety-Five Theses* that all the Christian life should be marked by repentance. Calvin also sees repentance as a lifelong process. Repentance is not merely the start of the Christian life; it *is* the Christian life, he says. It involves confession of sin as well as growth in holiness. Repentance is the lifelong response of the believer to the gospel in outward life, mind, heart, attitude, and will.[127]

Repentance begins with turning to God from the heart and proceeds from a pure, earnest fear of God. It involves dying to self and sin (mortification) and coming alive to righteousness (vivification) in Christ.[128] Calvin does not limit repentance to an inward grace but views it as the redirection of a person's entire being to righteousness. Without a pure, earnest fear of God, one will not be aware of the heinousness of sin or want to die to it. Mortification is essential because though sin ceases to reign in the believer, it does not cease to dwell within. Romans 7:14–25 shows that mortification is a lifelong process. With the Spirit's help, the believer must put sin to death every day through self-denial, cross-bearing, and meditation on the future life.

Repentance is also characterized by newness of life, however. Mortification is the means to vivification, which Calvin defines as "the desire to live in a holy and devoted manner, a desire arising from rebirth; as if it were said that man dies to himself that he may begin to live to God."[129] True self-denial results in a life devoted to justice and mercy. The pious both "cease to do evil" and "learn to do well." Through repentance they bow in the dust before their holy Judge, then are raised up to participate in the life, death, righteousness, and intercession of their Savior. As Calvin writes, "For if we truly partake in his death, 'our old man is crucified by his power, and the body of sin perishes' (Rom. 6:6), that the corruption of original nature may no longer thrive. If we share in his resurrection, through it we are raised up into newness of life to correspond with the righteousness of God."[130]

The words Calvin uses to describe the pious Christian life (*reparatio, regeneratio, reformatio, renovatio, restitutio*) point back to our original state of righteousness. They indicate that a life of *pietas* is restorative in nature. Through Spirit-worked repentance, believers are restored into the image of God.[131]

## Self-denial

Self-denial is the sacrificial dimension of *pietas*. We have seen that piety is rooted in the believer's union with Christ. The fruit of that union is self-denial, which includes the following:

(1) The realization we are not our own but belong to God. We live and die unto him, according to the rule of his Word. Thus, self-denial is not self-centered, as was often the case in medieval monasticism, but God-centered.[132] Our greatest enemy is neither the devil nor the world but ourselves.

(2) The desire to seek the things of the Lord throughout our lives. Self-denial leaves no room for pride, lasciviousness, or worldliness. It is the opposite of self-love because it is love for God.[133] The entire orientation of our life must be toward God.

(3) The commitment to yield ourselves and everything we own to God as a living sacrifice. We then are prepared to love others and to esteem them better than ourselves, not by viewing them as they are in themselves, but by viewing the image of God in them. This uproots our love of strife and self and replaces it with a spirit of gentleness and helpfulness.[134] Our love for others then flows from the heart, and our only limit to helping them is the limit of our resources.[135]

Believers are encouraged to persevere in self-denial by what the gospel promises about the future consummation of the kingdom of God. Such promises help us overcome every obstacle that opposes self-renunciation and assist us in bearing adversity.[136]

Furthermore, self-denial helps us find true happiness because it helps us do what we were created for. We were created to love God above all and our neighbor as ourselves. Happiness is the result of having that principle restored. As Calvin says, without self-denial we may possess everything without possessing one particle of real happiness.

### Cross-bearing

While self-denial focuses on inward conformity to Christ, cross-bearing centers on outward Christlikeness. Those who are in fellowship with Christ must prepare themselves for a hard, toilsome life filled with many kinds of evil, Calvin says. The reason for this is not simply sin's effect on this fallen world, but the believer's union with Christ. Because his life was a perpetual cross, ours must also include suffering.[137] In this we not only participate in the benefits of his atoning work on the cross, but also experience the Spirit's work of transforming us into the image of Christ.[138]

Cross-bearing tests piety, Calvin says. Through cross-bearing we are roused to hope, trained in patience, instructed in obedience, and chastened in pride. Cross-bearing is our medicine and our chastisement. Through cross-bearing we are shown the feebleness of our flesh and taught to suffer for the sake of righteousness.[139]

Happily, God promises to be with us in all our sufferings. God even trans-forms suffering associated with persecution into comfort and blessing.[140]

### The present and future life

Through cross-bearing, we learn to have contempt for the present life when compared to the blessings of heaven. This life is nothing compared to what is to come. It is like smoke or a shadow. "If heaven is our homeland, what else is the earth but our place of exile? If departure from the world is entry into life, what else is the world but a sepulcher?" Calvin asks.[141] "No one has made progress in the school of Christ who does not joyfully await the day of death and final resurrection," he concludes.[142]

Typically, Calvin uses the *complexio oppositorum* when explaining the Christian's relation to this world. In other words, he presents opposites to find a middle way between. So, on the one hand, through cross-bearing we are crucified to the world and the world to us. On the other hand, devout Christians enjoy this present life, albeit with due restraint and moderation, for they are taught to use things in this world for the purpose that God intended them. Calvin was no ascetic; he enjoyed good literature, good food, and the beauties of nature. But he rejected all forms of earthly excess. The believer is called to Christlike moderation, which includes modesty, prudence, avoidance of display, and contentment with our lot.[143] For it is the hope of the life to come that gives purpose to and enjoyment in our present life. This life is always straining after a better, heavenly life.[144]

How, then, is it possible for the truly pious Christian to maintain a proper balance, enjoying the gifts that God gives in this world while avoiding the snare of over-indulgence? Calvin offers four guiding principles:

(1) Recognize that God is the giver of every good and perfect gift. This should restrain our lusts because our gratitude to God for his gifts cannot be expressed by a greedy reception of them.
(2) Understand that if we have few possessions, we must bear our poverty patiently lest we be ensnared by inordinate desire.
(3) Remember that we are stewards of the world in which God has placed us. Soon we will have to give an account to him of our stewardship.
(4) Know that God has called us to himself and to his service. Because of that calling, we strive to fulfill our tasks in his service, for his glory, and under his watchful, benevolent eye.[145]

### Obedience

For Calvin, unconditional obedience to God's will is the essence of piety. Piety links love, freedom, and discipline by subjecting all to the will and

Word of God.[146] Love is the overarching principle that prevents piety from degenerating into legalism. At the same time, law provides the content for love.

Piety includes rules that govern the believer's response. Privately, those rules take the form of self-denial and cross-bearing; publicly, they are expressed in the exercise of church discipline, which Calvin implemented in Geneva. In either case, the glory of God compels disciplined obedience. For Calvin, the pious Christian is neither weak nor passive but dynamically active in the pursuit of obedience, much like a distance runner, a diligent scholar, or a heroic warrior submitting to God's will.[147]

In the preface of his commentary on the Psalms, Calvin writes: "Here is the true proof of obedience, where, bidding farewell to our own affections, we subject ourselves to God and allow our lives to be so governed by his will that things most bitter and harsh to us – because they come from him – become sweet to us."[148] "Sweet obedience" – Calvin welcomed such descriptions. According to Hesselink, Calvin used words such as *sweet*, *sweetly*, *sweetness* hundreds of times in his *Institutes*, commentaries, sermons, and treatises to describe the life of piety. Calvin writes of the sweetness of the law, the sweetness of Christ, the sweetness of consolation in the midst of adversity and persecution, the sweetness of prayer, the sweetness of the Lord's Supper, the sweetness of God's free offer of eternal life in Christ, and the sweetness of eternal glory.[149]

He writes of the sweet fruit of election, too, saying that ultimately this world and all its glories will pass away. What gives us assurance of salvation here and hope for the life to come is that we have been "chosen in Christ before the foundation of the world" (Eph. 1:4).[150] "We shall never be clearly persuaded . . . that our salvation flows from the wellspring of God's free mercy until we come to know the very sweet fruit of God's eternal election."[151]

## CONCLUSION

Calvin strove to live the life of *pietas* himself – theologically, ecclesiastically, and practically. At the end of his *Life of Calvin*, Theodore Beza wrote, "Having been a spectator of his conduct for sixteen years . . . I can now declare, that in him all men may see a most beautiful example of the Christian character, an example which it is as easy to slander as it is difficult to imitate."[152]

Calvin shows us the piety of a warm-hearted Reformed theologian who speaks from the heart. Having tasted the goodness and grace of God in Jesus Christ, he pursued piety by seeking to know and do God's will every day. He communed with Christ; practiced repentance, self-denial, and cross-bearing; and was involved in vigorous social improvements.[153] His theology worked itself out in heart-felt, Christ-centered piety.[154]

For Calvin and the reformers of sixteenth-century Europe, doctrine and prayer as well as faith and worship are integrally connected. For Calvin, the Reformation includes the reform of piety (*pietas*), or spirituality, as much as a reform of theology. The spirituality that had been cloistered behind monastery walls for centuries had broken down. Medieval spirituality was reduced to a celibate, ascetic, and penitential devotion in the convent or monastery. But Calvin helped Christians understand piety in terms of living and acting every day according to God's will (Rom. 12:1–2) in the midst of human society. Through Calvin's influence, Protestant spirituality focused on how one lived the Christian life in the family, the fields, the workshop, and the marketplace.[155] Calvin helped the Reformation change the entire focus of the Christian life.

Calvin's teaching, preaching, and catechizing fostered growth in the relationship between believers and God. Piety means experiencing sanctification as a divine work of renewal expressed in repentance and righteousness, which progresses through conflict and adversity in a Christlike manner. In such piety, prayer and worship are central, both privately and in the community of believers.

The worship of God is always primary, for one's relationship to God takes precedence over everything else. That worship, however, is expressed in how the believer lives his vocation and how he treats his neighbors, for one's relationship with God is most concretely seen in the transformation of every human relationship. Faith and prayer, because they transform every believer, cannot be hidden. Ultimately, therefore, they must transform the church, the community, and the world.

### Notes

1 Serene Jones, *Calvin and the Rhetoric of Piety* (Louisville: Westminster John Knox Press, 1995). Unfortunately, Jones exaggerates Calvin's use of rhetoric in the service of piety.

2 Cited in John Hesselink, "The Development and Purpose of Calvin's Institutes," in Richard C. Gamble, ed., *Articles on Calvin and Calvinism, vol. 4, Influences upon Calvin and Discussion of the 1559 Institutes* (New York: Garland, 1992), 215–16.

3 See Brian A. Gerrish, "Theology within the Limits of Piety Alone: Schleiermacher and Calvin's Doctrine of God," in B. A. Gerrish and Robert Benedetto, eds., *Reformatio Perennis: Essays on Calvin and the Reformation in Honor of Ford Lewis Battles* (Pittsburgh: Pickwick Press, 1981), 67–87, reprinted in *The Old Protestantism and the New: Essays on the Reformation Heritage* (Chicago: University of Chicago Press, 1982), ch. 12.

4 John Calvin, *Institutes of the Christian Religion* (hereafter, Inst.), ed. John T. McNeill, trans. Ford Lewis Battles (Philadelphia: Westminster Press, 1960), I.9.

5 Cf. Lucien Joseph Richard, *The Spirituality of John Calvin* (Atlanta: John Knox Press, 1974), 100–101; Sou-Young Lee, "Calvin's Understanding of *Pietas*," in W. H. Neuser and B. G. Armstrong, eds., *Calvinus Sincerioris Religionis Vindex* (Kirksville, MO: Sixteenth Century Studies, 1997), 226–33; H. W. Simpson, "*Pietas* in the *Institutes* of Calvin," in *Reformational Tradition: A Rich Heritage and Lasting Vocation* (Potchefstroom, South Africa: Potchefstroom University for Christian Higher Education, 1984), 179–91.

6 *John Calvin: Catechism 1538*, ed. and trans. Ford Lewis Battles (Pittsburgh: Pittsburgh Theological Seminary, 1972), 2.

7 *Inst.* I.2.1.

8 *Inst.* III.19.2.

9 *Institutes of the Christian Religion: 1536 Edition,* trans. Ford Lewis Battles, revised edition rpt. (Grand Rapids: Eerdmans, 1986). The original Latin title reads: *Christianae religionis institutio total fere pietatis summam et quidquid est in doctrina salutis cognitu necessarium complectens, omnibut pietatis studiosis lectu dignissimum opus ac recens editum* (*Joannis Calvini opera selecta*, ed. Peter Barth, Wilhelm Niesel, and Dora Scheuner, 5 vols. [Munich: C. Kaiser, 1926–52], I, 19 [hereafter *OS*]). From 1539 on the titles were simply *Institutio Christianae Religionis,* but the "zeal for piety" continued to be a great goal of Calvin's work. See Richard A. Muller, *The Unaccommodated Calvin: Studies in the Foundation of a Theological Tradition* (New York: Oxford University Press, 2000), 106–07.

10 *Calvin's New Testament Commentaries,* ed. David W. Torrance and Thomas F. Torrance, 12 vols. (Grand Rapids: Eerdmans, 1959–72), *The Second Epistle of Paul the Apostle to the Corinthians, and the Epistles to Timothy, Titus and Philemon,* trans. Thomas A. Smail (Grand Rapids: Eerdmans, 1964), 243–44. Hereafter, *Comm.* on text.

11 For the roots of Calvin's piety, see William J. Bouwsma, "The Spirituality of John Calvin," in Jill Raitt, ed., *Christian Spirituality: High Middle Ages and Reformation* (New York: Crossroad, 1987), 318–33.

12 Inst. III.2.1; Calvin, *Ioannis Calvini opera quae supersunt omnia,* ed. Wilhelm Baum, Edward Cunitz, and Edward Reuss, *Corpus Reformatorum,* vols. 29–87 (Brunswick: C. A. Schwetschke and Son, 1863–1900), XLIII, 428, XLVII, 316. Hereafter *CO.*

13 *CO* XXVI, 693.

14 *OS* I, 363–64.

15 *CO* XXIV, 362.

16 *Inst.* III.7.1.

17 *CO* XXVI, 225; XXIX, 5; LI, 147.

18 *CO* XLIX, 51.

19 *CO* XXVI, 166; XXXIII, 186; XLVII, 377–78; XLIX, 245; LI, 21.

20 *CO* VI, 9–10.

21 *CO* XXVI, 439–40.

22 D. Willis-Watkins, "The *Unio Mystica* and the Assurance of Faith According to Calvin," in Willem van 't Spijker, ed., *Calvin Erbe und Auftrag: Festschrift für Wilhelm Heinrich Neuser zum 65. Geburtstag* (Kampen: Kok, 1991), 78.

23 E.g., Charles Partee, "Calvin's Central Dogma Again," *Sixteenth Century Journal* 18/2 (1987), 194. Cf. Otto Gründler, "John Calvin: Ingrafting in Christ," in E. Rozanne Elder, ed., *The Spirituality of Western Christendom* (Kalamazoo, MI: Cistercian, 1976), 172–87; Brian G. Armstrong, "The Nature and Structure of Calvin's Thought According to the *Institutes:* Another Look," in *John Calvin's Magnum Opus* (Potchefstroom, South Africa: Institute for Reformational Studies, 1986), 55–82; Guenther Haas, *The Concept of Equity in Calvin's Ethics* (Waterloo, Ontario: Wilfred Laurier University Press, 1997).

24 *Inst.* III.11.9. Cf. *CO* XV, 722.

25 Howard G. Hageman, "Reformed Spirituality," in Frank C. Senn, ed., *Protestant Spiritual Traditions* (New York: Paulist Press, 1986), 61.

26 *Inst.* III.2.24.

27 Dennis Tamburello points out that "at least seven instances occur in the *Institutes* where Calvin uses the word *arcanus* or *incomprehensibilis* to describe union with Christ" (II.12.7; III.11.5; IV.17.1, 9, 31, 33; IV.19.35; *Union with Christ: John Calvin and the Mysticism of St. Bernard* [Louisville: Westminster John Knox Press, 1994], 89, 144). Cf. William Borden Evans, "Imputation and Impartation: The Problem of Union with Christ in Neneteenth-Century American Reformed Theology" (Ph.D. dissertation, Vanderbilt University, 1996), 6–68.

28 *Commentary* on John 6:51.

29 *Inst.* II.16.16.

30 Willem van 't Spijker, "*Extra nos* and *in nos* by Calvin in a Pneumatological Light," in Peter DeKlerk, ed., *Calvin and the Holy Spirit* (Grand Rapids: Calvin Studies Society, 1989), 39–62; Merwyn S. Johnson, "Calvin's Ethical Legacy," in David Foxgrover, ed., *The Legacy of John Calvin: Calvin Studies Society Papers, 1999* (Grand Rapids: CRC, 2000), 63–83.

31 *OS* I, 435–36; van 't Spijker, "*Extra nos* and *in nos*," 44.

32 *Inst.* III.1.4.

33 *Inst.* IV.17.6; *Commentary* on Acts 15:9.

34 *Commentary* on Ephesians 5:32.

35 *Inst.* III.1.1; IV.17.12.

36 "Calvinus Vermilio" (#2266, August 8, 1555), *CO* XV, 723–24.

37 *CO* L, 199. Cf. Barbara Pitkin, *What Pure Eyes Could See: Calvin's Doctrine of Faith in Its Exegetical Context* (New York: Oxford University Press, 1999).

38 *Inst.* II.9.2; *Commentary* on 1 Peter 1:25. Cf. David Foxgrover, "John Calvin's Understanding of Conscience" (Ph.D. dissertation, Claremont Graduate School, California, 1978), 407ff.

39 *Calvin's Commentaries*, 47 vols., rpt. of the Edinburgh edition (various editors and translators) (Grand Rapids: Eerdmans, 1948–50), on Genesis 15:6. Cf. *Comm. Luke 2:21.*

40 *Inst.* III.2.6.

41 *Inst.* III.2.30–32.

42 *Inst.* III.2.24; *Comm. 1 John 2:12.*

43 *Sermons on the Epistle to the Ephesians*, trans. Arthur Golding (1577; rpt. Edinburgh: Banner of Truth Trust, 1973), I, 17–18.

44 *Comm. Eph.* 3:12.

45 *Serm. Eph. 3:14–19.*

46 *Comm. Hab. 2:4.*

47  D. Willis-Watkins, "The Third Part of Christian Freedom Misplaced," in W. Fred Graham, ed., *Later Calvinism: International Perspectives* (Kirksville, MO: Sixteenth Century Journal, 1994), 484–85.

48  *Inst.* III.11.1.

49  *Sermons on Galatians*, trans. Kathy Childress (Edinburgh: Banner of Truth Trust, 1997), II, 17–18.

50  *Inst.* III.11.2.

51  Ibid.

52  *Inst.* III.11.1; III.15.7.

53  *Inst.* III.13.1.

54  *Inst.* I.7.5.

55  *Comm. John 17:17–19.*

56  *Inst.* III.11.6.

57  *Serm. Gal.* 2:17–18.

58  *Comm. Rom. 6:2.*

59  *Inst.* IV.1.1, 3–4; cf. Joel R. Beeke, "Glorious Things of Thee Are Spoken: The Doctrine of the Church," in Don Kistler, ed., *Onward, Christian Soldiers: Protestants Affirm the Church* (Morgan, PA: Soli Deo Gloria, 1999), 23–25.

60  *Inst.* IV.1.4–5.

61  *Comm. Ps. 20:10.*

62  *Comm. Rom. 12:6.*

63  *Comm. 1 Cor. 12:12.*

64  *Comm. 1 Cor. 4:7.*

65  *Comm. Eph. 4:12.*

66  *Comm. Ps. 18:31; 1 Cor. 13:12;* Inst. IV.1.5, 3.2.

67  *Sermons of M. John Calvin, on the Epistles of S. Paule to Timothie and Titus,* trans. L.T. (1579; rpt. facsimile, Edinburgh: Banner of Truth Trust, 1983), 1 Timothy 1:8–11.

68  *Calvin: Theological Treatises,* trans. and ed. J. K. S. Reid (Philadelphia: Westminster Press, 1954), 173. Cf. Brian Armstrong, "The Role of the Holy Spirit in Calvin's Teaching on the Ministry," in DeKlerk, ed., *Calvin and the Holy Spirit,* 99–111.

69  *Selected Works of John Calvin: Tracts and Letters,* 7 vols., ed. Henry Beveridge and Jules Bonnet (1849; rpt. Grand Rapids: Baker, 1983), II, 56, 69.

70  *Institutes of the Christian Religion: 1536 Edition,* 36.

71  *Inst.* II.7.12. Calvin gleans considerable support for his third use of the law from the Davidic psalms (cf. *Inst.* II.7.12 and his *Commentary on the Book of Psalms,* trans. James Anderson, 5 vols. [Grand Rapids: Eerdmans, 1949]).

72  I. John Hesselink, "Law," in Donald K. McKim, ed., *Encyclopedia of the Reformed Faith* (Louisville: Westminster John Knox Press, 1992), 215–16. Cf. Edward A. Dowey, Jr., "Law in Luther and Calvin," *Theology Today* 41/2 (1984), 146–53; I. John Hesslink, *Calvin's Concept of the Law* (Allison Park, PA: Pickwick Publications, 1992), 251–62.

73  Joel Beeke and Ray Lanning, "Glad Obedience: The Third Use of the Law," in Don Kistler, ed., *Trust and Obey: Obedience and the Christian* (Morgan, PA: Soli Deo Gloria, 1996), 154–200; W. Robert Godfrey, "Law and Gospel," in Sinclair B. Ferguson, David F. Wright, and J. I. Packer, eds., *New Dictionary of Theology,* (Downers Grove, IL: InterVarsity Press, 1988), 379.

74 *Inst.* IV.14.1.
75 *Inst.* IV.16.9; Ronald S. Wallace, *Calvin's Doctrine of the Word and Sacrament* (Edinburgh: Oliver and Boyd, 1953), 175–83. Cf. H. O. Old, *The Shaping of the Reformed Baptismal Rite in the Sixteenth Century* (Grand Rapids: Eerdmans, 1992).
76 *Inst.* IV.17.8–12.
77 Ibid.
78 *Inst.* IV.17.24, 33.
79 *Inst.* IV.17.12.
80 *CO* IX, 47, 522.
81 *Inst.* IV.14.18.
82 *Comm. 1 Cor. 11:25.*
83 *Comm. Matt. 3:11; Acts 2:38; 1 Pet. 3:21.*
84 *OS* I, 136, 145.
85 *Inst.* IV.18.3.
86 *Inst.* IV.18.17.
87 *Inst.* IV.17.44.
88 *Inst.* IV.18.13.
89 "Calvin's Eucharistic Piety," in David Foxgrover, ed., *Calvin Studies Society Papers, 1995–1997* (Grand Rapids: CRC, 1998), 53.
90 *OS* I, 76.
91 Brian A. Gerrish, *Grace and Gratitude: The Eucharistic Theology of John Calvin* (Minneapolis: Fortress Press, 1993), 19–20.
92 Lionel Greve, "Freedom and Discipline in the Theology of John Calvin, William Perkins and John Wesley: An Examination of the Origin and Nature of Pietism" (Ph.D., dissertation, Hartford Seminary Foundation; photocopy from Ann Arbor: Xerox University Microfilms, 1976), 124–25.
93 *CO* XXXI, 19; translation taken from Barbara Pitkin, "Imitation of David: David as a Paradigm for Faith in Calvin's Exegesis of the Psalms," *The Sixteenth Century Journal* 24/4 (1993), 847.
94 James Denney, *The Letters of Principal James Denney to His Family and Friends* (London: Hodder & Stoughton, n.d.), 9.
95 See James Luther Mays, "Calvin's Commentary on the Psalms: The Preface as Introduction," in *John Calvin and the Church: A Prism of Reform* (Louisville: Westminster John Knox Press, 1990), 201–204.
96 Allan M. Harman, "The Psalms and Reformed Spirituality," *The Reformed Theological Review* (Australia) 53/2 (1994), 58.
97 *Comm. Psalms*, I, xxxvi–xxxxix.
98 *Comm. Pss. 5:11, 118:5.*
99 Ibid., I, xxxix. See James A. De Jong, "'An Anatomy of All Parts of the Soul': Insights into Calvin's Spirituality from His Psalms Commentary," in Wilhelm H. Neuser, ed., *Calvinus Sacrae Scripturae Professor* (Grand Rapids: Eerdmans, 1994), 1–14.
100 *Comm. Psalms*, I, xxxix.
101 John Walchenbach, "The Influence of David and the Psalms on the Life and Thought of John Calvin" (Th.M. thesis, Pittsburgh Theological Seminary, 1969).
102 More than 30,000 copies of the first complete, 500-page, Genevan Psalter were printed by over fifty different French and Swiss publishers in the first year,

and at least 27,400 copies were published in Geneva in the first few months (Jeffrey T. VanderWilt, "John Calvin's Theology of Liturgical Song," *Christian Scholar's Review* 25 [1996], 67). Cf. *Le Psautier de Genève, 1562–1685: Images, commentées et essai de bibliographie*, intro. J. D. Candaus (Geneva: Bibliothèque publique et universitaire, 1986), I, 16–18; John Witvliet, "The Spirituality of the Psalter: Metrical Psalms in Liturgy and Life in Calvin's Geneva," in David Foxgrover, ed., *Calvin Studies Society Papers, 1995–1997* (Grand Rapids: CRC, 1998), 93–117.

103 Unlike Luther, Calvin tried to avoid mixing secular tunes with sacred singing and believed that all psalm-singing must be in the vernacular. The grounds for liturgical psalm-singing are found in the evidence of Scripture and in the practices of the ancient church, Calvin said (VanderWilt, "John Calvin's Theology of Liturgical Song," 72, 74).

104 Preface to the Genevan Psalter (1562) (Charles Garside, Jr., *The Origins of Calvin's Theology of Music: 1536–1543* [Philadelphia: American Philosophical Society, 1979], 32–33).

105 Elsie McKee, ed. and trans., *John Calvin: Writings on Pastoral Piety*, The Classics of Western Spirituality (New York: Paulist Press, 2001), Part 3.

106 *CO* X, 12; cited in Garside, *Origins of Calvin's Theology of Music*, 10.

107 Witvliet, "Spirituality of the Psalter," 117.

108 W. Stanford Reid, "The Battle Hymns of the Lord: Calvinist Psalmody of the Sixteenth Century," in C. S. Meyer, ed., *Sixteenth Century Essays and Studies* (St. Louis: Foundation for Reformation Research, 1971), II, 47.

109 T. Hartley Hall, "The Shape of Reformed Piety," in Robin Maas and Gabriel O'Donnell, eds., *Spiritual Traditions for the Contemporary Church* (Nashville: Abingdon Press, 1990), 215. Cf. Reid, "The Battle Hymns of the Lord," II, 36–54.

110 *Inst.* III.6.2.

111 *Inst.* III.6.3.

112 *Inst.* III.7; III.8.

113 *Comm. 1 Tim. 4:7–8*.

114 This section was first translated into English in 1549 as *The Life and Conversation of a Christian Man* and has been reprinted often as *The Golden Booklet of the True Christian Life*.

115 See R. D. Loggie, "Chief Exercise of Faith: An Exposition of Calvin's Doctrine of Prayer," *Hartford Quarterly* 5 (1965), 65–81; H. W. Maurer, "An Examination of Form and Content in John Calvin's Prayers" (Ph.D. diss., University of Edinburgh, 1960).

116 Due to space limitations, prayer is considered here in its personal dimension but for Calvin prayer was also of vast importance in its communal aspect. See McKee, ed., *John Calvin*, Part 4 for a selection of individual and family prayers Calvin prepared as patterns for Genevan children, adults, and households, as well as a number of prayers from his sermons and biblical lectures. Cf. Thomas A. Lambert, "Preaching, Praying, and Policing the Reform in Sixteenth Century Geneva" (Ph.D. diss., University of Wisconsin-Madison, 1998), 393–480.

117 *Inst.* III.20.3.

118 Ibid.

119 Charles Partee, "Prayer as the Practice of Predestination," in Wilhelm H. Neuser, ed., *Calvinus Servus Christi* (Budapest: Pressabteilung des Raday-Kollegiums, 1988), 254.

120 *Inst.* III.20.4–16.

121 *Inst.* III.20.11.

122 *Inst.* III.20.34.

123 *Inst.* III.20.14; Ronald S. Wallace, *Calvin's Doctrine of the Christian Life* (London: Oliver and Boyd, 1959), 276–79.

124 *Comm. Heb. 7:26.*

125 *Inst.* III.20.17.

126 Greve, "Freedom and Discipline," 143–44. For how Calvin's emphasis on prayer impacted the Reformed tradition, see Diane Karay Tripp, "Daily Prayer in the Reformed Tradition: An Initial Survey," *Studia Liturgica* 21 (1991), 76–107, 190–219.

127 *Inst.* III.3.1–2, 6, 18, 20.

128 *Inst.* III.3.5, 9.

129 *Inst.* III.3.3; Randall C. Gleason, *John Calvin and John Owen on Mortification: A Comparative Study in Reformed Spirituality* (New York: Peter Lang, 1995), 61.

130 *Inst.* III.3.8–9.

131 John H. Leith, *John Calvin's Doctrine of the Christian Life* (Louisville: Westminster John Knox Press, 1989), 70–74.

132 *Inst.* III.7.1.

133 *Inst.* III.7.2.

134 *Inst.* III.7.4–5.

135 *Inst.* III.7.7; Merwyn S. Johnson, "Calvin's Ethical Legacy," in Foxgrover, ed., *Legacy of John Calvin,* 74.

136 *Inst.* III.7.8–10.

137 Richard C. Gamble, "Calvin and Sixteenth-Century Spirituality," in Foxgrover, ed., *Calvin Studies Society Papers,* 34–35.

138 *Inst.* III.8.1–2.

139 *Inst.* III.8.3–9.

140 *Inst.* III.8.7–8.

141 *Inst.* III.9.4.

142 *Inst.* III.9.5.

143 Wallace, *Calvin's Doctrine,* 170–95.

144 *Inst.* III.9.3.

145 *Inst.* III.10.

146 Greve, "Freedom and Discipline," 20.

147 Leith, *John Calvin's Doctrine,* 82–86.

148 Ford Lewis Battles, *The Piety of John Calvin* (Grand Rapids: Baker, 1978), 29.

149 I. John Hesselink, "Calvin, Theologian of Sweetness" (unpublished paper delivered as The Henry Meeter Center for Calvin Studies Spring Lecture, March 9, 2000), 10–16.

150 For Calvin on assurance, see Randall Zachman, *The Assurance of Faith: Conscience in the Theology of Martin Luther and John Calvin* (Minneapolis: Fortress Press, 1993); Joel R. Beeke, "Making Sense of Calvin's Paradoxes on Assurance of Faith," in Foxgrover, ed., *Calvin Studies Society Papers,* 13–30; Joel R. Beeke, *The*

*Quest for Full Assurance: The Legacy of Calvin and His Successors* (Edinburgh: The Banner of Truth Trust, 1999), 39–72.

151 *Inst.* III.21.1.

152 In *Selected Works of Calvin: Tracts and Letters*, I, c. For piety in Calvin's own life, see Battles, *The Piety of John Calvin*, 16–20.

153 Johnson, "Calvin's Ethical Legacy," 79–83.

154 Cf. Erroll Hulse, "The Preacher and Piety," in Samuel T. Logan, Jr., ed., *The Preacher and Preaching* (Philippsburg, NJ: Presbyterian and Reformed, 1986), 71.

155 Hughes Oliphant Old, "What is Reformed Spirituality? Played Over Again Lightly," in John H. Leith, ed., *Calvin Studies VII* (Davidson, NC: n.p., 1994), 61.

# 9   Calvin and social-ethical issues

### JEANNINE E. OLSON

No successful reformer of the sixteenth century could ignore the needs of the society in which the reform took place, for the educational and welfare needs of people continued after the Reformation. Before regions became Protestant, the Catholic Church had funded schools and charity through its parishes and institutions. Catholic priests and nuns had staffed schools and hospitals and administered welfare. Catholic confraternities of lay and clerical members had engaged in charitable activities. There had been some centralization of welfare in lay and government hands, but to a large extent, schools and hospitals were run by the church and its clergy.

When regions became Protestant, the property and endowment of the Church of Rome and its institutions shifted over to the governments of the cities, regions, or nations that became Protestant, but some of it was lost to private hands in the process. Priests and nuns were asked to leave or to accept no new novices. Money was needed for staffing. Protestant regions needed to rebuild a new infrastructure in education and welfare.[1]

The Protestant reformers set out to establish a permanent institutional base for the Reformation and improve on what had gone before. Just as Luther influenced millions through his writings and established a base for the Reformation through the reform of the University of Wittenberg and the founding of Protestant universities and secondary schools, so John Calvin's influence was implemented through the founding of the academy in Geneva that later became the University of Geneva. These institutions attracted students from throughout Europe, many of whom advanced the reform when they returned home and founded educational institutions outside German and Swiss areas. Like Luther, Calvin promoted secondary school education and insisted on primary education for both boys and girls. Convinced that Scripture alone was the authority in the church, the Protestant reformers wanted everyone to be able to read, especially to read the Bible.

The reformers also understood the importance of charitable institutions to meet the needs of the indigent, the disadvantaged, and the victims of the historical events of the time. Luther urged the foundation of common chests for the poor just as Calvin urged the institutional organization of charity in step with the times.[2]

Ironically, for both of them, the foundational steps in reform of social welfare institutions in Wittenberg and in Geneva occurred when they were not in town. Luther, newly excommunicated and banned, was being held in hiding to protect him by the Elector of Saxony at Frederick's Wartburg Castle (1521–22) when Andreas Bodenstein von Karlstadt helped to set in place the Wittenberg Church Order of 1522, setting up a common chest for welfare work. Calvin had not even arrived in Geneva when the city council dissolved the small hospitals of the city and centralized them into one large general hospital.

Despite the fact he was not present when the reforms took place, Luther may have initiated the welfare reform in Wittenberg before he left for the Diet of Worms of 1521, but Calvin was not a part of the initial reform in Geneva.[3] He arrived there in 1536 after the city had voted in the Reformation and centralized the city's welfare program. Nevertheless, Calvin's personal impact on the Geneva Reformation and its expansion was tremendous.

Calvin stands head and shoulders above the leaders of the French and Swiss Reformations. Born in Noyon, France, in 1509 and educated in Paris, Orléans, and Bourges, he fled the rising persecution in France and settled in Protestant Basle in January, 1535.[4] The next year he published his first edition of the *Institutes of the Christian Religion*, but made his major impact on Europe and the rest of the world from Geneva, where he created institutions that were to be copied wherever Reformed churches spread throughout the world.

Calvin, a scholar, had no intention of moving to Geneva and getting enmeshed in its politics, but in the summer of 1536 he made a detour through the city on a trip to Strasbourg. William Farel, who had been instrumental in preaching the reform in Geneva, induced him to stay. The city council took Calvin on as a lecturer on Scripture and then as a pastor. Calvin continued to publish extensively, but one should look beyond his published works for the influence of his social and ethical ideas.

Unlike many would-be reformers, in Geneva Calvin had the opportunity to put his ideas into action, and the extent to which he did so gave evidence of an administrative genius for which he is seldom credited.[5] The lasting effectiveness of his reform owed much to the institutional structures through which he worked and which he also to an extent created in Geneva. These structures were a social welfare system headed by deacons, a Consistory or church court, a secondary school and academy, and a fourfold system of church office that included pastors, doctors (teachers), elders, and deacons. These structures institutionalized much of Calvin's social-ethical program for the church and society. They were replicated where Reformed churches spread.

This institutional framework was not to be realized at once upon Calvin's arrival, however. At first, the Geneva city council, the smallest of the city's councils and the most powerful, appeared to be more enthusiastic about his ability to control a turbulent audience than about his ideas about church order. He and the pastors got little of what they wanted when they presented the city council with "Articles concerning the Organization of the Church and of Worship at Geneva proposed by the Ministers at the Council January 16, 1537." The council turned down the proposals for the selection of disciplinary overseers and a system of excommunicating people from the church. It also turned down the proposal for a commission to supervise matrimonial matters, once controlled by the courts of the Church of Rome but now left in a void. The city council even turned down the request for monthly celebration of Communion in favor of continued quarterly observance.[6]

Matters came to a head between the city council and pastors in Geneva a year later at Easter, April 21, 1538, when Calvin and Farel preached after having been forbidden to do so by the city council, and then refused to serve Communion. The pastors disagreed with the city council over how much say the council should have over the details of church life and the liturgy in Geneva. The council was paying the pastors' salaries and keeping up the church buildings. From the city councilors' point of view, the pastors had overstepped their charge. Calvin, Farel, and another pastor were banished from Geneva.[7]

Calvin was not happy about this turn of events, but there was nothing he could do about it. The unwanted discharge from Geneva proved to be a reprieve. He was invited to Strasbourg where he did not have the responsibility of organizing the churches of the city. Strasbourg had already experienced a reformation in the 1520s under the leadership of Martin Bucer (1491–1551). On a much smaller scale, Calvin was put in charge of a congregation of French refugees who had gathered there. He was their pastor, for Strasbourg was German-speaking, a part of the Holy Roman Empire rather than of France as it is today. It was in the French-speaking congregation that Calvin found and, in August 1540, married his wife, Idelette de Bure, a widow with a son and a daughter.[8] Calvin also taught in Strasbourg, for the schools had been reorganized, and he attended international ecumenical councils.[9]

In Strasbourg, Calvin learned from the ideas of Bucer and saw another church order at work that may have impacted his later organization of the church in Geneva. William Bouwsma believes Bucer, almost a generation older than Calvin, was a father image for Calvin whose own father, Gérard Cauvin, had died on May 26, 1531, when John Calvin was still in France.[10]

Bucer often included deacons in his concept of ministry and church office.[11] Protestant reformers such as Bucer looked to deacons as the office in the church which should care for the poor, just as deacons had in the early church, but deacons as a church office in charge of social welfare was not realized in Strasbourg during Bucer's lifetime. What had happened in Strasbourg was that in the 1520s the city had dissolved the monasteries and abolished the Mass. For teachers' salaries the city used canonical prebends (the incomes used to support the priests or canons of a cathedral or church). The city authorities took over distribution of poor relief and asked that contributions to the poor be handed over to them. A weekly allowance was to be delivered to each needy home. There was to be no begging, but there were no deacons either, despite recommendations to amend the city's ecclesiastical ordinances to elect deacons and deaconesses to care for the sick and needy, following the example of the early church.[12]

Calvin's sojourn in Strasbourg lasted only until 1541, when he was called to return to Geneva. He hesitated, but then he accepted the invitation. Calvin now had the upper hand. He was in a good position to make changes in the organization of the church in Geneva if he worked fast and acted during the "honeymoon period" of his early arrival before disagreements arose. Prudently, he left his new wife and her children behind temporarily and lost no time in getting to work with a committee of pastors and six city councilors to rewrite the church laws of the city. Shortly, the committee produced draft ecclesiastical ordinances that were revised by the councils of Geneva. They became law on November 20, 1541, and thus became part of the governing structures of Geneva.[13]

The ordinances embodied Calvin's fourfold conception of church office, which was foundational to the institutional development of Geneva, its schools, its welfare program, and its church court or Consistory. The fourfold conception of church office was replicated elsewhere as Reformed churches spread throughout the world.

These four offices embodied much of Calvin's social and ethical plan for Geneva and for the church in general. Therefore, examining them is a logical way to begin to explore Calvin's position on social and ethical issues, rather than beginning with his more abstract writings and attempting to extrapolate from them what Calvin did or might have done in a practical setting.

Fundamental to the *Ecclesiastical Ordinances* is that Calvin felt that the fourfold office of ministry laid out therein was God-given: "There are four orders of office instituted by our Lord for the government of his Church . . . pastors; then doctors; next elders, and fourth deacons."[14]

Of what did these four orders of office consist? How did they function in the city?

## PASTORS

The first order, that of "pastor," was familiar to everyone. The church had had pastors over the centuries and the office of pastor was straightforward in the Geneva *Ecclesiastical Ordinances*: pastors were "to proclaim the Word of God" and to administer the sacraments as well as "to instruct, admonish, exhort, and censure" and to visit the sick and prisoners.[15] An additional provision was that the pastors in Geneva were to meet together once a week for discussion of Scripture. Pastors assigned to the outlying villages were to come as often as they could to the weekly gatherings, but at least once per month.[16]

This provision for weekly meetings of the pastors was a stroke of genius. Over the years, these gatherings would enhance the group solidarity of the pastors and further their missionary endeavors, for in addition to discussing Scripture, they talked about other business as well. The pastors came to be called "The Venerable Company of Pastors of Geneva." They kept minutes of business transacted by them when they met, and that business was more than just about local happenings, for the Geneva pastors had their eyes on the rest of the world. They were concerned with the expansion of the reform especially to France, the homeland of so many of the Genevan pastors.

For Calvin and the other pastors, there was no divide between social ethics and evangelism. The social ethics of Calvin included the spread of the "Reform of the Word," as the pastors called the Reformation. Theory flowed quickly into action. Geneva became an international center of the spread of the reform into the rest of Europe. The Company of Pastors of Geneva was instrumental in the expansion of the Reform of the Word. In the 1550s, the Company began to send pastors to newly formed congregations of Reformed Christians in Catholic areas. This was crucial to the growth and organization of those churches at both the local and national levels in the regions where they were located.[17] So important were the activities of the Geneva Company of Pastors that the minutes of their meetings are being transcribed, edited, and published.[18]

## SCHOOLS

The second order of office for the government of the church in the ecclesiastical ordinances of Geneva was doctor. This office was less well defined than the others as it was, in part, a project for the future. The title itself, Doctor of the Church, came out of the medieval universities. One thinks of Thomas Aquinas from the thirteenth century, for instance. In the Genevan ecclesiastical ordinances, the responsibility of the doctors was "the instruction of the faithful in true doctrine," but this second order was also called "the order of the schools."[19]

According to the *Ecclesiastical Ordinances* there was to be at least one lecturer in theology in Geneva, or better yet, two, one in Old Testament and one in New Testament. This was a role Calvin himself and William Farel had already undertaken. In fact, it was from Calvin's lectures that many of his commentaries on various books of the Bible originated, especially later in his life when he was overburdened and sick with tuberculosis and other physical problems. Calvin's friends Nicolas Des Gallars, Jean Budé, and Charles de Jonvilliers took notes on his lectures and, with Calvin's permission, published them.[20] These lectures were in a sense the origin of the Geneva Academy for the training of pastors.

Building on the provision for lectures, the *Ecclesiastical Ordinances* of Geneva also recommended the foundation of a *collège*, because it was only possible to profit from such lectures if one was first instructed in languages and the humanities, since the lectures were in Latin.[21] In addition, the *Ordinances* stated that a *collège* was needed to prepare children "for the ministry as well as for civil government."[22] This twofold purpose for the education of boys beyond the primary level, to prepare them for the ministry and for government service, is reminiscent of Luther's reasoning on this subject.[23]

*Collège*, in French, means an institution that is more the equivalent of a secondary school than of an institution of higher education or of a college in the sense of part of a university. Some seventeen years after the *Ecclesiastical Ordinances* of Geneva became law, between 1558 and 1562, a new *collège* was built in Geneva and still stands today where it stood then, at the edge of the old city. Theodore Beza (1519–1605), recruited from the Academy at Lausanne, Switzerland, and later to be Calvin's successor as moderator of the Company of Pastors of Geneva, was at its head as well as at the head of the Geneva Academy. Initially the two institutions were considered one, called *academia* in Latin and *collège* in French. This one institution consisted of two parts, a *Schola privata*, or private school, actually the city's preparatory school for boys, designed to educate the city's youth, and a *Schola publica*, or public school, the city's first institution of higher education, designed to provide advanced training, especially in theology. Over time in Geneva, *collège* came to refer to the preparatory school and *académie* to the school for higher education. The *collège* of the sixteenth century is now known as the Collège Calvin, one of three city-run college-preparatory schools in Geneva along with the Collège Rousseau and the Collège Voltaire.

Since the two institutions were initially considered one, at the same time the *collège* was instituted, the Academy was formally constituted but without a campus of its own. Lectures were held in church buildings as they had been before the Academy was officially instituted, such as in the Auditoire, the former church of Marie la Nove, situated next to the great Cathedral of S. Pierre in the center of the old city of Geneva. The Auditoire also housed the English church during the time that the refugees from England under Queen Mary (reigned, 1553–58) were in Geneva, and today it houses the Church of Scotland in Geneva.

At first, the Geneva Academy was largely intended to produce pastors for Reformed churches. The students studied the biblical languages, Hebrew and Greek, because it was considered important for a pastor to be able to read the Bible in the original languages. Eventually the Academy, with other courses of study and faculty added, would become the modern University of Geneva, Switzerland.[24]

The *Ecclesiastical Ordinances* also stated that there were to be primary schools for children of Geneva. The girls were to have their school apart, as had hitherto been the case.[25]

The *Ecclesiastical Ordinances* of 1541 did not initiate education in Geneva. There had been primary schools and a secondary school before, but the ordinances did forecast the expansion of education, the enlargement of the schools, the provision of buildings for a *collège*, and the formalization of higher education.

Because of these schools, Geneva became an educational center of the Reformed movement, attracting students from elsewhere and sending forth pastors from its Academy to serve Reformed churches in other parts of Europe. This was a role that a similar Reformed Academy at Lausanne, Switzerland, up the lake from Geneva, had played. The formal foundation of the Academy at Geneva in 1559 came at a good time, because in the late 1550s the faculty of the Academy of Lausanne and the pastors of Lausanne were at odds with the magistrates of Berne, their overlords and employers. Faculty members were leaving Lausanne and needed new positions. Some came to Geneva.[26]

## CONSISTORY

The third office of the church for Calvin was that of elder. The elders were to oversee the lives of all and to admonish those who were erring or leading a disorderly life.[27] To facilitate their keeping an eye on everyone, they were to be selected from all the quarters of the city.[28]

Particular faults mentioned in the *Ordinances* that the elders were to look out for were: (1) dogmatizing against the doctrines of the church and (2) negligence in coming to church, but there were many others as well.[29] Any action or word that transgressed the Ten Commandments given to Moses at Sinai were within the purview of the elders, as were any lapses into Catholic religious practices, such as attending Mass, which was considered idolatrous and therefore transgressed the First Commandment.[30]

This system of oversight of the people of Geneva was at the heart of the "discipline" that Calvin and the pastors had sought four years before in their proposed "Articles concerning the Organization of the Church and of Worship at Geneva," but this time the details were spelled out, and this time the proposals were put into effect. There were to be twelve elders. They were to be chosen from the membership of the city councils. They were to meet weekly with the pastors of the city on Thursday mornings, having summoned those people whom they wished to question or to admonish for wrongdoing.[31] This gathering of pastors and elders came to be called the "Consistory."

Those summoned before the Consistory were there either to witness to what someone else had done or to answer for what they had done themselves. The members of the Consistory gave wrongdoers an opportunity to confess, repent, and apologize for what they had done. In a sense, the Consistory replaced the confessional, for Calvin and other Reformed Christians objected to confession of one's sins to a pastor or to a priest. One should confess to God!

The Consistory admonished people, and if they persisted in refusing to admit wrongdoing, required them to abstain from the Lord's Supper (Communion) until they repented and changed their lives. In practice, just one time being forced to abstain from the Lord's Supper brought people around. If anyone attempted to partake of the Lord's Supper after having been thus excommunicated, the pastors were to turn the person away.[32]

When Calvin was at the Consistory meetings, which was much of the time when he was in Geneva, he was often charged with admonishing the wrongdoers. He was apparently very good at it. For crimes that merited more than just verbal remonstrance, that is, that merited chastisement, the *Ecclesiastical Ordinances* provided individuals were to abstain for some time from the Lord's Supper. This was to humble them and encourage them to acknowledge their faults the better. The object of this discipline of the Consistory was to move people to repentance and change of life, as the "Draft Ecclesiastical Ordinances" said, "to bring sinners to our Lord."[33]

If something that someone had done was very serious or a crime, he or she could be sent on to the city council of Geneva, which, unlike the

Consistory, could confiscate property and mete out corporal punishment: whipping, banishment, or death. Imprisonment was less common than it is today, and then it was only for short periods of time.

Calvin apparently had no strong objection to these penalties in principle or to "judicial torture," that is, torture administered to elicit a confession by the court from someone who was considered probably guilty. Calvin did not object to capital punishment, or to the burning of witches or of homosexuals, but he did object to particular punishments for individuals on specific occasions.

Because of his education in law in Orléans and Bourges, Calvin was capable of writing legal briefs to the court (the city council sitting as a court) and of expressing his opinion in legal matters, and he did so. In fact, besides the *Ecclesiastical Ordinances*, he had been asked to rewrite the laws of Geneva, and he had done so. Calvin had been educated in civil law, which was based on Roman law and was being revived in Europe in the medieval and Renaissance periods. In general, if some punishment or procedure was a part of the law code or of the generally accepted procedures of the time, Calvin was not opposed. He did oppose slavery and wanted it eliminated where it was still found, not in the society in which he lived, but in the Orient, in Greece, on the Barbary Coast.[34]

An individual could be called before the Consistory for a wide variety of reasons: for transgressions against the Ten Commandments; for gambling, playing games, or dancing; for drunkenness, for laziness and not working; for blasphemy; for not attending church; for criticizing the pastors, the deacons, or the government of Geneva; for relapsing into practices of the Roman Catholic Church; for praying in Latin; for poor supervision of one's  children or neglecting to ensure that one's children learned to read; for fornication and adultery or suspected fornication and adultery; for spouse-beating or for poor relations with one's spouse; or for a poor relationship with just about anyone at all. Though this system of discipline would only work in a society that esteemed right behavior and considered partaking in the Lord's Supper to be an important matter, Geneva was such a society. In the sixteenth century, excommunication worked well to bring people to repentance and amendment of life. Most cases before the Consistory did not go as far as excommunication, however. There were other restraints. People who could not say the Lord's Prayer or the Apostles' Creed in the vernacular would be required to attend the weekly catechism classes. People who were not getting along would be asked to reconcile.

In fact, in Geneva, as elsewhere where Consistories were formed, individuals sometimes presented themselves voluntarily before the Consistory for a formal act of reconciliation with someone else. Reconciling parties even embraced each other before the Consistory, as before the Lord, as they said. At its best, the Consistory was a court of reconciliation. In its ideal moments, the Consistory had healing qualities, and in many cases it led to amendment of life.

This was the "discipline" of Geneva. In the sixteenth century, the "discipline" of a church, when used by Protestants who had become reformed on the model of Geneva, meant both church order and the discipline of individuals, that is, adherence to the Ten Commandments by members of the church. The "discipline" of Geneva would be copied wherever Reformed churches spread. The emphasis on "discipline" was central to the character of the Reformed tradition, and, some would say, distinguished it from other Protestant denominations.

There was another role for the Consistory. It had a potentially large role to play in marital conflicts. It was, in effect, the commission to supervise matrimonial matters that the pastors had requested from the city council in 1537.

There were many marital cases that came before the Consistory. People, often women, came before the Consistory to protest breaches of promise to marry, for instance. People came hoping for divorces with the right to remarry. The Consistory preferred reconciliation and worked to that end. The grounds for divorce in Geneva were adultery or desertion. There were divorces granted in Calvin's Geneva, not by the Consistory, however, but by the city council. There were also applications for a divorce that were turned down. No one had a right to a divorce.[35]

Calvin tacitly approved of divorce in some cases. Galeazzo Caracciolo, a nobleman from Naples, wanted a divorce from his first wife on grounds of desertion because she refused to follow him to Geneva. Calvin first sent the question on to other theologians. The city council granted Caracciolo his divorce, and he remarried. The divorce of John Calvin's own brother, Antoine, from his first wife was the case in which Calvin seemed to become most personally involved. He was living with his brother and his sister-in-law at the time and was scandalized by her supposed adulterous behavior. Calvin had little patience with adultery. Later in the sixteenth century, the penalty in Geneva for repeated adultery would be death.

The Consistory had an indirect function beyond that of discipline and marital matters. It brought together the pastors of Geneva and city councilors (the twelve elders) in one body, working together on a regular basis. The provision that the elders of the church were to come from the city councils was politically wise, for Geneva's leading men sat on the city councils. As elders, twelve of the city councilors thus became directly involved in the church's work alongside the pastors.

In 1541 when the *Ordinances* were written, city councilors were from Geneva itself, whereas almost all the pastors within the next few decades would be French. There was feeling against foreigners in Geneva, including the French foreigners. There were restrictions against foreigners or immigrants participating in Geneva's government, but the pastors would have gotten nowhere in their program for the city without the cooperation of the city councilors. The Consistory bridged a gap by bringing the leaders of the Genevan community and the leaders of the French community in Geneva onto one body. Eventually foreigners were admitted into some of the governing councils of Geneva, especially after 1555 when the faction in the city that opposed Calvin had been defeated. In the meantime, the Consistory filled an important role in bringing the foreign French and the native Genevans together in a common effort.

As for an evaluation of the weekly activities of the Consistory itself: if one reads through the minutes, one is less impressed by any misuse of power than with the patience of the members of the Consistory. The pastors and city councilors were some of the busiest people in town, and they were dedicating at least one morning of each week to meet in the Consistory and to listen to the details of ordinary people's lives.

It is now possible to come to one's own conclusions about the Consistory. The minutes are being published, both in the original French and in English. The first volume of the edited transcriptions of the Consistory minutes in French came out in 1996.[36] Further volumes continue to be published. In turn, the French volumes are being translated into English and published.

## SOCIAL WELFARE

The fourth office of the church for Calvin was that of deacon. The ecclesiastical ordinances of Geneva seem to assume that the reader knows what a deacon is. Indeed, Calvin had already explained his conception of the office of deacon early on. In the first edition of his *Institutes of the Christian Religion* of 1536, he described deacons as those who "attend to the care of the poor and minister to them." He went on to refer to the sixth chapter of Luke's Acts of the Apostles in which the apostles of Jesus chose seven men to aid them with the widows and orphans: "Those they had chosen, he [Luke] says, they ordained in the presence of the apostles: praying, they laid their hands upon them [Acts 6:6]. Would that the church today had such deacons, and appointed them by such a ceremony; namely, the laying on of hands."[37] Calvin then went on to criticize the use of deacons in the Roman Catholic Church as essentially being too concerned with liturgical matters. He said that Catholic deacons had come to be assistants to the priest in the

Mass rather than helpers of the poor.[38] Indeed, the diaconate in the Catholic Church had become a stepping stone to the priesthood, the last office a man held in a hierarchy of offices before becoming a priest. Many of the social welfare functions of the early diaconate had been taken over by monks, nuns, parishes, and institutions of the Catholic Church such as hospitals.

As for the liturgical practices of deacons in Geneva, Calvin permitted the deacons to give the wine chalice to the communicants, for deacons had done this in the early church.[39] In general the reformers of the sixteenth century, as good humanists enthusiastic about Antiquity, were appreciative of what had been done in the early church under the Roman Empire, but, on the other hand, they were critical of changes that had come about during the medieval period.

The essential role of the deacon for Calvin was in social welfare. Social welfare in Geneva had been centered on the general hospital in the former convent of Saint Clare since its creation in 1535 during the Reformation in Geneva. To house the new hospital, the city had taken over the convent of the Poor Clares, whose nuns were forced to leave or turn Protestant. They had remained Catholic and re-established themselves in a neighboring Catholic town outside the control of Geneva.

The new hospital's budget was charged with the city's poor, who were housed either at home or in the hospital itself. It provided for the institutionalized poor as well as for those at home, for whom there was a weekly dole of bread cooked in the hospital ovens. The hospital was directed by a committee of trustees or procurators, as they were called, who were chosen by the city council from its own membership and from larger city councils of sixty and of two hundred.

The procurators oversaw the management and finances of the hospital. They met weekly, on Sundays at 6:00 a.m., before the sermon. They hired a hospital manager, known as the hospitaler, to do the day-to-day work. He and his wife made purchases and dealt with servants, outpatients, and the people housed in the hospital, who consisted of orphans and some of the poor, sick, or disabled people of the city.[40] The wealthier sick preferred to stay at home.

It was this institution and the plague hospital that Calvin described in the Geneva *Ecclesiastical Ordinances*. Calvin had an ongoing interest in the hospital, which he wanted to be run in an orderly manner. In 1545 he requested the city council to put the hospital's accounting in order, to list the revenue in writing, and to keep track of those who were given assistance. The city hospital directed the procurators of the hospital to do what Calvin had suggested.[41] Calvin suggested that the poor of the hospital be given a craft.[42] Eventually the silk industry was brought to the hospital.[43]

The procurators of the hospital and the hospitaler were already doing the work of deacons before Calvin gave them that title in the ecclesiastical ordinances of 1541. Their jobs fit into the model for two kinds of deacons that Calvin felt had existed in the ancient church: the one deputed to receive, dispense, and hold goods for the poor, not only daily alms, but also possessions, rents, and pensions; the other to tend and care for the sick and administer allowances to the poor.[44]

Calvin found biblical bases for this two-part division of the diaconate in Romans 12:6–8, which speaks of "gifts that differ according to the grace given to us." These verses include those who contribute and give aid and those who show mercy, which Calvin interpreted to be two different roles: (1) that of the procurators of the hospital "charged with the distribution of the public property of the Church" and (2) that of the hospitaler and others appointed to take care of the sick. "The functions of providing what is necessary for the poor, and of devoting care to their attention, are different."[45] For Calvin, there was, in effect, a double diaconate, as it has come to be called.

From a functional point of view this insistence on two types of diaconal care described well the division of labor of Genevan welfare and that of other cities. The double diaconate also made a place for women. Calvin saw the only appropriate public office of women in the church as that of caring for the poor.[46] Calvin looked back to the office of widow in the New Testament and early church and saw it as a female diaconate whose absence he regretted in contemporary Geneva.[47] The early Church had designated some mature widows for prayer and visitation of others. They had received charity from the Church.[48]

The deacons whom Calvin described in the *Ecclesiastical Ordinances* were not the only deacons in the city, although they were the only ones there in 1541. Others were created later as a response to the problem of what to do with the foreign poor in the city. By the middle of the 1540s the hospital was no longer able to handle all the social welfare needs in the city. The press of foreign refugees coming to Geneva from Catholic countries seeking freedom of religious expression was overwhelming the social welfare resources of the city. A typical reaction to such a dilemma in the sixteenth century would have been to have attempted to expel impoverished foreigners, because poor relief was geared to local residents, and Geneva was getting ready to do just that. Instead the foreign residents of Geneva formed funds for the poorer refugees flooding into town. These funds were formed by ethnic groups: French, Italian, German.

The first of these funds to come into being did so in the 1540s and was the fund for French refugees. Calvin seems to have had a direct hand in its formation, and he continued to be regularly involved through his contributions and recommendations to poor people to seek out the fund for help.[49] The first surviving account book in the archives of Geneva dates from September 30, 1550.

In the earliest years those in charge of the French Fund seem to have been called simply administrators of the fund. They were first formally referred to as deacons in the account books of July 1554 at an election at Calvin's house.[50] Legal documents of that era call them "administrators and deacons of the fund for the poor foreigners." "Deacons" was their enduring title. Their work and numbers increased with the growth in the refugee population. In the 1550s the fund appears to have added collectors to help gather money. The French Fund relied on an international network of resources, and gifts came in from other countries, especially France. The fund endured to the middle of the nineteenth century, and, even after its dissolution, the office of deacon in Geneva continued.[51]

The money of the fund was used for the poor, but the fund also sent books and pastors into France and paid a man to copy down Calvin's sermons as he preached them, a project that it was hoped would raise money for the poor through the eventual sale of the sermons. The French Fund had the right to the sale of Theodore Beza's Psalms as well. The lack of adequate copyright laws in the sixteenth century hampered these two money-raising efforts. Printers outside of Geneva simply published what they wanted without paying royalties to the original authors or to the deacons of the French Fund.

Despite these obstacles, much money was collected through contributions. Calvin contributed regularly himself and put an important emphasis on charity, but he did not abolish private property, nor demand that one sell all one had to give to the poor. Saint Francis was not his ideal.

The poor of the refugee funds were similar to the poor of the city hospital except that many of the refugees were only in temporary straits and, with a little help, were able to recover. Sometimes they later gave generously to the fund. Didier Rousseau, from Paris, the ancestor of Jean Jacques Rousseau, may have been such a case. He became an inhabitant of Geneva on June 24, 1550 as a wine merchant; received money for accommodations from the deacons on April 6, 1551, and remembered the French Fund in his will of 1570.[52]

The deacons found places for people to stay and jobs for them. The deacons employed people to care for the sick, wet nurses for infants, and foster homes for orphans. The deacons gave and lent clothing and bedding. They both gave money to the poor and lent money, especially if someone needed tools or was trying to set up a business. They appear sometimes to have given less money to the chronic poor than to the shame-faced poor, those who had been prosperous and had fallen on hard times. This was a common practice of the times. On the other hand, in the early years of the fund the deacons seem to have helped almost anyone who came to their door, in the beginning at least, including people of other nationalities and even a Jew who was on his way to England.[53]

The principle of encouraging foreign refugee communities to provide for their own proved to be a sound one. Other ethnic communities in Geneva (Italian, English, and German) established their own relief funds in conjunction with their own congregations in Geneva, which worshiped in Italian, English, or German rather than French. Deacons mentioned in sixteenth-century Genevan documents usually are those of one of these refugee funds. The title of deacon did not catch on as quickly for the procurators and hospitalers of the city hospital, perhaps because the hospital was already functioning when the ecclesiastical ordinances were written, and it was responsible to the city council. Toward the end of the century, the term "deacon" came into greater use with reference to hospital personnel.[54]

Calvin's model of the diaconate spread as Reformed churches spread. The deacons managed local church funds and also dealt with the poor. This provided a network of deacons' funds that helped Reformed religious refugees as they made their way out of Catholic countries, seeking refuge. The minority Reformed churches in Catholic countries could not have survived without this financial infrastructure. During the reign of Queen Elizabeth in England, there was a deacons' fund similar to that of Geneva in Sandwich, England, aiding refugees from the Low Countries where there was religious warfare, and even earlier than that in London, the Stranger Church, or reconstituted Reformed church for French-speaking foreigners (1560), had established a diaconate.[55] A similar pattern developed in France as Reformed churches emerged in the late 1550s and 1560s.

## A WORK ETHIC AND LENDING MONEY AT INTEREST

The *Ecclesiastical Ordinances* of Geneva cover much of Calvin's social and ethical program for the city and for the church, but there were other issues that arose, especially where money was involved. Now that the basic interaction of the pastors of Geneva and the city councilors has been laid out as one in which the pastors had to get the cooperation of the city councilors and sometimes give in to them, it is possible to look at other issues such as the lending of money at interest.

During the medieval period, lending money at interest had been considered usury and unchristian on the supposition that asking interest of a poor person was reprehensible. This left money-lending to the Jews, who were not allowed to do much else. Beginning in the thirteenth century, the Jews were asked to leave one European country after another. With the revival of a sophisticated money economy in Europe in the Middle Ages, there were other people who were lending capital for investment at interest.

Various contractual sleights-of-hand were developed to get around the Church's proscription of lending money at interest in the Middle Ages, but in the sixteenth century some of the reformers took the additional step of officially allowing the lending of money at interest as long as the rates were reasonable. The Wittenberg Church Order of 1522 provided for the refinancing of high-interest loans for its citizens at the lower rate of four percent annual interest, and Luther argued for a ceiling on interest in general.[56] Although Calvin did not introduce lending money at interest into Geneva (it was there when he arrived), pastors of Geneva lent money at interest. Usury was coming to be defined as not just any lending but as lending at exorbitant rates of interest, as it is today.

In Geneva the city council set the allowable rate of interest but was not able to control those who charged more. The problem was setting that allowable rate of interest at a just amount in the inflationary economy of the sixteenth century. After he returned to Geneva in 1541, Calvin worked hard with the city council to keep the rate of interest at no higher than five percent, but by November 12, 1557 it was raised to 6.67 percent per year. Even at that, even pastors of Geneva were tempted to lend money above the rate of interest, and some did so.[57] To do so blatantly and excessively could cost them their posts, however. The *Ecclesiastical Ordinances* proscribed usury as one of the faults of a pastor that was not to be tolerated.[58]

The rate of interest in Geneva and financial matters in general would continue to be an issue well after Calvin's death in 1564. Some of the pastors were deeply involved and opinionated and would get into trouble because of it if they disagreed with the city councilors. Such a man was Nicolas Colladon, a pastor of Geneva since 1560 and once secretary of the Venerable Company of Pastors, rector of the Academy (1564), and, with Theodore Beza, author of the first biography of Calvin.[59] On August 26, 1571, Colladon criticized from the pulpit the magistrates of Geneva, with whom he disagreed on financial policy. The city council would not accept his behavior. The affair occupied pages of the registers of the city council and culminated in Colladon being deposed in September 1571.[60] Fortunately for him, he found another position. After a brief stay in Heidelberg, Colladon began teaching in the Academy of Lausanne in January, 1572 and settled down there, ending up as rector.

With the lending of money at interest, a step was taken into the modern economic world, so much so that both Max Weber and R. H. Tawney give a special prominence to Calvinism in the development of modern capitalism. That, of course, is to partially ignore similar developments in other parts of Europe at this time, such as in Catholic Renaissance Italy. Weber gave a role to the Protestant ethic. Later, when there were Puritans in England and then in New England, others spoke of a Puritan work ethic as well. This "ethic" was based, in part, on the "discipline" that the Reformed churches emphasized and also, in part, on the suggestion that Puritans considered worldly success a sign of election by God for salvation (eternal life in heaven), but Calvin surely did not equate worldly success with election. On the contrary, he said:

> It is an error which is by far too common among men, to look upon those who are oppressed with afflictions as condemned and reprobate [that is, damned] . . . Most men, making judgments about the favor of God from an uncertain and transitory state of prosperity, applaud the rich, and those upon whom, as they say, fortune smiles; so, on the other hand, they insult contemptuously the wretched and miserable, and foolishly imagine that God hates them.[61]

Some have suggested that if Protestants seemed to work harder, it may be just that they worked more. The Reformation in Geneva and elsewhere did away with saints' days and other religious holidays, even Christmas, and made Sunday the only day of rest. Nevertheless, there was a different spirit abroad in the sixteenth century. In Calvin's Geneva one could not find essays on the virtue of the contemplative life (by oneself or in a monastery) versus the active life (in society) such as were written during the early Renaissance in Italy, but then, the early Renaissance in Italy took place in the fourteenth and fifteenth century in a society in which the religious life of monks and nuns was valued. The Reformation in Geneva was in the sixteenth century in a region that became Protestant and did away with monasticism.

When one considers social-ethical issues, it is evident, as André Biéler has said, that the Calvinist reform was a reform that was integral to society.[62] It remained integral to society after Calvin's death. Calvin and the pastors of Geneva had created institutions that would endure by delegating responsibilities to others so that their ideas did not die with them. The reform and Calvin's social ethics spread far beyond Geneva and the sixteenth century.

### Notes

1  I wish to thank the Rhode Island College Committee for Faculty Research, the National Endowment for the Humanities, the American Academy of Religion, and the Danforth Foundation for funding the research for this project.
2  Carter Lindberg, "Luther on Poverty," *Lutheran Quarterly* 15/1 (Spring 2001), 89–90.

3 Carter Lindberg, "'There Should Be No Beggars Among Christians': Karlstadt, Luther, and the Origins of Protestant Poor Relief," *Church History* 46 (September 1977), 326.

4 Alexandre Ganoczy, *The Young Calvin*, trans. David Foxgrover and Wade Provo (Philadelphia: Westminster Press, 1987), 91.

5 Jeannine Olson, "Calvin as Pastor-Administrator during the Reformation in Geneva," *Pacific Theological Review* 14/4 (Fall 1982), 78–83, reprinted in Richard Gamble, ed., *Articles on Calvin and Calvinism*, III, *Calvin's Work in Geneva* (New York: Garland Publishing, 1992), 2–9.

6 *Calvin: Theological Treatises*, trans. and ed. John K. S. Reid (Philadelphia: Westminster Press, 1954), 47–55 (hereafter *TT*).

7 Ganozcy, *The Young Calvin*, 121.

8 Richard Stauffer, *L'humanité de Calvin*, Cahiers Théologiques (Neuchatel, Switzerland: Éditions Delacaux et Niestlé, 1964), 24; available in English as *The Humanness of John Calvin*, trans. George Shriver (New York: Abingdon Press, 1971), 39.

9 For more on this school reform see Lewis W. Spitz and Barbara Tinsley, *Johann Sturm on Education: The Reformation and Humanist Learning* (St. Louis: Concordia Publishing House, 1995).

10 Ganoczy, *The Young Calvin*, 71. William Bouwsma, *John Calvin: A Sixteenth-Century Portrait* (New York: Oxford University Press, 1988), 21–24.

11 Martin Bucer, *The Restoration of Lawful Ordination for Ministers of the Church*, 254–83 in David F. Wright, trans. and ed., *Common Places of Martin Bucer*, The Courtenay Library of Reformation Classics, 4 (Abingdon, England: Sutton Courtenay Press, 1972), 254; Basil Hall, referring to Martin Bucer, *Enarratio Epistolae D. Pauli Ephesios* (Basle, 1562), in *Humanists and Protestants, 1500–1900* (Edinburgh: T. & T. Clark, 1990), 137–38.

12 Miriam Chrisman, *Strasbourg and the Reform: A Study in the Process of Change* (New Haven: Yale University Press, 1967), 42–44, 69–78, 235–40, 272, 279–80.

13 "Ordonnances ecclésiastiques, 1541," in *Registres de la Compagnie des Pasteurs de Genève au temps de Calvin*, published under the direction of the Archives of the State of Geneva, vol. 1, *1546–1553*, ed. Jean-François Bergier (Geneva: Librairie Droz, 1964), 1–13; for English translation see "Draft Ecclesiastical Ordinances," in *TT*, 56–72.

14 "Draft Ecclesiastical Ordinances," 58.

15 Ibid., 58, 66–69.

16 Ibid., 60.

17 For the seminal analysis of the role of the Genevan pastors in the spread of the Reformation into France see Robert M. Kingdon, *Geneva and the Coming of the Wars of Religion in France, 1555–1563* (Geneva: Librairie Droz, 1956).

18 *Registres de la Compagnie des Pasteurs de Genève au temps de Calvin*, published under the direction of the Archives of the State of Geneva (Geneva: Librairie Droz, 1962–).

19 "Draft Ecclesiastical Ordinances," 62.

20 Jean-François Gilmont, "Les sermons de Calvin: de l'oral à l'imprimé," *Bulletin de la Société de l'Histoire du Protestantisme Français* 141 (1995), 157–60.

21 "Draft Ecclesiastical Ordinances," 63.

22 Ibid.

23  See, for instance, Martin Luther, "To the Councilmen of All Cities in Germany That They Establish and Maintain Christian Schools," in *Luther's Works*, American Edition, 55 vols. (St. Louis and Philadelphia: Concordia and Fortress Press, 1958–86), XLV, pp. 339–78.

24  Karin Maag, *Seminary or University? The Genevan Academy and Reformed Higher Education, 1560–1620*, St. Andrews Studies in Reformation History (Aldershot, England: Scolar Press, 1995); Charles Borgeaud, *Histoire de l'Université de Genève*, I, *l'Académie de Calvin, 1559–1798* (Geneva: Georg, Librairies de l'Université, 1900).

25  "Draft Ecclesiastical Ordinances," 63.

26  For information on the Lausanne Academy see Henri Meylan, *La haute école de Lausanne, 1537–1937: Esquisse historique publiée à l'occasion de son quatrième centenaire* (Lausanne: F. Rouge & Cie, Librairie de l'Université, 1937).

27  "Draft Ecclesiastical Ordinances," 63.

28  Ibid., 64.

29  Ibid., 70.

30  For residual Catholic religious practices in Geneva after the city had formally become Protestant see Thomas Lambert, "Daily Religion in Early Reformed Geneva," in *Université de Genève Institut d'Histoire de la Réformation Bulletin Annuel*, XXI, *1999–2000* (Geneva: University of Geneva, February 2001), 33–54.

31  "Draft Ecclesiastical Ordinances," 63, 70.

32  Ibid., 70–71.

33  Ibid., 71.

34  Sermon XCV on Deuteronomy, chapter 5. John Calvin, *CO*, XXVII, 346 as quoted in André Biéler, *La pensée économique et sociale de Calvin* (Geneva: Librairie de l'Université, George & Cie, 1961), 171.

35  For the best book on this subject in English see Robert M. Kingdon, *Adultery and Divorce in Calvin's Geneva* (Cambridge, MA: Harvard University Press, 1995).

36  Thomas A. Lambert and Isabella M. Watt, eds., *Registres du Consistoire de Genève au temps de Calvin*, I. Travaux d'Humanisme et Renaissance 305 (Geneva: Librairie Droz, 1996).

37  John Calvin, *Institution of the Christian Religion Embracing almost the whole sum of piety, & whatever is necessary to know of the doctrine of salvation: A work most worthy to be read by all persons zealous for piety, and recently published*, trans. Ford Lewis Battles (Atlanta: John Knox Press, 1975), 235.

38  Ibid.

39  "Draft Ecclesiastical Ordinances," p. 67. *Constitutions of the Holy Apostles* 8.2 in *The Ante-Nicene Fathers*, VII, *The Fathers of the Third and Fourth Centuries: Lactantius, Venantius, Asterius, Victorinus, Dionysius, Apostolic Teaching and Constitutions, Homily, and Liturgies*, American rpt. of Edinburgh edition, ed. A. Cleveland Coxe (Grand Rapids: Eerdmans, n.d.), 491.

40  Robert Kingdon, "Social Welfare in Calvin's Geneva," *American Historical Review* 76 (February 1971), 52, 55–57.

41  March 9, 1545, Archives d'État de Genève, Registres du Conseil, vol. XL (February 8, 1545–February 7, 1546), fol. 42.

42  Archives d'État de Genève, Registres du Conseil, XXXIX, fols. 84v–85.

43  Liliane Mottu-Weber, "Des vers à soie à l'Hôpital en 1610: Un bref épisode de l'histoire de la soierie à Genève," *Revue du Vieux Genève* 12 (1982), 44–49.

44 "Draft Ecclesiastical Ordinances," 64.

45 *Ioannis Calvini opera quae supersunt omnia* (hereafter referred to as *CO*), XLIX, 240, translated in Elsie McKee, *John Calvin on the Diaconate and Liturgical Alms-giving* (Geneva: Librairie Droz, 1984), 195.

46 For Calvin's position on the role of women in the church see Jane Dempsey Douglass, *Women, Freedom, and Calvin*. The 1983 Annie Kinkead Warfield Lectures (Philadelphia: Westminster Press, 1985). See also *Inst.* IV.3.9, vol. II, p. 1061 of John Calvin, *Calvin: Institutes of the Christian Religion*, ed. John T. McNeill, trans. Ford Lewis Battles (Philadelphia: Westminster Press, 1960).

47 John Calvin, sermon 39, 1 Tim. 5:7–12, in *CO* LXXX, 475, quoted in McKee, *John Calvin*, 215–16.

48 See 1 Tim. 5:9–10 and Bonnie Thurston, *The Widows: A Women's Ministry in the Early Church* (Minneapolis: Fortress Press, 1989).

49 For more on this fund see Jeannine Olson, *Calvin and Social Welfare: Deacons and the Bourse française* (Selingsgrove: Susquehanna University Press; London and Toronto: Associated University Presses, 1989). For the origins of the fund see especially ch. two, 29–36.

50 Archives d'État de Genève, Archives hospitalières, Kg 15 (July 1554–July 1555), 1.

51 For the history of deacons and deaconesses, in particular their roles in the sixteenth century, see Jeannine Olson, *Deacons and Deaconesses through the Centuries: One Ministry/Many Roles* (St. Louis: Concordia Publishing House, 1992; 2nd edition, 2004).

52 Olson, *Calvin and Social Welfare*, 103, 133–34, 264 n. 28.

53 Archives d'État de Genève, Archives hospitalières, Kg 14, August 18, 1553.

54 Olson, *Calvin and Social Welfare*, 31–32.

55 W. J. C. Moens, "The Relief of the Poor Members of the French Churches in England as Exemplified by the Practice of the Walloon or French Church in Sandwich (1568–72)," *Proceedings of the Huguenot Society of London* (January 10 and March 14, 1894), 321–38.

56 Lindberg, *Luther on Poverty*, 89, 91.

57 W. Fred Graham, *The Constructive Revolutionary: John Calvin and His Socio-Economic Impact* (n.p.: Michigan State University Press, 1987), 120.

58 "Draft Ecclesiastical Ordinances," 61.

59 Théodore de Bèze and Nicolas Colladon, *Vie de Calvin*, in *CO* XXI, 1–118.

60 Archives d'État de Genève, Registres du Conseil, vol. LXVI, January 7, 1571 to January 4, 1572, folios 104–122v.

61 *CO* XXXI, 418, *Commentary* on the Psalms, Psalm 41:1, quoted in Graham, *Constructive Revolutionary*, 66.

62 Biéler, *La pensée économique et sociale de Calvin*, 1.

# 10 Calvin and political issues

WILLIAM R. STEVENSON, JR.

As a theologian and pastor, Calvin addressed political ideas and issues more from necessity than from direct inclination or intention. The proper relationship of the church to civil government inevitably became a major concern for each of the reformers. So Calvin was obliged to work out, at least in outline form, the foundational political ideas he perceived to be generated by Holy Scripture. Calvin's chapter "On Civil Government" from the last book of his *Institutes of the Christian Religion* remains his most explicit statement. But just as important for seeing fully his framework for thinking politically are his earlier pages on issues of church polity, his earlier chapter "On Christian Freedom," his extensive commentaries on scriptural references to political questions, and, of course, his many tracts and letters.

By exploring these various sources, we can form some coherent answers to the following key political questions: (1) What is the source and justification for civil government among human beings? (2) What is the purpose and proper role of civil government? (3) How ought civil government accomplish its rightful aims? and (4) Under what circumstances, if any, might Christians under government properly disobey or resist that government?

## WHAT IS THE SOURCE AND JUSTIFICATION FOR CIVIL GOVERNMENT?

For Calvin civil government is "divinely-established order" (IV.20.1).[1] It arises by God's providential ordination as both a consequence and a partial remedy for human sin. Sin makes government necessary because without it even minimally constructive relationships among human beings would be difficult to imagine. In a very real sense, then, Calvin reports in his *Romans* commentary, "the safety of mankind is secured" by means of civil order. For "except the fury of the wicked be resisted, and the innocent be protected from their violence, all things would come to an entire confusion." Civil government is more than a mere expedient to peace; it serves spiritual and pedagogical purposes as well. Nevertheless, the mere "ground of utility," which Paul proposes in Romans 13:3, ought to carry believers a long way toward full appreciation of God's manifest providence in civil government. Even if such government is imperfect, perhaps even despotic, it cannot help but "assist in consolidating the society of men." For rulers "do never so far abuse their power, by harassing the good and innocent, that they do not retain in their tyranny some kind of just government" (*Comm. Rom. 13:3*).

The gift of civil government thus demonstrates clearly the reality of God's providential care. For Calvin it is plain that in spite of the historical human perversion of God's good creation, God through his "common grace" (*generalis gratia*) continues to shower his world with small sources of comfort, pleasure, and enlightenment. For example, human understanding still "possesses some power of perception" (II.2.12), and can perceive the minimal requirements of "earthly" life, in particular, "certain civic fair dealings and order": "Hence no man is to be found who does not understand that every sort of human organization must be regulated by laws, and who does not comprehend the principles of those laws" (II.2.13).

A temporal ruler is then *primarily* a "minister of God," and his true accountability is to God alone. "[T]hat king who in ruling over his realm does not serve God's glory exercises not kingly rule but brigandage" (*Inst.* Pref., 12). In the same way, a subject's accountability is ultimately to God alone, recognizing of course that governmental officials work as primary instruments of God's *imperium* (e.g., IV.20.23; IV.20.32).

Calvin goes on to argue the necessity of civil government to be "no less among men than that of bread, water, sun, and air" (IV.20.3). Would any established government, therefore, to the extent it is able to accomplish its minimal tasks of maintaining civic peace and at least superficial harmony, be anything but a good gift of God? After all, Scripture plainly reveals that "the Lord has designed [civil government] to provide for the tranquility of the good and to restrain the waywardness of the wicked" (*Comm. Rom. 13:3*). Having foreseen human rebellion against his created order, God determined not to leave the human race "in a state of confusion, that they might live after the manner of beasts." Instead, he provided "as it were . . . a building regularly formed, and divided into several compartments." Serving as a mechanism to structure and confine human behavior, the "building" of political order – along with the "compartments" of civil institutions – provides "a mode of living" which is "well-arranged and duly ordered," and as such "is peculiar to men." Such order the Apostle Peter calls "a human ordination" precisely because God designs it so fittingly for human habitation (*Comm. 1 Pet. 2:13*).

## WHAT IS THE PURPOSE AND PROPER ROLE
## OF CIVIL GOVERNMENT?

The jurisdiction of the "civil order" is for Calvin dramatically distinct from that of the church; it has "a completely different nature" (IV.20.1). Civil government's responsibility is to see first "that men breathe, eat, drink, and are kept warm." It is to see second "that a public manifestation of religion may exist among Christians" (IV.20.3). In short, its purpose is to protect the physical integrity of its subjects and to ensure the legitimacy of the church. It should by no means try to *be* the church, for the salvation in Christ promised to believers "belongs to the kingdom of Christ," not to "some earthly kingdom" (*Comm. Jer. 33:16*). Yet strong, vital, and just social institutions are essential to the health and growth of all persons, Christian or otherwise.

*[margin handwriting: more than justice]*

Given the importance of both physical and spiritual growth and health Calvin sees as a primary duty of civil government to "cherish and protect the outward worship of God," and "to defend sound doctrine of piety and the position of the church" (IV.20.2).

What might this mean? If the primary marks of the true church are the preaching of the gospel and the administration of the sacraments (IV.1.10), and if preaching the gospel means the public proclamation of the key elements of God's Word (such as "God is one; Christ is God and the Son of God; our salvation rests in God's mercy; and the like" [IV.1.12]), and administration of the sacraments means the public performance of the biblically mandated ceremonies which signify God's forgiving and redeeming grace (namely baptism and the Lord's Supper [IV.14.22]), then not just any institution giving itself the name "church" can properly claim government "protection." The authentic church not only can claim protection, though, God mandates its protection.

At the same time, if keeping the peace means more than just ensuring lack of overt conflict, and includes thereby minimal "protection, . . . benevolence, and justice," then not just any terrorist regime can claim divine legitimacy (IV.20.6). Calvin insists that Scripture does provide some clear indications of God's specifically designated, and indeed limited, role for human governments. Government's role, Calvinist "revolutionary" movements notwithstanding, is less to radically re-orient than to point subjects toward orderly peaceableness. "So long as we live among men," civil government's "appointed end" is not only "to cherish and protect the outward worship of God, [and] to defend sound doctrine of piety and the position of the church," but also, and as important, "to adjust our life to the society of men, to form our social behavior to civil righteousness, to reconcile us with one another, and to promote general peace and tranquility." Civil government is thus one of those "helps" (*subsidia* or *auxilia*) that God provides while "we go as pilgrims upon the earth" ultimately "aspir[ing] to the true fatherland," and we ought never "stupidly [to] imagine" any "perfection" as can "never be found in a community of men" (IV.20.2). Hence, we ought never to assume that civil government can re-make the world but only that it might "provide that a public manifestation of religion may exist among Christians, and that humanity be maintained among men" (IV.20.3).

Perhaps most important here, though, is Calvin's determination to follow Scripture in emphasizing the duty of both church *and* civil polity (both as preaching the gospel and protecting the preaching of the gospel) to direct their attention to the disenfranchised and dispossessed. As Calvin puts the matter directly in his *Commentary* on Jeremiah 7:5–7, whenever God speaks of a "right government," he "mentions strangers and orphans and widows." This is so because when "*others* obtain their right, it is no matter of wonder, since they have advocates to defend their cause, and they have also the aid of friends." However, "strangers and orphans and widows . . . [are] almost destitute of protection." Such people are "subject to many wrongs, as though they were exposed as prey." A government that recognizes its responsibility to reflect and channel God's paternal care (IV.20.6) to all under its charge will thus take especial pains to enfold and protect those most vulnerable to exploitation. Imaging God means imaging God's communal construction work in the world; it means joining in the work of "edification" (IV.20.4).

For Calvin, civil government does indeed have "spiritual" responsibilities. Why would it not? Calvin sees, as did most of his Christian medieval forbears, an indissoluble link between religious faith and public order. This connection arises out of the humility imposed on humankind and their ordinary social relations by sound Christian doctrine. Precisely for this reason, healthy public order (rather than oppressive tyrannical rule) rests on a people's spiritual wellness. In the same way that a father oversees the physical, emotional, and spiritual development of his children, a civil government inevitably oversees the multi-dimensional growth, or else deterioration, of its subjects.

The temptation to classify people as "elect" or as "reprobate," and in this way to undertake a triumphal "cleansing" of the political order on behalf and in the name of the elect is one Calvin understands very well. Yet while he sees God prodding believers to act constructively in the world, he recognizes the need to understand that God still holds the prod. In God's mysterious providence the prod can metastasize into a club when believers forget or ignore the real ground of their salvation energy. In an ironic twist, then, election ought to breed not chauvinism but something more like servility. Calvin sheds further light on this issue when he speaks of "impiety" in reference to Deuteronomy 13:5. He notes that Moses "does not condemn" to earthly punishment those who "may have spread false doctrine," but who only did so because of some "particular or trifling error." Rather Moses condemns those "who are the authors of apostasy, and so who pluck up religion by the roots." As a result, "the crime of impiety," Calvin says, "would not otherwise merit punishment." Only if the sacrilege "had not only been received by public consent and the suffrages of the people, but, being supported also by (apparent) sure and indisputable proofs, should place its truth above the reach of doubt," should it be forcibly addressed (*Comm. Harm. Moses* on Deut. 13:5).

The practical implications of God's establishment of explicit limitations on human action should now be clear. God exercises his power for a *purpose*: he seeks through the rule of Christ and the work of his Spirit to reclaim, restore, renew, and revitalize all that is his own in order that he might live in eternal community with it. Human exercises of power are thus legitimate only when they work toward the same goals of renewal and revivification and do so in praise of God's incredible mercy. To illustrate the point, Calvin is fond of noting that temporal government does have specific duties, and that those duties consist of a good deal more than merely clearing the way for an oppressive and presumptuous institutional church. Were power itself the criterion of good government, Calvin would hardly be so quick to argue for gifted, attentive, and *responsive* rulers; for constitutional restraints on exercises of power; for governmental "modesty" in both style and substance; and for governmental duties both to protect the true church and to serve the socially and politically dispossessed.

## HOW OUGHT CIVIL GOVERNMENT ACCOMPLISH ITS RIGHTFUL AIMS?

Not power but attentive responsiveness to God's purposes marks rightful government. Any magistrate, in performing his duties, "does nothing by himself," says Calvin, but instead "carries out the very judgments of God" (IV.20.10). Even "they that rule unjustly and incompetently" do so by God's investment, for they have been "raised up by him to punish the wickedness of the people" (IV.20.25). God alone manifests the true source of political authority. To the extent that either rulers *or* subjects claim alternate sources of authority (for example, their own or the "people's" prerogative), they forfeit all legitimacy in God's eyes, and they prepare the way of their own demise. As Calvin puts the matter in his Prefatory Address in the *Institutes*, "this consideration makes a true king: to recognize himself a minister of

God in governing his kingdom" (Pref. 2). Ignoring the divine source of all political authority brings about its own punishment: "Before his face all kings [doing so] shall fall and be crushed" (IV.20.29).

Particular rulers, then, have no authority of their own, even though they are constantly tempted to assert their own. "The dignity, therefore, with which they are clothed is only temporary and will pass away with the fashion of the world" (*Comm. Ps. 82:6*). Tempted to "lift their heads above the clouds," kings may forget that "they, as well as the rest of mankind, are under the government of God (. . . *ut regantur sub Dei manu*)." Christians holding power, and using it to effect change, must understand that it is from God that they hold such power.

Good government will then be government that acknowledges those with the "calling" to administer. It does not assume that just anyone can govern. Rather, says Calvin, "ruling" is properly thought of as "among God's gifts," distributed to human beings "according to the diversity of grace," and *for* "the upbuilding of the church." By his words through the Apostle Paul in Romans 13, and by his actions in support of just rulers such as Moses, Joshua, David, and Josiah, God speaks clearly that "civil authority is a calling," and so, "not only holy and lawful before God, but also the most sacred and by far the most honorable of all callings in the whole of mortal life" (IV.20.4).

The signs of such a calling will be manifest to anyone inspired to see them. For those "who know that they have been ordained ministers of divine justice," qualities such as "zeal for uprightness, for prudence, gentleness, self-control, and for innocence" should be readily apparent. Indeed, "if they remember that they are vicars of God," then they will be especially diligent "to represent in themselves . . . some image of divine providence, protection, goodness, benevolence, and justice" (IV.20.6).

Good government is thus modest in its appearance and operation. In any number of places, Calvin castigates kings for their "pomp." For him, "moderation" (*moderatio*) is a vital concept and a living reality. Moderation, then, for Calvin implies both disciplined frugality and orderly restraint. Even those with whom Calvin shares political goals he condemns, on occasion, for their "inconsiderate zeal" (*Letter* dcxix of December 24, 1561 [VII, 251]), their "impetuosity," and their "pretensions" to the property of vanquished Roman church buildings (*Letter* dcxxx of May 13, 1562 [VII, 272]). Interestingly, therefore, as Harro Höpfl rightly notes, "*moderatio* is a term Calvin not infrequently employed to mean government, its connotations [being] those of containment and regulation rather than direction."[2]

A most significant part of the calling to govern, Calvin repeatedly asserts, is attention to the poor and dispossessed. "To treat such [persons] with cruelty argues a singular degree of impiety, and contempt of divine authority" (*Comm. Ps. 94:5–6*). Moreover, by clear evidence he understood his job as Genevan pastor as, among other things, to encourage Genevan political authorities to redefine governmental oversight of its subjects to include what we would now call social welfare programs. "The city authorities themselves," says Wallace, "had to be encouraged to think of their work in government as involving a social care for the welfare of each individual corresponding to the pastoral care exerted by the ministry of the Word."[3] Late in his career Calvin worked diligently to establish in Geneva a free public school, the Academy of Geneva, staffing it with the best teachers he could find among the other reformers.[4] In addition, he urged inclusion in the 1541 *Ecclesiastical Ordinances* of a section establishing in the Genevan church the biblical office of deacon, charged with nursing the sick and feeding the poor. His emphasis on the work of the diaconate played itself out in his continuing support of the public *hôpital général*, administered by lay church members and charged with the traditional diaconal duties.[5]

Are there particular structural instruments by which government's work should be done? In fact there are not. When Calvin distinguishes three kinds of law in *Institutes* IV.20, only the "moral law" (which "commands us to worship God with pure faith and piety" and "to embrace men with sincere affection") is the "true and eternal rule of righteousness," and is "prescribed for men of all nations and times." As to "judicial [i.e., civil] law," says Calvin, "surely every nation is left free to make such laws as it foresees to be profitable to itself," so long as they are "in conformity to that perpetual rule of love (*caritas*)" (IV.20.15). How "false and foolish," even "perilous and seditious," for example, says Calvin, to claim that no polity "is duly framed which neglects the political system of Moses" (IV.20.14).

Indeed, Calvin explicitly refuses to engage in "long discourse concerning the best kind of [civil] laws." His discussion of civil law, and its relationship to "moral law," he says, ought not to provide a "reason why anyone should expect" such a discourse, a discourse that would, ultimately, "be endless and would not pertain to the present purpose and place" (IV.20.14). Comprehending the moral law is fundamental to healthy politics, but in building on that foundation, human beings are free to exercise their own judgment and prudence.

Calvin thus proceeds, not unexpectedly, to place the subject of governmental "forms," which was a matter of grave concern to the ancient Greek and late medieval thinkers, into a category of only secondary import. The forms of government are a good deal less weighty than are the contents of men's hearts. While there may indeed be a proper governmental form for a particular society, such design "depends largely upon the circumstances."

God in his providence "has wisely arranged that various countries should be ruled by various kinds of government" (IV.20.8).

Good government will acknowledge essential human equality, at least to the extent that all persons under its authority have innate value and that all persons exercising authority are tempted to abuse it. As Monter has pointed out in his study *Calvin's Geneva*, Calvin worked unhesitatingly to put this sense of essential equality into institutional practice in the church. Upon his return to Geneva in 1541, Calvin's first public act was to ask the Genevan Small Council to name a committee to prepare a written constitution for the Genevan church. The adopted structure, with Calvin's full assent, worked to broaden considerably the measure of lay supervision within the church.[6] Perhaps even more noteworthy, throughout Calvin's long career as a pastor mediating ecclesiastical and pastoral disputes, he held to an equality of disciplinary treatment for all Genevans, rich or poor, celebrated or inglorious.[7] In his *Institutes* and elsewhere, Calvin encouraged Christians of all social ranks to make use, as needed, of civil courts of law, and even, if appropriate, act to instigate judicial proceedings. If one understands, Calvin wrote, the civil magistrate to be "a minister of God for our good," if "he has been given by the Lord for our defense," then the Lord's "purpose" cannot be borne out "unless we are allowed to enjoy such benefit," unless we may "without impiety . . . call upon and . . . appeal to" such magistrates (IV.20.18).[8]

No doubt Calvin's instinct for minimal egalitarianism is behind his rather consistent disdain for hereditary monarchy, and the established hierarchy it implies. *Because* of their special status, kings, perhaps especially kings by birth, "think themselves to be, as it were, cut off from the company of men," and not "anymore to be counted in the common array" (*Serm. Deut.* 17:16–20). In his explicit discussion of governmental forms, then, Calvin states his general conclusion that elective aristocracy, "or a system compounded of aristocracy and democracy . . . far excels all others." The excellence of a non-monarchical form, however, arises not "of itself, but because it is very rare for kings so to control themselves that their will never disagrees with what is just and right." As a result, "men's fault or failing (*vitium vel defectus*) causes it to be safer and more bearable for a number to hold governmental power." This number, then, will be in a position to "help one another, teach and admonish one another," and, if one's personal ambition improperly asserts itself, "there may be a number of censors and masters to restrain his willfulness (*libidem*)" (IV.20.8). In the final analysis, though, Calvin looks to Galatians 3:28 and Colossians 3:11: "[I]t makes no difference what your condition among men may be or under what nation's laws you live, since the Kingdom of Christ does not at all consist in these things" (IV.20.1).

## UNDER WHAT CIRCUMSTANCES, IF EVER, MIGHT CHRISTIANS UNDER GOVERNMENT PROPERLY DISOBEY OR RESIST SUCH GOVERNMENT?

Calvin grounds his view of justified resistance to temporal authority in his doctrine of providence. God's providence reveals not only his sovereignty and majesty, but also his determination through ways often unexpected and wearisome to hem in and care for his creatures. The providence of God in carefully setting before each human being and each human society what each needs at that moment and what each can bear takes on much more significance here than God's predestined choosing of his own. While predestination can energize believers to live out what they understand to be God's call in history, it can tempt them to do so in a posture almost headlong. But providence as nourishing care provided by and *through* existing institutions and circumstances (be they comfortable or uncomfortable) works to restrain fanatical manifestations of belief by reminding believers that God knows them better than they know themselves, and that he often hems them in by certain social, political, and cultural institutions, in order to restrain them for their own good.

As clear manifestation of God's providential care, existing, established civil government deserves both obedience and respect. To resist or rebel against such government would be not only to "avow ourselves as the public enemies of the human race" (*Comm. Rom. 13:3*), but as well, and consequently, "to despise the providence of him who is the founder of civil power." Magistrates are indeed "constituted by God's ordination," which is the primary reason "why we ought to be subject" to them. As Paul states explicitly, "it ought to be enough for us" that the particular governing authorities believers face "*do rule*" (*Comm. Rom. 13:1*; Calvin's emphasis).

In working through the subject of civil government, Paul points directly to God's loving providence by way of the "higher powers." He does this, says Calvin, primarily in order "to take away the frivolous curiosity of men." For Paul understands that stubborn human beings have an ingrained tendency "to inquire by what right they who rule have obtained their authority." More to the point, by declaring that "*every soul*" be subject to existing government, Paul "removes every exception, lest anyone should claim an immunity from the common duty of obedience" (*Comm. Rom. 13:1*; Calvin's emphasis). Likewise the Apostle Peter exhorts believers to submit themselves "to every ordination of man" (New International Version: "to every authority instituted among men"). Not only is every person under government subject to that government, in other words, but every government is worthy of such obedience. "[O]bedience is due to all who rule, because they have been raised to that honor not by chance, but by God's providence" (*Comm. 1 Pet. 2:13*).

God might allow particular hardships "to instruct his own people in patience," "to correct their wicked affections and tame their lust," "to subjugate them to self-denial," or even "to arouse them from sluggishness." In sum, says Calvin in the *Institutes*, he undoubtedly seeks "to bring low the proud, to shatter the cunning of the impious and to overthrow their devices" (I.17.1). Ironically, then, while "violent men dash themselves to pieces by their own eagerness," it is in just the quiet patience of godly people that the real "vigor" of faith, "though it has less display, and often appears to lie buried," is thereby "refreshed and renewed" (*Comm. Isa. 40:31*).

In his many letters Calvin finds numerous occasions to confirm this truth in his own and in his fellow believers' daily experience. To the Admiral de Coligny, taken prisoner by the Spanish in August, 1558, Calvin is blunt: "(I)n sending you this affliction (God) has intended to set you apart, as it were, that you might listen to him more attentively." How difficult it is, Calvin points out, "in the midst of worldly honors, riches, and power to lend to him an attentive ear, because these things draw our attention too much in different directions." Personal deprivation thus promises a new insight into God's mercy and grace (*Letter* dxii of September 4, 1558 [VI, 466]).

Existing regimes are no accident, Calvin proclaims, and believers need to recognize God's hand in precisely those regimes. In his providence, God does not merely "permit" particular institutions and structures to arise, he "commands" them (I.18.1). Indeed, Calvin insists in another place, "if we admit that God is invested with prescience," that he "superintends and governs the world he has made," and that he "does not overlook any part of it," then it must follow that "everything which takes place is done according to his will" (*Comm. Ps. 115:3*). God's manifest will "may be mysterious (*abscondita nobis*)," but such occlusion ought not to keep believers from regarding it "with reverence," it being "the fountain of all justice and rectitude" (*Comm. Ps. 135:6*).

Most remarkable on this score is Calvin's continuous flow of letters cautioning believers against heedless and impious disruption of established institutions. Writing to Englishman William Cecil in May, 1559, for example, Calvin responds to John Knox's inflammatory pamphlet against the government of women. As troublesome as the reign of a woman, in this case Queen Mary, might be, Calvin can think of a number of examples of women "raised up by the providence of God," such ascension "either because he willed . . . to condemn the supineness of men, or thus to show more distinctly his own glory." More to the point, says Calvin, "in my judgment it is not permitted to unsettle governments that have been set up by the peculiar providence of God" however they may appear to indignant but mortal eyes (*Letter* dxxxviii [VII, 47]).

In sum, as Calvin wrote to the church in Paris in September, 1557 (a church burdened with violent persecution), "better it were that we were all involved in ruin than that the gospel of God should be exposed to the reproach of arming men to sedition and tumult." God will ever, declares Calvin, "cause the ashes of his servants to fructify, but excesses and violence will bring them nothing but barrenness" (*Letter* cccclxxv [VI, 361]). In this way, then, "humility will restrain our impatience" (IV.20.29).

Clearly Calvin does work to distinguish legitimate government from tyranny. In his *Commentary on Genesis*, for example, he marks the distinction by attributing to "lawful government" a place for "counselors," who, with the ruler "should administer public affairs rightly and in good order" (*Comm. Gen. 49:10*). A rightful government, then, is one which both knows its true ends, opens itself to outside criticism as to how it might best pursue them, and then pursues them with diligence and determination. Tyranny, on the other hand, consists of rulership by those who "give the reins to their lust, and think all things lawful to themselves" (*Comm. Dan. 2:5*).

Generalizing from Isaiah's prophecy, Calvin notes that in tyrants "[a]rrogance [is] joined, as it usually is, to violence and cruelty." The tyrannical impulse in all human beings, the impulse to "despise others," leads almost inevitably to deeds of "violence and injustice and oppression." Indeed, "it is impossible for men to abstain from doing harm to others, if they do not lay aside all conceit and high estimation of themselves." Henceforth, Calvin tells believers, "let us willingly . . . bring down our minds to true humility, if we do not wish to be cast down and laid low to our destruction" (*Comm. Isa. 13:11*). To impersonate such humility, a public persona is far from sufficient.

As to *resistance* to tyrannical rule, Calvin's language does on occasion appear benedictory. For example, in his Dedicatory Epistle to the *Commentaries on Daniel*, addressed, in 1561, "to all the pious worshippers of God who desire the kingdom of Christ to be rightly constituted in France," Calvin makes clear his judgment of the then current French regime, a place "from which the truth of God, pure religion, and the doctrine of eternal salvation are banished, and the very kingdom of Christ laid prostrate." Further, he calls upon his fellow believers "as far as lies in your power, and your calling demands it," to exercise their "duty . . . to use your hearty endeavors, that true religion may recover its perfect state."

Indeed, Calvin's convictions regarding both the power and place of individual conscience, and the role and place of government in God's providential order, would appear to steer one logically to the appearance of Christian individuals publicly defying ungodly magistrates. In saying that "God always retain[s] the highest authority," Calvin asserted in his *Commentary on the Harmony of the Gospels* (1555), Christ means that "those who destroy political order are rebellious against God." Therefore, "obedience to princes and magistrates is always joined to the worship and fear of God." If, on the contrary, "princes claim any part of the authority of God, we ought not to obey them any farther than can be done without offending God" (*Comm. on Matt. 22:21, Mark 12:17,* and *Luke 20:25*).

Whatever the case, Calvin's words in the letter and in the final chapter of the 1559 *Institutes* still appear plain. Telling Francis that from him and his followers "not one seditious word was ever heard," and that "when we lived under you, [our] life . . . was always acknowledged to be quiet and simple" (Pref. 8), he concluded his work, and his final chapter on civil government, with strong words of obedience. "Let no man deceive himself here," asserts Calvin, "the magistrate cannot be resisted without God being resisted at the same time" (IV.20.23).

Moreover, Calvin goes on to detail the obedience believers owe even to unjust and "wicked" rulers. For, in the end, obedience is about the recognition of the *office* of magistrate and not about affection for the particular *holder* of the office. Even "a very wicked man utterly unworthy of all honor," so long as he "has the public power in his hands," should be "held in the same reverence and esteem by his subjects, in so far as obedience is concerned, in which they would hold the best of kings if he were given to them." For in his public office "that noble and divine power resides which the Lord has by his Word given to the ministers of his justice and judgment" (IV.20.25). Those who rule "have been raised to that honor not by chance, but by God's providence" (*Comm. 1 Pet. 2:13*). Christian believers ought to be concerned "not to inquire about another's duties, but every man should keep in mind that one duty which is his own," and in the case of subjects under government, that duty is responsible obedience (IV.20.29).

Calvin does appear to open the door to resisting public authority when he speaks of "popular magistrates" (IV.20.31). In so doing, though, he distinguishes "private individuals," who are bound to obey even wicked tyrants, from those lesser magistrates who have been "appointed to restrain the willfulness of kings." These latter (and Calvin mentions in particular the Spartan ephors, the Roman tribunes, and the Athenian demarchs) are imbued with public authority and therefore should rein in the temptation to "wink at kings who violently fall upon and assault the lowly common folk," a temptation which involves them only in "nefarious perfidy." Instead, they should "withstand" (*intercedere*) such behavior. If they fail to uphold this responsibility, they "dishonestly betray the freedom of the people, of which they know that they have been appointed protectors by God's ordinance" (IV.20.31). *Intercedere* (literally, "to go between") can imply a range of actions, of course, from verbal objection to physical resistance. As a result, perhaps only one aspect of Calvin's point is clear: any public official is answerable to God for the performance of his public duty to shepherd his charges. Such persons must have been explicitly given public office and authority, however.

What about those whom Calvin calls "open avengers" (*manifestos vindices*), the individuals whom God on occasion "raises up . . . from among his servants," and "arms . . . with his command to punish the wicked government and deliver his people . . . from miserable calamity"? In such a case, "when they had been sent by God's lawful calling to carry out such acts" (that is, "taking up arms against kings"), they clearly "did not at all violate that majesty which is implanted in kings by God's ordination." Rather, "armed from heaven, they subdued the lesser power with the greater, just as it is lawful for kings to punish their subordinates" (IV.20.30). But by using Moses as his primary example, one might justifiably say Calvin is trying to contain this "exception" to scriptural figures only. Indeed, given that the ground and impetus for divinely-authorized "resistance" can come only from God's specific and explicit revelation, Calvin seems clearly to be asserting less a benedictory license to subjects seeking to revolt and more a warning to tyrants that both God and the affected subjects are watching.

Calvin does envision the possibility of resolution to the sometimes-explicit conflict between the civil authority and God's revealed Word in Scripture. Such resolution is modeled, for Calvin, by the example of Daniel under King Darius. In explicitly addressing "the inhabitants of France" he dedicates his 1561 *Commentaries on Daniel* to them, thereby pointing to Daniel as their best example. The Book of Daniel shows clearly not only "how God proves the faith of his people . . . by various trials," but also how his goodness "shines forth" in the midst of such trials (*Comm. Dan.,* Dedic.). To follow the *example* of Daniel may be to disclaim, dissent from, and even disobey the government in question, but not to provoke, or participate in, outright rebellion. In Daniel's case, Calvin points out, "The stone by which those kingdoms, which had made war on God, were destroyed . . . was not formed by the hand of man." Indeed, although Calvin is well aware of the "very great indignities" which the French Protestants have endured over the thirty years prior to 1561, but especially during "the last six months"; and although "more atrocious things should be yet at hand," nevertheless, he says, "you must use every effort, that no madness of the impious who act . . . intemperately, should deprive you of that moderation by which alone [French officialdom has] thus far been conquered and broken down" (*Comm. Dan.*, Dedic.).

Calvin is quite aware of the dangers of triumphalism. He understands that the story of salvation in history works its way through trials and persecutions as well as triumphs. Civil government does have distinct responsibilities, and the church should continually call temporal rulers to those God-ordained duties. Yet no matter the circumstances within which a people finds itself, no matter the day or the hour, and no matter the political structures or policies with which they must contend, the promise and vision of God deliberately, obstinately, persistently, sculpting his kingdom within history inspires a hope out of which one can generate incredible energy and perseverance. Reading the story of God's people in Old Testament Scripture is for Calvin a loud reminder of God's determination and faithfulness: "History certainly bears ample testimony that the people of God had not to deal with a few enemies, but they were assaulted by almost the whole world; and further, that they were molested not only by external foes, but also by those of an internal kind, by such as professed to belong to the Church." Yet in spite of this experience (yea, *because* of this experience), says the Psalmist, God's people retain a hope undergirded by "the encouraging consideration that the Church, by patient endurance, has uniformly proved victorious" (*Comm. Ps. 129:1*). Indeed, "he who shall entrust the keeping of his life to God's care, will not doubt of its safety even in the midst of death" (*Comm. Ps. 31:5*).

### Notes

1  Unless otherwise noted, all citations to the *Institutes* will consist only of the book, chapter, and part numbers from the McNeill edition (trans. Battles). *Institutes* IV.20 is, of course, Calvin's chapter "On Civil Government." Citations to the *Commentaries* are from the Calvin Translation Society (Edinburgh) edition. Citations to Calvin's letters point to the numbering of Henry Beveridge and Jules Bonnet, and show the volume and page numbers from the Baker Books reprint edition, *Selected Works of John Calvin: Tracts and Letters*.

2  Harro Höpfl, *The Christian Polity of John Calvin* (Cambridge: Cambridge University Press, 1982), 159. See, e.g., *Inst.* I.15.8 (where Battles translates *moderatio* as "guidance"); II.8.32 ("regulation"); III.4.12 ("rule"); III.15.3 ("restraint"); III.19.12 ("control"); and IV.20.2 ("government").

3  Ronald S. Wallace, *Calvin, Geneva and the Reformation* (Edinburgh: Scottish Academic Press, 1988), 125.

4  E. William Monter, *Calvin's Geneva* (New York: John Wiley and Sons, 1967), 111–14.

5 Ibid., 139.
6 Ibid., 71.
7 Ibid., 75.
8 Calvin does not wish to encourage unhealthy litigiousness, however. The purpose of magisterial help, for ordinary people, is thus to "preserve their possessions, while maintaining friendliness toward their enemies" (IV.20.20). See also IV.20.18; and IV.20.21.

## 11  Calvin's controversies

RICHARD C. GAMBLE

The literary style of sixteenth-century polemical writings is quite foreign to modern readers. For those theologians, religion was a matter of life and death, literally. Phrases and expressions that should not be used in "polite company" today are found heavily seasoning the writings of both Roman and Protestant polemical authors.

As an example of sixteenth-century polemic writing style, listen to Sir Thomas More speak of Martin Luther in his Latin work *Response to Luther*:

> What wonder, then if the stupid scoundrel slanders the prince, since he has already long ago scorned both the apostle James and the whole catholic church and now proceeds to such a degree of impiety that he openly blasphemes the Holy Spirit, since that which everyone sees the Holy Spirit has inspired in all the faithful, this buffoon worse than any infidel dares to blaspheme with his cursed tongue which should be cut out by the roots.
>
> But since the foundation of such a facetious fiction [on the element of wine in the Eucharist] is not any word of the prince but the dull-witted device of Luther himself, by which everyone sees that he imputes to the king a statement which the king nowhere makes, who is so foolish that he will not laugh at this fool so foolishly fashioning fools?[1]

The enlightened and elegant author, More, was able write in such a strong fashion against Luther. Moreover, Luther could reply in a similar manner! This type of clever, sharp, and brutal writing was the accepted literary genre.

Since this literary genre is rather "strong" for contemporary readers, so also sixteenth-century pulpit polemics sound foreign to our ears. In similar fashion, John Calvin used very "strong" language in the pulpit. In 1549 Calvin referred to certain Genevan citizens as "dogs chasing dogs in heat," as "drunkards," as "worse than brute beasts." He had not calmed down in 1551 when he referred to the entire city of Geneva as a "stinking cesspool of hell."

Likewise, he would not allow the powerful magistrates to get off free from such a standard; in a sermon from 1552, he addressed their godlessness: "I say this that the Senators, Judges and Advocates of Geneva not only attempt to argue against God, thereby hoping to gain for themselves the right to mock him, but rejecting all the Holy Scriptures, they vomit forth their blasphemies as supreme decrees. These gargoyle monkeys have become so proud . . . that they allow no place for reason or truth."[2]

Calvin's work played an important polemical role at the time. Still, his work as a controversialist can only be understood as an overall part of his ministry in Geneva. Primarily, his role as pastor, biblical commentator, and theological author was characteristic of his ministry.[3] Since Calvin's literary corpus is substantial, the sum of his writings that fall under polemical or controversial categories is quite significant; his polemical writings can be divided into at least five different sections.[4]

## I. TREATISES *AGAINST THE ANABAPTISTS*; *AGAINST THE LIBERTINES*; AND THE *PSYCHOPANNYCHIA*

This group of writings includes Calvin's polemics against Protestants in general, and closer to home, Protestants in Geneva, Strasbourg and Paris.

The *Psychopannychia*[5] is one of Calvin's earliest works, first published in 1534. Calvin attacked the position of many who taught that when one dies, instead of going directly to heaven or hell, the human soul "sleeps." Though this view originated from within the Anabaptist community, it apparently spread rather quickly through the Protestant communities. The matter was significant enough that a few British theologians translated the treatise into English in London in 1581.[6]

Calvin's *Against the Anabaptists*[7] was first published in Latin at Geneva in 1544. A few months later it came out in French, and in 1549 it was translated and published in the English language.[8] In this work Calvin first refuted what we now call the Schleithem Confession, which was an anabaptistic "confession" of the Swiss Brethren written in 1527. The Anabaptists, as Calvin understood their differences, were divided into two sects. One faction held to the authority of the Bible and engaged in theology, though greatly lacking at its foundation; it was against this group that Calvin wrote the tract. The other group was quite different from the first. They were radical Spiritualists and Libertines, and they received their own polemical treatise.

Calvin's treatise *Against the Libertines*[9] was published in French in 1545. The main protagonist as described in the writing was a man named

Quintin whom Calvin had previously met somewhere near Paris. Quintin was then enjoying the patronage of Marguerite of Angoulême. The Libertines were likely dispersed throughout Holland, Belgium, and parts of Germany; Calvin estimated that they were between four and ten thousand in number.[10] These radicals developed a hermeneutic that separated the "letter" from the "spirit," and they likely propagated a pantheistic and speculative spiritualism.[11]

## II. HIS *RESPONSE TO SADOLET* AND THE *ANTIDOTE TO TRENT*

This grouping includes technical theological works against the Roman Catholic Church. Calvin's *Response to Sadolet* was published in 1539.[12] The historical situation that gave rise to the timely *Response* was very interesting considering the concurrent Reformation in Geneva. Calvin and two other pastors had been banished from the city for refusing to serve the Communion (Eucharist); thus there existed a power struggle between the pastors and the leaders of the city, who had set out to control access to the partaking of the Lord's Supper. This turmoil provided a fine opportunity for the Roman Church to attempt to win back the jewel of the city of Geneva. Cardinal Sadolet, author of a "Letter by James Sadolet, a Roman Cardinal, to the Senate and People of Geneva," was an accomplished scholar. He thought that Calvin would not bother to respond to him because of the dishonour of being banished. On that political point, he was badly mistaken.

Calvin's rejoinder is uncharacteristically mild. Perhaps his mildness was in response to the charge made by Sadolet and others that Calvin was never able to engage in polemics without hurling insults at his opponent and losing his temper.

Continuing with technical responses to the Roman Church, the *Antidote to Trent* is very thorough.[13] In this treatise, Calvin addressed a number of issues. In religious matters, Calvin asked, how much do people need to submit to human authority? Calvin articulated in this work what is called a great Protestant principle: that the Scriptures alone are the infallible standard of authority.

Calvin analysed the teaching found among the leaders of the ongoing Council of Trent, a formative assembly of theologians that would provide a standard for Roman Catholic theology. Needless to say, he was not impressed! He was also not overwhelmed with admiration for their opening address. Their own confession demonstrated to Calvin that it was right for those who had attempted to purify the church to leave it.

Calvin proceeded to consider each of the canons of the Council of Trent verbatim, and refuted each of them in what he called the "antidote", which thus forms the title of the work. The main issues dealt with were the rule of faith, original sin, justification, and the sacrifice and merits of Christ.

Calvin reminded his readers that the Roman Church decided that all who refused to receive what the Protestants call the Apocrypha (books not properly in the Bible) as inspired of God and authoritative, were anathematized. Calvin was furthermore disappointed that instead of going to the original Greek and Hebrew texts of the Bible, it chose the Latin Vulgate as the authoritative version.

### III. HIS WORKS *TREATISE ON RELICS*; *THE ADULTERO-GERMAN INTERIM, WITH THEIR REFUTATION: THE NECESSITY OF REFORMING THE CHURCH*; *SINFULNESS OF OUTWARD CONFORMITY*; *AGAINST ASTROLOGY*; *ON SCANDALS*

These polemical writings are all pointed at the Roman Church as well, but have a different character than the preceding. These are not technical theological polemics, but are aimed at the heart and mind of members of the church.

The *Treatise on Relics* appeared in French 1543 and in Latin in 1548.[14] That it appeared first in the French language is significant; Calvin usually wrote complex theologies in Latin but obviously wanted to reach the people with this text which he thus chose to write in French. Subsequently, soon after the Latin text appeared, Cochlaeus, the Roman controversialist, attacked Calvin.[15] This work was written not only in French, but in a different style than Calvin's theological treatises. Here he outlines some of the absurdities connected with many of the relics. Calvin concluded that image or relic worship is comparable to the gross idolatry of the heathen.[16]

*The Adultero-German Interim, with their Refutation*: Although most of Calvin's polemical writings concentrated on the city of Geneva, French Protestantism, or the Roman Church, here he was forced to deal with matters concerning the Emperor Charles V and the German world.[17] The emperor had drawn up a confession of faith (written by three theologians – two Catholic and one Protestant) which was aimed at settling the religious controversy in Germany. Quickly, results of the Confession's allowances followed: priests who married were permitted to retain their wives, and the laity was permitted to commune with both bread and wine. The interim certainly succeeded in at least one thing: it infuriated both Catholics and Protestants!

After presenting the full twenty-six sections of the text of the Confession, Calvin laboriously refuted each one. His introduction gives us a flavour of his writing style:

> I am not here debating with Turks and Jews, who would wish the name of Christ utterly extinguished, or with grosser Papists, who demand from us an open abjuration of true doctrine, but with the contrivers of a kind of specious pacification, who leave us a half Christ, but in such a manner that there is no part of His doctrine which they do not obscure or bespatter with some stain of falsehood. And, this artifice of deforming piety that they send forth – so help them! Under the name of reformation![18]

*The Necessity of Reforming the Church*[19] is an address presented to the Diet of Spiers in 1543 and is presented "in the name of all who would have Christ to reign." Calvin considered three main issues here: "*First*, I must briefly enumerate the evils that compelled us to seek for remedies. *Secondly*, I must show that the particular remedies that the Reformers employed were apt and salutary. *Thirdly*, I must make it plain that we were not at liberty any longer to delay putting forth our hand, in as much as the matter demanded instant amendment." The necessity was so great because it concerned, according to Calvin, "the whole substance of Christianity. This includes a knowledge of both the mode in which God is duly worshipped and of the source from which salvation is to be obtained."[20]

The *Sinfulness of Outward Conformity to Romish Rites*[21] came out at a time when individual members of the church found themselves in the midst of tremendous social and financial pressure. Converting to Protestantism from Catholicism could in fact spell death. The question that Calvin addressed in this work is how should someone live as a Protestant while dwelling in a land under Papal control? Another way that the question could be addressed is whether or not it is lawful for a person who had personally renounced the Roman Church and her theology in his heart to conform outwardly, that is with his body, to its rites so that he or she could avoid persecution.

Calvin's answer was that even when a person's heart does not conform to the ceremony, it is not right to perform the Roman ceremony. This answer caused many Protestants to be displeased with Calvin. The criticism was levelled against him that it is easy to get such a response when one is safely placed in the city of Geneva. The censure against Calvin's position was strong enough for him to elicit confirmation of his views by Peter Martyr Vermigli as well as Martin Bucer and Philip Melanchthon, which he did.

*Against Astrology* was made public in 1549.[22] The topic of this tract, unlike most of his polemical material, does not appear in any detail in the *Institutes*. Calvin dealt with the importance of having a clear conscience before God and thus avoiding astrology. However, to avoid astrology, a good working definition must be supplied. Calvin defined the differences between true and false astrology this way: false astrology is the attempt to ascertain the future by reading the stars. True astrology is what we would call today "astronomy."

He then demonstrated how the Scriptures condemn astrology and provided what he called a "remedy" for the evils of astrology. The remedy would follow these rules: "To dedicate our souls and our bodies to God and to serve him without pretence . . . Each person [should] attend closely to the end to which he has been called in order that he might apply himself to the duties of his office . . . [so that] the end of their actions might be to edify both themselves and others in the fear of God."[23]

*On Scandals* appeared in 1550 in Geneva.[24] A "scandal" was defined as an offence or stumbling block. The stumbling blocks addressed places where the gospel was being attacked. The work has a surprisingly contemporary flavor. Certain learned humanists thought poorly of anyone who did not mock God; these scholars thought that no one could be learned and hold to the gospel. Calvin acknowledged that there are offences from the gospel itself, particularly Christ's demand of self-surrender. In his own day, another cause of potential offence was the socio-political upheaval that sometimes accompanied the turn to Protestantism. Infighting in the church was another perennial source of scandal.[25]

## IV. THE EUCHARISTIC CONTROVERSY

One of the saddest segments of sixteenth-century history concerns these heated debates between the Swiss Reformed and the German Lutherans surrounding the nature of the Lord's Supper.[26]

Some outline is needed of the historical context of John Calvin's *Defensio sanae et orthodoxae doctrinae de sacramentis* of 1555. By 1528, Martin Bucer of Strasbourg, Johannes Oecolampadius of Basle, and Ulrich Zwingli of Zurich unanimously held ". . . that it may not be proved from Scripture that the body and blood of Christ are actually bodily received in the bread of the Eucharist".[27] Luther disagreed with this interpretation of the Supper, and a meeting was organized to discuss the issues. That meeting, or colloquy, held at the castle of Marburg in 1529, produced no harmony between the two Protestant groups but left the Swiss Reformed smarting from Luther's condemnation.[28]

Later, Bucer and Philip Melanchthon agreed on what is called the *Cassel Formula* on the Lord's Supper. They affirmed that "Christ was truly and really received; that the bread and wine were *signia exhibitiva* with which were received at the same time the body and blood of Christ . . . what is posited of the one may be posited of the other."[29] The Second Swiss Confession, known as the *Confessio fidei de eucharistia*, bolstered what may be called a "non-Lutheran" position on the Supper.[30]

Martin Luther answered the Swiss confession with his *Kurzes Bekenntnis vom heiligen Sakrament wider Schwenckfeld und die Schweizer* in 1544. As expected, a Zurich response appeared swiftly, the *Wahrhaftes Bekenntnis der Diener der Kirche zu Zurich* in 1545.

The sphere of politics always played a role in theological debate, even in what appears to be a purely theological issue. In 1547, Emperor Charles V had successfully attacked south Germany, forcing it to come under his political control. The city of Geneva, concerned about the situation, sent Calvin to the other Swiss cities, including Zurich, to confer upon the political conditions. While he was in Zurich, Heinrich Bullinger gave Calvin a copy of his treatise on the Lord's Supper, called *Absoluta de Christi Domini et catholicae ecclesiae Sacramentis tractatio*.[31]

The apex of Swiss unity was reached on the Supper a few years later with the Zurich Agreement or *Consensus Tigurinus* of 1549.[32] The *Consensus Tigurinus* was ratified in May, 1549, but was not published until two years later. After the Latin original, a German translation by Bullinger and a French translation by Calvin followed.

It was in the midst of this turmoil that Joachim Westphal, a pastor in Hamburg, published the *Farrago of Confused and Divergent Opinions on the Lord's Supper* in 1552 against the *Consensus Tigurinus* of 1549.[33] Westphal condemned both Zwingli and Calvin as heretics for denying a literal eating of Christ's body in the Lord's Supper.[34] John Calvin's *Defensio sanae et orthodoxae doctrinae de sacramentis* (1555)[35] was his response to Westphal.

John à Lasko had informed Calvin that he was going to respond to Westphal's *Farrago*. Heinrich Bullinger fully supported that idea and had hoped that Calvin would respond to Westphal's book entitled *Right Belief*, as well. Moreover, Pierre Viret of Lausanne thought that he would respond to Westphal, and Calvin wrote to encourage him to take up the pen, thus sparing Calvin the effort. However, months passed and no one had begun his work.

However, in September of 1554, Calvin informed Bullinger that a response was forthcoming and, within a month, the draft was sent to Zurich. Calvin solicited Zurich's input on the work, and consequently received it.[36] He promptly responded to the suggestions and submitted a second draft by

the end of the week. The *Defensio sanae et orthodoxae doctrinae de sacramentis* was approved and published in Zurich in 1555, but Calvin did not
explicitly name Westphal in it.[37] The hope of many of the Swiss was that
the controversy would now end. Calvin also believed that he had Philip
Melanchthon's support on the nature of the Lord's Supper, and thus carried
a hope for peace – though it was evidently a false hope in the end.[38] However, this theological defence did not satisfy the Germans, nor did it stop
their attacks. In response, Calvin published his second defense, *Secunda
Defensio piae et orthodoxae de Sacramentis fidei contra Ioachimi Westphali
calumnias*, in 1556.[39]

In the *Secunda Defensio*[40] Calvin reminded his readers that neither in
the *Consensus Tigurinus* nor in later writings on the Lord's Supper had
anyone been attacked by name. The peace that had been coveted by the
*Consensus Tigurinus* was, as Calvin said ironically, used "as a kind of Furies'
torch to rekindle the flame."[41]

The main issues, as Calvin saw them, were threefold: first, whether "the
bread of the Supper is substantially the body of Christ"; second, whether
the body of Christ "is immense, and exists everywhere without place";
finally, whether or not there may be a "figure of speech" in Christ's words
of institution.[42]

The Swiss maintained that "the flesh of Christ gives life, and that we
are truly made partakers of it in the Supper," but they would not affirm that
the "bread is substantially the body." The Swiss also argued that the Holy
Spirit "transfuses life into us from the flesh of Christ," but again would not
agree that "the body of Christ is actually placed before us."[43] They also
believed that there was sufficient warrant from Scripture concerning the
sacraments, that "an analogy is drawn between the sign and the visible
action and the spiritual reality."[44]

Calvin's *Second Defence* against Westphal was presented in the style
typical of sixteenth-century theological polemic. "If he is to be believed,"
asserted Calvin, then "I exhibit canine eloquence."

> Although I long not for the praise of eloquence, I am not so devoid of
> the gift of speaking as to [be] obliged to be eloquent by barking . . .
> From the withered flowers which he sheds over his discourse, it is
> plain how very jejune a rhetorician he is, while his intemperance
> sounds more of the Cyclops than anything human. One thing I deny
> not: I am not less alert in pursuing the sacrilegious, than the faithful
> dog in hunting off thieves.[45]

Nonetheless, the publication of Calvin's 172-page treatise did not end his
conflict with Westphal. The *Last Admonition to Westphal*, subtitled: *Who if
he heeds it not, must henceforth be treated in the way which Paul prescribes*

*for obstinate heretics*,[46] contains quite a bit of heat. Calvin's methodological approach in the treatise hinges upon a few presuppositions. Calvin accuses Westphal of three crimes: first, charges of heresy against the Swiss were unwarranted.[47] Second, Westphal unfairly slandered both the living and the dead, even when Westphal's own name was never mentioned in public.[48] Finally, Westphal's debating presupposition, that heretics should be treated harshly and be silent when proven wrong, was true in principle but rightly applied to Westphal as opposed to the Swiss![49]

Armed with those rules of debate Calvin had decided to sharpen his pen. And sharp it was! It was the sharpness of Calvin's pen that Westphal protested. In response, Calvin did not deny Westphal's charge that his response was "full of sting and virulence." Rather, he retorted, "I am not surprised at the former epithet, nor am I sorry that men so stupid have, at least, felt some pricks."[50] Westphal charged that Calvin threw every possible insult at him, to which Calvin countered, "When he says in another place that I have anxiously laboured not to omit any kind of insult, how much he is mistaken will best appear from the fact."[51] Perhaps with a silent sigh, Calvin noted:

> [S]ince his ferocity has proved intractable, it is easy to see the frivolousness and childishness of all his declamation. As if lions and bears, after rushing madly at every one in their way, should complain that they do not meet with soothing treatment, this delicate little man, after atrociously attacking the doctrine of Christ and his ministers, regards it as a great crime that he is not treated like a brother.[52]

Furthermore, concerning the charges that Westphal was being unjustly persecuted by Calvin, "One would say, that we have here Julian the apostate, while he cruelly rages against the whole Christian name, discoursing in mockery about bearing the cross."[53]

Westphal refused to be silenced. After Calvin's final reply, he published *Some Apologetic Writings* in 1558 and *Answer to Some of the Outrageous Lies of John Calvin* for Calvin personally. The debates continued, but Calvin no longer joined in the fray.

## V. THEOLOGICAL CONTROVERSY: *AGAINST SERVETUS*; *AGAINST MENNO*; *AGAINST PIGHIUS AND BOLSEC*; *AGAINST CAROLI*

These are theological works written against Protestants. Calvin's *Defence of the Doctrine of the Trinity Against Servetus* was published in 1554, after Servetus' death.[54]

In much of the popular literature concerning Calvin, certain misconceptions are tacitly accepted without a critical analysis of historical sources and historical circumstances. The force of the misconception regarding Calvin and Servetus could be summarized like this: Calvin the religious zealot was directly responsible for the execution of an extremely talented medical doctor and theologian named Servetus. The reason was that Servetus would not become a "Calvinist," and was just as talented as Calvin; Calvin had him executed because of either jealousy or religious fanaticism on the same level as any current Ayatollah. This vision of the circumstances, although popular, is false.

Michael Servetus was in fact an extremely talented person. He was capable in both theology and medicine. He is even credited with making some pioneering discoveries in the latter field. However, perhaps in light of his great abilities, he also had some serious personality flaws. In 1531, Servetus published his first book, entitled *On the Trinity*, which was roundly condemned by the reformers. Nevertheless, in that same decade, Calvin made a special trip to Paris to meet with Servetus, to, as Calvin recalled, "gain him for the Lord." However, Servetus failed to show up for the meeting. We must remember that Calvin's trip to Paris was made at great risk. He had been condemned to death in France, and Calvin put his very life on the line. However, Calvin considered a theological reconciliation with Servetus to be sufficiently important.

Communication between Calvin and Servetus continued into the forties. As one reads the letters, it is easy to get the distinct impression that there was something seriously wrong with Servetus, mentally. One outstanding Calvin scholar has found it hard to believe that Servetus was completely sane at that time.[55] In the 1550s, Servetus' pen was again active, this time authoring *The Restoration of Christianity*; this work was condemned as blasphemous and heretical by Protestants and Roman Catholics alike.

Servetus had been arrested by the Roman Catholic authorities in France and condemned to death as a heretic, but he escaped from jail. For some very strange reason Servetus travelled to Geneva and was sitting in the congregation when Calvin was preaching. He was recognized, and the city magistrates had him arrested. Previously, Calvin had warned Servetus that his safety could not be guaranteed in the city of Geneva.

Servetus was tried by the city for heresy and his sad story ends in execution, being declared an unrepentant heretic. Although Calvin approved of the death sentence, as did all Protestants at the time, he was not legally responsible for the execution of Servetus; only the city magistrates could perform such acts. All this will hardly sound like much of a defense to those who attempt to believe the worst about John Calvin! However, it should also be added that Calvin was persistent in his personal appeals to Servetus that he change his mind as he visited him in prison. Calvin furthermore requested that Servetus' sentence be reduced from burning to beheading, a much more humane means of execution, but that request was denied by the city authorities.[56]

Today there are no "Christian governments" who exercise the option of death for blasphemy. That type of activity would be relegated only to certain extreme Islamic groups. Furthermore, that type of action would have been rightly condemned by other governments and medias. Nevertheless, whether we believe it to be proper for any government to execute heretics of the church is a moot question. In the sixteenth century, no enlightened civil leader believed that the government did not have the right to execute blasphemers and heretics, and John Calvin was certainly a child of the sixteenth century. Thus, when contemporary readers understand the sixteenth-century cultural context in which Calvin lived, this act of execution, although not to be regarded with approval, is much more understandable. The sixteenth century was not necessarily any more violent than our own, but the doctrine and purity of the church were guarded with much more passion and care than is comfortable for us today.[57]

Calvin's *Contra Mennonem* (*Against Menno*) was an answer to the request of his friend Martin Micron for help against Menno. We note from Calvin's correspondence that he had heard about Menno's theology as early as 1545, and that is also the year of à Lasco's book against Menno.[58] Calvin's work analyzed each of Menno's twenty articles on the incarnation. Menno thought that Christ was incarnate without partaking of Mary's flesh. His was a heavenly humanity, becoming a man in Mary but not of Mary. Menno wondered how Jesus could be formed of Mary's flesh and not come under sin. It was a birth "without a mother"; she only fed him but gave nothing of her substance. The second Adam corresponded to the first Adam as he was before the Fall in Paradise.[59]

Albert Pighius was a Dutch Roman Catholic theologian who responded against Calvin's 1539 *Institutes*.[60] Calvin's work *Against Pigius*[61] came out in 1543. Calvin had addressed only six of Pighius' ten subjects, focusing on the bondage and liberation of the human will. Before he could address predestination and the last four books, Pighius died.[62]

Not that the issue of predestination would lack attention! Jerome Bolsec had served as a monk and lived in Paris. Leaving the Roman Church, he became a court physician outside of Geneva. Bolsec was against Calvin's notion of predestination, accusing Calvin of making God the author of sin. The ministers of Geneva asked for advice on what to do with him from the other Swiss Protestant churches. The theological issue on the table concerned the universality of salvation. As a result, Bolsec was banished from Geneva.[63]

The Bolsec controversy led Calvin to address the issue of predestination more fully. He wrote *De aeterna Dei praedestinatione . . . (Concerning the Eternal Predestination of God)* in 1552.[64] In it he returned to the debate with Pighius which had happened nine years before. This is the largest and most sustained treatment Calvin wrote on the doctrine of predestination.

Peter Caroli, recipient of the work *Against Caroli*,[65] was a doctor of theology and a theologian of Sorbonne who turned to Protestantism and was forced to flee from France in 1533. After some time in Geneva and Basle (August, 1535–March, 1536), Caroli was chosen to be the professor of Old Testament and the primary preaching minister in the Swiss city of Lausanne. That was the same year as Calvin's arrival at Geneva. Immediately upon his arrival, Caroli caused a disturbance in Lausanne in that he apparently still held to the efficacy of prayers for the dead. Perhaps to counter-attack his accusers, Caroli charged Viret, who was a pastor in Lausanne, Calvin, and Farel with Arianism. To resolve the situation, there were discussions in Lausanne in October of 1536, and later in Berne, and finally a synod met in Lausanne in May of 1537. These meetings supported Farel and Viret. But it was Farel and Caroli who were to debate the issues in Berne in June of 1537. However, the debate never occurred because Caroli returned to the Roman Church. Shortly thereafter (1539), Caroli went back to Protestantism, was forgiven and received, and given a pastorate. However, in 1543, Caroli published a tract against Calvin and Farel which in turn produced Calvin's *Pro G. Farello et collegis ejus* in 1545.[66]

## CONCLUSION

Calvin was a prolific controversialist. The body of works examined is extensive, but not everything has been analysed here, including his writings against the Italian anti-trinitarians,[67] and the Pole Stancarius.[68] For the contemporary reader, once the very foreign genre of controversial works is overcome, tremendous insight into the theological, political, and social issues of the day is gained through the polemical works.

### Notes

1 *Responsio ad Lutherum*, ed. John M. Headley, trans. Sister Scholastic Mandeville, 2 vols. (New Haven: Yale University Press, 1969), II/10, pp. 433 and 434.
2 William G. Naphy, *Calvin and the Consolidation of the Genevan Reformation with a New Preface* (rpt., Louisville: Westminster John Knox Press, 2003), 157–60.
3 See the chapters by Thompson, DeVries, etc.

4 See Alfred Erichson, *Bibliographia Calviniana: Catalogus chronologicus operum Calvini. Catalogus systematicus operum quae sunt de Calvino; cum indice auctorum alphabetico* (Nieuwkoop: B. De Graef, 1960), 115 ff.

5 An English translation is found in *T&T* vol. III. For further literature see W. de Greef, *The Writings of John Calvin: An Introductory Guide*, trans. Lyle Bierma (Grand Rapids: Baker, 1993), 165–67.

6 "An excellent treatise of the immortalytie of the soule By which is proued, that the soules, after their departure out of the bodies, are avvake and doe lyue, contrary to that erronious opinion of certen ignorant persons, who thinke them to lye asleape vntill the day of iudgement. Set fourth by M. Iohn Caluin, and englished from the French by T[homas]. Stocker" (London: John Day, 1581).

7 *Brieve instruction pour armer tous bons fideles contre les erreurs de la secte commune des Anabaptistes. CO* VII, 49–142. A modern English translation can be found in Calvin, *Treatises against the Anabaptists and against the Libertines*, ed. and trans. Benjamin W. Farley (Grand Rapids: Baker, 1982), 11–158.

8 For more information, see Karl H. Wyneken, "Calvin and Anabaptism," in Richard C. Gamble, ed., *Articles on Calvin and Calvinism*, V, and de Greef, *Writings of John Calvin*, 167 n. 4.

9 *Contre la secte phantastique et furieuse des Libertins que se nomment Spirituelz. CO* VII, 149–248. For an English translation see Calvin, *Treatises*, ed. Farley, 159–326. The following year, still in French, a work was published in Strasbourg that combined the two.

10 Zwingli had many dealings with Anabaptists before Calvin. He wrote *In catabaptistarum strophas elemenchus.* See Richard Stauffer, "Zwingli et Calvin, critiques de la confession de Schleitheim," in Marc Kienhard, ed., *The Origins and Characteristics of Anabaptism* (The Hague: Nijhof, 1977).

11 For more information, see Benjamin Farley, "The Theology of Calvin's Tract *Against the Libertines*" and Allen Verhey and Robert G. Wilkie, "*Against the Libertines,*" both in Gamble, ed., *Articles on Calvin and Calvinism*, V; and de Greef, *Writings of John Calvin*, 169–71.

12 It came out with the Strasbourg publisher Rithelius. It was published again in 1540 in Geneva in Latin and in French. See de Greef, *Writings of John Calvin*, 152 n. 8 for bibliography. An English translation is found in *T&T*, I, 91–129.

13 An English translation is in *T&T*, III, 13–169.

14 *Traité des reliques.* For text history see de Greef, *Writings of John Calvin*, 156 n. 15.

15 *De sacris reliquiis Christi et sanctorum eius, Brevis contra Ioannis Calvini calumnias et blasphemias responsio* (Mainz, 1549).

16 The English translation is titled *An Admonition, Showing the Advantages Which Christendom May Derive from an Inventory of Relics.* See *T&T*, I, 330–74.

17 *Interim adultero-germanum, cui adiecta est Vera Christianae pacificationis et ecclesiae reformandae ratio. CO* VII, 54–674. It was published in French in 1549. There was also a German translation. De Greef says concerning it: "The peculiar thing about the German edition is that a section of the original work was left out, and in a critical note Calvin was accused of Pelagianism in connection with his conception of infant baptism." To correct this and make other editorial changes, Calvin published *Appendix libelli adversus Interim adultero-germanum* in 1550. See De Greef, *Writings of John Calvin*, 163. For an English translation see *T&T*, III, 170–220.

18  *T&T*, III, 240–41.
19  English translation in *T&T*, vol. I, 193–288.
20  *The Necessity of Reforming the Church*, *T&T*, I, 196.
21  Found in *T&T*, as *On Shunning the Unlawful Rites of the Ungodly, and Preserving the Purity of the Christian Religion*, vol. III, 330–76.
22  *Advertissement contre l'astrologie qu'on appelle iudiciaire: et autres curiositez qui regnent auiourd'huy au monde*. First translated into English in 1561 and published in London. A modern French edition is *Advertissement contre l'astrologie judiciaire*, ed. Olivier Millet (Geneva: Librairie Droz, 1985).
23  Calvin, "A warning against judiciary astrology and other prevalent curiosities," translated and introduced by Mary Potter, *Calvin Theological Journal* 18/2 (November 1983), 189.
24  *De scandalis quibus hodie plerique absterrentur, nonnulli etiam alienantur a pura evangelii doctrina. CO* VIII, 1–84. Printed by Crispin; there was also a French edition at the same time.
25  An English translation is John Calvin, *Concerning Scandals*, trans. John W. Fraser (Grand Rapids: Eerdmans, 1978).
26  Parts of this section will be published as "Calvin and Vermigli: a Study in the Foundations of Reformed Eucharistic Theology," in Frank A. James III, ed., *Peter Martyr Vermigli and the European Reformations*, Studies in the History of Christian Thought (Leiden: E. J. Brill, forthcoming).
27  See Hastings Eels, *Martin Bucer* (New York: Russell & Russell, rpt. 1971), 70–92.
28  Literature on the Marburg colloquy is vast. See Walther Koehler, *Zwingli und Luther: Ihr Streit uber das Abendmahl nach sinen politischen und religiousen bezeiehungen* (2 vols., rpt., London: Johnson, 1971). Peter Buhler, "Der Abendmahlsstreit der Reformatoren und seine aktuellen Implikationen," *Theologische Zeitschrift* 35 (1979), 228–41. Eels, *Martin Bucer*, lists literature at p. 452 n. 151.
29  December 30, 1534. See Eels, *Martin Bucer*, 173–82.
30  Ibid., p. 214. English translation in John K. S. Reid, trans. and ed., *Calvin: Theological Treatises* (Philadelphia: Westminster Press, 1954), 167–69.
31  Greef, *Writings of John Calvin*, 190–93. Also during the First Schmalkaldic War Peter Martyr Vermigli was forced to flee the continent, leaving Strasbourg, and made his way to England. Cf. John Patrick Donnelly, trans. and ed., *Peter Martyr Vermigli: Dialogue on the Two Natures in Christ*, Sixteenth Century Essays and Studies, vol. 2 (Kirksville, MO: Thomas Jefferson University Press, 1995), xi. Vermigli was later joined by Bucer, who went to Cambridge.
32  Text in B. J. Kidd, *Documents of the Continental Reformation* (Oxford, 1911), "The Consensus Tigurinus," May 1549, no. 319, pp. 652–56. English translation by Ian D. Bunting, *Journal of Presbyterian History* 44 (1966), 45–61. See also P. Schaff, *The Creeds of Christendom*, 3 vols. (rpt., Grand Rapids: Baker, 1977), I, 471–73. See also Timothy George, "John Calvin and the Agreement of Zurich (1549)," in *John Calvin and the Church: A Prism of Reform* (Louisville: Westminster John Knox Press, 1990), 42–58.
33  *Farrago confusanearum et inter se dissiduntium opinionum de Coena Domini, ex Sacramentariorium libris congesta* (Magdeburg, 1552). Cf. Karl Moenckeberg, *Ioachim Westphal und Iohannes Calvin* (Hamburg, 1865). Cf. Joseph N. Tylenda, "The Calvin–Westphal Exchange: The Genesis of Calvin's treatises against Westphal," *Calvin Theological Journal* 9 (1974), 182–209.

34  Donnelly, *Peter Martyr Vermigli*, xiii.

35  *OS* II, 263–87. French translation by Calvin in 1555. Cf. Uwe Plath, *Calvin und Basel in den Jahren 1552–1556* (Zurich: Theologischer Verlag, 1974), 174–92. Cf. Bernard Cottret, "Pour une semiotique de la Reforme: Le consensus Tigurinus et La Brève Resolution . . . (1555) de Calvin," *Annales: Economies, Sociétés, Civilisation* 39 (1984), 265–85. Cf. Kilian McDonnell, *John Calvin, the Church, and the Eucharist* (Princeton: Princeton University Press, 1967), 177.

36  Tylenda, "The Calvin–Westphal Exchange," 192.

37  *T&T*, II. The text had three sections: a dedication letter, a defense of the *Consensus Tigurinus*, and the text of the *Consensus*.

38  See Tylenda, "The Calvin–Westphal Exchange", 197 f. "How lamentably Calvin had misjudged the strength of the Westphal party, and how incautiously he had overestimated Melanchthon's popularity!," p. 204.

39  *CO* IX, 41–120. Cf. *TT*, 258–324, and *T&T*, II, 245 ff.

40  *Secunda Defensio piae et orthodoxae . . .* (Jean Crispin, Geneva 1556). *OC* IX, 45–120; English translation in *T&T*, II, 236–318.

41  *T&T*, II, 231.

42  Ibid., 232.

43  Ibid., 233.

44  Ibid., 289.

45  Ibid., 311. The *Secunda Defensio* continues: "But while all see it to be your purpose completely to destroy the reputation of Oecolampadius, Zuinglius, Bucer, Peter Martyr, Bullinger, John à Lasco, do you think there is any pious and impartial man in the world who does not feel indignant at your malicious detraction?" Ibid., 245. Furthermore, "with regard to the discussions which have taken place in England, I would rather leave it to Peter Martyr, a faithful teacher of the church of Strasburg, to give the answer, which, I trust, he is now preparing." Ibid., 291.

46  *Ultimo admonitio Ioannis Calvini ad Ioachimum Westphalum, cui nisi obtemperet, eo loco posthac habendus erit, quo pertinaces haereticos haberit iubet Paulus* (Jean Crispin, Geneva 1557). *OC* IX, 137–252. English Translation *T&T*, II, 319–449.

47  *Calvin's Selected Works*, II, 321. "Why did Joachim, when so mildly requested, choose to cry out heresy, rather than to point out the error, if any there was?"

48  Ibid., 323. "After our Agreement was published, and Westphal had full liberty to correct any thing that was faulty, calumniously searching in all quarters for an appearance of repugnance, he in savage mood lashed the living and the dead. I, in repelling this savage attack, refrained from giving his name, in order that if he was of a temper that admitted of cure his ignominy might be buried." "Considering that this obstinate intemperance was not to be cured by gentle remedies, I took the liberty to sharpen my pen."

49  Ibid., 324. "Joachim insists that anything is lawful to him against us, because, as he says, he is defending true doctrine against impious error."

50  Ibid., 320.

51  Ibid., 321.

52  Ibid., 323.

53  Ibid., 320.

54  *Defensio orthodoxas fidei de sacro Trinitat, contra prodigiousos errores Michaelis Serviti Hispani. CO* VIII, 453–644. Published in 1554 with a French translation, it appeared in Latin, by Stephanus, and in French in Geneva by Crispin.

55 T. H. L. Parker, *John Calvin: A Biography* (Philadelphia: Westminster Press, 1975), 118.

56 The acts against Servetus can be found in *CO* VIII, 721–872. Servetus was accused of 38 points of departure in religion and responded to the charges. Cf. *CO* VIII, 501–53 and 799–801.

57 For further information, see Roland Bainton, "Servetus and the Genevan Libertines," and G. Coleman Luck, "Calvin and Servetus," in Gamble, ed., *Articles on Calvin and Calvinism*, V. See also Jerome Friedman, *Michael Servetus: A Case Study in Total Heresy* (Geneva: Librairie Droz, 1978).

58 W. Balke, *Calvin and the Anabaptist Radicals*, trans. William J. Heynen (Grand Rapids: Eerdmans, 1981), 202 ff.

59 Ibid., 206: "one cannot imageine anthing to be prouder than an ass, more impudent than this dog." "But who beyond the communal opinon of all people would believe the figments of an unlearned man". Menno is "a writer in blood, a man of blood who approved of the persecution of the faithful children of God."

60 *De libero hominis arbitrio et divina gratia, libri decem* (1542).

61 *Defensio sanae et orthodoxae doctrinae de servitute et liberatione humani arbitrii adversus calumnia Alberti Pighii Campensis* (Gerard, Geneva 1543). *CO* VI, 225–404. English text, *Calvin's Calvinism: Treatises on the Eternal Predestination of God and the Secret Providence of God*, trans. Henry P. Cole (Grand Rapids: Eerdmans, 1987). See L. F. Schulze, *Calvin's Reply to Pighius* (Potchefstroom, South Africa: Pro Rege, 1971). John Calvin, *The Bondage and Liberation of the Will. A Defence of the Orthodox doctrine of human choice against Pighius*, ed. A. N. S. Lane, trans. G. I. Davies (Grand Rapids: Baker, 1996).

62 For further information see L. F. Schulze, "Calvin's Reply to Pighius – A Micro and a Macro View," in Gamble, ed., *Articles on Calvin and Calvinism*, V.

63 De Greef, *Writings of John Calvin*, 118–19; For a further account see P. C. Holtrop, *The Bolsec Controversy on Predestination from 1551 to 1555*, I (Lewiston, NY: Edwin Mellen Press, 1993).

64 See *Concerning the Eternal Predestination of God*, trans. and introduction by J. K. S. Reid (rpt., Louisville: Westminster John Knox Press, 1997).

65 *Confessio de Trinitate propter calumnias P. Caroli. CO* IX, 703–10. Cf. also Calvin's letter to Caroli, *CO* XI, 72–75 and the *Pro Farello et collegis eius adversus Petri Caroli calumnias defensio Nicolai Gallasii*, which was written by Calvin, *CO* VII, 289–340.

66 For further information see Richard C. Gamble, "Calvin's Theological Method. The Case of Caroli", in W. Van 't Spijker, ed., *Calvin. Erbe und Auftrag. Feschrift für Wilhelm Neuser* (Kampen: Kok, 1991), 130–37. See also Calvin, *Defense de Guillaume Farel et de ses collègues Contre les calomnies de Pierre Caroli par Nicoal Des Gallars. Avec diverses lettres de Calvin, Caroli, Farel, Viret et autres documents traduits et presentés par Jean-Francois Gounelle* (Paris: Presses Universitaires de France 1994).

67 *Impietas Velentini Gentilis detecta et palam traducta, qui Christum non sine sacrilege blasphemia Deum essentiatium esse fingit. CO* IX, 361–420.

68 *Responsum ad fratres Polonos, quomodo mediator sit Christus, ad refutandum Stancaro errorem* (1560). *CO* IX, 333–42. *Ministorum ecclesia Genevensis responsio ad nobiles Polonos et Franciscum Stancarum Mantuanum ad controversia mediatoris* (1561). *CO* IX, 345–58.

# Part III

*After Calvin*

## 12  The spread of Calvin's thought

ANDREW PETTEGREE

In the spring of 1552 John Calvin in Geneva received a letter from the Polish reformer John à Lasco, recently appointed superintendent of the new Stranger Church in London. The church had two congregations, a Dutch and a French, and the French had recently been disturbed by controversy when a newcomer criticized an aspect of the church's teaching on the grounds that it diverged from that of the Genevan church. At issue was whether the Virgin Mary should be given the title the Mother of God. Calvin's reply was careful but firm. While not denying the difference of opinion he nevertheless sharply reproved those who had disturbed the church by invoking his name, or as he put it, making "an idol of me, and a Jerusalem of Geneva." For as he went on, the more critical issue was that of church order, and unity: "If those who have stirred up these strifes among you have taken occasion to do so through the diversity of your ceremonies, they have ill understood in what the unity of Christians consists, and how every member ought to conform himself to the body of the Church in which he lives."[1]

For some modern readers this answer might come as a surprise, as it no doubt was to the disappointed advocates of Genevan practice in London. For over the centuries Calvin has become almost a byword for doctrinal rigor and remorseless immutability – an image formed, as much as anything, by the relentless pursuit of those few foolhardy spirits that dared to question his teaching in Geneva itself. But as his influence spread through Europe Calvin understood clearly enough that different circumstances demanded a variety of approaches to church-building.

The exchange with the London French church came early, at a stage when Calvin was only beginning to be a force in the wider Protestant movement. But in fact the principles he laid down here were ones he followed with commendable consistency. When in 1554 a portion of the now dispersed London French community arrived in the Rhineland city of Wesel, the local Lutheran authorities granted permission to settle and establish a new community only on the condition that the newcomers attended Communion in the local parish churches. To the refugees this was too much to stomach, and they appealed to Calvin for endorsement of this view. But Calvin once again counseled caution, and conformity. The Genevan reformer thought it better to accept the distasteful Lutheran practices than to lose the chance of a refuge altogether. This advice was all the more remarkable since at precisely this time Calvin had embarked on a bitter polemical exchange with the Lutheran minister Joachim Westphal. But he did not deny (and this was the crucial point) that Lutherans were for all their differences members of the true church; and this was the overriding principle that guided his advice to those who found themselves in Lutheran territories.[2]

What was true of Calvin's lifetime was all the more so after his death. As Calvin's movement spread and took root in the years after 1560 it necessarily adapted itself to a whole variety of different circumstances: sometimes in national churches, sometimes in city environments, sometimes where the state power was as cooperative as in Geneva, elsewhere frankly hostile. In different parts of Europe different aspects of Calvin's teaching would at different times seem more or less appropriate and applicable. There would be churches that held the Genevan reformer in great reverence but would, nevertheless, when occasion demanded, totally disregard his teaching on quite critical issues.

Here I will tease out some of these issues by considering, for the latter part of the sixteenth century, three aspects of Calvin's wider European influence. First I will survey the general scope of his writings, which circulated widely and in many European languages. Then I will consider the more specific examples of his teaching with regard to relations with the state and its interpretation in time of tension and civil strife (endemic in this most turbulent period of the Reformation era). Finally I will consider his prescriptions for church organization, often regarded (then and now) as the defining feature of a true Calvinist polity.

## CALVIN'S WRITINGS

We now honor Calvin most of all as the founder of an enduring family of churches; and as an author, especially of the *Institutes*, one of the core texts of Protestantism. So it is as well to remind ourselves that Calvin's contemporary fame came very largely through his reputation as a preacher. Calvin preached indefatigably (at least five sermons a fortnight throughout his time in Geneva) and well; these were, as we know both from contemporary reports and surviving texts, spell-binding performances, which moved their audience to both tears and anger. Early modern cities vied for the best and most renowned preachers, and the Genevan city fathers had reason to bless their good fortune even as they smarted from Calvin's forthright denunciation of their failings; for people came from far and wide simply to hear Calvin.[3] Of course his preaching also acted as a magnet for his fellow French citizens when they too chose exile.

Calvin took immense pains over his sermons, which moved systematically through exposition of books of the Bible. Yet he personally regarded his sermons as essentially ephemeral, things of the moment, intended for his Genevan congregation alone. Those texts that survive as manuscripts are packed with contemporary references to current Genevan issues, to which he devoted the same forthright clear-mindedness as in his biblical expositions. But in his own mind the sermons certainly did not have the same status as his biblical commentaries, which he prepared with an eye to a wider and more scholarly audience. That the sermons survive at all we owe not to Calvin but to an inner circle of admirers who arranged for them to be taken down verbatim by a specially designated scribe. This was paid for, for reasons that are not entirely clear, by the *Bourse Française*, the fund established to support poor French immigrants.[4] Although a considerable number of sermons were published during Calvin's lifetime Calvin himself did little to assist their preparation for the press.[5] A large number, however, languished unpublished in the city archives until the nineteenth century, when they were disposed of. Most were sold for waste paper and have been lost; only a few volumes have been preserved.

Even among those works that Calvin himself prepared for publication he preserved a clear mental hierarchy of merit. During his early years in Geneva he published a number of vernacular works that were intended to address a particular audience or contemporary issue; these were small, often polemical, works which he would have regarded as of limited importance. In his mature years most of his time and most sustained effort was devoted to the great biblical commentaries, written and published in Latin for a scholarly audience. These ran to many thousands, even hundreds of thousands, of words, and might occupy him for over a year at a time. For this work too he often relied heavily on the editorial assistance of close colleagues, such as his devoted secretary Nicolas des Gallars. Several editions were prepared largely by des Gallars based on notes taken during Calvin's exegetical lectures.

The publication of Calvin's works during his own lifetime thus had regard for two principal audiences: the evangelicals of his own native land, France, and the wider international, Latinate, scholarly community. The concern for France was evident in the rush of small vernacular writings during the mid-1540s: the treatise on relics, the *Petit traité de la Cene*, the anti-Nicodemite writings. Many of these small vernacular works enjoyed a second vogue in the years immediately before the outbreak of the French wars of religion. The establishment of formally recognized churches right at the end of Calvin's life brought a new wave of French editions, this time of the more substantial biblical commentaries. The pattern of publication, however, changed abruptly with Calvin's death in 1564. The following year saw a fresh wave of editions in French, perhaps stimulated by news of Calvin's passing (they included Beza's life of Calvin). But between 1567 and the end of the century there were only nine further editions of works by Calvin in French. Calvin's works represent less than 1 percent of Protestant works published in French in the remaining thirty-two years of the century.[6] For answers to more contemporary concerns in the unsettled years of the French wars of religion Huguenot readers now looked to a new generation of authors: Theodore de Bèze, of course, but also Antoine de la Roche Chandieu, Jean de l'Espine, Philippe du Plessis Mornay, and others.

By far the largest market for Calvin's writings in the later part of the sixteenth century was not his native France, but England.[7] This may initially come as something of a surprise, for commentators on the English Reformation have often presented England as at best a semi-detached part of the international Calvinist community.[8] Evidence from a painstaking reconstruction of the publishing history suggests that this is wildly exaggerated, for English readers apparently had an almost insatiable appetite for Calvin's works. Among the nearly fifty editions of Calvin's works published in English during the reign of Elizabeth were a full range of Calvin's weightiest works: the *Institutes* and his biblical commentaries. England was also the only European tradition that developed a popular abridgement of Calvin's *Institutes*. This was the work of Edmund Bunny, a shrewd and enterprising popular writer who also published a Protestant version of the popular devotional text, the *Imitation of Christ*.[9] The largest wave of publication came during the 1580s, a period in which English printing houses were also turning out large numbers of English translations of the works of other great figures of continental Protestantism, including Pierre Viret and Martin Luther. But if such a concentrated effort hints at official encouragement, then these publications were also clearly a commercial success. Evidence from surviving wills and inventories suggests that Calvin clearly outstripped all other authors, English or continental, in English book collections.

By whatever measure one adopts, Calvin emerges as the dominant force in the theology of the Elizabethan church. This is even more the case if one considers that his theological influence would be mediated primarily not through English translations, however impressively numerous, but through Latin editions. Between Calvin's death and the end of the century there were a further sixty-five editions of his works in Latin, almost without exception substantial folios of the *Institutes* and his biblical commentaries. Only a small number of these editions were actually published in England, but that is hardly material. The market in Latin books during the sixteenth century was a full international one, and little can be inferred about a likely market from place of publication.

One can, however, see some straws in the wind from a close inspection of surviving copies, as for instance the 1568 Genevan Latin edition of Calvin's *Institutes*. Of the forty surviving copies eighteen are located in British libraries and ten in the United States; evidence of both the contemporary impact of Calvin in the English-speaking world and that of English-language libraries on modern book science.[10] Another clear indication of the almost inexhaustible appetite for Calvin is the great Latin edition of Calvin's correspondence, published at Geneva in 1575. Over seventy copies of this magnificent folio still survive in public collections, and the following year saw both a further issue and a genuine second edition, published at Lausanne (together, a further hundred listed copies).[11] These are some of the most non-rare books of the sixteenth century.

Calvin's influence on other European vernacular cultures was less striking than in England, but still profound. Late-century editions of Calvin in French were outstripped by the quantities published in both Dutch and German. The number of editions in Dutch of course greatly understates Calvin's influence in the Netherlands, since large proportions of the interested public would have had access to his works either in Latin or in French. Even after the collapse of the principal Calvinist churches in the southern Netherlands in 1582–85 during Parma's campaign of reconquest the internal exile movement stimulated by this ensured that Walloon (that is, French-speaking) Calvinism would find a prominent place in the religious culture of the new Dutch Free State.

Meanwhile Dutch admirers of the Genevan reformer ensured a steady stream of translations of his work into their own language. The first Dutch translation of the *Institutes* appeared in Emden in 1560, the work of the exiled Ghent jurist Jan Dyrkinus.[12] Dyrkinus explained in his preface that he had worked mostly from the Latin edition, referring to the French also in cases of obscurity. Dyrkinus was also responsible for a fine Dutch translation of Heinrich Bullinger's *Decades*, another hugely popular and influential book in the Netherlands. After the success of the revolt had rendered Emden redundant the new Protestant presses of Antwerp and Amsterdam took up the task of rendering Calvin into the vernacular, with further fine editions of Calvin's biblical commentaries and Gospel Harmony.[13]

The German Empire represented Calvinism's hardest and most controversial mission ground. The Peace of Augsburg that brought to an end the conflict between Charles V and the Lutheran princes of the Empire envisaged no place for any other competing Protestant confession. In the longer term, this fatally undermined what was at the time seen as a visionary accommodation between competing religious confessions. In his own homeland the zealous defenders of Luther's memory saw no place for the heirs of the Swiss reform, as Calvin found to his cost when he locked horns with Joachim Westphal of Hamburg over the issue of the sacraments. Calvin mocked Westphal as an ignorant provincial, and was genuinely surprised when German opinion lined up solidly behind the local man. Even Melanchthon (who the Swiss always thought of in some ways as one of them) was forced to beat a tactical retreat. Calvin swiftly came to realize that so public a confrontation had been a bad tactical error, and his subsequent engagement with the affairs of the Empire was far more restrained and circumspect.

Nevertheless, from these unpromising beginnings the influence of Calvinism in the Empire grew steadily as the century wore on. The conversion of the Rhineland Palatinate was the most public early success, but as important in the longer term was the insidious progress of Calvinist theological views in the German universities.[14] These found their most powerful expression in a Calvinist/Melanchthonite syncretism. The highpoint of Philippist influence in the University of Wittenberg was reached with the publication in 1571 of a new catechism of Christoph Pezel that clearly contained a Reformed understanding of the Lord's Supper. The success of Crypto-Calvinism brought an inevitable backlash, first political and then theological, stimulating the arrest or exile of the leading Saxon Calvinists and the dismissal of all Philippists from the University of Wittenberg. The Calvinist threat also brought a theological response with the Formula of Concord, an attempt to unite the German states behind an agreed statement of orthodox Lutheran theology (1580). The development of Calvinism in the Empire was arrested but not reversed, and the last two decades of the century brought a steady wave of conversions among the smaller princely states, particularly of the Rhineland and north-west.[15]

The two major centers of Calvinist intellectual life in the Empire were successively Heidelberg and Herborn. From Heidelberg emanated the first major German editions of Calvin's works; when the reconversion of the Palatinate to Lutheranism closed Heidelberg University to Calvinist influences, many of the professors and students found a home in the new academy of Herborn.[16] In the far north, the city of Emden remained an important beacon of civic Calvinism. The long struggle for supremacy with the counts of East Friesland led ultimately to a final trial of strength and the revolution of 1595. The presiding genius of the Emden church in these years was Menso Alting, one of the emerging cohort of churchmen whose gift lay in interpreting the teachings of Calvin to a new generation. As was the case in Emden, these situations often led Calvin's disciples into theological positions and political actions of which the reformer himself would scarcely have approved.

## THE RIGHT OF RESISTANCE

Calvin's influence radiated out from Geneva through three principal means: his published writings; his correspondence; and the leadership of those men who, trained in Geneva, carried the precepts of the reformer and the practice of his church back to their homelands. Calvin, of course, was an indefatigable correspondent, and a master of the epistolary art. Even in an age that valued the letter as one of the highest literary forms, Calvin achieved in his letters a mastery of style that makes them compelling reading today: many are masterpieces of controlled passion, patient advocacy, and clear-minded exposition.

Nevertheless, the influence of the correspondence, though profound, was far less straightforward than might be inferred from an uncritical reading. For one thing, the period when Calvin was in a position to exercise direct influence over the burgeoning international movement was remarkably brief. Although Calvin returned to Geneva in 1541, it was only in 1555 that the final defeat of his domestic opponents gave him real freedom to direct his gaze abroad. Before this his forays into international church affairs had been extremely hesitant (as with England during the reign of Edward VI) or – remembering the Westphal affair – ill advised.

Even in France, which received the lion's share of Calvin's attention before and after 1555, the real impact of his guiding hand is far from obvious. From the time of the first foundation of churches in France that honored Calvin as their inspiration (1554–56) he pursued a strategy for France of remarkable consistency. To the churches he urged patience and restraint, first in the face of continuing persecution, then, when the political situation turned in their favor, counseling against triumphalism and confrontation. Meanwhile he attempted to effect the conversion of France by winning to the Reformed cause the natural leaders of French society, the Princes of the Blood and the nobility.

In the years between 1555 and Calvin's death in 1564 both parts of this strategy can be seen to have failed spectacularly. As the churches grew in size and ambition, the congregations of urban France seemed increasingly deaf to the reformers' pleas for restraint. Demonstrations, provocation, iconoclasm, and attacks on Catholic clergy became the order of the day as France tumbled increasingly into anarchy.[17] Meanwhile the noble leaders, whom

Calvin had trusted to provide for the orderly transition to true religion, proved slippery friends. Anthony of Navarre, on whom Calvin had lavished endless time and patience, ended his life fighting on the Catholic side in the first of the French wars of religion.[18] His brother Louis of Condé would sign a peace that while protecting the position of the Huguenot nobility would consign the urban churches, the real lifeblood of the movement, to a slow decline.

The conduct of the two brothers was sharply condemned in Geneva, but in truth the extent to which Calvin had been much more than a distant observer of these tumultuous events may truly be doubted. In the mid-1550s the French churches had looked to Geneva for advice and leadership, but as the movement took wing after the death of Henry II (1559) the pace of events overwhelmed the stately strategies of Geneva. The demand for resources – principally ministers and books – far outran what Geneva could provide. To Calvin's evident distress, as France hurtled toward confrontation, the congregations took inspiration not from the repeated counsels of restraint expressed in his letters, but from the more confrontational tone of his youthful polemics. The brilliant excoriating satire of the treatise on relics, which catalogued in humiliating detail the fragments of saints' bodies hoarded by a credulous church, enjoyed an ominous second vogue during these years.

This was important, for over a long writing career Calvin's own views inevitably shifted and refined, as his own perspective developed. The mature patriarch of the Geneva church was not the same man as the young reformer, recently exiled from Paris, contemplating the ruins of a once promising evangelical movement. The mature Calvin believed images should only be removed as part of an orderly process presided over by the properly constituted authorities. This was the position carefully articulated in his most systematic treatment of the issue in the *Institutes*. But the *tone* of his early polemical writings was very different; and it was this that struck a more forceful chord with young churches finding their way in a hostile Catholic environment, as was the case in France around the year 1560. While Calvin the Genevan statesman might deplore the iconoclasm and destructiveness that accompanied the church-building in France, Calvin the author could not be entirely absolved of responsibility.

The true measure of Calvin's receding influence in France during these years can be seen in his changing attitude to armed resistance. Calvin believed, and this is a position articulated with some clarity in the *Institutes*, that changes in religion should only be instituted by the properly constituted powers. Beyond this, God would provide; and in the extraordinary events of 1559–60 (the unexpected deaths in short order of two persecuting kings, Henry II and Francis II) there seemed to be plentiful evidence of God's providential involvement on the Protestant side.[19] But as France's Huguenot communities moved toward open confrontation with the Crown Calvin was increasingly marginalized. The Conspiracy of Amboise, hatched under his nose in Geneva itself, brought forth angry protestations. But as France drifted into war Calvin had little choice but to revise his position to provide a fig-leaf of justification for his too-hasty disciples. His last known sermons addressing these issues show a troubled mind and an angry heart: the prophet of a troubled apocalypse in a homeland he loved but no longer understood.[20]

By the time war broke out in France in 1562 Calvin's life was moving towards its end. Even though the Genevan reformer would live to see (and deplore) the Peace of Amboise that brought the first fighting to a close, where French affairs were concerned leadership had already passed to his trusted lieutenant and eventual successor, Theodore de Bèze. De Bèze had led the Genevan delegation at the Colloquy of Poissy in 1561, and he remained in France throughout the first war. His actions during this period reveal that he was already much more than merely Calvin's loyal plenipotentiary.

Even before assuming the burdens of leadership in Geneva de Bèze was a powerful independent voice, and far more prepared than the cautious Calvin to contemplate military action in defense of the faith. To the extent that the Huguenots were ready to take on the royal army in 1562, this must be attributed in almost equal measure to the leadership of the Huguenot nobility and to the work of de Bèze in raising military contributions from the congregations.[21]

Meanwhile in the south of France (already by this point emerging as the real stronghold of the movement) the leading role was played by Pierre Viret, dispatched as Geneva's representative in 1561 but soon playing a largely independent hand. He, again, proved a far from passive observer of the wave of destruction that accompanied the Calvinist takeover of Nîmes, Montpellier, and Montauban at the beginning of the first war.[22]

It is from this more forthright activist strand of Calvinism that one can trace the doctrines of resistance that found their most developed form in the famous Monarchomach tracts: François Hotman's *Francogallia*, the *Droit des Magistrats* of de Bèze, and the anonymous *Vindiciae contra Tyrannos*. These most famous tracts, published in the wake of the St. Bartholomew's Day Massacre, have dominated discussion of Huguenot resistance theory, but their real contemporary political importance is highly questionable. By this point the survival of the Huguenot movement would depend more on political factors than published pamphlets; in their radicalism the Monarchomach tracts in any case went far beyond what most leaders of the movement, noble or civic, would have contemplated in practice. But if it was only now that Calvinist theorists articulated a complete and convincing theory of resistance, their spirit had dominated the movement from the first days of the fighting in France in 1562, or indeed in the Netherlands in 1566.[23] Their earliest practical expression was the successful coup that installed a Calvinist regime in Scotland in 1559–60. Calvin, still alive at this point, would will the ends but not the means. But the international Calvinist tradition certainly owed its greatest successes to the fact that in moments of crisis and opportunity it chose to ignore the more legalistic scruples of its founding father.

Here a comparison (and contrast) with Luther's church is instructive. Luther and Calvin were alike in their instinctive distrust of disorder; although otherwise temperamentally distant here the clerical conservative and the cautious lawyer converged. When Luther was consulted by a group of admirers in Antwerp who wished to set up a separate church in the still Catholic city, Luther was emphatic and discouraging. They should wait upon a change in the political climate, and until then, continue to attend Mass. The early promising beginnings of Netherlandish Lutheranism were soon stifled. There are no doubt many reasons why Luther's movement made such faltering progress outside his own homeland, but Luther's own ingrained respect for political authority was an important factor. Calvinism, crucially, found the means to put down roots and grow in places where the state power was still hostile. That these young Calvinist churches were prepared to face the issue of resistance and seize their chance of power violated every instinct of their Genevan preceptor. But it was crucial to their success.

## CHURCH ORGANIZATION

The other vital ingredient of the success of Calvinism as an international movement was church organization. From the point at which Luther's own sense of the apocalyptic end-time receded sufficiently for him to devote his attention to the education of the Christian people, church organization was a preoccupation of all Protestant confessions. Those charged with the responsibilities of church-forming gave close attention to what had been achieved elsewhere: first in the German Princely territories and the city-states of the Empire, latterly in Scandinavia. In consequence, when one talks of an individual reformer and their church order – the work of Martin Bucer in Strasbourg, John à Lasco in London and Emden, or Calvin in Geneva – one must take it as read that each new church order builds on those that came before, adapted and molded to suit local circumstances and to accommodate local cultural traditions.

For all that, Calvin's organization of the Genevan church, the *Ecclesiastical Ordinances* of 1541, is rightly viewed as a milestone of church-forming. In the *Ecclesiastical Ordinances*, Calvin's talents and personal experiences, his lawyer's training and his recent observation of Bucer's work in Strasbourg, combined to inspire a brilliant synthesis of previous Protestant church orders. For this, Geneva provided an almost perfect laboratory. Recently reformed, and chastened by the experience of turbulence during Calvin's recent exile, there was a hunger for order. Crucially, the city was of a size that gave some hope that the prescriptions of the *Ordinances* might actually be enforced. Meanwhile, and no less important, the presence of a body of educated French exiles allowed Calvin to pack the Genevan ministry with men who shared his vision and commitment.[24]

All this gave a fair wind to the most revolutionary aspect of Calvin's blueprint, the Consistory, a joint committee of magistrates and ministers charged with enforcing social discipline and morals. The result was, by any measure, remarkable. When John Knox famously spoke of Geneva as "the most famous school of Christ" he articulated a perception that was widespread (if not shared by Calvin himself). By the time of Calvin's death in 1564 if was widely believed that the relentless, dogged application to discipline and good order had succeeded in creating a society in which the common moral precepts of the age (for Geneva was in no way exceptional in the values it espoused) were actually applied. When Calvinist ministers elsewhere in Europe urged greater zeal, the godliness of Geneva was assumed. No aspect of Calvin's achievement was so influential in sixteenth-century society as this perception of the perfectibility of the Christian commonwealth.

The vision of Geneva, the city on the hill, was thus extremely powerful. But it was by no means certain how appropriate, in practice, the structures of the Genevan church would prove when exported to other parts of Protestant Europe. Here, again, the distance between myth and reality needs careful investigation. Through the ages Calvinism as a system of church government has been widely admired for its perceived clarity of structure and the apparently uniform application of the Genevan template through different parts of Europe. In practice Calvinism succeeded for precisely the opposite reason: because, as with the application of Calvin's views on resistance, it proved itself extremely flexible and adaptable.

That this was so was immediately apparent in Calvin's own lifetime, with the rapid growth of Calvinist churches in France. As congregations multiplied in the towns and cities of France in the years after 1555, it quickly became clear that the churches would benefit from a national church order: a clear statement of agreed doctrine, and a structure of church organization encompassing the whole national church. At the first National Synod of 1559 both of these objectives were achieved. The church adopted a Confession of Faith, based on (but not identical to) one supplied by Geneva, and a system of church government articulating a pyramid of authority from the local congregation to the national synod.[25] Here the ministers who met in Paris had to be congratulated on their inventiveness, for the city-state of Geneva obviously offered no clear model for such a national church. But the structure of government adopted for the French national church, refined over successive meetings of the synod between 1559 and 1572, in fact proved extremely effective. The competing claims of congregational initiative and due order were finely balanced; effective mechanisms were put in place to monitor the quality of candidates for the ministry (a major problem at a period of such rapid growth) and to regulate what was published in the name of the church's ministers.

The church order created at the Paris synod of 1559 was an enduring success. It would provide the model and inspiration for churches elsewhere in Europe where opportunity arose to create national churches: most immediately in Scotland when the revolution of 1559–60 created a rather unexpected opportunity to create a Calvinist polity with little prior preparation. The French order also profoundly influenced events in the Netherlands, where the Dutch and Walloon churches quickly articulated a skeleton structure of colloquies and provincial synods in imitation of that created in France. But this undoubted organizational cross-fertilization masked a great deal of local variety. This was true even of France. Here the church fathers soon discovered that it was easier to devise a structure for a national church than to insure true unity of practice in its many provinces and congregations.

In the first ten years of the French church successive national synods gave considerable attention to two main issues: the regulation of the quality of those who presented themselves as candidates for the ministry, and the structure of authority within and above each congregation. In both cases they drew broadly on the experience of the Genevan mother church. For each congregation they anticipated a threefold ministerial order of ministers, elders, and deacons. This was patterned on Geneva, but already with a significant variation: little is heard of the order of "doctors" or teachers described in the Genevan *Ecclesiastical Ordinances*. Presumably this was regarded as more appropriate for the Swiss city-state, where the doctors articulated Calvin's stress on education, and prefigured the later role of the Professors of the Genevan Academy. Obviously not every church would have such a critical educational role, and in the early days, at least, the French churches could not expect to exercise any control over the schoolmasters operating in the town. Most other churches followed the French, rather than

Genevan, example in building round the classic threefold order, though the Scottish Discipline flirted with an additional tier of "readers," auxiliary ministers who would lead the congregation if there were no properly established minister.[26] This was regarded as an emergency measure specific to a young church; in the French experience deacons sometimes performed the same function as licensed readers of Scripture to lead the service.

As this example suggests, even the articulation of a common threefold order of ministry often masked a considerable variety of practice. In some congregations deacons sat on the consistory alongside the ministers and elders; in others they did not. This was the Genevan practice; but in a number of French churches deacons were given considerably more responsibility than merely the maintenance and administration of poor relief, their core duty under the classic Genevan scheme. As the churches grew, further variations arose as congregations took practical steps to cope with the great influx of new persons. At the beginning of the religious wars, in many places the Calvin congregations seized control of the city government. The Catholic Mass was abolished, and churches turned over to the congregations. In these new circumstances French Calvinist communities sometimes established a separate church council alongside, and quite distinct from, both the city government (which they sometimes now controlled) and the Consistory. Both Lyon and Nîmes had such a council, but how responsibilities were divided between this body and the Consistory is never entirely clear.

The greatest and most controversial differences emerged over the question of where ultimate responsibility rested for the discipline and for the election of ministers. In Geneva, a church that was at the same time a single city community, the problem did not arise. The appointment of ministers was vested in the city council, advised by Calvin and his colleagues: after 1541, in effect, the ministers were a self-selecting (and very high-quality) group. In disciplinary matters there was no appeal from the decision of the local Consistory. In the first instance the French church boldly adopted the Genevan model, envisaging each church as an independent entity. The first national synod boldly stated that "no church should aspire to any precedence or domination over another," clearly implying that responsibility for selection of ministers would rest with each congregation. This mirrored the existing practice of the first "churches under the cross," where ministers were often elected by the members of the congregation themselves in an essentially democratic process, following the example of the apostles.

In the years that followed the French church swiftly rowed back from this bold expression of confidence in the judgment of the ordinary members of the congregation. The first national synod vested responsibility for the selection of ministers in the Consistory alone; by the time of the second meeting (Poitiers, 1561) the church was expected to be guided by the ministers of neighboring churches.[27] This increased clericalism in part reflected great anxiety at the unsuitable nature of many who had proposed themselves and been accepted as ministers: each national synod published a long list of deposed ministers, some of whom had fraudulently presented themselves to more than one church. But the change was not uncontested. Many in the French church resented the erosion of local autonomy, and this faction found its most eloquent advocate in Jean Morély, who published his *Traité de la Discipline* in 1562. Morély was an old foe of the Genevan fathers, and they quickly marshaled forces to have his book condemned and Morély excommunicated. But the support for Morély's position, though cowed into silence, was clearly broad. The *Traité de la Discipline* was dedicated to Pierre Viret, who had promoted many of the same ideas in his organizational work for the churches of Languedoc.[28] Noble supporters of the church also instinctively expected the right to nominate their own ministers, unguided by the local *colloque* or synod; we know very little, in fact, about how these noble churches operated in practice. The conflict over Morély's ideas rumbled on until 1572, when the St. Bartholomew's Day massacre rendered the dispute largely irrelevant.

What these French debates demonstrate is a circumstance that has wider application for a study of Calvinism as an international movement: that even within a single national church the position of the church within each community encompassed very wide variations. Some French churches came close to the total domination of society enjoyed in Geneva, and a very similar level of cooperation from the town magistrates. This was the case, for instance, in Montauban and Nîmes, the two principal centers of Huguenot strength in the south.[29] At the other end of the scale churches in some of the northern cities enjoyed a barely tolerated existence in conditions of great danger. The church in Paris seldom emerged from the conditions of the early "churches under the cross," before being effectively wiped out in the St. Bartholomew's Day massacre.[30] Most French churches enjoyed a status somewhere between these two extremes. They were tolerated, often very grudgingly, but only alongside the established Catholic Church which maintained the support of the majority of the population and continued to dominate the town council. In these circumstances the Calvinist community took on the character of a voluntary community; there was nothing to compel obedience to the discipline beyond the social and moral pressure exerted by ministers and fellow members. Obviously this had its impact on the type of social discipline churches could hope to enforce. Issues that could be successfully addressed in a fully Calvinistic community like Geneva (or Montauban) lay outside the compass of congregations in places like Caen or Angers, where if pressed too hard members could simply abandon the church.

This typology of churches proves equally valid if we turn our attention to the Calvinist churches in other parts of Europe. Scotland and the Netherlands, for instance, both at first sight present examples of a successful established Reformed church. Yet both in fact enjoyed only a very conditional support from the state. In Scotland the Revolution of 1559–60 established Calvinism as the sole authorized church. The Mass was abolished and churches turned over to the new congregations. But the natural leaders of society did little to address the pressing issue of impropriated property (that is church lands that had fallen into lay hands), and the support for the exercise of social discipline was extremely tenuous. In due course Calvinism became deeply embedded in Scottish culture; but it was at the cost of a long process of compromise and negotiation with the local lairds.[31] The churches in the Netherlands hardly even enjoyed this success. Their role in the war of independence earned the Calvinists privileged status in the new free state, and they swiftly laid their hands on the best city churches. But a system of state salaries, though reasonably generous, was a double-edged sword, and the frustrated *dominees* were soon expressing their frustration at the magistrates' manifest lack of interest in assisting them in the creation of a new Geneva. Key parts of community life, such as schooling and poor relief, remained securely under magisterial control; and the magistrates made little effort to suppress the many competing sects and confessions that flourished in the relatively tolerant society of the Dutch Republic. Most crucially of all, ecclesiastical discipline could only be applied to those who voluntarily subjected themselves to full membership of the community. As a result there arose in the Netherlands a curious two-tier church society. While a good half of the population, including most of the magisterial classes, supported the churches in a broad sense, only a much smaller group (perhaps 10 percent) chose to become full communicating members of the church, and subject themselves to the discipline. These were the *lidmaten* (members) as opposed to the *liefhebbers* (or well-wishers).[32]

This was a distinction that Calvin would certainly have deplored as an aspect of church order, and certainly not have tolerated in Geneva. To him, this sort of voluntarism was antithetical to good order. But curiously this two-tier system with an inner core of enthusiasts made reasonable sense as a crude articulation of Calvinist theology. For if one asks oneself why in these circumstances anyone would have subjected themselves to the full rigors of the discipline, when attendance at the church was not otherwise barred to them, then the search for assurance of salvation must surely offer the key. Calvinists knew that only a small number would be saved, and the gathered community offered a plausible visible manifestation of this community of the elect. The desire to create even within a nominally Christian population an inner core of the elect was thus strong in all Calvinist churches – what one might call the Puritan urge. This was a distinctive aspect of English Reformed culture, and its most important legacy to the New World communities of the seventeenth century, but in truth it was evident in all parts of the Calvinist movement from the first days of the church. It can be seen even in Calvin's own mind in the sermons where he lambasts Geneva – his own Reformed city on a hill – as a cesspool of iniquity.[33]

## CONCLUSION

Calvin did not live to see the foundation of a true international movement; he certainly had no experience of leading one. First and foremost he was, like other first-generation figures, a preacher and an evangelist. He aimed at the conversion of society, and inevitably pursued traditional conversion strategies: the call to repentance; the appeal to political elites; the call to witness and, if necessary, exile or martyrdom.

These were all strategies and gifts suited to a period when the church was a minority. If one asks how the evangelical movement in western Europe was revived from the low point of the 1540s, then Calvin's restless, tireless, uncompromising preaching and teaching plays a major role. There could have been no Protestant revival in the "wonder-years" of 1559–66 without his remarkable gifts. But they were gifts of a particular moment, and at times when it was necessary to move beyond prophetic utterance to careful weighing of political opportunity the Genevan reformer was sometimes too far distant from events to give an effective lead. Calvinism succeeded as an international movement because his disciples honored Calvin as inspiration, teacher, and theologian. But they also appreciated that their churches had to grow out of the shadow of Geneva. In the turbulent world of the sixteenth century they did so with remarkable speed.

*Notes*

1  Calvin to the French Church in London, Geneva, September 27, 1552. Cited in George C. Gorham, *Gleanings of a few scattered ears during the period of the Reformation in England* (London: Bell and Daldy, 1857), 283–86.

2  On these events see Wilhelm Neuser, "Die Aufnahme des Flüchtlinge aus England in Wesel (1553) und ihre Ausweisung trotz der Vermittlung Calvins und Melanchthons," in *Weseler Knovent, 1568–1968* (Düsseldorf: Presseverband der Evangelischen Kirche im Rheinland, 1968); Andrew Pettegree, "The London Exile

Community and the Second Sacramentarian Controversy, 1553–1560," in *Marian Protestantism: Six Studies* (Aldershot, England; Brookfield, VT: Scolar Press, 1996), 55–85.

3 As is revealed by the story told by Florimond de Raemond of a Catholic nobleman, returning from the wars, who rode by Geneva out of curiosity to hear Calvin. He was astonished to find also in the congregation his wife and daughter, whom he imagined safely at home. The document, in English translation, is in Alastair Duke, Gillian Lewis, and Andrew Pettegree, eds., *Calvinism in Europe 1540–1610: A Collection of Documents* (Manchester: Manchester University Press, 1992), 37–38.

4 Jeannine Olson, *Calvin and Social Welfare: Deacons and the Bourse française* (Selingsgrove: Susquehanna University Press; London and Toronto: Associated University Presses, 1989), 47–49.

5 Jean-François Gilmont, *Calvin et le livre imprimé* (Geneva: Librairie Droz, 1997), 104–14.

6 According to my own calculations, between 1568 and 1599, 1197 Protestant works were published in French. This data has been gathered as part of the work of the St Andrews Sixteenth Century French Book project.

7 For what follows, see Francis Higman, "Calvin's Works in Translation," in Andrew Pettegree, Alastair Duke, and Gillian Lewis, eds., *Calvinism in Europe: 1540–1620* (Cambridge: Cambridge University Press, 1994), 82–99; Andrew Pettegree, "The Reception of Calvinism in Britain," in William H. Neuser and Brian G. Armstrong, eds., *Calvinus Sincerioris Religionius Vindex: Calvin as Protector of the Purer Religion*, Sixteenth Century Essays & Studies, XXXVI (Kirksville, MO: Sixteenth Century Journal Publishers, 1997), 267–89.

8 For instance Patrick Collinson, "England and International Calvinism, 1558–1640," in Menna Prestwich, ed., *International Calvinism 1541–1715* (Oxford: Clarendon Press, 1985), 197–223.

9 *Bibliotheca Calviniana* (*BC*), III, 76/5 etc. A further abridgment for the English market was the work of the French Huguenot exile Guillaume Delaune. This too appeared in both Latin and French editions: III, 83/5, 85/1 etc.

10 Ibid., 68/2.

11 Ibid., 75/1, 76/1, 76/2.

12 Ibid., 60/7. On Emden printing, see Andrew Pettegree, *Emden and the Dutch Revolt: Exile and the Development of Reformed Protestantism* (Oxford: Clarendon Press, 1992), ch. 4.

13 *BC* III, 82/1, 82/2, 82/6.

14 Bodo Nischan, "Germany after 1550," in Andrew Pettegree, ed., *The Reformation World* (London: Routledge, 2000), 387–409; Bodo Nischan, *Lutherans and Calvinists in the Age of Confessionalism* (Aldershot, England; Brookfield, VT: Ashgate, 1999).

15 Bodo Nischan, *Prince, People and Confession: The Second Reformation in Brandenburg* (Philadelphia: University of Pennsylvania Press, 1994).

16 Gerhard Menk, *Die Hohne Schule Herborn in ihrer Frühzeit (1584–1660)* (Wiesbaden: Selbstverlag der Historischen Kommission für Nassau, 1981).

17 The spirit of these years is brilliantly evoked in Philip Benedict, *Rouen During the Wars of Religion* (Cambridge: Cambridge University Press, 1972).

18 N. M. Sutherland, "Antoine de Bourbon, King of Navarre and the French Crisis of Authority, 1559–1562," in *Princes, Politics and Religion 1547–1589* (London: Hambledon Press, 1984), 55–72.

19 For Calvin and Beza's reaction to the deaths of the two kings see Duke et al., eds., *Calvinism in Europe*, 80–81.

20 Willem Nijenhuis, "The Limits of Civil Disobedience in Calvin's Latest Known Sermons," in *Ecclesia Reformata: Studies on the Reformation*, 2 vols. (Leiden, Brill, 1972; 1994), 73–97.

21 Mark Greengrass, "Financing the Cause: Protestant Mobilization and Accountability in France (1562–1589)," in Philip Benedict et al., eds., *Reformation, Revolt and Civil War in France and the Netherlands 1555–1585* (Amsterdam: Royal Netherlands Academy of Arts and Sciences, 1999), 233–54; Kristen B. Neuschel, *Word of Honor: Interpreting Noble Culture in Sixteenth-Century France* (Ithaca: Cornell University Press, 1989).

22 Stuart Foster, "Pierre Viret and France, 1559–1565," Diss. University of St. Andrews, 2000.

23 Martin Van Gelderen, *The Political Thought of the Dutch Revolt 1555–1590* (Cambridge: Cambridge University Press, 1992).

24 William G. Naphy, *Calvin and the Consolidation of the Genevan Reformation* (Manchester: Manchester University Press, 1994).

25 John Quick, ed., *Synodicon in Gallia Reformata* (London, 1692).

26 James K. Cameron, ed., *The First Book of Discipline* (Edinburgh: St. Andrew Press, 1972), 105–107.

27 The relevant articles in translation can be found in Duke et al., eds., *Calvinism in Europe*, 72, 76.

28 Foster, "Pierre Viret and France."

29 Philip Conner, *Huguenot Heartland: Montauban and southern French Calvinism during the wars of religion* (Aldershot, England; Burlington, VT: Ashgate, 2002).

30 Barbara B. Diefendorf, *Beneath the Cross: Catholics and Huguenots in Sixteenth-Century Paris* (New York: Oxford University Press, 1991).

31 Michael F. Graham, *The Uses of Reform: 'Godly Discipline' and Popular Behaviour in Scotland and Beyond 1560–1610* (Leiden: Brill, 1996).

32 Andrew Pettegree, "Coming to Terms with Victory: The Upbuilding of a Calvinist Church in Holland 1572–1590," in Pettegree et al., eds., *Calvinism in Europe*, 160–80. For a splendid portrait of multi-confessional religion in the Dutch Republic see A. Th. van Deursen, *Plain Lives in a Golden Age: Popular culture, religion, and society in seventeenth-century Holland*, trans. Maarten Ultee (Cambridge: Cambridge University Press, 1991).

33 Jean Calvin, *Sermons sur le livre de Michée*, ed. J. D. Bênoit, vol. V of *Supplementa Calviniana* (Neukirchen: Neukirchen Verlag der Buchhandlung des Erziehungsvereins, 1964), 63–64, 151, 163.

# 13 Calvin and Calvinism

### CARL R. TRUEMAN

The question of the relationship between the theology of John Calvin and later Reformed theology has been the subject of considerable debate since at least the rise of the School of Saumur and the subsequent controversies over Amyraldianism in the seventeenth century. On the whole, the issue has been pressed in terms of the extent to which certain later theologians can be seen to stand in continuity or discontinuity with the thought of Calvin. The method involved in this particular tradition of debate has been to identify certain doctrinal positions held by Calvin and to regard these as normative standards by which later theologians can be judged. This trajectory of scholarship is epitomized in the title of Basil Hall's famous article "Calvin against the Calvinists," though Hall represents merely one example of such scholarship.[1]

Underlying the various examples of this approach are a number of assumptions which, on close examination, can be seen to be somewhat inadequate as proper historical criteria. First, it is too often assumed that Calvin's theology has, or had at some point in the past, some kind of normative status within the Reformed tradition. This is historically and ecclesiastically not so. While it is certainly true that the writings of Luther enjoyed unique influence among Lutheran confessional communities, the writings of Calvin never occupied anything approaching such a position. The historic identity of Reformed theology has always been expressed through public confessional documents such as the First and Second Helvetic Confessions, the *Consensus Tigurinus*, the Heidelberg Catechism, the Belgic Confession, the Canons of Dordt and the Westminster Standards. These were the productions of committees and of historical circumstances and thus embody a certain theological catholicity; they certainly did not represent either the work or the thought of any one individual. Thus, the conflation of Calvin's theology with normative Reformed theology at any point, or the use of his theology as some kind of criterion for confessional statement, are moves which have no historical foundation or justification in the actual history of Reformed churches.[2]

Second, the constant quest for points of identity or difference between Calvin and later Reformed theologians has often been driven by the desire to claim Calvin as some kind of theological authority for the present day. Thus, on the one hand the separation of Calvin from, say, the Westminster Confession has been used by some of a neo-orthodox persuasion as a means of undermining the position of certain factions within the modern theological world;[3] on the other hand, the close identification of the two is used by other groups or traditional Calvinists as a means of undermining claims to historical antecedents by the neo-orthodox.[4]

Given these two basic flaws in much previous "Calvin and Calvinism" scholarship, we need to make a number of methodological points before we begin our brief survey of the question. First, we need to understand that the term "Calvinism" is profoundly unhelpful. It was coined as a polemical tool for tarnishing the reputation of the Reformed, and it is of no real use to modern intellectual history. Far better are the terms "Reformed theology" and "Reformed Orthodoxy" as these actually reflect the fact that so-called Calvinists were not those who looked to Calvin as the major theological authority but rather those who looked to the tradition of Reformed confessions. This thus makes room for Calvin as an important source for the tradition without making him the sole dominating theological force, a point that reflects both his status in his own day, as witnessed by his far-from-absolute control even of Geneva, let alone the Reformed churches in the neighbouring Swiss cantons, and in the years following his death, where Reformed writers generally allude more frequently to Augustine than to Calvin in their writings.

Second, we need to move beyond the language of *identity* and *difference*, and even, perhaps, to be careful in the use of that of *continuity* and *discontinuity* – though the latter, when understood in the correct way, is not objectionable. A better approach to the question is to use the category of *development*. Much has been written over the last two decades by Richard A. Muller and a number of scholars associated with him concerning the continuities between Calvin and later Reformed theology.[5] It might be possible to read this material as stressing the identity between the two, but this would in fact be a misreading of the argument. What the newer scholarship has tried to do is to indicate the way in which Reformed theology *developed* in the century and a half after Calvin. The result of this has been that the importance of points of identity and difference has been dramatically relativized; the question has been not so much, for example, "Is the theology of Calvin identical or different to that of the Westminster Confession?" but more "How does the Westminster Confession come to be formulated in the way it was, given the century of Reformed theology which preceded it?"

This kind of historicism is far removed from the old dogmatically driven scholarship, a point which could well be lost on those who read it using the same categories as used by the "Calvin against or for the Calvinists" school.

This leads to a third preliminary methodological point: Reformed theology is expressed in historical texts, whether confessions, commentaries, catechisms, or systems; and these are historical actions which need to be understood in context, not isolated from that context and treated as self-standing, autonomous artefacts. There has been a tendency to view the issue of the development of Reformed theology as a purely, or at least primarily, dogmatic problem. Obviously, the development of a dogmatic tradition is, by definition, *partly* a dogmatic problem; but to understand the development of Reformed theology, we must take into account the context in which Reformed theology was developing, and that involves attention to factors other than those which are purely Reformed and those which are purely dogmatic. For example, the trajectories of theological and philosophical reflection in which Reformed theology stood reach back through the Middle Ages to the early church, and any study of Reformed theology must take this into account at the outset. Second, the libraries the Reformed thinkers used provide a key link with the past, and, as with the thought of any thinker or writer, we must take serious account of the literature which was available, which was read, and which thus helped to forge the linguistic and conceptual worlds within which Reformed theologians lived and worked. Further, the power struggles within church and society impacted upon the lives of theologians at various points, and much of their writing is not simply theology for the sake of theology but theology for the purpose of achieving some end, which may actually be somewhat less than purely theological. In addition, the literary genres in which they wrote were crucial to the ways in which they expressed themselves, and therefore must also be crucial to the way in which modern students of their thought read and compare their works. This is far from an exhaustive list but it serves as a reminder that theology is done by real people in real situations; thus, the problems which such theology poses for the historian may appear on the surface to be purely dogmatic and to require purely dogmatic solutions; but this is deceptive – problems in historical theology require, first and foremost, historical solutions. Hard though it may seem for systematic theologians and hard-line social historians to believe, sound historical analysis of the development of Reformed theology does not require the historian of theology to have a vested interest in either vilifying or vindicating either Calvin or the so-called Calvinists.[6]

At the heart of the scholarly conflict that has proved most central to debates about the relationship of Calvin to later Reformed theology is the

228 Carl R. Trueman

issue of scholasticism. The basic thesis underlying much of the scholarship which regards later Reformed thought as fundamentally deviating
from Calvin's Reformation original is that the use of medieval scholastic
method, language, and concepts by later Reformed theologians involves a
basic change of theological substance.

This is the thesis put forward most powerfully by Brian Armstrong and
those scholars who take his basic definition of scholasticism as their starting
point, though claims about the substantial logical, metaphysical, and theological effects of scholasticism predate his work. Armstrong's definition,
in brief, asserts that scholasticism is a theological system which logically
deduces doctrine from axioms, usually via a syllogism; which places reason on a par with, or even superior to, revelation; which treats Scripture
as a unified or coherent whole; and which exhibits extensive interest in
metaphysical thought and speculative abstraction.[7]

What this definition does is to enclose a series of issues under the single rubric of scholasticism, with the result that, if it is a valid definition,
the presence of one aspect of such scholasticism (e.g., a syllogism) might
well be taken to signify the presence of all the rest. The account of the
development of Reformed theology which this definition of scholasticism
promotes is one whereby the pristine, non-metaphysical, exegetical theology
of Calvin is slowly replaced by a speculative, metaphysical, overly-rational,
and hair-splitting dogmatism, as represented by later theologians such as
Voetius, Turretin, and John Owen. Later Calvinism or Reformed Orthodoxy
thus comes to represent a proto-rationalist movement which points forward to the various philosophies and theologies which emerge from the
Enlightenment.[8]

The problems with such an account of the development of Reformed
theology can be exposed when the definition of scholasticism proposed
by Armstrong is subjected to careful critique. What the definition does is
conflate a series of separate issues that need to be looked at individually
in order to establish an accurate historical picture of what is going on in
Reformed theology in the century after Calvin. These issues are the nature of
scholasticism as a method; and the role of metaphysics and "Aristotelianism"
within later Reformed theology.

## SCHOLASTICISM AS METHOD

Scholasticism is defined with succinctness by van Asselt and Dekker:
"Scholasticism is a scientific method of research and teaching, and does not
have a doctrinal content, neither does it have reason as its foundation."[9] Such
a definition, while standing in stark contrast to the conflation of method

and content so typical of many Protestant treatments of the subject, is, in fact, hardly innovative, being a commonplace among Roman Catholic scholars.[10] What it does is allow scholasticism to define itself rather than bringing to bear upon the subject the various connotations of rationalism and hair-splitting that the term has come to possess over the years. Scholasticism is, literally, the method of the school: it was a means of teaching and writing which originated in the founding of the great cathedral schools and then the universities of the Middle Ages. When we consider the broad array of medieval theologies which one might legitimately characterize as "scholastic" – Thomist, Scotist, Occamist, radical Avverroist, etc. – it becomes clear that there is very little binding them together as a single entity other than the fact that they all participate in the methods of university discourse and pedagogy of the time.

Given the establishment of university discourse as the dominant pattern of pedagogy in Europe, it becomes clear that the rise of institutions of higher learning committed to the teaching of Reformed theology was of crucial importance to the shape and development of Reformed thought. Driven by the need to train ministers at the highest level in order to facilitate the propagation of the faith and the combating of heresy, the Reformed church inevitably both penetrated established seats of learning and founded a number of its own. Most famous of such institutions was, of course, the Academy at Geneva. Founded in 1559, its first rector was Theodore Beza, French humanist and Calvin's successor as theological leader of Geneva. The Academy attracted students from all over Europe, and thus became the most significant center for the transmission of Reformed thinking to the broader European context.[11] Among its students, it numbered the English Puritan, Thomas Cartwright, and the Dutchmen, Arminius and Uitenbogaert, both of whom were later to become leaders in the Dutch Remonstrant faction. While Geneva was arguably the earliest of the significant Reformed higher educational institutions, other universities soon emerged to help further the cause. Thus, in Holland Leiden emerged as an intellectual center for Reformed Protestantism, as did the Universities of Utrecht, Franeker, and Groningen. In England, while no specifically Protestant universities were founded, in the mid-sixteenth century the brief sojourns of Martin Bucer and Peter Martyr Vermigli at Cambridge and Oxford served to influence a generation of early English reformers, such as John Bradford, and the widespread experience of exile in Reformed cities during the Marian regime (1553–58) ensured that the influence of continental Reformed thinking was a powerful, if never dominant, force within the Anglican Church throughout the late sixteenth and early seventeenth century.[12] Thus, for example, the intellectual make-up of Oxford and Cambridge remained eclectic even during the

Commonwealth and Protectorate of the 1650s, but most of the significant English Reformed thinkers of the time were linked with these institutions either through undergraduate studies, Fellowships, or even high office, as in the case of John Owen, England's preeminent Reformed theologian, who was for a while Dean of Christ Church and Vice-Chancellor of Oxford.[13]

In addition to the changing institutional placement of Reformed education in the century after Calvin, one further factor must be noted at the outset: the increasingly complex polemical environment. When we look at the work of Calvin, we see a number of classic opponents: the various early church heretics; the medieval schoolmen; Anabaptists and Radicals; contemporary Catholics; and some of the more extreme Lutherans. In addition, the level of contemporary polemic is itself not as widespread or as sophisticated as it was to become. It was not until after the Council of Trent (1545–63) that Catholicism started to frame a clear and consistent response to Protestantism, something that greatly enhanced the precision of theological debate. Further, the rise of the Jesuits in the sixteenth century gave renewed intellectual impetus to the Catholic Reformation and again dramatically sharpened the terms of dispute, which in turn demanded responses of increasing sophistication from within the ranks of the Protestants. The work of Robert Bellarmine (1542–1621) is of particular significance in this matter.

Of course, it was not only the increasing precision and sophistication of Catholic polemics that affected Reformed Orthodoxy; the increasing diversity of sophisticated Protestant heterodoxy also put great pressure on the Reformed. Central to this were the Arminians and the Socinians, who used the same basic scriptural principle as the Reformed Orthodox and yet came to dramatically different conclusions. This, as we shall see, had particular significance when it came to the increasingly high profile given to metaphysical discussion in later Reformed theology. For the moment, however, it is sufficient to note that the development of Catholic and heterodox Protestant theology and polemic placed great demands upon the Reformed Orthodox of which those in the generation of Calvin were blissfully unaware.

These questions of the institutional location of Reformed theology and the increasingly complex polemical scene are highly significant for understanding how Reformed theology developed in the century and a half after the founding of the Genevan Academy, involving as they do fundamental changes in the context and purpose of Reformed teaching. A good example of this can be seen by making a comparison between the *Institutes* of John Calvin and those of a later professor at Geneva, Francis Turretin.[14]

The former work is perhaps the classic statement of Reformed theology from the era prior to the elaborate development of Reformed university pedagogy, while the latter represents a fine example of precisely the kind of university discourse that later, university-based, Reformed teaching produced.[15] Even the most superficial reading of the two works indicates profound differences. For a start, the order of topics is not the same: Calvin starts with a discussion of the nature of knowledge of God and of humanity; Turretin starts with a more elaborate prolegomenal discourse concerning the nature, object, and genus of theology, followed by an exploration of its cognitive grounding in the Holy Scriptures. This different opening reflects a fundamental difference in topical ordering throughout the two works. The differences, however, do not stop here: throughout his work, Turretin uses language which has a more obvious debt to the medieval philosophical discourse than Calvin. Most significant for our discussion of the relationship between Reformed Orthodoxy and scholasticism, he also deploys the medieval technique of the disputed question in a manner which is much more widespread, obvious, and self-conscious than any such which might be found in Calvin. Indeed, the whole of Turretin's work is structured around such questions. Take, for example, the first topic, "Theology" which is discussed by means of four questions:

I. Should the word 'theology' be used in the Christian schools, and in how many ways can it be understood?
II. Whether there is a theology and its divisions.
III. Whether natural theology may be granted.
IV. Is natural theology sufficient for salvation; or is there a common religion by which all promiscuously may be saved? We deny against the Socinians and the Remonstrants.[16]

This use of what is clearly a technique of discourse which has its roots in the Middle Ages and which does not function in an analogous way in Calvin's *Institutes* raises the obvious question of why such a development takes place. It is perhaps tempting to answer, as many have done in line with the Armstrong definition, that this represents a substantial dogmatic change from a theological approach which places biblical exegesis and warm-hearted piety at the center of the theological agenda to one which stresses the careful, logical ordering and investigation of topics by theologians more concerned with logical and philosophical consistency. Certainly, this is how the shape of the development has been narrated by some scholars.[17]

Before we draw such sweeping dogmatic conclusions from such formal differences, however, it is necessary to ask a more fundamental question than that which concerns only the form of theological discourse: what are Calvin and Turretin *doing* in their respective works? What actions are they performing? There are, after all, many reasons why two texts, written in two different contexts by two different people, might exhibit differences, none of which need necessarily indicate radical substantial change in theological matter; and thus it may well be that the differences between them can be explained to a large extent by changes in context and intention. After all, the dramatic differences between, say, a poem about a daffodil and a discussion of the same daffodil in a botany textbook can be explained by differing genres and intentions without the need to resort to qualitative categories of truth and falsehood, or superiority and inferiority.

If we look at Calvin's *Institutes* first, we have at the very start the famous letter to King Francis I of France that lays out Calvin's purpose in writing. First, we should note that the letter is pitched to a large extent as a plea for persecuted Protestants in France, and the reminders scattered throughout the text, along with the specific refutations of allegations of novelty and of an inextricable link between Protestantism and social chaos, indicate quite clearly the broader political concerns which underlie the treatise: the desire to win over the French authorities to the cause of Reform.[18] This gives us the overarching intention of the work.

Next, if we look at the prefatory letter to the reader, Calvin gives a significant clue to the purpose of the work. Having declared his intention in the *Institutes* to instruct the reader in sacred theology, he adds the following:

> If, after this road . . . has been paved, I shall publish any
> interpretations of Scripture, I shall always condense them, because I
> shall have no need to undertake long doctrinal discussions, and to
> digress into commonplaces. In this way, the godly reader will be
> spared great annoyance and boredom, provided he approach Scripture
> armed with a knowledge of the present work, as a necessary tool.[19]

In other words, Calvin's more narrowly theological intention in the *Institutes* is to produce a work which will operate in tandem with his project of biblical commentary, whereby the prolixity of some of his predecessors in their commentaries will be avoided by the discussion of the various theological loci raised by the scriptural text in a separate handbook, the *Institutes*.[20] It is true that, in this letter, Calvin also stresses his intention to produce a work wherein the sum of religion is presented in a series of carefully ordered theological topics, and this perhaps legitimates the use of the term "systematic theology" to describe what he is writing – but only with the important proviso that we realise this is systematic theology as pursued within a trajectory stemming from the twelfth century and not to be understood by the crude imposition of later models of systematic theology onto the sixteenth century.[21]

If we turn now to the *Institutio* of Turretin, we find that he, too, addresses his work to the political realm, though this time it is to the Senate of Geneva, not the King of France.[22] This is a fairly predictable piece, recounting the struggles in Geneva with fanatics and heretics, and praising the politicians for their role in maintaining stability and the true religion. What is extremely interesting – and repays careful reading – is the prefatory letter to the reader wherein Turretin lays out his agenda. First – and most significantly – he sets his work firmly within the context of his teaching role at the Genevan Academy:

> For while I was endeavoring according to my strength to inform the youth from the requisitions of the entrusted office (not only publicly but privately), among other things I proposed for their investigation the *Decades* of the most celebrated Maresius. And that this might be to them a more useful exercise, I thought that the state and foundation of the controversies treated there should be explained in a few words (some distinctions and observations being also added) by which the *proton pseudos* ('principal falsehoods') of opponents might be revealed and the principal objections solved.[23]

In other words, the origins of his *Institutes* lie, not, like those of Calvin, in a desire to produce a theological commonplace book which will act as a companion to the reading of biblical commentaries, but in the demands of classroom discussion of matters in dispute between the Reformed and their opponents. This is confirmed later in the same letter, where Turretin emphatically rejects any notion that his *Institutes* should be read as a comprehensive system or statement of theology:

> Let no one think that a full and accurate system of theology is delivered here. For this was not indeed the design proposed to me, but only to explain the importance of the principal controversies which lie between us and our adversaries (ancient and modern) and supply to the young the thread of Ariadne, by the help of which they may more easily extricate themselves from their labyrinth.[24]

Thus, while Turretin's work might well be more verbose than that of Calvin, and while the professors at the nineteenth-century Princeton Seminary may well have used it as their textbook in systematic theology, it was in fact far more modest in its aim than either fact would suggest: it was a textbook of polemical theology, focusing not on theology as a whole but on those topics or aspects of topics which were in dispute.[25] This difference in intention has ramifications for the method that Turretin employs. In the same preface, he states that his purpose recommends four aspects of method to him: the clear exposition of the views on all sides of the questions in dispute; the subsequent positive exposition of truth and negative refutation of error; the answering of specific objections; and the summary resolution of the question.[26]

What Turretin has outlined is, of course, the basic framework of the disputed question, the fundamental building block of university education from the thirteenth century onwards. Given the context and purpose of his *Institutes*, the adoption of such a method is hardly surprising: here is a man working with the framework of university discourse – and that a discourse little changed in terms of basic form for four centuries – who needs to lay out in detail the reasons why he is a Reformed Protestant and not, say, a Catholic, a Lutheran, or a Socinian; and he has, at his disposal, the ideal pedagogical tool for so doing – the disputed question.

Indeed, in his use of this he is not even innovative as a Protestant. Recent studies by both David Steinmetz and Richard Muller have indicated that there are elements of this approach, albeit subject to modification by Renaissance developments, in Calvin himself.[27] Then, by the late sixteenth and early seventeenth centuries, the disputation was a well-established method of approach, evidenced particularly by the writings of Dutch theologians such as Jacob Arminius and Gisbert Voetius.[28] When we look at Turretin's *Institutes*, therefore, we have to beware of drawing simplistic conclusions based on a straightforward comparison with those of Calvin. When we ask whether the two works differ in terms of the way they present their theology, we must answer in the affirmative, but this actually tells us very little about the relationship of the two pieces. If we ask the more subtle question of whether the two authors are trying to do two different things in their respective works, we must also answer in the affirmative, and when we explore this answer further, we go a long way to explaining the differences without having to resort to notions of degeneration or massive theological change: Calvin is presenting his students with a handbook to accompany biblical exegesis and is writing at a time when Protestantism had yet to establish itself within the university; Turretin is writing a polemical handbook from within the context of a university and at a time when the polemical and systematic theological world was far more complex than when Calvin had been writing. They are doing two different things at two different times, albeit within the same broad Reformed theological trajectory. I would submit that dramatic formal differences between the two works were not only to be expected but were completely unavoidable. Thus, the question of scholasticism is in fact a question first and foremost of context and genre, not of theological content.

## THE ROLE OF METAPHYSICS

If we accept that *scholasticism* is a methodological category and that its adoption by the Reformed is satisfactorily explicable in terms of the institutional context of theological education, this still leaves us with the question of the role of metaphysical argumentation within later Reformed theology. This has been part and parcel of much of the literature devoted to tracing the development of Reformed thought, for example, in the arguments that the later Orthodoxy came to rest upon the doctrine of predestination, abstractly considered, which was then used as a metaphysical axiom from which all other theology could be deduced (the so-called "centraldogma" theory).[29] This theory has been subjected to devastating criticism in recent years, and so there is little need to elaborate further on this topic in particular, other than to direct the reader to the relevant secondary literature.[30]

Regarding the use of metaphysics in general, however, the following points are worth noting:

1. The Reformation never marked a complete break with the ongoing university traditions of metaphysics that extend back to the Middle Ages.[31] There was, of course, much anti-metaphysical rhetoric produced by the early Reformers, but recent research has demonstrated that this must be taken with more than a mere pinch of salt, since the real relationship is somewhat more complex. In fact, so much of the world was steeped in implicit metaphysical and logical assumptions that it would have been virtually impossible for the reformers to free themselves from its influence even if they had wished to do so.[32]

A good example of this is provided by Calvin's rejection of the medieval notion of the absolute will of God in his discussion at *Institutes* I.17.2. As David Steinmetz has convincingly demonstrated, he may have thought he was rejecting the distinction, but he actually misunderstood it, and in fact adopted the substance of the medieval notion.[33] In addition, Richard Muller's careful comparison of the Latin and French editions of Calvin's works has revealed that attacks on scholastics in general in the Latin are frequently more restricted in the parallel French texts, focused on the theologians at the Sorbonne in Calvin's beloved France.[34]

2. The changing nature of Reformed theological education and polemics demanded a more self-conscious attitude to metaphysics. The move to the university inevitably required deeper reflection upon how Reformed theology connected with the wider university arts curriculum, and this inevitably involved engagement with the metaphysical traditions which underlay that curriculum.[35] Then, the need to engage Jesuit polemic inevitably demanded close attention to metaphysical questions, given the highly sophisticated

level at which Jesuit thinkers in the sixteenth and seventeenth centuries operated as they marshaled and developed the vast field of medieval and Renaissance Christian thought at their disposal in order to combat the Protestants. This, of course, drove the Protestants themselves back to precisely the same sources.[36] In addition, the close connection between Jesuit thinking on contingency and related issues and that of leading Remonstrant thinkers such as Arminius and Episcopius further reinforced the need for the Reformed Orthodox to address the metaphysical implications of their own theology in order to defend and articulate it in a coherent and competent manner.[37]

Finally, the rise of Arminianism and, even more so, Socinianism, confronted the Orthodox with deviant theologies which operated with the same formal Scripture principle as they did themselves. No longer was it enough to combat heresy with a straightforward appeal to the authority of Scripture, as they had done to a large extent with the Catholics: now there was need to tease out the metaphysical implications of the scriptural record and also to mount a defense of the coherence of standard theological doctrines such as that of the Trinity. The demands this placed upon theologians required a much greater self-awareness regarding metaphysical questions.[38]

3. The impact of the use of metaphysical argumentation in Reformed Orthodoxy needs to be understood in a nuanced way as determined by the texts themselves and not by the role of metaphysics in medieval thought or clichéd generalizations about how metaphysics impacts upon theology. This is an extremely important point. First, it is important to note that the use made of metaphysical argumentation by the Reformed Orthodox exhibits a much greater preoccupation with exegetical considerations than many of the medieval precedents, precisely as a result of the exegetical turn which takes place at the Reformation. Thus, the use of metaphysics is not so much an intentional break with the approach of Calvin and other earlier reformers but a positive attempt to build upon their legacy by bringing a subordinate metaphysics into relationship with exegesis.[39] The veritable cornucopia of exegetical and philological studies generated by the Reformed Orthodox in the late sixteenth and seventeenth centuries (and, indeed, by their Catholic opponents) is a sure sign of the vital importance of exegesis to their overall theological project.[40]

Second, the Orthodox use of metaphysical argumentation is distinctly different to that of the medievals in a number of ways. For example, in discussion of the proofs of God's existence, it is quite clear that the Reformed Orthodox place the traditional proofs within an argumentative context which is decisively shaped by the tradition of classical rhetoric, thus rendering the whole not as tight philosophical *proofs* as such but rather as rhetorical *persuasions* to belief. A classic example is provided by Stephen Charnock in the relevant chapters of his unfinished sermons series, *The Existence and Attributes of God,* where arguments from causality rub shoulders with arguments based on the consent of the nations in what amounts to an attempt to overwhelm his audience with persuasions to God's existence.[41] Given that Calvin himself can on occasion use arguments based on the consent of the nations, it is clear that the gap between himself and the Orthodox on this issue is perhaps nowhere near as great as might be assumed by a superficial reading of the texts. In the context of Renaissance rhetorical practice, it is arguable that Charnock represents simply a later, more elaborate, expression of the same intention we find in Calvin.[42]

Finally, the impact of metaphysics upon individual theologians must be judged by the results themselves and not by the kind of *a priori* models of which theologians are so fond but which too often fail to work when applied to real historical actions. First, we need to remember that the Reformed Orthodox did not have a universal metaphysical framework which they all shared but, as was typical of their thinking as a whole, were eclectic, with, say, John Owen opting for a modified Thomism while a thinker like Twisse could opt for a more Scotist position while yet rejecting the univocity of being and accepting the real distinction between existence and essence. Then, the results of metaphysical argumentation frequently run counter to expectations. For example, I have often heard it said in seminar discussion that later Reformed Orthodoxy was more rigidly deterministic than the Reformation thought of Calvin, a view which, I presume, derives from the acceptance of the kind of centraldogma theories outlined above. In fact, the opposite would appear to be the case. Central to any deterministic view of the divine–human relationship is the denial of a permissive will in God, whereby God can, say, permit a certain action but, in some mysterious way, not positively and actively will it. This is emphatically the position of Calvin who rejects the notion of divine permission as "babble" and "absurd talk."[43] When we come to later Reformed Orthodoxy, however, we find that the notion of a permissive will in God is a commonplace, albeit nuanced in such a way, with references to secondary causes and contingency, that Arminian and Pelagian constructions are precluded. The concern of Calvin – the preservation of God's priority and sovereignty – is thus safeguarded, but the medieval metaphysical heritage, with its careful distinctions regarding necessity and its use of levels of causality and its discussion of contingents, is thus useful in producing a more subtle expression of this sovereignty than one finds in Calvin who simply lacked sufficient medieval background to avoid the blunt determinism of the expressions we find in his writings.[44] Given this, Calvin's placement of predestination under the doctrine of salvation rather than the doctrine of God becomes theologically less than significant and implausible as an attempt to relativize his predestinarianism; in fact, this can be satisfactorily explained in terms of the changing genre of the *Institutes* and Calvin's reading and use of Melanchthon, without the need to resort to unsupportable speculation about Calvin's alleged theological motives.[45] This is not the only example where the texts contradict the scholarly myths: research has demonstrated that supralapsarian understandings of the divine decretal order are actually less dependent upon metaphysical constructions than their infralapsarian counterparts;[46] that formulations of "limited atonement" derive from reflections upon the relationship of orthodox trinitarianism to the economy of anti-Pelagian understandings of salvation and not from logical deduction from the decrees;[47] and that use of such concepts as the analogy of being could, in the context of seventeenth-century controversy, be used to undergird rather than undermine the christocentric nature of Reformed theology.[48]

Finally, while there is not space here to deal thoroughly with claims such as those by Bizer and Armstrong regarding the use of human reason and Aristotle in later Reformed Orthodoxy, the following brief comments are in order. First, there is a great difference between the use of syllogisms and a commitment to rationalism in a Cartesian or Enlightenment sense of the word. The point at issue is not the use of logic – it is simple enough to find examples of logical reasoning in John Calvin (hardly surprising since the Aristotelian syllogism was not rejected until the advent of Fregean analysis in the nineteenth century, as any history of logic primer will tell us) – but the premises upon which that logic operates. We need to distinguish here between *rationality* and *rationalism*: the former takes its axioms from the givens of faith but assumes that theology is not nonsense and has a certain coherence – the classic "faith seeking understanding" model; the latter takes its axioms from elsewhere, whether from human psychological self-awareness (Descartes) or sense perception (Locke) or some other non-revelatory source. Given the unswerving commitment of the Reformed Orthodox to total depravity, the absence of natural analogies to the Trinity, and the supernatural nature of faith, it is hard to see how accusations of *rationalism* can be made to stick. More care is needed in the use of terminology in this area.

Second, the wide variety of schools of Aristotelian interpretation in the Middle Ages and the Renaissance, from medieval Thomism and Scotism to the schools at Paris and Padua, combined with the way in which Aristotelian conceptual terminology underwent dramatic transformations at the hands of Christian thinkers (e.g., accidents and substance in discussions of transubstantiation), renders the whole notion of a coherent entity to which we can give the title "Aristotelianism" highly problematic. As with other "isms", most notably in this context "Augustinianism", by the time of the Reformation, we can apply the term "Aristotelianism" only in the broadest sense of a tradition which regards the canon of Aristotle's works, and/or the trajectories of thought which have engaged with it, as in some sense useful for contemporary discussion. In short, the term is probably meaningless with regard to content, as are arguments which assume it has an identifiable content, and it would be best abandoned by later scholarship.[49]

## CONCLUSION

Clearly, there is a lot more to be said about the relationship between Calvin and later Reformed thought than we have been able to cover in this article. The rise of federal theology, the increasing emphasis upon pastoral concerns in Dutch, English, and New England Puritanism, and the eventual collapse of Orthodoxy in the early eighteenth century are all important parts of the historical narrative.[50] Nevertheless, from the above it is clear that any account of the development of Reformed thinking has to take a number of issues into consideration:

1. The development of Reformed theology is not simply a dogmatic problem and must not be treated as such. It involves wider cultural issues, such as the placement of theological education in the university setting, which require the historian to pay attention to the impact upon method and self-understanding that this required. Reformed theology was written by real people in real historical circumstances; such historical actions require historical explanations which seek to understand the particular text in relation to the general context.

2. Scholarship cannot treat Reformed theology as a discrete entity that flows from the writings of one individual, John Calvin. It represents a movement which is pluriform in origin and eclectic with regard to its sources. It is one part of the ongoing western trinitarian and anti-Pelagian tradition that sought to draw its theology from the broad western intellectual tradition, patristic, medieval, Renaissance, and Reformation, in order to give it coherent expression in its own day. In doing so, it also focused on exegesis and philology in its desire to understand more deeply the biblical text, the cognitive foundation of theology. These concerns are what bind, say, Calvin and Voetius together, and to judge each simply in relation to the other is really to miss the whole point of what they were doing. We must not be sidetracked by analytical models which isolate Calvin from the western tradition

as if he were some peculiar authority – he was not that even within his own narrower tradition. We must adopt a more eclectic approach that does justice to the intellectual and cultural eclecticism of the Reformed tradition itself.

3. The development and continuity for which I have argued should not be taken to mean identity. It is vital to stress this fact since the revised picture of the relationship between Calvin and Reformed Orthodoxy which has emerged in the last twenty years is emphatically not an attempt to posit identity between the two; it is rather to demand a more sound historical approach to the problem which broadens the context and eschews the qualitative language of decline and fall as obscuring the problem; and an attempt to demonstrate how theology developed from 1559 to approximately 1680 in a manner which is explicable by historians without resorting to the kind of non-verifiable speculative theological models which various nineteenth- and twentieth-century theologians sought to impose upon the material. When textual and contextual factors are given analytical priority, a coherent narrative of *development* emerges. Whether this represents theological improvement or decline is a task for theologians, but those theologians must make sure they get their history right first.

### Notes

1  B. Hall, "Calvin against the Calvinists," in G. E. Duffield, ed., *John Calvin* (Appleford: Sutton Courtenay Press, 1996), 12–37. One of the most influential and detailed works in English that stands in this tradition of scholarship is Brian G. Armstrong: *Calvinism and the Amyraut Heresy* (Madison: University of Wisconsin Press, 1969). For a thorough survey and a critique of the literature in this tradition, see the two-part article by Richard A. Muller, "Calvin and the 'Calvinists'; Assessing Continuities and Discontinuities between the Reformation and Orthodoxy," *Calvin Theological Journal* 30 (1995), 345–75; 31 (1996), 125–60.

2  The pluriformity and catholicity of Reformed theology has been emphasized most clearly in the work of Richard Muller: see his *Christ and the Decree: Christology and Predestination from Calvin to Perkins* (Grand Rapids: Baker, 1988) and *Post-Reformation Reformed Dogmatics 1: Prolegomena to Theology* (Grand Rapids: Baker, 1987).

3  For example, Holmes Rolston III, *John Calvin versus the Westminster Confession* (Richmond, VA: John Knox Press, 1972); James B. Torrance, "Strengths and Weaknesses of the Westminster Theology," in Alasdiar I. C. Heron, *The Westminster Confession in the Church Today* (Edinburgh: St Andrews Press, 1982).

4  For example, The Banner of Truth Trust, through its monthly magazine, has promoted at a popular level the notion that the five points of Calvinism contain the essence of Calvinism and bind Calvin together with later Orthodoxy.

5  See especially the two following collections: Carl R. Trueman and R. S. Clark, eds., *Protestant Scholasticism: Essays in Reassessment* (Carlisle: Paternoster, 1998); Willem J. van Asselt and Eef Dekker, eds., *Reformation and Scholasticism: an*

*Ecumenical Enterprise* (Grand Rapids: Baker, 2001). Both contain useful methodological introductions and surveys of the scholarship.

6  I am indebted on this score to the work of the intellectual historian, Quentin Skinner, who has done much to give clear expression to the basics of sound method in the field of intellectual history in general: see the collection of his writings in James Tully, ed., *Meaning and Context: Quentin Skinner and His Critics* (Oxford: Polity Press, 1988).

7  For Armstrong's definition, see *Calvinism and the Amyraut Heresy*, 31. For its elevation to the level of textbook definition, whereby the author apparently does not feel it necessary to acknowledge the source, see Alister E. McGrath, *Reformation Thought: An Introduction* (Oxford: Blackwell, 1993).

8  This point was made with force by Ernst Bizer, *Frühorthodoxie und Rationalismus* (Zurich: EVZ, 1963); also his introduction to Heinrich Heppe, *Die Dogmatik der Evangelisch-Reformierten Kirche* (Neukirchen: Neukirchener Verlag, 1958), xvii–xcvi.

9  Van Asselt and Dekker, eds., *Reformation and Scholasticism*, 39.

10  For example, see James Weisheipl, "Scholastic Method," and I. C. Brady, "Scholasticism: Medieval Scholasticism," in *New Catholic Encyclopedia*, 19 vols. (New York: McGraw-Hill, 1967–95), XII, 1145–46 and 1153–58.

11  On the Academy, see Karin Maag, *Seminary or University? The Genevan Academy and Reformed Higher Education, 1560–1620* (Aldershot: Ashgate, 1995).

12  On the broad impact of continental theology on early English Reformation theology, see Carl R. Trueman, *Luther's Legacy: Salvation and English Reformers, 1525–1556* (Oxford: Clarendon Press, 1994). While I disagree with the theological analysis at significant points, a good survey of the impact of the exile on the shaping of English Protestantism can be found in Dan G. Danner, *Pilgrimage to Puritanism: History and Theology of the Marian Exiles at Geneva, 1555–1560* (New York: Peter Lang, 1999); on the Marian experience in general, see Andrew Pettegree, ed., *Marian Protestantism: Six Studies* (Aldershot: Scolar Press, 1996).

13  On Oxford in the seventeenth century, see Nicholas Tyacke, ed., *The History of the University of Oxford IV: Seventeenth Century Oxford* (Oxford: Clarendon Press, 1997); on John Owen's life, see Peter Toon, *God's Statesman* (Exeter: Paternoster, 1971).

14  I have chosen this specific example because I have seen it used so often in postgraduate seminars to argue for precisely the kind of radical disjunction between earlier and later Reformed thought that I seek to deny.

15  On the publishing history of Calvin's *Institutes*, see B. B. Warfield, "On the Literary History of Calvin's *Institutes*," in *The Works of B. B. Warfield*, 10 vols. (Oxford: Oxford University Press, 1932), V, 373–428; also "Introduction," in John Calvin, *The Institutes of the Christian Religion*, 2 vols. (London: SCM, 1960), I, xxix–lxxi. Turretin's *Institutio Theologiae Elencticae* (Geneva, 1679–85) was translated into English in the nineteenth century by George Musgrave Giger. It has been edited and reissued by James T. Dennison as *Institutes of Elenctic Theology*, 3 vols. (Phillipsburg: Presbyterian and Reformed, 1992–94).

16  Turretin, *Institutes*, I, vii.

17  See the works cited above by Armstrong, Bizer, McGrath, Rolston, and Torrance.

18  The letter is translated in the Library of Christian Classics edition. See John Calvin, *Institutes of the Christian Religion*, ed. John T. McNeill, trans. Ford Lewis

Battles. Library of Christian Classics (Philadelphia: Westminster Press, 1960), I, 9–31.

19 Ibid., I, 4–5.

20 For a variety of views on the purpose and structure of Calvin's *Institutes*, see the discussions in B. B. Warfield, "On the Literary History of Calvin's *Institutes*"; Wilhelm Niesel, *The Theology of Calvin*, trans. Harold Knight (London: Lutterworth, 1956); François Wendel, *Calvin: The Origin and Development of His Religious Thought*, trans. Philip Mairet (London: Fontana, 1963); Ford Lewis Battles, "*Calculus Fidei*: Some Ruminations on the Structure of the Theology of John Calvin," in *Interpreting John Calvin*, ed. Robert Benedetto (Grand Rapids: Baker, 1996); Richard A. Muller, *The Unaccommodated Calvin; Studies in the Foundation of a Theological Tradition* (Oxford: Oxford University Press, 2000).

21 See the comments of Muller, *The Unaccommodated Calvin*, p. 101.

22 Turretin, *Institutes*, xxxiii–xxxviii.

23 Ibid., xxxix.

24 Ibid., xl.

25 Turretin goes on to explain the absence of certain topics on the grounds that he does not wish to add to the mass of literature and pointless controversies which surround the Reformed faith: Ibid., xli.

26 Ibid., xl.

27 David C. Steinmetz, "The Scholastic Calvin," in Trueman and Clark, eds., *Protestant Scholasticism*, 16–30; Muller, *The Unaccommodated Calvin*, ch. 3.

28 See Jacob Arminius, *Opera Theologica*, 3 vols. (Leiden, 1629); Gisbertus Voetius, *Selectae Disputationes*, 5 vols. (Utrecht, 1648–69). On Arminius' relation to medieval pedagogy, see Richard A. Muller, *God, Creation and Providence in the Thought of Jacob Arminius* (Grand Rapids: Baker, 1991); on Voetius, see the introduction and selection in Willem van Asselt and Eef Dekker, eds., *De Scholastieke Voetius* (Zoetermeer: Boekencentrum, 1995).

29 Alexander Schweizer, "Die Synthese des Determinismus und der Freiheit in der reformierten Dogmatik. Zur Vertheidigung gegen Ebrard," *Theologische Jahrbücher* 8 (1849), 153–209; Paul Althaus, *Die Prinzipien der deutschen reformierten Dogmatik im Zeitalter der aristotelischen Scholastik* (Leipzig: Deichert, 1914); Hans Emil Weber, *Reformation, Orthodoxie und Rationalismus*, 2 vols. (Darmstadt: Wissenschaftliche Buchgesellschaft, 1966); Bizer, *Frühorthodoxie und Rationalismus*; Johannes Dantine, "Les Tabelles sur la doctrine de la prédestination par Thèodore de Béze," *Revue de théologie et de philosophie* 16 (1966), 365–77; Walter Kickel, *Vernunft und Offenbarung bei Theodore Beza* (Neukirchen: Neukirchner Verlag, 1967). Not all authors regarded the predestinarian "centraldogma" in the same way: Schweizer, in contrast to others, regarded it as a good thing; Schweizer, Heppe, and Althaus saw it as marking a point of continuity between Calvin and later Reformed thought; while Bizer, Dantine, and Kickel, under the impact of Barthian reconstructions of christology and predestination, considered it to mark a point of discontinuity between Calvin and later Orthodoxy.

30 See the following by Richard A. Muller: *Christ and the Decree*; *Post-Reformation Reformed Dogmatics I* (where the complete absence of predestination from Orthodox prolegomenal discussions is indicative of its lack of "centraldogmatic"

status); "Found (No Thanks to Theodore Beza): One 'Decretal' Theology," *Calvin Theological Journal* 32 (1997), 145–51; "The Use and Abuse of a Document: Beza's *Tabula praedestinationis*, the Bolsec Controversy, and the Origins of Reformed Orthodoxy," in Trueman and Clark, eds., *Protestant Scholasticism*, 33–61.

31  In this context, see especially the work of Charles Schmitt: *Aristotle and the Renaissance* (Cambridge: Harvard University Press, 1983); *The Aristotelian Tradition and Renaissance Universities* (London: Variorum Reprints, 1984).

32  D. V. N. Bagchi, "*Sic et Non*: Luther and Scholasticism," in Trueman and Clark, eds., *Protestant Scholasticism*, 3–15; Irena Backus, "'Aristotelianism' in Some of Calvin's and Beza's Expository and Exegetical Writings on the Doctrine of the Trinity, with Particular Reference to the Terms *ousia* and *hypostasis*," in *Histoire de l'exégèse au XVIe siècle* (Geneva: Librairie Droz, 1978), 251–60; Antonie Vos, "Scholasticism and Reformation," in van Asselt and Dekker, eds., *Reformation and Scholasticism*, 99–119; Muller, *The Unaccommodated Calvin*, 156–57.

33  David C. Steinmetz, "Calvin and the Absolute Power of God," *Journal of Medieval and Renaissance Studies* 18 (1988), 65–79.

34  Muller, *The Unaccommodated Calvin*, 50–52.

35  On the university curriculum in the period of Reformed Orthodoxy, see Tyacke, ed., *The History of the University of Oxford IV*; William T. Costello, *The Scholastic Curriculum at Early Seventeenth Century Cambridge* (Cambridge, MA: Harvard University Press, 1958).

36  For example, William Twisse, *Vindiciae Gratiae, Potestatis ac Providentiae Dei* (Amsterdam, 1632) and *De Scientia Media* (Arnhem, 1639), both of which engage Jesuit and Arminian thinking on their own metaphysical territory. For discussion of this point, see Eef Dekker, "An Ecumenical Debate between Reformation and Counter-Reformation? Bellarmine and Ames on *liberum arbitrium*," in van Asselt and Dekker, eds., *Reformation and Scholasticism*, 141–54.

37  On the use of Jesuit thought by Arminius, with particular reference to the issue of middle knowledge, see E. Dekker, "Was Arminius a Molinist?," *Sixteenth Century Journal* 27 (1996), 337–52; also his *Rijker dan Midas: Vrijheid, genade en predestinatie in de theologie van Jacobus Arminius (1559–1609)* (Zoetermeer: Boekencentrum, 1993).

38  For example, see John Owen's major anti-Socinian work, *Vindiciae Evangelicae*, which opens with a grudging acknowledgment that Socinians appear to hold to the Protestant Scripture principle: *The Works of John Owen*, 24 vols. (London: Johnstone and Hunter, 1850–55), vol. XII.

39  On the exegetical orientation of Reformed thought, see the essays in Richard A. Muller and James E. Bradley, *Biblical Interpretation in the Era of the Reformation: Essays Presented to David Steinmetz in Honor of His Sixtieth Birthday* (Grand Rapids: Eerdmans, 1996); also Richard A. Muller, *Post-Reformation Reformed Dogmatics 2: Holy Scripture* (Grand Rapids: Baker, 1993); Richard A. Muller, "*Ad fontes argumentorum*: the Sources of Reformed Theology in the 17th Century," *Utrechtse Theologische Reeks* 40 (1999), esp. pp. 9–11; Muller, "Calvin and the 'Calvinists,'" 130–33.

40  See the survey by Richard A. Muller, "Biblical Interpretation in the Sixteenth and Seventeenth Centuries" in Donald K. McKim, ed., *Historical Handbook of Major Biblical Interpreters* (Leicester: Inter-Varsity Press, 1998).

41  Stephen Charnock, *Discourses upon the Existence and Attributes of God*, 2 vols. (Grand Rapids: Baker, 1979), esp. I, 25–175.

42  See *Inst.* I.3.1–2; cf. the comments of Muller, "*Ad fontes argumentorum*", 18.

43  See *Inst.* I.18.1.

44  See *The Westminster Confession of Faith*, ch. 5, "Of Providence." See Philip Schaff, *Creeds of Christendom*, 3 vols. (rpt., Grand Rapids: Baker, 1977), III, 612–14.

45  See Richard A. Muller, "*Ordo Docendi*: Melanchthon and the Organization of Calvin's *Institutes*, 1536–1543," in Karin Maag, ed., *Melanchthon in Europe* (Grand Rapids: Baker, 1999), 123–40.

46  See Lynn Courter Boughton, "Supralapsarianism and the Role of Metaphysics in Sixteenth-Century Reformed Theology," *Westminster Theological Journal* 48 (1986), 63–96; cf. Richard A. Muller, "Perkins' *A Golden Chaine*: Predestinarian System or Schematized Ordo Salutis?," *Sixteenth Century Journal* 9 (1978), 69–81.

47  See Carl R. Trueman, *The Claims of Truth: John Owen's Trinitarian Theology* (Carlisle: Paternoster, 1998).

48  See Carl R. Trueman, "John Owen's *Dissertation on Divine Justice*: An Exercise in Christocentric Scholasticism," *Calvin Theological Journal* 33 (1998), 87–103.

49  It is perhaps worth noting that Calvin himself recommends Aristotle to those who wish to have a clearer grasp of the distinction between coercion and necessity. See John Calvin, *The Bondage and Liberation of the Will: A Defence of the Orthodox Doctrine of Human Choice against Pighius*, ed. A. N. S. Lane, trans. G. I. Davies. Texts and Studies in Reformation and Post Reformation Thought (Grand Rapids: Baker, 1996), 146–50.

50  On the issue of assurance, see R. T. Kendall, *Calvin and English Calvinism to 1649*, 2nd edn (Carlisle: Paternoster, 1997), and the reply by Paul Helm, *Calvin and the Calvinists*, 2nd edn (Edinburgh: Banner of Truth, 1998). On the issue of Calvin and federal theology, see Peter A. Lillback, *The Binding of God: Calvin's Role in the Development of Covenant Theology* (Grand Rapids: Baker, 2001). Cf. Willem J. van Asselt, *The Federal Theology of Johannes Cocceius (1603–1669)*, trans. Raymond A. Blacketer. Studies in the History of Christian Thought (Leiden: E. J. Brill, 2001).

# 14 Calvin's heritage

R. WARD HOLDER

It can safely be assumed that John Calvin had an enormous impact on the world of the sixteenth century.[1] From language, to models of community life, to habits of mind, to ideals of interpretation of religious texts – in these and numerous other areas, Calvin's effect can only be calculated, it cannot be argued.[2] However, if that historical heritage of the Genevan reformer can be presumed, we are left with the question of the present. Certainly Calvin had great achievements in his own time.[3] But what of his legacy? Where does Calvin's thought live today?

This is not an easy question. How can one consider where the influence of John Calvin still lives today? The difficulties are somewhat daunting. Some may deny Calvin the lion's share of influence, noting that he is not the most original thinker in the broad Reformed tradition.[4] Others might attempt a Calvinistic "maximalism," which seeks, for good or for ill, to see Calvin's influence almost everywhere.[5] Neither approach is correct. When John Calvin died in 1564, he left a tremendous literary corpus, which might alone have secured his heritage.

But he also had endeavored, through an extensive network of acquaintances and a widespread correspondence, to influence the world outside of Geneva. Beyond that, the number of his students, protégés, and colleagues is vast. In leaving such a legacy, he made some questions almost impossible to answer. For instance, who is more to be credited for the modern range of Reformed beliefs about the presence of Christ in the Eucharist, Calvin or Bullinger, or their students?

Thus, I do not propose to limit the issue of Calvin's heritage merely to those issues for which a pure genealogy can be supplied. This would necessarily leave so many topics out that we might quickly conclude that Calvin has no contemporary significance. Yet, a quick glance at Amazon.com will reveal that more books are in print about or by Calvin than most of his contemporaries.[6] If we can assume that publishers still keep books in print for a profit motive, it seems reasonable to assume that there is some greater level of thought about Calvin in society than many of his contemporaries. But how do we measure that?

Recently, work has been done upon the possibility of considering theological traditions as practices, rather than as confined to the doctrinal *tradita* that are handed down.[7] This model of knowing what a tradition is by paying attention to its practitioners balances the model of historical tracing that one might find argued in a strictly historical work. What I propose, then, is a consideration of some key areas where Calvin's influence, considered either negatively or positively, can in practice be seen to live. To qualify, Calvin clearly will have had to have taught or supplied the impetus in question. However, clarifying the streams of influence from the sixteenth to the twenty-first centuries will not be attempted – to do so would take volumes. The areas, while not exhaustive, demonstrate the wide variety of ways in which Calvin's heritage still exerts influence in the world today.

The first area we shall consider is the geographic heritage Calvin has enjoyed. The second area to be considered will be rather uninspired, but also central: that is, Calvin's ongoing significance in contemporary theology. The third and fourth topics will no doubt engender more debate. These are Calvin's economic heritage and Calvin's political heritage. Fifth will be an even more slippery topic, Calvin's cultural heritage.

## CALVIN'S GEOGRAPHICAL HERITAGE

The problems of heritage are quite clear when we begin to consider Calvin's geographical heritage, or the geographical spread of Calvinist churches. Certainly those churches that are presbyterian in their polity seem to be Calvinist, and are frequently accounted so. But are they? Does having elders mean holding a particular set of doctrines? Does the holding of a particular doctrine mean being a Calvinist?[8] Further complicating matters is the fact that that for some countries, differing Calvinistic streams have been imported from various tributaries. For the purpose of this consideration, two different criteria will be observed. First, and most easily, Presbyterian polity will be considered a mark of the survival of the Calvinist tradition. Second, and with far greater difficulty, I shall consider the notion of doctrinal tradition, and doctrinal impact, both positive and negative. However, what this portion of the chapter must not attempt is even a brief tracing of the genealogy of Calvinism through its introduction to various places, concluding in the present day. There simply is not space for such a study!

### United Kingdom

Calvinism in the United Kingdom presents, as a microcosm, the immediate problems of tracing the Calvinistic heritage in a particular realm. The patterns of Calvinism within the various areas of the British Isles are quite distinct, in fact sometimes contradictory. The Church of England's formation had little or nothing to do with any great need for Calvinist doctrine, and everything to do with the king's choice to divorce.[9] Yet British voices could be quite Calvinistic, either from reading Calvin, or from influence by a colleague of Calvin's, the most important example being Martin Bucer. The Scottish situation differed from that of England by moving directly from Roman observance to a Reformed ordering of the kirk. The Welsh pattern of Calvinism was an eighteenth-century product of Methodist evangelical revivals, led especially by Howel Harris, Daniel Rowlands and others. This Methodism was tempered by the Calvinism of George Whitefield, creating the almost oxymoronic Welsh Calvinistic Methodism. Finally, the case of Northern Ireland is absolutely one of colonization. This former haven of Roman Catholicism became dominated by English Puritan and Scottish landholders in Ulster in the seventeenth century. This broadness of pattern allows for some of the idiosyncratic varieties of "Calvinism" that appear in the United Kingdom.

### England

The formation of the Church of England began with the "King's Great Matter." Denied a divorce by Pope Clement VII, King Henry VIII established the Church of England in 1534. Certainly, Henry was no Calvinist. Most likely, he died a religious Catholic. However, both inside and outside the Church of England, Calvinist strains were felt. Inside the Church of England, Cranmer's doctrines were far more Reformed than Roman, especially after Henry's death. Outside the Church of England, Puritans of both Presbyterian and Congregationalist sympathies were important minority voices in Great Britain.

After Henry's death in 1547, his son Edward VI took the throne. This was the moment seen as the true possibility for the reform of the Church by those of Calvinist sympathies. Calvin himself wrote the dedicatory epistle to his commentary on the Pastoral Epistles to the Duke of Somerset, Edward's regent. Throughout, this lauds the Duke, and enjoins him to protect true religion. However, Edward died an early death, leaving the throne to his half-sister Mary. Her reign imposed Roman allegiance again upon England, and she sought with all the means at her disposal to root out the heretics. It was this effort, perhaps more than anything else, that gave the young evangelical movement its strength and martyr character.[10] After Mary's death in 1558, the daughter of Henry and Ann Boleyn, Elizabeth, came to the throne. It was under her reign that the Church of England took on its most definitive form, set out as a *via media* in the Elizabethan Settlement of 1559.[11]

The settlement was a compromise that was generally opposed by those of Puritan sympathies. The Puritans wanted greater conformity with continental reforms, and less of the forms of Rome. Presbyterian Puritans wished for a presbyterian polity, but were unsuccessful until the 1640s. Then, for a brief moment, the Presbyterians held the English Parliament. With their majority, they were able to convene the Westminster Assembly. The confession that came out of that Assembly has had its greatest impact outside of England, becoming the confessional standard for Presbyterians in Scotland, the United States, and Canada. However, it was not to make such a mark in England itself. Cromwell favored the Congregationalists, and purged the Presbyterians from Parliament. Under the reign of Charles II, episcopal polity was restored.[12]

Both Presbyterianism and Congregationalism continued as forces within English church life. Congregationalists generally were separatists from the Church of England, while Presbyterians eventually accommodated, or left. However, it is not enough to see the impact of Calvinism in Britain as only represented in the dissenting bodies. The Elizabethan Settlement itself, which Presbyterians and Congregationalists so strenuously rejected, can be seen as an acceptance of some Calvinistic theological principles within the Church of England.

Today, the Church of England and the United Reformed Church coexist peacefully. These two bodies account for over 60 percent of the population, with the Church of England having the larger share of those adherents.[13]

### Scotland

Scotland was reformed in the Calvinist pattern independently of England. The work of John Knox is generally seen as the most significant impetus to reform,[14] and Knox had spent time in Geneva, terming it the most perfect community of saints since the apostles. It was Knox and five other church leaders who in 1560 wrote the Scots Confession. Knox then added to this the Book of Common Order. The Reformation of the Church of Scotland, since it received its vigor from Knox, received its order from Geneva. The church adopted a Presbyterian polity with judicial levels of the local church (kirk) session, presbytery, synod, and general assembly.[15]

Throughout the nineteenth century, schism rent the Church of Scotland.[16] Evangelicals, led by Thomas Chalmers, disputed with moderates about the mission of the church, especially the support for foreign missions. The greatest schism was the Disruption of 1843.[17] However, the early twentieth century was a time of healing of division, and in 1929 the United Free Church and the Church of Scotland united, to form the Church of Scotland. Effectively, this was a reconstitution of the national church.[18]

Today, the Church of Scotland can still claim pride of place within Scotland, though its numbers are declining.[19]

### Wales

The Presbyterian Church of Wales was a latecomer to the United Kingdom family of Calvinist churches. Its true roots lie not directly in the Reformation, but in the eighteenth-century revivals of the English evangelicals. Hence its other name, the Welsh Calvinistic Methodist Church.[20] This "other" Methodist body differed from its counterpart in England by holding a Calvinist, rather than an Arminian, theology. This Calvinism was bequeathed to the church by George Whitefield.[21]

Originally, the Calvinist Methodist movement was simply that – a movement within the Church of England. However, the ordination of nine "lay exhorters" in 1811, performed by Thomas Charles of Bala, led to a break with the Church of England.[22] The church drafted its own confession in 1823, based on the Westminster Confession. The churches retain a fierce independence, and almost three quarters of the congregations still hold their services in Welsh.[23] This is also the pattern for the other Calvinist body, the Union of Welsh Independents, which holds its services wholly in Welsh.[24] Thus, this latecomer to the Calvinistic fold mixes nationalism with doctrinal Calvinism.

### Northern Ireland

The Presbyterian Church in Ireland began, as noted above, with colonization from England and Scotland. The Ulster region became the home of foreign aristocracy and merchant classes, while the Irish sank deeper into the underclass. Though divisions led to revolts, British military force supported the continuation of the Ulster Plantation, which was augmented by the arrival of Huguenots fleeing French persecution in the seventeenth and eighteenth centuries.[25]

In 1800, the British Parliament passed the Act of Union, which placed Irish Protestants under the protection of the British government. The social and economic divisions in Ireland that were the root cause of the problems between Presbyterians and Roman Catholics did not change, and many Scots-Irish emigrated to America, Australia, and other countries, forming strong new communities with deeply felt identities such as that in Nova Scotia. In 1922, full political partition was created, with the formation of a British-ruled Northern Ireland. The Presbyterian Church in Ireland was formed in 1840 by the merger of congregations linked to the Scottish schisms, and Presbyterian congregations organized as the Synod of Ulster.[26] Though the Church did not recognize the partition, Presbyterians eventually became concentrated in Northern Ireland, where they make up approximately a quarter of the population, approximately 330,000 members.[27]

### The Netherlands

Although some scholars have wished to concentrate upon the preparation for the Reformation in the Low Countries made by the Brethren of the Common Life and their characteristic Augustinianism,[28] and the latest research on the progress of the Reformation in the Netherlands has concentrated upon the slowness of the "Protestantization,"[29] the Calvinistic strains of the Reformed faith in the Netherlands are comparatively easy to trace. Calvinism was brought to the Netherlands by refugees, especially French and English; however, Calvin himself directed some of his work toward the Low Countries.[30] The first synod of the Dutch Reformed Church was held in 1571, and the church adopted the Belgic Confession and the Heidelberg Catechism as its confessional standards. The adoption of the Belgic Confession is especially significant for tracing a particularly Calvinist brand of Reformed religion, for it was written by Guy de Bres, who thought highly enough of Calvin to receive his opinion of it.[31] In the seventeenth century, theological disputes broke out over the issue of predestination. The teachings of Jacob Arminius were opposed by those of Francis Gomar, with Arminius condemning predestination, and thus lending his name to that movement. The Synod of Dort, convened in 1618, condemned the Arminian position, and its canons were accepted as the third doctrinal standard of the Dutch Reformed Church.[32] Even today, Calvinistic churches retain the greatest proportion of Protestant Christians in the Netherlands, though the claim of the Dutch Reformed Church to remain the folk church cannot be supported statistically.[33]

The Dutch were a major colonial power in the seventeenth and eighteenth centuries. This contributed to the spread of Calvinism, as they formed outposts in South Africa and North America. In the nineteenth century, several changes occurred in Dutch Calvinism, which caused the church to take on the characteristics it bears today. In 1816, the Dutch Reformed state church was reorganized under William I and renamed the Netherlands Reformed Church.[34] This church generally accepted theological liberalism, causing a backlash and secession of some groups. The two largest groups that had separated from the Netherlands Reformed Church united in 1892 to form the Reformed Churches in the Netherlands.[35] These two denominations have customarily represented the doctrinally liberal and doctrinally conservative strands, respectively, of Dutch Calvinism. However, in recent years the Reformed Churches in the Netherlands has become more moderate in its views. The churches united, along with the Evangelical Lutheran

Church in the Kingdom of the Netherlands, to form the Protestant Church in the Netherlands in May 2004.[36]

### North America

There can be little doubt that Calvinism has been one of the dominant theological paradigms for the North American continent for most of the history of European commerce with it. This is especially true when one considers that some of the Anglican strains that came ashore from England were Calvinist in theology. As well, the theology of Calvin was a constant influence in the Puritan havens in Massachusetts and New England.[37] The likeness between the Congregationalists and Presbyterians in doctrine was attested even by Cotton Mather who assured his audience that the English Protestants planting churches in America were "nothing in doctrine, little in discipline, different from [those] of Geneva."[38] If Mather thought the discipline little different, there were others who disagreed enough to bring a more Genevan polity. Calvin's polity was brought by Dutch Calvinists to New Netherlands, and later fortified by Scotch Presbyterians such as Francis Makemie.[39] By the middle of the seventeenth century, formal declaration had been made that only the Reformed Church should be accepted in New Netherlands.[40]

American Presbyterianism broke into various strands. The Dutch Reformed churches followed the lead of the Netherlands, and remained, until the middle of the twentieth century, ethnic churches, heavily concentrated in some areas of the country, such as Michigan. The Presbyterians were fed by streams of Scots and Scots-Irish; English, and especially the Welsh Calvinistic Methodists; and some American conversions. Within America, however, this unity of ethnic heritage quickly foundered on the shoals of doctrinal schism, with several divisions over the years. Even today, the largest Presbyterian denomination, the Presbyterian Church (USA), is a union of the former United Presbyterian Church in the United States of America, and the Presbyterian Church in the United States. But this church has sister Presbyterian denominations in the Presbyterian Church of America, the Orthodox Presbyterian Church, and the Evangelical Presbyterian Church. Today, the PC(USA) is the most doctrinally liberal, but also the most divided on theological stands.

Congregational Calvinism was brought to North America by the Pilgrims and their pastor, John Robinson, in 1620.[41] This heritage of Calvinism was organized by the Cambridge Platform of 1648 and the Saybrook Platform of 1708. Strengthened by the preaching of the Great Awakening, with such figures as Jonathan Edwards and George Whitefield, Congregational churches became the most influential Reformed bodies of the colonial period.[42] Although the impact of the Great Awakening was to increase the membership of the churches, it was not without cost. The New Light–Old Light split,[43] with the New Light group supporting and the Old Light group opposing revival, broke the burgeoning power of the churches. Many New Light churches later became Baptist, while numerous Old Light churches moved toward Unitarianism.[44] The Congregationalists followed the Presbyterian pattern of division and reunion, finally arriving at the widest denomination today, the United Church of Christ. Interestingly, the Congregationalist and Presbyterian experiment in cooperation in the nineteenth century is being replayed today, with a Formula of Concord, in which the ministries and sacraments of each denomination are recognized by the other.[45]

### South Africa

As far as the Calvinism of South Africa goes, for its earliest historical roots one need look no further than the Netherlands. Reformed Christianity came to South Africa with the settlement of Cape Town by the Dutch East India Company in 1652.[46] However, though the Dutch certainly brought the first wave of Reformed Christianity to South Africa, they are far from the only stream of Calvinistic thought to feed that pool. British influences were introduced during Great Britain's occupation of the Cape, when the London Missionary Society sent Johannes T. Vanderkemp.[47] Scottish influence also made an impression, when in the nineteenth century the Glasgow Missionary Society sent missionaries Robert Moffat and David Livingstone. This mixture has caused a unique Calvinist heritage to spring up, as much a product of a peculiar trajectory of Calvinism as it is an outgrowth of a cultural-ethnic identity that was defined against another ethnicity in a racially severe manner.[48]

The Dutch Reformed Church served exclusively among white South Africans until 1836. After that point, some effort was made to reach out and evangelize the native populations (Bantu), but this was not universally accepted. For instance, one of the defining characteristics of the Nederduitse Hervormde Kerk, founded in the Transvaal in 1853, was its opposition to missions among the blacks.[49] The Calvinist theology of providence was frequently used (or mis-used) to justify this division.

As noted above, the Dutch were not the only Calvinistic influence on the nation of South Africa. Presbyterian churches were planted by the Scots and English in the nineteenth century, especially among the Bantu people of the eastern Cape.[50] As well, the London Missionary Society had begun an English-speaking Congregationalist missionary effort, marked by the arrival of Theophilus Van der Kemp in 1799.[51] Unlike the Dutch churches, which tended to see their mission as being to the white immigrant populations, the Scots and English were inclined to identify their task as taking the gospel to the African populations.

In both the Dutch and other European models, native churches came to be formed. This became a point of crisis for the Christians in South Africa in the middle years of the twentieth century. The political policy of apartheid, which was formally enacted into law in South Africa after World War II, represented a fundamental crisis for Reformed Christians in South Africa. Several of the denominations supported the policy, on theological as well as on practical grounds.[52] On the other hand, the World Alliance of Reformed Churches denounced the policy, and eventually suspended the membership of the Nederduitse Gereformeerde Kerk and the Nederduitse Hervormde Kerk in 1982 over their continuing support of the policy.[53] The support of the Reformed International for outrage against this racism allowed Reformed African theologians such as Desmond Tutu and Alan Boesak to gain a fuller hearing of their critiques. In 1986, the Nederduitse Gereformeerde Kerk began to reconsider apartheid, and in 1990, formally renounced its support for the policy.[54] Today, one is as likely to see Calvinist thought used to defend the policy as it is to decry it – demonstrating that Calvinism is not necessarily an automatic guarantor of any particular outcome.

### Equatorial Africa

Another successful planting site of Calvinist Christianity remains the equatorial region of Africa, especially nearer the coasts. The Presbyterian Church was the first Protestant denomination on the Gold Coast, a mission site of the Swiss Basel Mission, begun in 1828.[55] The Presbyterian Church in Ghana is presently the largest Protestant denomination in the country, with 814,000 members, and trails only Roman Catholicism for number of adherents.[56] The opposite coast is home to the Reformed Church of East Africa, and the Presbyterian Church of East Africa. Together, these two denominations make up the fourth largest denominational group in Kenya, trailing the Roman Catholic, Anglican, and Africa Inland Church.[57]

Kenya and Ghana followed similar paths in the spread of Calvinism, though the Ghana mission was much earlier. Beginning as mission churches staffed from Europe, in the twentieth century the churches became autonomous. However, many of the cultural and societal functions which were hallmarks of the early missionary days of these churches still remain. Thus, education is still central in Reformed Christianity in both Kenya and Ghana, as are the medical missions.[58]

## Korea

Presbyterianism is one of the hallmarks of Korean Christianity. Though Christianity was first introduced to Korea through a Scottish mission founded in Manchuria to train Koreans as missionaries, the greater expansion of Calvinism and Christianity followed the Korean treaty with the United States in 1882. This allowed western missionaries access to Korea.[59] The arrival of Horace Underwood in 1885 and Samuel A. Moffett in 1890 began the great expansion of Korean Presbyterianism. The Presbyterian mission was the center of a great revival that took place between 1903 and 1907; at its end, the various western missions united to form the Presbyterian Church of Korea.[60] One of the crucial aspects of Korean Calvinism is its strong evangelical sense. Frequently, South Korean Christians will speak confidently of the time in the future when they will be able to bring the gospel to their neighbors in the North, and their concrete plans to bring this about. However, schism has also been a hallmark of Korean Presbyterian and Reformed Christianity. Though the Methodist mission in South Korea has managed to overcome this tendency in the late twentieth century, the number of Presbyterian denominations, normally formed by schismatic fracture, continues to grow.[61]

### Impact of the geographical heritage

Certainly, the geographical family tree of Calvinism can be traced, and has been much more thoroughly than this brief effort. But what impact has that spread of Calvinism had on the present day? Two points are worth mentioning. First, the constant presence of Calvinist congregations, whether Congregationalist, Presbyterian, or even Episcopalian, makes a difference in the religious consciousness of the adherents. This can act as a dominant cultural paradigm, as it has in Scotland, Korea, and the Netherlands. Or it can be the significant "leavening" voice, as has occurred in the rest of the United Kingdom. Or finally, it can be the salt, that exercises an influence far out of proportion to its occurrence within the culture, as seen in North America.

This can be measured in various ways, and some of them are other subject headings within this chapter. However, to offer up just one topic, not otherwise covered, let us consider education. Wherever they have been successfully planted,[62] Calvinist churches have sown or come to dominate schools. These schools have become agents of belief, handing down patterns of thought, ideas of propriety, and an ethos of community life built around the relationship between the divine and the human. Though this heritage is significantly different in some of its strains, as for instance one can argue that Dutch Kuyperianism is simply not always compatible with Welsh

Calvinistic Methodism, the influence these streams have had is undeniable. Just as undeniable is the source of these streams, in the thought of John Calvin.

Another, more anecdotal, way to measure this impact of Calvin's heritage in areas where Calvinist churches have been successfully planted can be related. A convocation of Presbyterian scholars was sponsored by the Presbyterian Church (USA).[63] These scholars, coming from widely different schools and very different teaching specialties, were asked to introduce their thoughts on the vocation of the Presbyterian teacher with a brief, 1–2 page, reflection. Twenty-six reflections were collected. Of these, eleven mentioned Calvin and Calvinism specifically. Further, the great majority of these, nine of the eleven, were attempting to make their cases about the Presbyterian vocation of teaching by specific reference to Calvin himself. Interestingly, some of the theses were almost flatly contradictory in their use of Calvin, and their interpretation of his significance. However, that is not the point. What must be seen is that without prompting, more than a third of Presbyterian educators offered a relationship to Calvin in their thought.[64]

Another, frankly less salutary, effect of Calvinism on the religious consciousness of any country where it is planted is the stark tendency toward schism. While Calvin himself may have written strongly against leaving the true church, the fact remains that he believed himself to be an accurate arbiter of where the true church was. This tendency was passed on to his descendants. The divisions in Scotland, America, the Netherlands, South Africa, Korea, and Equatorial Africa are simply too prevalent to ignore. Within the genius of historical Calvinism is at least one seed of the destruction of unity, which is the impulse to become doctrinally pure. While Calvin spoke with great force against the gathered churches of the Anabaptists, and against the ideal of a sinless body on earth, his efforts at communal piety based on credal subscription left a heritage to his followers that has resulted in a sometimes bewildering array of Calvinist denominations, which frequently claim to be the Church in contradistinction to each other.

These are the real reasons to consider the geography of Calvinism. Where Calvinist churches have been successfully planted, Calvin's thought retains a normative character. In fact, Calvin sometimes fulfills a mythic function, where good ideas are "attached" to Calvin to give them greater weight. We can see this not only in church publications where the level of reference can be quite low. The same can be seen in the work of academics of the first rank. Calvin's own ideals aside, his function as a desirable authority seems clear. Because of that enduring mythic and originating function in areas where Calvinist churches have been successfully and continuously nurtured, seeing the geographical spread of Calvinism helps explain the modern impact of Calvin's thought.

## CALVIN'S THEOLOGICAL HERITAGE

It is almost impossible to consider modern theology without acknowledging the influence of John Calvin's heritage. Of course, the issues of predestination and the will are frequently noted in any quick survey of Calvin's impression in later theological models. But far more interesting are the ways in which Calvin's theology impacted the grounding of theology. Certainly, one can remember the story of Karl Barth placing the bust of Friedrich Schleiermacher upon his desk, and note that both considered themselves to be in continuity with the tradition that flowed through Calvin. However, arguing about who was the truer "Calvinist," or painted the more accurate "trajectory" from Calvin, though entertaining, does not amply illustrate Calvin's ongoing influence. Other loci do. Though it is impossible to exhaust this topic, there are three issues where Calvin's impact can still be seen in the working of theologians today. These are his grounding of theology in the divine and human dynamic, his utter reliance on grace, and his notions of interpretation of revelation.[65] Each of these has exercised considerable influence in the Reformed tradition, and continues to be significant in the theological currents of contemporary Christian thought.

### Dynamic of human and divine

Calvin begins the *Institutes* with the words, "Nearly all the wisdom we possess, that is to say, true and sound wisdom, consists of two parts: the knowledge of God and of ourselves."[66] This linking of the divine and human is characteristic of Calvin's thought.[67] Calvin finds it impossible to look at oneself without being almost driven to contemplate God, forced by the unhappiness of the human condition to that knowledge.[68] We find it in his trinitarian development of the pattern of salvation,[69] in his epistemology,[70] and in his consideration of the task of preaching.[71] But more important for our considerations is how we find that tendency still alive in the theological conversations of today.

Where does this tendency live today? One can hardly imagine the Neo-Orthodox movement of the first half of the twentieth century without it. When the (gratuitously ugly) term "theo-anthropology" was coined, what could it signify except the necessity of considering the divine and human objects together? The whole character of twentieth-century theology has the quality of this type of thought. It is found in disparate places – Barth's linking of the knowledge of God and the knowledge of the self is balanced by Tillich's consideration of the principle of correlation, which he explicitly applied to Calvin.[72] Frequently, there is no tipping of the hat to Calvin in this, nor should there be. This is simply a site where Calvin's ongoing influence can be seen.

### Radical grace

Did Calvin have a radical doctrine of grace? Of course he did. This is one of the few questions in Calvin's thought which does seem settled. Calvin took an essentially Augustinian turn in his doctrine of grace, and this was available to him both through his study of Luther, and through reading Augustine himself. This is a commonplace, so much so that Benjamin B. Warfield could write that the Reformation represented the triumph of Augustine's doctrine of grace over his doctrine of the church.[73]

Yet does this idea still live today? In a sense, it seems unable to die. In considering Calvin's doctrine of the will, a recent book seems at pains to correct Calvin, and allow for a greater functioning of human freedom.[74] Further, much feminist theological critique aimed at contemporary theologians can be seen as a "working out" of the ongoing impact of Calvin's thought. For instance, in Valerie Saiving Goldstein's reproach of Reinhold Niebuhr's doctrine of sin, certainly Calvin and Augustine are directly in the background.[75] Her criticism that the nature of sin is oversimplified by the Niebuhrian acceptance of sin as sins of power is potent but, to some degree, what Goldstein must see is that she is arguing against Niebuhr's acceptance of a particular theological tradition, which carried Calvin's imprint. Further, Goldstein's argument about the particular sins of women can itself be seen as a "gendered" response to Calvinistic thought. Though she draws a different tone in her conclusion, does her point not seem to argue that women have accepted the effects of the Augustinian/Calvinistic doctrine of the radicality of sin too well? That the main problem may not be the doctrine, but its inappropriate, or too strenuous, or simply imbalanced, application? In any case, whatever the answer to the question, one cannot deny Calvin's impact on this question.

### Interpretation of divine revelation

Since long before the famous Barth–Brunner debate,[76] the issue of the interpretation of Calvin's thought upon the correct way to understand the revelation(s) of God was an issue of concern. Francis Turretin could allow for no possible difference between the truths of right reason and faith, and found this in the tradition stemming from Calvin.[77] The matter continues to be played out in scholarship dedicated to discussing what Calvin actually thought, as several recent studies can demonstrate. However, what about the present impact of such a locus?

First, what is Calvin's notion of divine revelation? Where is God's most clear revelation located, and how is it grasped? We must begin by stating that for Calvin, the clearest revelation of God to humanity is in Jesus Christ. Though Calvin could speak with the highest reverence for the text of the Bible, he never confused the gospel content – the Christ – with the words of Scripture.[78] Christ was made available most clearly through the ministry of the Word. However, once that ministry had done its task, wider possibilities were opened up before the believer.[79]

Additionally, Calvin influences the modern theological tradition in his understanding of the whole of God's revelation as accommodated.[80] Essentially, Calvin claimed that God, in all forms of divine revelation, gives knowledge through simplified language, and simplified communication. Calvin uses a metaphor to explain this, that of a nurse babbling (*balbutire*) to a child.[81] The possibilities for interpreting revelation inherent in this tool are obvious. Further, the clarity of the impact of this understanding can be seen in a work such as Philip Walker Butin's *Revelation, Redemption and Response*, where Butin approvingly uses this notion as a solution to the problem of the sharp divine/human antithesis that some students of Calvin have seen.[82] Some theologians who would like to use Calvin's thought have ignored this dynamic in Calvin's thought to the detriment of their consideration of his theology.[83]

Another item in the interpretation of the revelation of God which Calvin certainly has affected is the consideration of the providence of God in the world. Calvin raises the question, quite radically, of how much of the world God directly controls. Historically speaking, there is little doubt that Calvin was a proponent of the belief in God's direct action in the world. He sought to tie secondary causality, such as the work of the angels, natural law, and governments, particularly closely to God's direct intervention in the world, in order to avoid deflating the importance of the actual providence of God in favor of some lesser causality.[84] But does that original stance still have an impact today?

For an answer, consider Anna Case-Winters' *God's Power: Traditional Understandings and Contemporary Challenges*. Case-Winters' book concentrates on the doctrine of divine omnipotence, both because of difficulties that arise from the traditional formulation of this doctrine, and to consider different answers to the issue. Basically, Case-Winters argues that when the omnipotence of God is affirmed, the problem of evil gives rise to the ugly head of the problem of theodicy.[85] Her argument is nuanced, and too long to summarize here. Suffice to say that Case-Winters attacks the problem by looking at its roots in the theological tradition. She begins with Calvin.

Case-Winters states her own reservations about this choice, and then her beliefs that cause her to use Calvin. She writes:

> The tradition is by no means monolithic in its answer to the question of the meaning of omnipotence. Nor is John Calvin necessarily the example par excellence of the tradition's common wisdom on the subject. Neither of these points is being presumed, nor is either a necessary prerequisite for the line of argumentation being pursued here. Nevertheless there are within the tradition shared convictions that create a certain "family resemblance" in which Calvin, in his own way, participates. At a bare minimum, these convictions include the belief that God's power is expressed in creating the world, governing it, and bringing it to its "proper end." . . . Calvin's understanding is being identified as 'classic' in the sense that it is representative of a way of thinking about divine power which was both widely held and strongly influential within the broader tradition.[86]

In her conclusion, Case-Winters proposes a synthesis of positions of process thought and feminist theology to construct a doctrine of omnipotence where omnipotence is defined as "the power to influence all and to be influenced by all." This power is characterized by being " 'life-giving' and 'world-generating.' Its operation is synergistic and empowering rather than overpowering."[87]

Arguing about which model might more correctly meet the needs of the modern faith community as well as most accurately depict God cannot be done here. However, what is important to this study is the way in which Case-Winters proceeded. Without too much discussion or defense of the choice, Calvin was picked as the representative of the tradition with whom one had to deal. When looking for the figure of (Protestant) orthodoxy, Case-Winters turned to Calvin. Perhaps, in this case, the choice is as simple as knowing that this is the voice most difficult to quell. On the other hand, perhaps the choice is instead indicative that Calvin's doctrine represents the mainstream of traditional thought, which raises the problem which Case-Winters wishes to discuss. In any case, Calvin's influence in the modern issue is clearly demonstrated.

Calvin's theological heritage has been traced in these three areas. But what of the question raised by Richard A. Muller? Is the effort to use Calvin's thought as an inspiration, a conversation partner, or a point of departure a twisting of Calvin's thought out of context? Yes and no. Certainly, Calvin does not share a significant historically situated context with those thinkers who wish to consider his thought. But he does share the desire for the knowledge of God, and the efforts at understanding the will of God, with later Christians.

Further, if Calvin's thought cannot be a spur to "Calvinist" theologies, what becomes of his own pattern? Calvin liberally drew on Chrysostom, Augustine, and Bernard of Clairvaux, to name only a few. Certainly, no thoughtful historian would argue that Calvin's Geneva was a reproduction of fifth-century Hippo, or fifth-century Constantinople, or even twelfth-century France – at least when that final situation is placed within a monastery. If the statement that Calvin is an "Augustinian" raises as much ire as admiration, cannot modern theologians' efforts at being in contact with this part of the Christian tradition do much the same?

Thus, it seems that Calvin's theological heritage can consider two divergent paths. First, it can be caught on the horns of a dilemma – trapped between those who would use Calvin for contemporary theological purposes, and those who deny the possibility of this, those who argue that Calvin's historical situatedness makes this move impossible with genuine integrity. Or, that same issue can be one of creative tension. Constructive theologians can use Calvin as a conversation partner and theological source, while historians serve as the keepers of Calvin's context, critiquing efforts that stray too far afield. But this is not a one-way street. Constructive theologians may find approaches to the historical questions that still surround Calvin and can coax historians from hide-bound orthodoxies toward innovative ways of understanding Calvin. In both cases, Calvin's ongoing sway in the modern theological conversation is noted, while inappropriate efforts at grasping his imprimatur without his thought are denied.

## CALVIN'S ECONOMIC HERITAGE

If many scholars of the Reformation will agree that Calvin had an economic heritage that is sturdy enough to be an actual object of study, much less consensus can be gained when considering the nature of that heritage. The starting point is Max Weber's celebrated thesis, *The Protestant Ethic and the Spirit of Capitalism* (1905).[88] However, if this is the starting point of the conversation, it cannot be considered the final word.

First, as has often been noted, Weber's thesis deals not so much with Calvin as with what might arguably be his heritage. This thesis connects the accumulation of capital to the need to prove one's salvation by economic success, linked with an ascetic lifestyle which did not allow great consumption of the fruits of that success. Without getting too deeply into some of the historical difficulties with this thesis,[89] it is not arguable that Calvin's heritage has made great impact on the present consideration of economic history.

Second, one of the great impacts of Calvin's thought that still is present in the modern world is his conclusion that the economic sphere is particularly a sphere for Christian action and even stewardship. Mark Valeri has pointed out that the trade laws that were enacted during Calvin's time in Geneva were exactly calculated to support Calvin's ideals of Christian commerce, rather than to allow a *laissez-faire* approach,[90] which might have anticipated a later model of "private vices becoming public virtue." Though Valeri was commenting most particularly on laws, Calvin's own religious writing supports this thesis. In his Genesis commentary, Calvin expresses an economic theme as he comments on the necessity of the stewardship of God's gifts:

> Moses adds, that the custody of the garden was given in charge to Adam, to show that we possess the things which God has committed to our hands, on the condition, that being content with a frugal and moderate use of them, we should take care of what shall remain. Let him who possesses a field, so partake of its yearly fruits, that he may not suffer the ground to be injured by his negligence: but let him endeavour to hand it down to posterity as he received it, or even better cultivated. Let him so feed on its fruits, that he neither dissipates it by luxury, nor permits it to be marred or ruined by neglect. Moreover, that this economy, and this diligence, with respect to those good things which God has given us to enjoy, may flourish among us; let every one regard himself as the steward of God in all things which he possesses. Then he will neither conduct himself dissolutely, nor corrupt by abuse those things which God requires to be preserved.[91]

Calvin made it clear that the Christian community simply could not pay attention solely to the accumulation of wealth, even should that wealth be gained legally. Instead, he put forward a vision of the Christian community where every person, even the poor, fulfills a part of God's economy. In his ninety-fifth sermon on Deuteronomy, Calvin declared that "God sends us the poor as his receivers. And although the alms are given to mortal creatures, yet God accepts and approves them and puts them to one's account, as if we had placed in his hands that which we give to the poor."[92] The poor, in their reception of alms, are not just a scale or yardstick of faith and charity. Rather, they provide an opportunity for the practice of Christian charity. Without the poor, Christians could not grow in love through the acts of gracious giving.

Does this Calvinist dynamic of giving still have influence today? Proving that it does is almost too easy. In one ecclesiastical pronouncement after another, Calvinist denominations worldwide have taken up the task of poverty relief. They have set up foundations; worked at the root causes of poverty such as lack of housing, lack of education, and lack of healthcare; and have given millions of dollars toward these efforts. Though this could be said to be common to all Christian traditions, Calvinist bodies tend to be able to avoid the excesses of some groups, by seeing this effort as their duty, rather than a task that is to be judged by its worldly success. For that reason, Calvinist churches tend to be some of the hardiest in their mission efforts, continuing to savor their founder's grasp of the twin poles of sin and duty.

## CALVIN'S POLITICAL HERITAGE

Calvin's political heritage again opens up a wide range of possible evaluations. Frequently, Calvin's or Calvinism's effect on democracy or other representative forms of governing are almost assumed. It has been noted that the impression of Calvin's thought on a wide range of "secular" topics that are acknowledged to have their roots in the sixteenth century has been generally ignored.[93] However, as noted above, some have conjectured that Calvin's success in his own day had to do with his skill at law and politics.[94] Certainly, he did have a wide influence in the making of laws in Geneva itself. But can his effect still be traced in the modern world?

A survey of the history of political philosophy can give an intermediate answer. Simply put, surveys of the history of political thought generally include Calvin.[95] But what of Calvin's influence today? Two different theorists have given very different answers. Quentin Skinner, in his *Foundations of Modern Political Thought*, takes up the question of Calvin's contributions to modern political theory, mostly in order to deny that Calvin and his followers had significant theoretical impact upon political thought.[96] This is not to deny their importance, but to shift the theoretical credit to earlier ages, from which Calvin and Calvinism borrowed. Michael Walzer, on the other hand, sees in Calvinism the formation of a disciplined radical activist.[97] Though not systematic about whether religious affections can be theoretically the basis of secular order, Walzer links the ideals of the Christian Calvinist believer to a certain secular life, which supports views linked to modernity.[98]

Are Calvin and Calvinism a force in modern politics? Yes, both for foundational and for contemporary reasons. We might conclude this simply from the amount of ink spilt arguing the question. At the foundations,

Calvin took positions that separated him from some of the other reformers, and definitely from the medieval tradition. He drew consideration of the civil government within Christian theology, as a necessary component of an ordered society. His Geneva provided for some representation of citizens, though it truly cannot be called a democracy, and he maintained the right of lower magistrates to revolt against the higher when those higher lords had gone irretrievably astray. In the hands of theorists such as Beza and Huguenot writers, these theories became radicalized, to include a broader right of revolution, and practical theories of political toleration of religious difference. These early theories on political processes in the godly society were immediately grasped by Roman Catholics and Protestants, and have become classical formulations.[99]

But Calvin also exerts influence through more contemporary actions. John Witherspoon was a Presbyterian pastor, who signed the American Declaration of Independence. More than once, the colonial rebellion was termed a "Presbyterian rebellion" by British and loyalists. Over two hundred years later, Alan Boesak was a Reformed voice speaking against apartheid in South Africa. For Calvinists, the principle of total division between faith and government has never been acceptable. Each has its own sphere, and neither should interfere with the other! But for Calvin, the question "Can the believer serve God and the state?" is simply out of the question. The rightly ordered state can only exist when believers participate. The Calvinist tradition has accepted this, and married the activist political life to Christian activity.

## CALVIN'S CULTURAL HERITAGE

The impress of Calvin's mind on the culture of the modern world is evident in a number of ways. Certainly, scholars of the French language have noted his formative influence upon that language as it began to take its modern form. As well, the habits of mind of theologians, economists, and politicians have been undeniably changed through the continuing influence of Calvin. Several of my previous headings could be lumped together under "culture." But in this slippery discussion, it is necessary to consider three topics, not considered elsewhere, that seem to be important portions of culture. The first of these is Calvin's impact on the French language. The second is how theological historiography has been changed by the consideration of Calvin. And finally, it is necessary to consider the common culture, shared by people of all walks of life. Calvin's effect is evident here, both for those who consider Calvin as one of the roots of our common consciousness, and for those who may never have heard of Calvin.

### French language

Calvin changed the nature of the French language. Along with Rabelais, he is generally seen as the most influential writer of the period.[100] Abiding by the Reformation principle of doctrine in the vulgar tongue, Calvin preached in French, wrote treatises in French, and even twice translated his theological masterwork, the *Institutes*, into French. This represented a truly new phenomenon, for the *Institutes* was a radically new standard for theological works in French.[101] Part of the growth of French censorship can be directly correlated to the efforts of Genevan presses to evangelize France.

But aside from the great literary contribution, Calvin changed the French language itself. He did this in two ways. First and most importantly, Calvin contributed to French habits of speech. An example is his dependence on the short sentence. Higman writes, "Not, of course, that Calvin's sentences are always short. But when his syntax does become more complex, one of its most notable features is the strength of the 'connectives,' the syntactic signposts which make clear to the reader which way the sense is going."[102] Likewise, Calvin's vocabulary introduced a new standard to French of precision and careful choice.[103]

A second, and equally important, impact of Calvin upon the French language is his creation of French as a truly theological language. Olivier Millet considers this one of Calvin's finer achievements, his development of French into a technically precise language through the instrument of the *Institutes*.[104] This work, though not always appreciated,[105] allowed Calvin to fulfill the effort of making the laity participants in their faith, through the consideration of important theological texts. Both of these efforts have influenced the French language, contributing toward making it the instrument of philosophy and theology that it is today, and giving it some of its characteristic features.

### Theological historiography

This is an odd category, seeming perhaps more fittingly to belong to a discussion of theology. However, after the discussion, it will be more clear why this discussion belongs with Calvin's cultural heritage. Along with Luther, Calvin has excited the most extreme reactions of the classical reformers. Some of this has been a tendency to hagiography, as has been the critique of Emil Doumergue's classical study.[106] Some of this has been a tendency to demonology.[107]

This tendency to see Calvin as either the root of evil to be yanked out and burned, or as a perfected apostle to be emulated, has begun to be calmed in modern theological historiography. Biographies such as William Bouwsma's *John Calvin: A Sixteenth Century Portrait*, have sought to find methods to portray neither a demon nor a saint, but rather a complex human being, navigating an extraordinarily difficult time with very human emotions.[108] Critiques of ahistorical efforts to grasp Calvin have begun to receive significant scholarly attention.[109] Why?

The simplest and best answer is that Calvin's own personality, available through his voluminous writings, demands this. The imprint of Calvin's nature demonstrates to us that too-facile clutching of him, to fit our own needs in the twenty-first century, falls short of the truth. In providing such a stimulus, Calvin's heritage provides the grist for our modern mills to come up with more appropriate historical and theological models for the engagement with tradition, and forwards the aims of both the academy and the faith community.

### Common culture

What is the common culture? This is an impossible question.[110] Culture may be several things, and it certainly must be linked to its own geography. But for the purpose of discussion, culture must include, it seems, all those things that we take for granted, that which is below recognition. This is true both for the "cultured" discussion, and for the living of life that is wholly unexamined. In Calvinist countries, Calvin's heritage impacts both.[111]

To begin with the more academic consideration of Calvin, consider a series of essays by Marilynne Robinson, entitled *The Death of Adam*. Time after time, Robinson points out the Calvinistic heritage which lies at the foundations of American culture, and which modernity has purposely abandoned or derided. She notes that some of the greatest hallmarks of early American culture, the *New England Primer*, and the *McGuffey Reader*, had Calvinist traces through and through. Yet because of the later decision to erase those normative models in favor of a liberal elitism, these basic texts are known with their covers tight shut.[112] This is another form of what was mentioned above – Calvin's negative impact. In part, Calvin's heritage must be measured in how important it has been to this culture to reject his thought and the tradition that bears his name.

Within Calvinism, transferred to America through the Puritans, Robinson found generosity, liberality, morality, and a basic humility that was reflected in the doctrine of total depravity. This doctrine, far from being problematic, was salutary in that it kept the Puritans and other Calvinist communities from attempts at earthly utopianism. We have replaced that culture with one that holds out the ideal of an American salvation, where everything can be achieved, and sin, or failure, can finally be eradicated. The cost of that transformation is around us, and the social critics who point it out are the heirs of the Calvinists.

But what of the popular culture? What about those who have never heard of Calvin, or of Calvinism in any significant manner? Speaking of the American culture, the answer must again be given in the affirmative. Consider, for instance, the simple issue of liquor sales in Massachusetts. Certainly, this area has never been very Presbyterian, the dominant Protestant form of Christianity being Congregational. Further, Massachusetts is quite multicultural, with sizable populations of non-Christian religions, as well as many self-identifying agnostics and atheists. Yet, it is illegal to buy liquor on Sundays. In a liberal state, where the rights of the individual are frequently exalted, one simply cannot buy a bottle of wine, or whiskey, on Sunday. Is the example so simple as to be banal? Perhaps. Yet perhaps the make-up of culture that does not enjoy the celebration of the salons is the simple everyday material, too common to be worthy of consideration, too normal to be changed. Perhaps it is this culture where we can find those things which are "just so," and thus find a mirror of what is so basic to us that it is beneath our recognition. The foundation and subsequent survival of blue laws into the twenty-first century must be laid at the feet of the Calvinist tradition. The tempering of the civil society by the activism of the believing community is a basic fact of American culture, and one of the stronger fountains of that tendency is found in Calvinism.

Once we have begun to look for Calvin's and Calvinism's influence in modern culture, we can begin to let things get out of hand, and begin to see Geneva everywhere. Some of this material is necessarily anecdotal, some of it a polemic in itself. What is not deniable is Calvin's impact on some cultural phenomena.

## CALVIN'S HERITAGE

In this survey, we have seen a variety of ways in which Calvinism and the mind of John Calvin continue to impact the modern world. Are the answers always clear? Far from it. An underlying question in this survey has been to examine why Calvin is still such a topic of discussion! For this, there are two final answers.

The first answer is theological. In Calvin's ongoing theological influence, the reason for his continued impact is comparatively simple. Calvin is one of the best theologians the Christian tradition has to offer. His melding of the edification of the church with an effort at being true to the biblical witness cannot be ignored, though it can be critiqued, denied, or built upon. He stands in the first rank of theologians, and the continuing influence he exerts is unremarkable.

The second answer is social and religious. As Professor Oberman pointed out, Calvin offered the Genevans and the evangelical refugees the survival mechanism of moral self-control. More than that, Calvin offered a powerful view of a Christian society. This is evident in his impact on economics, politics, and culture. Calvin's vision is hardly the only Christian model of a society. On the other hand, in the close attention that he gave to the details of communal living, Calvin gave practical guides to the formation of Christian communities which, even when pushed into the subconscious of the later society, exert powerful influence. For our examination of Calvin, that impact must be considered even more influential than his theology proper, from which it flowed.

### Notes

1 Originally, Professor Heiko A. Oberman was invited to write this chapter. His increasingly poor health prevented him from accepting. Sadly, Professor Oberman died on April 22, 2001. It is poignantly appropriate that as we consider the impact of Calvin on the modern world, we mark the passing of a scholar whose career has so deeply influenced contemporary ways of examining John Calvin and his time. In 1990, Oberman presented a paper, "*Initia Calvini*: The Matrix of Calvin's Reformation," at the International Congress on Calvin Research held in Grand Rapids. As some have remarked, this was another beginning, the re-entry of Professor Oberman into Calvin studies. That promise was not to come to full fruition, but in generations of students formed in the careful study of history and theology which eschews clichéd models of understanding in favor of honest grappling with thoughts and worlds not our own, Heiko Augustinus Oberman has given an even richer gift to scholarship of the early modern period.

2 A survey of the histories of the Reformation would be tiresome, and prove the point *ad nauseam*. However, an illustrative point comes in John W. O'Malley's *Trent and All That: Renaming Catholicism in the Early Modern Era* (Cambridge: Harvard University Press, 2000), 122. In a book self-consciously written for the purpose of clarifying a historiographical question about Catholicism, O'Malley backhandedly compliments Calvin for clarity of exposition and "wallop" in setting out the Protestant vision, linking him only with Martin Luther as his equal in evangelical reform.

3 It is interesting to note that Professor Oberman gave an address to the Sixth Colloquium on Calvin Studies at Davidson College, in 1992, entitled "John Calvin: The Mystery of His Impact." In the address, Oberman argued that the reason for Calvin's comparably greater impact than that of his contemporaries can be attributed especially to six attributes. These were the structural significance of Calvin's innovative institutions, the group of friends who communicated his work, the new way of reading Scripture that identified Reformation Christians with exilic Jews in the Old Testament, the placement of the message of Scripture in a context of persecution and displacement, the survival mechanism of high moral

self-control, and finally the religious psychological attraction of Calvin for those who were deprived of priestly absolution. Unfortunately for our present purpose, Professor Oberman did not carry his project forward into the twenty-first century, but the issues which he raised are at the heart of Calvin's ongoing influence. See Heiko A. Oberman, "John Calvin: The Mystery of His Impact," in John H. Leith, ed., *Calvin Studies VI*, Presented at a Colloquium on Calvin Studies at Davidson College and Davidson College Presbyterian Church, Davidson, North Carolina (Davidson, NC: Davidson Presbyterian Church, 1992), 1–11.

4  The difficulties in simply defining the "Reformed" tradition have already been discussed by other authors. See Robert Benedetto, Darrell L. Guder, and Donald K. McKim, *Historical Dictionary of Reformed Churches* (Lanham, MD: Scarecrow Press, 1999), xlvi–l. Benedetto, Guder, and McKim offer up a guideline from the Constitution of the World Alliance of Reformed Churches (xlix), but refuse to define what identifies this tradition's theology.

5  Further, the term "Calvinism" gives just as great a range of difficulty as "Reformed" does. For instance, even such a "Calvinist" as Benjamin Warfield, writing in 1908, could identify that it was an "ambiguous term," and catalogued three distinct meanings. See his "Calvinism," in *The New Schaff-Herzog Encyclopedia of Religious Knowledge*, edited by Samuel Macauley Jackson (New York: Funk and Wagnalls, 1908), 359–64.

6  The great exception, of course, is Luther. My unscientific survey found that Calvin had 55 titles attributed to him as author, and another 42 in print about him or his thought. Luther had over 600 titles about him, though Calvin was covered in some of those as well, and not catalogued under his own name. Of Melanchthon, Bullinger, Cranmer, Zwingli, and Erasmus, only Erasmus approached the amount of material in print, none of the others reaching double digits, and Erasmus did so only when volumes of his collected works were considered works about him, rather than those by him.

7  See Terrence W. Tilley, *Inventing Catholic Tradition* (Maryknoll, NY: Orbis Books, 2000), esp. ch. 1 and ch. 4.

8  For instance, can one not imagine a church with elders, which would deny predestination? Or for that matter, cannot a Roman Catholic who holds double predestination be theoretically considered?

9  This is not to say that Henry VIII did not have honest reservations about the legitimacy of his marriage to Catherine of Aragon. Instead, it is to note that Henry did not accept some of the most characteristic Protestant doctrines, and that his separation of the Church of England from the papacy was political and ecclesiastical, rather than wholly religious.

10  For an interesting overview of this time, see Lacey Baldwin Smith, *Fools, Martyrs, Traitors: The Story of Martyrdom in the Western World* (New York: Knopf, 1997), ch. 7.

11  Benedetto et al., eds., *Historical Dictionary*, 324.

12  Ibid.

13  *World Christian Encyclopedia*, 2nd edn, ed. David B. Barrett, George T. Kurian, and Todd M. Johnson (Oxford: Oxford University Press, 2001) I, 144–45.

14  Though for a different point of view, see Michael Lynch, "Calvinism in Scotland, 1559–1638," in Menna Prestwich, ed., *International Calvinism 1541–1715* (Oxford: Oxford University Press, 1985), 225–56.

15 Benedetto et al., eds., *Historical Dictionary*, 326.
16 Perhaps Calvinism itself was responsible for the argumentative turn in Scottish church life. See J. D. Douglas, "Calvinism's Contribution to Scotland," in W. Stanford Reid, ed., *John Calvin: His Influence in the Western World* (Grand Rapids: Zondervan, 1982), 230.
17 Benedetto et al., eds., *Historical Dictionary*, 326.
18 Ibid., 327.
19 *World Christian Encyclopedia*, I, 146.
20 Benedetto et al., eds., *Historical Dictionary*, 325.
21 Ibid., 326.
22 Ibid.
23 Ibid.
24 *World Christian Encyclopedia*, I, 147.
25 Benedetto et al., eds., *Historical Dictionary*, 328.
26 Ibid.
27 *World Christian Encyclopedia*, I, 147.
28 John T. McNeill, *The History and Character of Calvinism* (New York: Oxford University Press, 1954), 255–56.
29 See Alastair Duke, "The Ambivalent Face of Calvinism in the Netherlands, 1561–1618," in Prestwich, ed., *International Calvinism 1541–1715*, 109–12.
30 W. Robert Godfrey, "Calvin and Calvinism in the Netherlands," in Reid, ed., *John Calvin*, 98.
31 McNeill, *History and Character of Calvinism*, 260.
32 Ibid., 265.
33 *World Christian Encyclopedia*, 1, 532–35.
34 Benedetto et al., eds., *Historical Dictionary*, 228.
35 Ibid.
36 Ibid.
37 See McNeill, *History and Character of Calvinism*, 334–35. McNeill points out the especially un-Calvinist nature of the church polity of the Pilgrims.
38 Cotton Mather, *Magnalia Christi Americana*, quoted in W. A. Speck and L. Billington, "Calvinism in Colonial North America, 1630–1715," in Prestwich, ed., *International Calvinism 1541–1715*, 258.
39 Benedetto et al., eds., *Historical Dictionary*, 329.
40 McNeill, *History and Character of Calvinism*, 342.
41 Benedetto et al., eds., *Historical Dictionary*, 329.
42 Ibid.
43 This is similar to the Presbyterian New Side–Old Side split of the same period.
44 Benedetto et al., eds., *Historical Dictionary*, 329.
45 The Evangelical Lutheran Church in America also participates in this concord.
46 Benedetto et al., eds., *Historical Dictionary*, 282.
47 Ibid.
48 Ibid., 283.
49 Ibid.
50 Ibid., 284.
51 Ibid., 285.
52 This must be noted, as well as the fact that Calvinist theology was used to support this. Most Calvinist doctrinal histories display an advanced degree of discomfort

with this. For an example, see Gideon Thom's "Calvinism in South Africa," in Reid, ed., *John Calvin*, esp. 358–62.

53  Benedetto et al., eds., *Historical Dictionary*, 284.

54  Ibid.

55  *World Christian Encyclopedia*, I, 308.

56  Ibid., 311.

57  Ibid., 431.

58  Ibid., 309 and 428.

59  Benedetto et al., eds., *Historical Dictionary*, 221–22.

60  Ibid., 222.

61  *World Christian Encyclopedia*, I, 683–86.

62  One can even argue that where it has not been perpetually planted, as in the case of the French academy at Saumur, or the Genevan Academy.

63  Consultation on the Vocation of the Presbyterian Teacher, Louisville, KY, August 10–13, 2000.

64  This particular Calvinist denomination makes the point best. The PC(USA) is one of the more liberal historically Calvinist bodies in the United States, which often does not spend great effort on relating to its historical roots. *The Book of Confessions*, which contains the doctrinal standards to which ordination questions pertain, does not even contain a document which Calvin would have helped to write, such as the Geneva Catechism, or the Gallican Confession. Yet even without those supports, Calvin remains a touchstone.

65  An immediate problem arises when considering Calvin's connection to modern theology. When one deliberates the reason for delving into Calvin's thought, there is an academic disagreement about the right and wrong ways to do this. This divisive issue is best painted in the preface to Richard Muller's *The Unaccommodated Calvin* (Oxford: Oxford University Press, 2000), vii–viii, where Muller writes: "In the last decade, we have clearly come to such a shift – or to a series of shifts – in the interpretation of Calvin and Calvinism. Without making any claim to finality, we can review the history of recent scholarship and note that an older model, typical of the heyday of Barthian studies of Calvin, has become outmoded, albeit not entirely set aside. Movement away from the Barthian or neo-orthodox approach has taken at least two directions, the one quite promising, the other (to borrow a phrase from Calvin and his contemporaries) pressing deeper into a labyrinth of twentieth-century theologizing. The positive, promising shift in Calvin historiography is a movement, evidenced among historians of ideas as well as among social and political historians, away from the dogmatically motivated study of Calvin's theology and from the related assumption that the primary purpose of an exposition of Calvin's doctrine is to provide a significant point of departure for contemporary theologizing." This evaluation will be considered later, but must be in the back of the reader's mind – there is a very real debate about "how to read" Calvin in our own time.

66  John Calvin, *Institutes of the Christian Religion*, ed. John T. McNeill, trans. Ford Lewis Battles. Library of Christian Classics, 2 vols. (Philadelphia: Westminster Press, 1960), I.1.1.

67  In pointing this out, I do not seek to argue that Calvin is the only thinker to proceed this way in his analysis of the task of theology. It is to point out that Calvin's method prohibits the division of the consideration of the divine from the

human. This is seen in distinct contrast with some of the scholastic theologians of the thirteenth century. To use Aquinas as an example, when one considers his starting point in the *Summa Theologiae*, it is the definition of the theological science (Ia. 1), which leads directly into a consideration of the doctrine of God (Ia. 2 ff).

68  *Inst.* I.1.1.
69  See Philip Walker Butin, *Revelation, Redemption, and Response: Calvin's Trinitarian Understanding of the Divine-Human Relationship* (New York: Oxford University Press, 1995).
70  See Edward A. Dowey Jr., *The Knowledge of God in Calvin's Theology*, 3rd edn (Grand Rapids: Eerdmans, 1994).
71  See Wilhelmus T. H. Moehn, *God Calls Us to His Service: The Relation Between God and His Audience in Calvin's Sermons on Acts* (Geneva: Librairie Droz, 2001).
72  See Dowey, *The Knowledge of God*, p. 18 where Dowey relates this from a seminar of Tillich's.
73  Benjamin Breckenridge Warfield, "Augustine," in Samuel G. Craig, ed., *Calvin and Augustine* (Philadelphia: Presbyterian and Reformed Publishing Co., 1980), 322. "For the Reformation, inwardly considered, was just the ultimate triumph of Augustine's doctrine of grace over Augustine's doctrine of the Church."
74  See Dewey Hoitenga, *John Calvin and the Will: A Critique and Corrective* (Grand Rapids: Baker, 1997).
75  See Valerie Saiving Goldstein, "The Human Situation: A Feminine View," *Journal of Religion* 40 (1960), 100–13.
76  See *Natural Theology: Comprising "Nature and Grace" by Professor Dr. Emil Brunner and the reply "No!" by Dr. Karl Barth*, trans. Peter Fraenkel (London: Geoffrey Bles: The Centenary Press, 1946).
77  See Francis Turretin, *Institutes of Elenctic Theology*, trans. George Musgrave Giger, 3 vols. (Philipsburg, NJ: Presbyterian and Reformed Publishing Co., 1992), vol. I; and Charles Hodge, *Systematic Theology*, 3 vols. (Grand Rapids: Eerdmans, rpt. 1986).
78  Dowey, *The Knowledge of God*, 155–61. See also Dawn DeVries, *Jesus Christ in the Preaching of Calvin and Schleiermacher*, Columbia Series in Reformed Theology (Louisville: Westminster John Knox Press, 1996), 15–16.
79  *Inst.* I.6.1.
80  The literature on Calvin and accommodation is quite wide. See Ford Lewis Battles, "God Was Accommodating Himself to Human Capacity," in Donald K. McKim, ed., *Readings in Calvin's Theology* (Grand Rapids: Baker, 1984), 21–42. Though several articles have added to the discussion, most helpful is David F. Wright's "Calvin's Accommodating God," 3–20 in *Calvinus Sincerioris Religionis Vindex*, ed. Wilhelm Neuser and Brian Armstrong (Kirksville, MO: Sixteenth Century Journal Publishers, 1997). This contains a helpful overview of the literature.
81  *Inst.* I.13.1.
82  Butin, *Revelation, Redemption, and Response*, 17.
83  A case in point could be Anna Case-Winters' *God's Power: Traditional Understandings and Contemporary Challenges* (Louisville: Westminster John Knox Press, 1990), where Case-Winters never considers the possibility of accommodation softening some of the imagery that Calvin uses.

84  See Susan E. Schreiner, *The Theatre of His Glory: Nature and the Natural Order in the Thought of John Calvin* (Durham, NC: Labyrinth Press, 1991), esp. chs. 1–2.

85  Case-Winters, *God's Power*, 17.

86  Ibid., 39. Here Case-Winters agrees with the historical conclusions of Schreiner, *The Theater of His Glory*, 35, who stated that "In his discussions about providence, Calvin relied, to a large extent, on the tradition."

87  Case-Winters, *God's Power*, 241.

88  Max Weber, *The Protestant Ethic and the Spirit of Capitalism*, trans. Talcott Parsons (rpt. New York: Scribner, 1958).

89  Some of those might have been the prior appearance of "capitalistic" examples in Italy earlier than Protestantism, and other possible explanations for the differentations between Protestant and Catholic countries. For an interesting opposing view, see Herbert Lüthy, "Variations on a Theme by Max Weber," in Prestwich, ed., *International Calvinism 1541–1715*, 369–90.

90  See Mark Valeri, "Religion, Discipline, and the Economy in Calvin's Geneva," *Sixteenth Century Journal* 28 (1997), 123–42.

91  Calvin, *Comm. Genesis 2:15* (Calvin Translation Society, I, 125).

92  Cited in Donald K. McKim, "John Calvin: A Theologian for an Age of Limits," in McKim, ed., *Readings in Calvin's Theology*, 300. Cf. W. Fred Graham, *The Constructive Revolutionary: John Calvin and His Socio-Economic Impact* (Richmond, VA: John Knox Press, 1971), 69.

93  Especially by William Bouwsma, in his *John Calvin: A Sixteenth Century Portrait* (Oxford: Oxford University Press, 1988), 1.

94  See Oberman, "John Calvin: The Mystery of His Impact"; and William Naphy, *Calvin and the Consolidation of the Genevan Reformation* (Manchester: Manchester University Press, 1994).

95  See Douglas F. Kelly, *The Emergence of Liberty in the Modern World: The Influence of Calvin on Five Governments from the 16th through the 18th Centuries* (Philipsburg, NJ: Presbyterian and Reformed Publishing Co., 1992); Duncan Forrester, "Martin Luther and John Calvin," in Leo Strauss and Joseph Cropsey, eds., *History of Political Philosophy*, 3rd edn (Chicago: University of Chicago Press, 1987), 318–65; and Eric Voegelin, "The Great Confusion I: Luther and Calvin," in *The Collected Works of Eric Voegelin, vol. 22, The History of Political Ideas, vol. IV, Renaissance and Reformation*, ed. David L. Morse and William M. Thompson (Columbia, MO: University of Missouri Press, 1998), 217–91.

96  Quentin Skinner, *Foundations of Modern Political Thought*, 2 vols. (Cambridge: Cambridge University Press, 1978), II, 233 ff.

97  Michael Walzer, *The Revolution of the Saints: A Study in the Origins of Radical Politics* (Cambridge, MA: Harvard University Press, 1966).

98  For clarification, see Ralph C. Hancock, *Calvin and the Foundations of Modern Politics* (Ithaca: Cornell University Press, 1989).

99  For more on this, see Robert Kingdon, *Geneva and the Consolidation of the French Protestant Movement, 1564–1572: A Contribution to the History of Congregationalism, Presbyterianism, and Calvinist Resistance Theory* (Madison: University of Wisconsin Press, 1967); and Richard Muller, "Calvin, Beza, and the Exegetical History of Romans 13:1–7," in John B. Roney and Martin Klauber, eds., *The Identity of Geneva: The Christian Commonwealth 1564–1864* (Westport, CT: Greenwood Press, 1998), 39–56.

100 Higman points out that W. von Wartburg, in the *Evolution et structure de la langue française,* "illustrates the language of the sixteenth century by quotations from Calvin and Rabelais only." Francis Higman, "The Reformation and the French Language," *Esprit Créateur* (Winter 1976), 21.

101 Ibid.

102 Ibid., 30.

103 Ibid.

104 Olivier Millet, *Calvin et la dynamique de la parole: étude de rhétorique réformée* (Geneva: Editions Slatkine, 1992), esp. Quatrième Partie.

105 Higman notes that Calvin according to the precepts of his own day became a better translator between the 1541 and 1560 *Institutes.* But he then suffered in the estimation of later ages. See "Calvin and the Art of Translation," *Western Canadian Studies in Modern Languages and Literature* 2 (1970), 5–27.

106 Emil Doumergue, *Jean Calvin, les hommes et les choses de son temps,* 7 vols. (Paris: Librairie Fischbacher, 1899–1927).

107 Higman has drawn out some of the roots of the Calvin and Geneva myth in his "The Origins of the Image of Geneva," in Roney and Klauber, eds., *The Identity of Geneva,* 21–38. T. H. L. Parker points out a similar kneejerk distaste in the preface to his *Portrait of Calvin* (London: Lutterworth Press, 1953), 7–9.

108 See Bouwsma, *John Calvin: A Sixteenth Century Portrait.*

109 See Muller, *The Unaccommodated Calvin.*

110 Marilynne Robinson has considered the difficulty of discussing cultural assumptions because of their subterranean nature in her "McGuffey and the Abolitionists," in *The Death of Adam: Essays on Modern Thought* (Boston: Houghton Mifflin Company, 1998), 126–49.

111 To understand a culture, I believe one must live there. Thus, this section will concentrate upon the culture of the United States of America.

112 Robinson, "McGuffey and the Abolitionists," and "Puritans and Prigs," in *The Death of Adam,* 150–73.

**Part IV**

*Calvin Today*

# 15 Calvin's role in church history

DAVID F. WRIGHT

John Calvin was born on July 10, 1509 in the small French town of Noyon about sixty miles north-east of Paris, and died on May 27, 1564 in Geneva, an independent city-state whose common interests increasingly lay with the major cities of Switzerland. Noyon would remain a fairly unimportant place, but the fact that Calvin was a Frenchman – originally Jean Cauvin by name – is integral to understanding his role in church history. This made him an outsider in Geneva, but paradoxically it was his achievement, far more than anyone else's, that promoted Geneva to a city of European stature. Most of Calvin's adult career was spent in Geneva, from 1536 to his death, with a break during 1538–41. Prior to his time, it was a place of modest size with scant claim to distinction. It had no university nor leading light of the new learning of Renaissance humanism, it housed no major industries or finance enterprise, it was home to no significant printing press and wielded little or no political or military clout. It was, however, a regional trade center and not far from routes carrying traffic of all kinds between northern and southern Europe.

It was the Reformation, formally accepted by the citizen assembly in 1536 before Calvin's arrival, which would make Geneva internationally influential. The successful introduction of the Reformation was inseparable from the city's equally successful struggle for independence from the traditional sovereignty of its prince-bishop backed by the duchy of Savoy. Its liberty was won in a revolution in which Geneva's liberation depended crucially on the military aid of Berne. Geneva's achievement in both winning and maintaining its political freedom was almost unparalleled among European cities during the turmoil of the Reformation.

Calvin's place in church history belongs first to his role as the leader of the Reformation in Geneva. He is often depicted as a second-generation reformer. Zwingli had died in 1531 and Luther would follow in 1546. Critical issues had already been fought through to a conclusion years before Calvin was recruited in 1536 to lend his support to evangelical preachers like Guillaume Farel, active in Geneva from the early 1530s. Yet in his death-bed farewell to his fellow pastors Calvin commented that on his arrival in the city there was preaching and destruction of idols but "no reformation."

For this needed "reformation," Calvin insisted on the formation of an ordered church structure, which in time served as an inspiration for churches elsewhere and eventually for the disparate family of Reformed and Presbyterian bodies worldwide. This he attempted with only limited success during his first years in the city, 1536–38, which ended in a clash with the city council and the banishment of Farel and Calvin. What Calvin observed and learned during his exile in Strasbourg in 1538–41 was fed into the *Ecclesiastical Ordinances*, which were rapidly drafted and approved after his recall in 1541 and formed the blueprint for Geneva's reformed church order. It was this framework, especially after its transcription onto a national scale in France and then in Scotland, which would constitute Calvin's most enduring ecclesiastical legacy to world Christianity at the outset of its third millennium.

This fact is often concealed by the dominant use of the noun "Calvinism" to denote first and foremost a distinctive brand of Protestant theology, or, less frequently, a Christian ordering of society or shaping of culture. These dimensions of Calvin's work are dealt with elsewhere in this book, but it is necessary in this chapter to say something about both, since his church-historical significance encompasses both.

Calvin's intellectual and religious formation in France can be traced more confidently in its main outlines than in precise details. He was a student in Paris, Orléans, and Bourges, and was powerfully influenced in all three universities by fresh currents of humanist learning, with its commitment to the historical, literary, and linguistic study of classical and Christian antiquity. Calvin would never be less than a humanist scholar. His first published work was a commentary on a treatise on *Clemency* by the second-century Roman Stoic moralist, Seneca (1532). It reflects Calvin's interest in Roman law, especially the collected legislation of the Christian emperors of Rome, which he pursued under stimulating humanist professors at Orléans and Bourges. Later in Geneva Calvin would be useful to the city authorities for his skills as a legal and constitutional draughtsman, and even in diplomacy. His sure touch in these areas also served him well when it came to drawing up the *Ecclesiastical Ordinances*.

Calvin's native tongue was of course French. He soon acquired fluency in Latin, the international medium of the academy and the church and of professional intercourse in most fields. The impulse of humanism, as much classical as biblical, provided Calvin with initiation into Greek. He also embarked on Hebrew, whose position within a humanist context was much less obvious.

Through whom and when and where Calvin came to embrace the new Lutheran gospel remains a matter of scholarly debate. Many years later, in the preface to his commentary on the Psalms, he wrote of God's subduing his obstinate spirit by "a sudden conversion," making him teachable and extricating him from the murky abyss of Papal superstitions. Paris in the early 1530s appears a likely setting for this birth of Calvin's new allegiance to the evangelical faith. Luther's writings had circulated – and been banned – there throughout the 1520s. Erasmian and Lutheran currents had together won over a number of Calvin's fellow students, friends, and teachers, including his cousin Pierre Robert Olivétan. Such movements also animated more conservative reforming circles led by Lefèvre d'Étaples and Guillaume Briçonnet, bishop of Meaux to the east of Paris.

Calvin's fortunes became caught up in the backlash to overt, even provocative, displays of Protestant zeal in Paris during 1533–34. Late in 1534 he fled France to travel to Basle in Switzerland via Strasbourg. Though he made only one brief return trip to France, his homeland remained near the center of his affections. Later in Geneva he devoted extensive efforts to a mission to France, directed towards supplying small and often harassed congregations of believers with rigorously trained pastors. Even in exile, Calvin may be said to have become the architect of the nascent French Reformed Church. In turn, his own initiation into evangelical faith among radical, informal, and insecure groups of French believers equipped him to implement in Geneva what the late Heiko Oberman suggestively called a reformation of the refugees.

Calvin's French writings also left Francophone Reformed Christianity permanently in his debt. His very first Protestant publication was a foreword to Olivétan's French translation of the Bible (June 1535) – an ongoing task to which Calvin long contributed in Geneva. Most editions of his *Institutes* he produced in French as well as Latin, the last in 1560. These marked an important advance in the use of the French language for extended publications in the field of theology or philosophy. A full assessment of Calvin's qualities as a speaker and writer of French will be possible only when all his extant sermons, over 1600 in total, have been published.

The interval between Calvin's flight from France in 1534 and his entrapment in Geneva by Farel in 1536 was spent mostly in Basle, where he may even have met Erasmus near the end of his life. More significantly, he became acquainted with the progress, and the leadership, of different patterns of reform in Swiss cities and elsewhere, such as Strasbourg.

March 1536 saw the publication in Basle of the first edition (in Latin) of his *Institutio*, his *Introduction to Christianity*, written for the benefit of ordinary believers (despite not appearing in a French version). The prefaced letter dedicated to King Francis I of France discloses also an apologetic purpose. Calvin wished to kill the lie that slandered the evangelicals of France as Anabaptist rebels deserving of suppression. Though Calvin would experience fewer direct encounters with religious radicals than most reformers, his hostility toward them was no less sharp. The reform he championed was closer to a purification and renewal of catholic Christianity than to their drastic program for a clean sweep and a fresh start.

The 1536 *Institutio* was more like a catechism than anything else, based mostly on the Decalogue, the Apostles' Creed, the Lord's Prayer and the sacraments of baptism and the Lord's Supper. It owed not only its shape to Luther. Two additional chapters, on topics such as spiritual and temporal government, dealt with issues of contemporary controversy. They pointed the way to the extensive expansion and reorganization of the work through four editions, in 1539, 1543, 1550, and finally 1559, each followed by a French version (1541, 1545, 1551, 1560).

The *Institutio* of 1559 became Calvin's best-known publication and probably the most influential theological work to come out of the Reformation. An English translation was issued in London in 1561. Eighty chapters in four books, perhaps arranged loosely according to the order of the Apostles' Creed, gathered up not only the harvest of Calvin's mature understanding of the Bible and earlier theology, especially the early church fathers and supremely Augustine, but also his resolution of numerous issues, in dispute with the Roman Church, with Anabaptists and other radicals, including the anti-trinitarian Servetus, and with other versions of mainstream Reformation teaching, such as Joachim Westphal's Lutheran view of the Lord's Supper. The work also reflected Calvin's indebtedness to other reformers, from Luther and Zwingli to Bucer and Melanchthon.

The end product was a massive manual of biblical and controversial theology, both a guide to the reading of Scripture and a summation of its teaching, intended now particularly for candidates for church ministry. Yet this is not academic theology in the modern sense, for it embodies also the sum of piety for Christian believers. The praises of the *Institutes* (as the work is generally, if a little loosely, known in English) have often been sung. It is understandable, if not excusable, why Calvin should for too long have been read as the author of this one book alone. From the 1539 edition onwards, Calvin's preface explicitly correlated the *Institutio* with his biblical commentaries. They would be free of lengthy doctrinal discussions because these had been drawn together in the *Institutio*. For the book's detailed exegetical groundwork the commentaries would be indispensable.

In highlighting Calvin's role in Christian history, however, pride of place must be given to the *Institutes* as the unrivaled medium of his magisterial doctrinal formation of the Reformed tradition. This theological tradition extends beyond the churches of the Reformed-Presbyterian family into Congregational, Anglican, Baptist, and even Methodist circles. The *Institutes* earned this far-reaching influence as the weightiest intellectual presentation, less tidily systematic than was often assumed, of what the Reformation was all about. It was by no means the only long-lasting instrument issuing from Calvin's life-work to stamp its mark upon generations of evangelical faith and churchmanship, but it may be regarded as his most personal achievement. The *Institutes*, it may be argued, owed less to Calvin's efforts as the leading reformer of Geneva than other significant embodiments of his reforming genius, which this chapter will discuss. To the extent the *Institutio* unfolded its understanding of Reformation teaching and practice on a European rather than local canvas – drawing upon the best catholic tradition, in engagement with far-reaching controversies, from almost a second-generation vantage-point (the Council of Trent had demonstrated Rome's clear rejection of the Protestant challenge) – the book was well suited to exercise an influence regardless of what happened to Calvin in Geneva.

The first edition of the *Institutes* of March, 1536 sold out quickly, and Calvin soon set to work on an improved version. (This may well explain why no French translation was published.) It was while he was en route to Strasbourg, there to pursue his preferred vocation as a scholar in the mold of biblical humanism, that he stopped off in Geneva in the summer of 1536. There Farel conscripted him into the service of the Word of God in Geneva. In September he began to lecture on Paul's epistles in Latin, and within a couple of months he was working also as a pastor. The rest of his life was bound up with the progress of evangelical reform in Geneva. This remained true even in his exile during 1538–41 which was spent mostly in Strasbourg, for the possibility of his return to Geneva was rarely out of his mind.

Apart from this enforced absence, Calvin seldom traveled far from the city. His growing and eventually Europe-wide influence came about by other means – his writings and not least his far-flung correspondence, and the numerous people who were drawn to Geneva for a variety of reasons, united only by its reputation as a place where the Reformation was making powerful waves. Particularly significant among the incomers were pastors and theological teachers, students in training for the pastorate and hordes of refugees from many countries – from England and Scotland, more often from Italy, and most by far from France. Some of them, to be sure, brought trouble. This was true of some of the independent-minded, even anti-trinitarian, Italians. But others arrived with invaluable financial resources and industrial or commercial skills. Chief among these was the

Estienne (Stephanus) family of scholar-printers from Paris. Their presses were among a number of new publishing houses whose productions played an indispensable role in spreading the good news of Calvinian and Genevan reform. The stature of Geneva grew *pari passu* with that of Calvin, and to some extent also vice versa.

But for most of Calvin's years in Geneva the path of reform was anything but smooth. The price of political independence, whose achievement was inseparable from the acceptance of the Reformation by the Genevan people, was a degree of subservience to Berne, a Protestant city but committed to a more conservative Lutheran pattern of reform. Calvin's first sojourn in Geneva came to an end in April, 1538 as a result of the city council's insistence on acceding to Berne's demands for some church practices unwelcome to Calvin and Farel. They seemed modest enough (e.g., the observance of the four major festivals of the Christian year) but at stake was the basic principle of freedom of determination. In addition, the central thrust of the pastors' reform program had already run into choppy water among Geneva's city fathers and populace.

Calvin's agenda for true reform of the church always focused on two, or perhaps three, essentials. These were the doctrine and the "discipline." Little could be hoped for without an agreed statement of evangelical doctrine and an established church polity, which included provision for pastoral discipline in the narrower sense, that is, a system for ensuring that people's beliefs and behavior conformed to the gospel. These twin concerns were met by *Articles concerning the Organization of the Church and of Worship*, drafted by Calvin and approved in early 1537, and a *Confession of Faith* (1536/7), quite possibly by Farel and apparently a shorter version of Geneva's first reformed catechism, *Instruction and Confession of Faith* (1537; the Latin version of 1538 entitled it a *Catechism*). The *Articles* required city-wide individual subscription to the *Confession*, and also provided for district wardens to monitor residents' misconduct, which would entail exclusion from the Lord's Supper if censure was not followed by amendment of life. The attempt to secure this one-off person-by-person adherence to the *Confession of Faith* was intended by Calvin to clarify the religious situation in the city: how many could be counted on to support the reform? But together with the measures for discipline it involved a wholly unprecedented degree of intrusiveness into individuals' lives. It was no surprise that the council members sided with Berne's representations.

So in April, 1538 Calvin repaired to Basle, but his renewed hopes of freedom for scholarly work were overtaken by Martin Bucer's insistent invitation to Strasbourg. There he spent the rest of his exile from Geneva. His main responsibility was to pastor a new congregation of French refugees, from September, 1538, and in early 1539 he began lecturing on the New Testament in the city's new academy. The second edition of the *Institutes* was published the same year, but it had been largely completed before his arrival in Strasbourg. Hence its revision and enlargement of the first edition could take little account of Calvin's Strasbourg experiences. His first biblical commentary, on Paul's letter to the Romans, came out in 1540, followed the next year by a *Short Treatise on the Lord's Supper*. Written in French, this masterly and elegant exposition was Calvin's first essay in resolving the stubborn dispute between Lutherans and Zwinglians about Christ's presence in the Supper.

In August, 1540 Calvin married Idelette de Bure, widow of an Anabaptist with two children. Their only child, a son, died soon after birth in 1542, but when his wife died in 1549 he continued to look after her two children.

Strasbourg's Reformation offered several object lessons to a keen observer like Calvin, particularly on the pastors' unsuccessful struggle for church-controlled discipline, which the numerous radicals of various brands who had been attracted to Strasbourg made essential if the homogeneity of the city–church community was not to be broken up. Calvin learned a great deal, on the Bible, theology, church order, and perhaps also irenicism, from Bucer, the erudite, consensus-minded, but sometimes slippery senior pastor in Strasbourg.

These years broadened Calvin's horizons on the Reformation in Germany and gave him the opportunity to attend the colloquies with sympathetic Catholic representatives at Haguenau, Worms, and Regensburg during 1540–41. The Protestant side was led by Bucer and Philip Melanchthon, in whom Calvin recognized a kindred spirit, although not in everything. The Regensburg talks achieved a notable agreed statement on justification by faith. Calvin reported that it contained nothing not found in his own writings, but the conversation process as a whole left him disillusioned.

The chances of Calvin's return to Geneva were widely and openly discussed. In 1539 he found himself called upon to compose a *Reply to Sadoleto*, which is widely regarded as one of his most attractive and skilful writings. Cardinal Jacopo Sadoleto, bishop of Carpentras in southern France and a Catholic reformer of a biblical and humanist bent, had addressed to Geneva a plausible appeal to return to the Catholic fold. In the absence of Calvin and Farel Geneva must have seemed vulnerable to such an approach. That Calvin should have been asked to reply, albeit not by Geneva but through Berne, suggested that his commitment to Geneva still bound him. But bitter memories of his first tribulations in the city aroused deep anguish in his mind, until at last, in September 1541, he arrived back in Geneva. Immediately he picked up the threads as if he had never been away.

He had in effect negotiated the terms of his return with the city authorities to his own satisfaction. They covered not only his stipend but also more crucially a guarantee "to preserve the catechism and the discipline," as he put it in his farewell message to his fellow ministers a month before he died. Calvin produced a new *Catechism of the Church of Geneva* in November, 1541 (Latin, 1545). It was this, and not the *Institutio*, that served as the official statement of Genevan church doctrine for most of Calvin's life. Its 373 questions-and-answers were divided into weekly assignments for the whole year for the Sunday afternoon catechizing in which the children of Geneva were drilled. The *Catechism* in English translation also played a prominent role in the Scottish Reformation.

The "discipline" came in the *Ecclesiastical Ordinances*, which Calvin drafted and the councils revised and approved within two months of his setting foot again on Genevan soil in the autumn of 1541. It is hard to exaggerate the significance of this formulation of the new church order to be implemented in Geneva. It gathered up all the points of the abortive 1537 *Articles*. Though revision at the hands of the councils weakened some of its provisions and left others ambiguous, it very largely represented what through Calvin in particular became a distinctive feature of the Reformed tradition, namely, a clearly defined ordering of congregational life. For Calvin this meant the one church of Geneva, which had three parishes and three church buildings but functioned as one congregation, not three. It would be in France first of all and then Scotland that the Genevan model was elaborated to fit a national church.

The *Ordinances* in essence dealt with what Calvin, following Bucer's Strasbourg pattern, called "the four orders of office instituted by our Lord for the government of his church" – namely, pastors, doctors (i.e., teachers, lecturers), elders, and deacons. Virtually everything in the *Ordinances* fell under one or other of these four heads. The pastors were the lynch-pin, and Calvin himself never enjoyed a position higher than that of chair of the Company of Pastors in Geneva. Their careful selection and examination, with final approval resting with the city council, emphasized their high responsibility. Discipline appears first in the *Ordinances* in connection with the pastors, including two lists of offenses, those which are "quite intolerable in a minister and those which may be corrected through admonition." To conserve their "purity and concord of doctrine among themselves," they were required to meet weekly (on Fridays) for corporate study of the Scriptures. These meetings were known by the French word *congrégations* (they were not open to the public) and were in fact one of the origins of the later presbytery.

The doctors were in reality almost a sub-set of the pastors or ministers. They were subject to the same discipline and attended the *congrégations*. Calvin doubled as a lecturer throughout his time in Geneva. Only in 1559 was it possible to inaugurate the Academy of Geneva when the expulsion of ministers from Lausanne, including Theodore Beza, provided the necessary personnel. The Academy would develop into the University of Geneva, but in Calvin's time, in addition to a secondary or high school, it offered little beyond instruction in Greek and Hebrew and the Old and New Testaments, together with the classical disciplines of rhetoric, dialectic, and the like. Later it would extend into Law and Medicine.

Years before the Academy began, Geneva's pastors and lecturers were running a demanding ministerial training program, chiefly for Reformed congregations in France. The Company of Pastors supervised specifically their proficiency in preaching and spiritual formation, which were viewed as essential, in addition to their academic certification, if they were to survive, let alone function effectively, in the testing situation of France's persecuted Protestants. This was a tightly controlled scheme to provide rigorously equipped personnel for mission in France. The minutes of the Company show that month after month it consumed most of the pastors' corporate attention.

Calvin insisted on regarding the eldership as an order of apostolic ministry, but in reality in Geneva the elders were representatives of the city councils, albeit required to be God-fearing and spiritually wise and chosen in consultation with the pastors. Together with the pastors they were to meet weekly on Thursdays in the Consistory, the organ of discipline and one of the most distinctive and controversial features of Reformed church polity. Only recently has publication of the minutes of the Consistory begun, but enough was already known for us to recognize it as the storm-center of the process of reform in Calvin's Geneva. The long reach of the Consistory's disciplinary arm extended impartially to members of some of Geneva's most eminent families no less than to humbler residents, which contributed to factional tensions in the city. These were rarely absent, but during the years of reform were fueled by resentment at the increasingly intrusive part played by the ministers, who by the mid-1540s were all of French, not Genevan, origin. Final control of the right of excommunication was contested – in reality retained by the council – until 1555, when at last it was recognized as lying in the hands of the Consistory.

Calvinian church discipline has too often been judged from the records of the later Kirk session, to which the Consistory gave rise. Reconciliation was often its aim in Calvin's time, especially between feuding family members or neighbors. It has been described as akin to a compulsory marriage counseling service, and the outcome of its hearings was commonly no more than an instruction to "frequent the sermons" and a biblically based admonition often delivered by Calvin himself. As Calvin's early biographer, Nicholas Colladon, recognized, these remonstrances were another form of Calvin's ministry of the Word of God in Geneva, along with preaching, lecturing, and contributing virtually another exposition week by week to the biblical colloquy known as the *congrégation*.

The sheer weight of Calvin's preaching ministry in Geneva gave it unparalleled significance within the Reformation as a whole. Almost a generation earlier Zwingli had recovered the patristic practice of expounding books of the Bible in their entirety, working through passage by passage or verse by verse in a homiletic commentary by *lectio continua*. Calvin followed this procedure for nearly all his average output of some ten sermons a fortnight, at least from 1549. A good number were published during or shortly after Calvin's lifetime, and many also appeared in early English translation.

Calvin's commentaries cover almost the whole Bible. Most of those on Old Testament books originated as his Latin lectures, while the New Testament ones were composed as written works. They display Calvin's strengths as a humanist-trained student of texts in ancient languages, and the measure of success he attained in aiming for "lucid brevity," as he put it in the preface to his first commentary, on Romans, in 1540. The economy and scholarly discipline of Calvin's exegesis – unfolding the mind of the writer was in his judgment almost the sole task of the interpreter – secured for his commentaries a continuing usefulness far beyond that of any other preacher's corpus from the sixteenth century. Greater accessibility has made his commentaries better known than his sermons.

Calvin bequeathed to later generations in the Reformed churches and further afield an extensive legacy which may be summed up under two main heads – a massive body of biblical theology, and a firmly ordered pattern of church polity. Each commended the other, though the mutually reinforcing relationship between the two has not always been recognized. John Knox's eulogy of Geneva in 1556 is often quoted: "The most perfect school of Christ that ever was in the earth since the days of the apostles." But by stopping at this point, the real force of Knox's appreciation is commonly lost: "In other places I confess Christ to be truly preached, but manners and religion so sincerely reformed I have not yet seen in any other place." Calvin and his colleagues achieved, in the admittedly small compass of sixteenth-century Geneva, as successful a realization of evangelical ideals as could be found anywhere in Reformation Europe – religion (faith, worship, piety) and manners (behavior, practice, morals) as purely reformed as nowhere else.

This was not Calvin's own estimate at the end of his life. He could not forget the conflicts entailed in the pursuit of an evangelically reformed church, which dogged him to the last. But an impressively efficient set of organs was in place: the Company of Pastors, the Consistory, the Academy, the "General Hospital" presided over by the deacons and rather like a modern multi-purpose community welfare center, the weekly catechizing and *congrégations*, the ever-so-frequent sermons. If the pastors constituted the key corps of personnel, the role of the elder in the contested sphere of discipline was a major distinctive. (This is not to forget that, like several other elements in Calvin's reformed Geneva, it derived chiefly from Martin Bucer's Strasbourg.) The eventual vindication of the exercise of discipline independent of the city's government was itself unparalleled in the Reformation movement.

By no means all the ordered instruments of reform in the small city of Geneva could be translated onto a regional or national canvas without major adaptation or development. Yet the possibilities of meaningful translation without discontinuity were to be seen in Scotland in the *First Book of Discipline* (1560) and the *Second Book* (1578). A more direct transfer to Scotland was the service book used in the English congregation in Geneva as *The Forme of Prayers*, which became the Scottish church's *Book of Common Order*. The French Genevan book of the same title had been brought back by Calvin from his Strasbourg congregation.

Driving what this chapter dares to call Geneva's successful Reformation was not only a man of singular gifts and determination but a biblical theology which could cope with the opposition – and which in good part explains the ability of the Calvinian model of reform to survive transplantation to hostile regimes such as France. It is undeniable that this Calvinism proved itself eminently more exportable than Lutheranism. The two were of course at one on the evangelical fundamentals of the Reformation – Scripture alone, grace alone, Christ alone, faith alone – even if each of these was distinctively nuanced in Geneva and Wittenberg. But the more characteristic emphases of Calvin's theological mind informed his and similar programs of reform with a conspicuous confidence and sense of irrevocable divine purpose. These emphases must include the honor of God, the "useful" character of true knowledge of God, zealous adherence to God's self-revelation and rejection both of free-thinking speculation in theology and of human inventions and intrusions in the worship of God, the so-called third use of the law of God focused in the Decalogue as the publication of his continuing will for his people and his world, and, not least, the predestinating providence and grace of God. The relationship between Calvin's own theology and later Calvinist theologies is the subject of another chapter in this book. Those who saw themselves as standing in his succession did not always endeavor, nor succeed if they did, in replicating the multi-motif proportions of his teaching. After all, the theological bequest was enormous and came in different shapes and sizes: *Institutio*, commentaries, catechism, controversial treatises, sermons, letters.

A third summary head should finally be mentioned to do fuller justice to the Calvinian legacy in the round. It too receives proper attention elsewhere in this *Companion*. It is that pursuit of the godly commonwealth encompassing every dimension of a community's life that in Calvin's mind gave the highest dignity to the vocation of councilors, princes, and statesmen. This vision represented an evangelical version of the *corpus christianum* of pre-Reformation Europe. In the crumbling Christendom of the western world today it looks to be the least durable of Calvinian legacies. Cultural and religious pluralism excludes that earnest ordering of a unitary Christian society witnessed in earlier centuries in various configurations in the Netherlands, in Dutch-Reformed South Africa, in Scotland, and in Puritan England and New England. By contrast, as rapid church growth in Korea has demonstrated, the day of Calvinian theology and church polity is by no means past.

# 16  The place of Calvin in Christian theology

### B. A. GERRISH

> God has never seen fit to bestow such favour on his servants that each
> individually should be endowed with full and perfect knowledge on
> every point. No doubt, his design was to keep us both humble and
> eager for brotherly communication.
>
> John Calvin

Anyone, whether historian or theologian, who writes on John Calvin is
likely to venture judgments concerning his place in Christian theology.
Over the years the judgments have varied widely. Calvin's admirer Benjamin
B. Warfield, for example, argued that the man the Roman Catholic Church
judged a heretic actually marked a fresh epoch in the history of the catholic
dogma of the Trinity. A less generous opinion, made from another ecclesiastical corner, is that Calvin was at best a mere epigone of Martin Luther,
at worst a debaser of pure Reformation doctrine. At the end of the nineteenth century, it was said that Calvin represented a certain "atrophy" or
"degeneration" of the idea of Protestantism (Ferdinand Kattenbusch), and
in the mid-twentieth century one of the most widely used textbooks of
church history in Germany could still present Calvin's theology in the form
of six "deviations" from the theology of Luther (Kurt Dietrich Schmidt).
Yet another well-known estimate from the last century judged Calvinism a
more creative intellectual force in the modern world than Lutheranism but
placed Calvin himself, with Luther, on the side of the "old Protestantism,"
which only tried to give a new answer to an old medieval question, "What
must I do to be saved?" (Ernst Troeltsch).

  These sample judgments could be multiplied indefinitely. But they suffice to forewarn us that Calvin's place in Christian theology is a wide-ranging
and controversial question. It could be asked with respect to every topic of
Christian theology on which he voiced an opinion, and the evidence goes
to show that the answer given may betray the theological location of the
person asking the question. The present chapter addresses the *historical*
question of Calvin's place in the story of Christian theology, not the

*theological* question of what he might have to say in the current theological conversation. The task certainly calls for insight, even theological insight, not merely for juxtaposing statements Calvin made with statements others have made before and since, and the author of this chapter may not be any more successful in hiding his own theological leanings than others have been in curbing theirs. The very selection of topics and material, as always in studies of the past, already says something about an author's standpoint. Nevertheless, the criterion of a defensible historical assertion is the historical evidence advanced, not norms appropriate to systematic theology. And the conclusions reached here are not intended to promote Calvin unduly even in the context of historical theology, but rather, as he himself would wish, to note some of the contributions he made, sound or not, to the "brotherly [add "sisterly"!] communication" on which theological progress depends.

A suitable point of entry is Calvin's relation to the Augustinian tradition, especially on the Christian understanding of grace. In Augustine's struggle with Pelagianism, a profound gratitude for the grace of God led him inexorably to the thorny question of predestination or *the election of grace*. The Augustinian piety of gratitude for divine grace shines through the theology of Calvin, but "Calvinism" became virtually synonymous in the minds of its critics with the enigma of predestination and the bondage of the will. Questions of *free will and merit*, bequeathed by the Pelagian controversy, continued to exercise the theologians of the Middle Ages; among them Calvin had a special regard for Bernard of Clairvaux, in whom he found the witness of a kindred spirit to the cardinal theme of God's grace. In Calvin's own day, the Augustinian heritage remained a major reference point in the Reformation debates. Partly inherited from Augustine were two issues on which Calvin thought differently than Luther: *spirituality and sacramental signs*. After the Protestant Reformation, a good deal of theological attention turned to *the task of Christian theology* itself, and a few reflections will be added in conclusion on Calvin in relation to Friedrich Schleiermacher and Karl Barth, the two most influential theologians of the Reformed or Calvinist family in modern times. All these themes have generated complex, controversial discussions. Exploration of them here can do little more than open the door to further "brotherly communication."

## THE ELECTION OF GRACE

In the Address to the King of France that served as a preface to the first edition of the *Institutes* (March, 1536) and to every subsequent edition, Calvin defended the evangelical cause against the charge of novelty.

The defense expressed his twofold persuasion that while patristic authority mostly favored the evangelicals, the patristic consensus from which they allegedly deviated was a fiction. His adversaries, as he put it in the acerbic style of the time, were bent on gathering dung amid the gold. Calvin's facility for marshaling citations from the Fathers, demonstrated in the address to Francis I, stood him in good stead at the Lausanne Disputation (October, 1536), where he made his first public appearance as a reformer. Being the newcomer in the Genevan party, he was silent until the Catholics charged the Reformed with rejecting "the holy doctors of antiquity." He then rose and delivered from memory a discourse on the eucharistic opinions of Tertullian, pseudo-Chrysostom, and especially Augustine, five of whose writings he cited. With a touch of vanity, he regretted that he could not recall whether his citation of one of Augustine's homilies on John came from the eighth or the ninth section.

These early statements from 1536 set a pattern for Calvin's subsequent writing. As he explained at Lausanne, we listen to the Word of God with the Fathers, but the highest authority belongs to the Word itself. Scholarly tabulation has shown that in the *Opera omnia* (*OC*) Calvin's explicit references to the early church fathers number more than 3,200; some 1,700 of them are references, often with extended quotations, to Augustine. The numbers are greatly increased when echoes and allusions are taken into account.[1] But the principle Calvin laid down at the Lausanne Disputation is never in doubt: we use the help of the Fathers' teaching as it serves and as occasion offers. When his teaching on the bondage of the will and predestination was challenged by the Roman Catholic theologian Albert Pighius, Augustine's anti-Pelagian writings served Calvin well. In his reply he made his forthright claim, "Augustine is wholly ours," borrowed recently as the title for a major study of Calvin and Augustine.[2]

Augustine's understanding of predestination grew out of his passionate celebration of divine grace. He testified that, even before the Pelagian controversy, a crucial change of mind came to him as he reflected on Paul's words, "What do you have that you did not receive? And if you received it, why do you boast as if it were not a gift?" (1 Cor. 4:7). He had long believed that conversion to God is a work of God's grace, which alone, by an "infusion" of love for God, can bring about a radical reorientation from the fault of seeking life in one's own self to receiving life in faith from the true Fountain of Life. And he had understood that the ability to accept the gospel in faith must itself be the gift of grace, or it would not be true that we have nothing we did not receive. But why is it that one person comes to faith while another does not? In one of his last writings, the anti-Pelagian treatise *On the Predestination of the Saints* (428 or 429), Augustine recalls his change of mind (chs. 7–10 [iii–v]). He once supposed that at least our consent to the gospel, when it is preached to us, must be our own doing and come from ourselves. This, he now realizes, was a mistake: he had not yet grasped *the election of grace*. Everyone has the ability to believe, just as everyone has the ability to love; but it doesn't follow that everyone has faith, any more than everyone loves. If a person comes to faith, it is because the Lord prepares the wills of those he has chosen for himself. Ability to believe (*fidem posse habere*), then, is a gift of nature; believing (*fidem habere*) is the gift of a special grace, given only to God's elect.

For Calvin, too, the divine election was the final proof that everything is of grace, including the division between those who come to faith and those who do not. "We shall never be clearly persuaded, as we ought to be, that our salvation flows from the wellspring of God's free mercy until we come to know his eternal election, which illumines God's grace by this contrast: that he does not indiscriminately adopt all into the hope of salvation but gives to some what he denies to others."[3] Here, clearly, the Augustinian concern to maintain the utter gratuitousness of God's grace or mercy is fundamental, and the eternal election of grace explains the observed fact that some accept the gospel while others don't. Calvin further agrees with Augustine that while the division between the elect and the non-elect is inescapably the teaching of Scripture, the reason *why* God chooses some, not all, is hidden in God's inscrutable justice. It could surely be said that, in this doctrine if not in others, the proper placement of Calvin's theology will see in it "a great revival of Augustinianism" (Warfield). But this need not exclude differences between them even on grace and election.

It is often asserted, for instance, that what is distinctive of Calvin is the doctrine of a *double* predestination, to eternal life or to eternal damnation (see the definition in *Inst.* III.21.5), whereas Augustine wrote of a *single* predestination of the saints that simply passes by the rest of humanity. The assertion is not entirely true. Their emphasis differs, but Calvin often used the language of "passing by" the non-elect, and Augustine occasionally wrote of predestination to death or eternal death. The reason for the two ways of speaking is that both are found in Scripture: the Fourth Gospel represents Jesus as calling his chosen disciples out of the world (e.g., John 15:19, 17:6), whereas Paul contrasts "the vessels of mercy" with "the vessels of wrath made for destruction" (Rom. 9:22–23). In any case, the supposedly milder language of "preterition" (passing by) is no comfort to the non-elect, who will be damned either way.

Connected with election and predestination is a point on which Calvin explicitly rejects an opinion of Augustine's. Baptism was so essential to salvation in Augustine's view that he felt constrained to draw the logical inference: unbaptized infants who die in infancy cannot be numbered among the predestined but are condemned to hell. Their penalty is by no means unjust; though they have not yet committed actual sins, they inherit the guilt of Adam. Augustine took no pleasure in this terrible inference. The best he could find to say by way of mitigation, however, was that such infants would suffer only the mildest of pains. Calvin, too, believed infants are tainted by original sin, but he could reject the Augustinian opinion on their fate, if they die without baptism, because for him election takes precedence over the sacrament of baptism. "God declares that he adopts our babies as his own before they are born [that is, the babies of the elect, the people of the covenant], when he promises that he will be our God and the God of our descendants after us" (*Inst.* IV.15.20; cf. IV.16.26). God can call those who are his without the ordinary means even of preaching, and sometimes he certainly does (IV.16.19).

A third difference between Augustine and Calvin on election has less to do with the content of the doctrine than with the use to which they put it. They were agreed that only the doctrine of election can safeguard the sovereign freedom of grace. But Calvin had also a secondary use for it: to establish assurance of salvation. Augustine, by contrast, held that none can know whether or not they are elect; the doctrine accordingly inspires fear rather than assurance. And this is a point on which Catholics and Calvinists took opposing sides at the time of the Reformation. For the followers of Calvin, assurance of election was a duty and a privilege (they appealed to 2 Pet. 1:10); for the Council of Trent, Calvinist assurance was only "the vain confidence of heretics."

## FREE WILL AND MERIT

Predestination was not, in Calvin's eyes, a useless topic, good only for contentious arguments. As he wrote in his second treatise against Pighius, the doctrine "lifts us up into an admiration of the unbounded goodness of God towards us [i.e., the elect!]."[4] Like Augustine, Calvin contended for an awareness of total dependence on the free grace of God, an awareness that would nurture in believers a piety of humility and thankfulness. But the witness to grace that inspired them has again and again been buried under a mountain of indignant objections to the determinism they inferred from it. The Pelagian controversy led on, after Augustine's death, to the so-called semi-Pelagian controversy, which the Second Council of Orange (529) calmed by a judicious compromise, affirming the prevenience of grace without Augustine's election of grace. Controversy reawakened in the ninth century (Gottschalk), and throughout the Middle Ages predestination remained a *quaestio disputata* in the schools. The fourteenth century saw a revival of Augustinianism, partly (Thomas Bradwardine, Gregory of Rimini) in reaction against the alleged Pelagianizing of the times, partly in defense of an inward definition of the church as the "number of the elect" (John Wycliffe, followed in the fifteenth century by John Hus).

In contrast to his abundant references to the Fathers, Calvin rarely cited the medieval doctors by name: Anselm and Bonaventure only once each, Duns Scotus and William of Ockham twice each, Thomas Aquinas four times. Peter Lombard, the "master of the sentences," who gave the medieval schools their textbook of theology, fared better with thirty-nine citations.[5] Attempts to trace the medieval influences on Calvin's theology have naturally foundered on the paucity of his references to medieval authors, which has given rise to doubts about the extent of his reading. His place in Christian theology cannot, of course, be settled by gathering his references to his predecessors, nor by speculation about possible influences on his intellectual development from predecessors he seldom or never mentions.[6] The question of his "place" has more to do with affinities and dissimilarities. But, as it happens, how Calvin saw the implications of grace for *free will and merit* is admirably reflected in references to his favorite medieval theologian: Bernard of Clairvaux, whom he cites forty-one times.[7] He thought Bernard's use of the two controverted terms "free will" and "merit" invited misunderstanding, but he could not bring himself to believe there was any material difference between him and the medieval monk whom he honored among "the ancient doctors" of the church.

In his influential treatise *On Grace and Free Choice* (c. 1128), Bernard followed Augustine in holding that the first man fell into servitude to sin and took the entire human race into slavery with him. Once he had fallen, Adam lacked the ability to get up again. Sinners cannot not sin, for it is not so easy to climb out of a pit as to fall into one (vii.23). Nevertheless, Bernard could still affirm that the sinner has an inalienable *free will* (viii.24), and to Calvin this was a misuse of language. *Liberum arbitrium* properly means "free choice" and is commonly taken to imply that the agent is poised between two equally possible courses of action. But this could not have been what Bernard meant by an inalienable human freedom, because, in agreement with Augustine, he spoke expressly of the agent's powerlessness to do anything but sin until the Holy Spirit liberates the will. By "free" Bernard meant "voluntary." Sinners remain free in the sense that they are *voluntary* slaves of sin: that is, although they cannot will not to sin, they are not *forced* to sin against their will (*Inst.* II.2.7).[8]

In that case, however, Bernard invites misunderstanding when he defines the inalienable freedom of the will as freedom from *necessity*: rather, it is freedom from *coercion*. The sinner sins necessarily because that is what he is, a sinner; he is not compelled to sin against his will by some external force (*Inst.* II.3.5). Still, Calvin professes himself reluctant to quibble over words. With a modest caveat, he is content to accept the distinction Bernard used between three freedoms: from necessity, from sin, and from misery, the first inalienable and the other two lost through sin. Calvin comments: "I willingly accept this distinction, except in so far as necessity is falsely confused with compulsion" (II.2.5). Likewise, he thinks the expression *liberum arbitrium* could be used without misunderstanding, but he prefers not to use it himself and recommends others also to avoid it (II.2.8). For Calvin, as (he thinks) for Augustine and Bernard, the condition for moral responsibility is not free choice but voluntary action – doing what, in fact, one wills to do. He makes no claim to originality (II.3.5); he only suggests greater care in the use of language.

The other controverted term, *merit*, leads to a similar conclusion. Luther had agonized over the Nominalist belief that God gives grace to those who merit grace by first doing the best they can without it – a belief he finally dismissed as crassly Pelagian. But even Augustine and Bernard, though they denied that any human merit can *precede* the gift of justifying grace, held that merit should *follow* grace, which, once it is given, frees the will from the necessity of sinning. Calvin could write, "[O]n the beginning of justification there is no quarrel between us and the sounder Schoolmen" (*Inst.* III.14.11). However, he located a continuing problem in the universal scholastic teaching that after the reception of grace the acquisition of merit is a possibility and a duty, and he had to face the difficulty that the Schoolmen had his two favorite theologians on their side. Once again, he took the line that, as far as Augustine and Bernard were concerned, the problem was semantic. "Merit" is a prideful term foreign to Scripture (III.15.2), mistakenly defended by appeal to biblical talk of "reward." For the kingdom of heaven is not servants' pay; the reward is the inheritance of God's children (III.18.2). Still, like Augustine, Bernard acknowledged that all our merits are gifts of God and continually pointed away from our good works to the gracious giver, who forgives what is still lacking in them (III.2.25; III.11.22; III:12.8). Accordingly, "the fact that he uses the term 'merits' freely for good works, we must excuse as the custom of the time" (III.12.3).

No one is likely to suspect Calvin of belittling the demand for good works. Some may be willing to commend him for his criticism that talk of "merit" puts the good works of the Christian life under the wrong metaphor – hired service instead of filial obedience. One might even venture to conclude that, although he did not invent the distinction between necessity and coercion, his use of it introduced greater conceptual clarity and consistency into the understanding of the term "free will" in the Augustinian tradition. Not everyone will applaud him for so doing. The bondage of the will remains an obstinately problematic idea, and a little unclarity about it may seem welcome. But it is worth noting that present-day philosophers, to say nothing of the behavioral scientists, often take the limitations of human freedom more earnestly than Calvin's theological critics. His reply to Pighius was what we should call these days a species of "compatibilism": he sought to show "how self-determination and necessity can be combined together."[9] Calvin's case resembles the well-known argument of G. E. Moore, for instance, that right and wrong depend not on what we absolutely *can* do, but on what we can do *if* we choose. We have free will if we do what we will to do. Moore remained doubtful whether it is also true that we could sometimes have willed differently than we did. But, be that as it may, moral responsibility does not require us to assert that acts of will are uncaused.[10]

## SPIRITUALITY AND SACRAMENTAL SIGNS

Within the overall theme of Calvin's place in Christian theology, his relation to Luther deserves more generous attention than can be given here.[11] The German reformer displayed a respect for Calvin that he was notoriously unwilling to extend to Ulrich Zwingli, the reformer of Zurich, and his generosity won an answering generosity from Calvin. In 1539, when it was pointed out to him that the younger man had criticized his teaching on Christ's presence in the Eucharist, Luther still refused to think ill of him. Calvin, in turn, steadfastly defended his "most respected father" throughout the later eucharistic controversies that embittered Luther against the Swiss and, after Luther's death, turned many Lutherans against Calvin. Even on the sacraments, Calvin sensed a greater kinship with Luther than with Zwingli. But it by no means followed that he could agree with all Luther's opinions: rather, he did not permit their disagreements to annul the essential harmony between them. Among their differences, Calvin did not endorse Luther's assertion, in refutation of free choice, that "to purpose anything either evil or good is in no one's control, but . . . everything happens by absolute necessity" (an assertion borrowed from Wycliffe).[12] That, we might say, was to confuse a psychological with a metaphysical necessity. Calvin, of course, could not escape the metaphysical problem, but when he turned to it, in his doctrine of providence, he was willing to make use of careful scholastic distinctions that Luther had dismissed (*Inst.* I.16.9). Two further differences between them had to do with *spirituality and sacramental signs*.

A common stereotype contrasts "Calvinist activism" with "Lutheran quietism," and sometimes the explanation is added that Lutheranism nurtures an intensely inward and individual religiousness. The question of Lutheran and Calvinist social ethics is much too complicated to be brought under such simple formulas. But a difference of *spirituality* (as we call it these days), whether or not it can account for their different programs for reform, has been well-nigh universally detected in the respective utterances of Luther and Calvin on the Christian life. It is reflected, in particular, in the way they spoke of grace and law in the life of the Christian. For Luther, "grace" was nothing but the favor or good will of God in freely justifying the sinner. Not that Luther was uninterested in "sanctification": as he put it in his treatise *Against Latomus* (1521), appealing to Romans 5:15, besides the *grace* that forgives the sinner there is the *gift* that little by little heals the sin. But Luther's great boon to the church was his profile of the Christian as one who lives in the liberating joy of unconditional forgiveness, and he was ever watchful for the least trace of a resurgent works-righteousness. Calvin, by contrast, taught a "double grace" that both justifies and sanctifies (*Inst.* III.11.1; cf. III.3.1), and his thinking was marked by a concern to balance these two gifts of participation in Christ. In a sense, he even gave the preeminence to sanctification, or the cultivation of purity of life, since he could say that the Lord freely justifies his own *in order that* he may restore them to true righteousness by sanctification (III.3.19). True piety, its loss and restoration, was in fact the subject of his *Institutes* from beginning to end: the title page of the first edition fittingly described the work as a *pietatis summa*, a "summary of piety." To be sure, Calvin could call justification "the sum of all piety" (III.15.7), but it was more characteristic of him to describe justification as the main *hinge* on which religion turns, or the *foundation* on which to build piety toward God (III.11.1; cf. III.15.1). The Calvinist profile of the Christian portrays a dutiful son, pledged to willing obedience, although it is not filial obedience but fatherly indulgence alone that secures the relationship (III.11.6, 16, 22; III.19.5).

Consistent with this image of the Christian as called to the obedience of the children of God is a distinctive perception of God's "law." Luther spoke of two uses of law: a civil use, to restrain wrongdoing, and a theological use, to bring about conviction of sin and drive the sinner to Christ. Calvin, following Luther's colleague Philip Melanchthon, spoke of a threefold use. "The third and principal use, which pertains more closely to the proper purpose of the law, finds its place among believers in whose hearts the Spirit of God already lives and reigns" (*Inst.* II.7.12). There it serves both as instruction in God's will and as a stimulus to obey it. The nature of God's law is misinterpreted, in Calvin's view, when seen only in the context of Paul's struggle against the *legalism* of false religion (II.9.4). The "proper purpose of law" is to be understood from the *covenant* context, in which the law is seen as God's gracious gift to his people (II.7.1; cf. III.11.20). Though it has sometimes led to mutual recriminations between the Lutherans and the Calvinists, the contrast in spiritualities is not absolute: Luther could in fact say many things that Calvin would have placed under the third use of the law. It is a question of where the accent falls.

A trace of anti-Lutheran polemic can perhaps be detected in Calvin's remark about "those who always erroneously compare the law with the gospel by contrasting the merit of works with the free imputation of righteousness" (*Inst.* II.9.4). On our other theme, *sacramental signs*, he saw himself unambiguously as Luther's champion and was indignant that, after Luther's death, not all the German reformers were able to see him in the same light. Before the controversy with the Swiss, Luther had freely used the notion of a sacramental sign in the Eucharist, though sometimes in a peculiar sense. In his *Prelude on the Babylonian Captivity of the Church* (1520), he identified the "sign" not with the elements but with the actual presence of Christ's body and blood *in* the bread and wine to confirm the promise of forgiveness. Zwingli and the Swiss reformers also used the notion of a sign and claimed the support of Augustine. In their view, when Jesus said "This is my body," he must have meant that the bread signified, or was a sign of, his body. Further, the Swiss thought that the primary reference of sacramental signs was to the past: they signal the fact that something has taken place. The Eucharist, then, was a *remembrance* of the crucifixion – of the body slain for our salvation – not a celebration of the real, bodily *presence*. Luther was appalled. The "fanatics," he scoffed, were stupidly misinterpreting Augustine, for whom a sacrament was not a sign of something absent but of something invisibly present. And yet Luther did not counter the Swiss blunder with a more authentically Augustinian understanding of sacramental signs; he sought to exclude sign talk from the interpretation of the words of institution.

A third option – neither Luther's nor Zwingli's – was obviously open: to interpret the sacramental signs as bearers of the reality they signify. This was the option that Calvin, among others, tirelessly commended as the only way to reconcile the parties in the dispute. When Paul says that the bread we break in the Lord's Supper is "a participation in the body of Christ" (1 Cor. 10:16), there is no reason to protest that the language is figurative. "I indeed admit that the breaking of bread is a symbol; it is not the thing itself. But, having admitted this, we shall nevertheless duly infer that by the showing of the symbol the thing itself is also shown . . . [T]here ought not to be the least doubt that [the Lord] truly presents and shows (*vere praestet atque exhibeat*) his body" (*Inst.* IV.17.10). In Calvin's opinion, it was the notion of "exhibitive signs" that provided the basis for settling the eucharistic debate. And by *exhibere*, as is plain from the tandem expression "presents and shows," he meant more than the English word "show" might seem to imply. Christ once gave his body to be crucified: he gives it to us daily, and in the Supper he inwardly fulfills what he outwardly signifies (IV.17.5).

In his understanding of both the "graced" life and the function of sacramental signs, Calvin stood closer than Luther to Augustine. But he remained uneasy with Augustine's failure to distinguish the grace of justification sharply enough from sanctification, or at any rate with his manner of putting it (III.11.15), and was convinced that Luther, were he still alive, would gladly have accepted the view "that what the sacraments figure is truly presented to us" (Calvin to John Marbach, August 24, 1554). Much more could be said. But it hardly seems appropriate to assign Calvin a place in the sixteenth century either as a mere epigone of Luther or as a debaser of pure Lutheran doctrine. They represent, rather, two interesting and perhaps complementary variants of a common evangelical witness, rooted in the New Testament and the Augustinian tradition.

## THE TASK OF CHRISTIAN THEOLOGY

Like every other great intellectual of the past, Calvin left a legacy that his heirs have received in more ways than one. The uses to which his theology has been put, partisan though they may be, have served to highlight aspects of it that certainly belong to the assessment of his place in Christian theology. Much discussion has turned around the question of whether Reformed scholasticism developed or distorted his legacy. Very little serious reflection has been given to Schleiermacher's thoughts on Calvin, though he was the most eminent theologian of the Reformed family between Calvin and Barth.[13] The neglect is largely due to uncritical echoing of Barth's verdict that Schleiermacher's theology marked a break with the Reformation heritage. Our interest is in Calvin's place in Christian theology, not Schleiermacher's – or Barth's. But the remarks made on Calvin by these two Reformed theologians of modern times may draw attention to some features of *the task of Christian theology*, as he understood and practiced it.

Schleiermacher commended Calvin's masterwork, the 1559 *Institutes*, for two main reasons: because it never loses touch with the religious affections, and because it is distinguished by sharpness of method and *systematic compass*. Evidently, he admired most in the *Institutes* what he himself strove for in his own dogmatic work, *The Christian Faith* (2nd edn, 1830–31). To be sure, it was sometimes denied during the twentieth century that Calvin could properly be seen as a systematic theologian. The denial appears to have arisen out of a limited notion of a "system" as a deductive construct in which everything is derived with logical precision from a first principle. The *Institutes* is certainly not a deductive system. Neither was Calvin interested in contriving an intellectual edifice for its own sake. From Desiderius Erasmus and Martin Bucer he learned that genuine theology, unlike the "sophistry" of the late medieval schoolmen, is eminently practical: its aim is piety or, as Bucer said, "a godlike life." Calvin nonetheless earns a special place among the sixteenth-century Protestant reformers not least because, in the final edition of his *Institutes*, he produced a comprehensive and organized whole, in which he took care to establish the interconnections between one doctrine and another. His *pietatis summa* was a true systematic theology. Schleiermacher's theme also was Christian piety, though he intended his *Christian Faith* to be a "scientific" rather than a directly edifying work, and he clearly stated the nature of a systematic theology when he wrote that the meaning of a dogmatic proposition is partly determined by its place (its "definite context") in the work as a whole (*Christian Faith*, § 28.2). To take the *Institutes* as a systematic theology in *this* sense is always to ask, not just what Calvin said on any topic, but where the topic fits in. Though this is not, of course, all that needs to be said about the design of the *Institutes*, neglect of it is bound to give rise to misunderstandings: for example, the misunderstanding that predestination was his "central dogma."

For his part, Karl Barth warned against any theological system that might prejudge what is heard when God speaks. He didn't direct this warning at Calvin. But he did think that the title of the *Institutes* – "instruction in the Christian *religion*" – was unfortunate if taken (erroneously) as comfort to those who want a "theology of religious consciousness." God's activity, not human activity, is the proper theme of the theologian. In his early Göttingen lectures on the theology of John Calvin (1922), Barth found in Calvin's dominant concern for living out evangelical faith in the real world his special place in the Protestant Reformation. A "second turn" of the Reformation, Calvin's notion of faith as obedience and his preoccupation with Christian ethics completed Luther's achievement – but also, Barth thought, jeopardized it (a judgment with which many Lutherans would agree). Later, in *The Holy Spirit and the Christian Life* (1929), Barth showed himself less inclined than Calvin to excuse Augustine's shortcomings or to interpret him *in optimam partem*. Barthian grace comes to us moment by moment as a totally free act of the Holy Spirit in the word of promise: Augustine, by his notion of an infused grace and his mixing of justification with sanctification, made man's own actions a condition of fellowship with God. The reformers (this time Luther is included!) held firmly to Augustine's anti-Pelagian polemics but "neglected to warn, with sufficient clearness and force, against the sweet poison that is meant when Augustine speaks of 'grace.' "[14]

In principle, Calvin could not complain about this attempt to open a greater distance between Augustine and the Protestant reformers: he held the task of theology to be not only systematic but also open-ended or *progressive*. In his reply to Pighius on free will, Calvin pointed out that not even Augustine arrived at the truth all at once. One could hardly expect more from Luther. If Luther's language was sometimes unguarded and exaggerated, it was justified by the needs of the day. But we are not obliged to repeat his every word, since we don't merely echo him but honor him as the one who opened up a path for us. "If Pighius does not know it, I want to make this plain to him: our constant endeavour, day and night, is to *form* in the manner we think will be best whatever is faithfully *handed on* by us."[15] As Calvin sees it, *fideliter tradere* is always *formare*; or, as he puts it less technically, there is a difference between a disciple and an ape (see, e.g., Calvin to Martin Seidemann, March 14, 1555).

The determination of Calvin's place in Christian theology must surely include recognition of his insistence on the development of Christian doctrine. Many of his heirs, in turn, have claimed a similar right to wrestle with *his* teaching and propose revisions of it. Particularly interesting is the way Schleiermacher and Barth both felt bound to acknowledge the importance of Calvin's doctrine of election, but free to re-form it. Schleiermacher astonished his contemporaries by coming to Calvin's defense in a long article on election (1819). His argument was carried over into *The Christian Faith*. There is indeed an antithesis between those who do, and those who do not, belong to the fellowship of redemption, and we must agree with Calvin that the antithesis is grounded solely in the divine good pleasure. But the reason for the antithesis is that Christ established the kingdom of God as a phenomenon of history: not everyone can be taken up into the kingdom at one time. However, it is a *vanishing* antithesis (*Christian Faith*, §§ 117–18). It is not, as Calvin supposed, unalterably fixed by an irrevocable foreordination of some to blessedness and others to damnation. There is but one divine foreordination – the decree to assume the human race into fellowship with Christ. It is *humanity* that is elect in Christ (§ 119.3; cf. § 109.3). In this fundamental assertion Schleiermacher was followed by Barth (in the *Church Dogmatics*, II/2, §§ 32–35). The only antithesis, then, that we are entitled to draw is not between the elect and the non-elect, but between the regenerate and the not yet regenerate (Schleiermacher), or those who live as God's elect and those who don't (Barth).

There is, of course, a great deal more to the theme of election in Schleiermacher and Barth, but even this much raises the question of *legitimate* development. There is no foothold in Calvin's theology for the notion of a single divine decree, which in fact resembles what he dismissed as the "absurd invention" of Pighius: that the whole human race was chosen in Christ but some deprive themselves of the benefit of universal election.[16] We can only conclude that Calvin's powerful argument for the election of grace has gripped even disciples, or heirs, who have no wish to be "apes," and his place in the history of Christian theology is partly given by his ability to set an agenda and incite dissent.

Many pertinent issues have been left untouched, or touched on only obliquely, in this chapter: Calvin's "Scripture principle" and correlation of Word and Spirit, for example, or his thoughts on such diverse matters as the person and threefold "office" of Christ, the organization and discipline of the church, and the cause of unity among the evangelical churches. It would be unwise to reduce even the themes explored here to a single formula descriptive of Calvin's place in Christian theology. No doubt, his relation to the Augustinian heritage is pivotal. But it hardly locates him in relation to others of whom one might wish to say the same. Warfield held that Calvin's Augustinianism was not peculiar to him but common to all the Protestant reformers. Calvin learned it from Luther and especially from Bucer, "into whose practical, ethical point of view he perfectly entered," only adding clearness and religious depth to what he learned. Bucer "was above all others . . . Calvin's master in theology."[17] Moreover, Protestant Augustinianism, as Warfield conceded, was highly selective; hence his famous aphorism, "[T]he Reformation, inwardly considered, was just the ultimate triumph of Augustine's doctrine of grace over Augustine's doctrine of the Church."[18]

Calvin cared about continuity of doctrine. But he was not interested in a repristination of the whole Augustine, and he was no mere echo of Luther (or of Bucer either). Any such characterization of him and his work would go against his explicit theological principles. Lange van Ravenswaay's suggestion is that, instead of always looking back on Calvin's debts to Augustine, we might think of him as "the initiator of a *distinctive* 'Schola Augustiniana' [Augustinian school] whose program goes far beyond the Wittenberg program."[19] Whatever Calvin learned from the Fathers, the medieval doctors, and his fellow reformers, he made his own and integrated into his own comprehensive interpretation of the Christian faith, establishing a Reformed theological tradition which, insofar as it is true to his understanding of the theological task, does not merely repristinate *his* teaching either but remains open to further "brotherly communication" and development.

## Notes

1 A useful guide in English, building on the earlier work of R. J. Mooi and Luchesius Smits, is Anthony N. S. Lane, *John Calvin: Student of the Church Fathers* (Edinburgh: T.&T. Clark, 1999); see pp. 28 n.96, 41 n.198.

2 J[an] Marius J. Lange van Ravenswaay, *Augustinus totus noster: Das Augustinverständnis bei Johannes Calvin*, Forschungen zur Kirchen- und Dogmengeschichte, 45 (Göttingen: Vandenhoeck & Ruprecht, 1990).

3 John Calvin, *Institutes of the Christian Religion* [1559 edition], ed. John T. McNeill, trans. Ford Lewis Battles, 2 vols., Library of Christian Classics, vols. XX–XXI (Philadelphia: Westminster Press, 1960), III.21.1; hereafter cited in parentheses in the text by book, chapter, and section.

4 Calvin, *Of the Eternal Predestination of God* (1552), trans. Henry Cole in *Calvin's Calvinism* (1856; rpt., Grand Rapids: Eerdmans, 1956), 29.

5 See Lane, *Student of the Church Fathers*, 44 n.231, 61–66.

6 On Calvin's relation to the various streams of late medieval thought, see Heiko A. Oberman, "*Initia Calvini*: The Matrix of Calvin's Reformation," in *Calvinus sacrae scripturae professor: Calvin as Confessor of Holy Scripture*, Papers from the International Congress on Calvin Research 1990, ed. Wilhelm H. Neuser (Grand Rapids: Eerdmans, 1994), 113–54. Oberman notes "a close proximity to Scotus" in Calvin's theological vocabulary (124–7).

7 Lane, *Student of the Church Fathers*, 101–14; cf. Anthony N. S. Lane, *Calvin and Bernard of Clairvaux*, Studies in Reformed Theology and History, new series 1 (Princeton: Princeton Theological Seminary, 1996).

8 Calvin's most careful discussion of the term "free will" appears in his first reply to Pighius: *The Bondage and Liberation of the Will: A Defence of the Orthodox Doctrine of Human Choice against Pighius*, ed. A[nthony] N. S. Lane, trans. G. I. Davies, Texts and Studies in Reformation and Post-Reformation Thought, 2 (Grand Rapids: Baker, 1996). See, in particular, pp. 103, 114, 122, 140, 146.

9 Ibid., 70. Cf. the rhetorical question (ibid., 101) concerning Augustine's talk of *liberum arbitrium:* "But does it therefore follow that nothing is at the same time both voluntary and necessary?"

10 G[eorge] E. Moore, *Ethics*, Home University Library (London: Oxford University Press, 1912; rpt., 1952), ch. 6.

11 I have dealt with the question more fully elsewhere. See B. A. Gerrish, *The Old Protestantism and the New: Essays on the Reformation Heritage* (Chicago: University of Chicago Press, 1982), 27–48, 135–36, 179–95, 258–62, 342 n.69. On sacramental signs, see further B. A. Gerrish, *Grace and Gratitude: The Eucharistic Theology of John Calvin* (Minneapolis: Fortress, 1993), 62–86, 160–73, 182 n.78.

12 Calvin, *Bondage and Liberation*, 28, 35–36.

13 In several essays, I have attempted to fill the gap in the literature, and I may refer to them for details and documentation: Gerrish, *The Old Protestantism*, 196–207; *Continuing the Reformation: Essays on Modern Religious Thought* (Chicago: University of Chicago Press, 1993), 178–216; "Constructing Tradition: Schleiermacher, Hodge, and the Theological Legacy of Calvin," in David Foxgrover, ed., *The Legacy of John Calvin: Calvin Studies Society Papers, 1999* (Grand Rapids: CRC, 2000), 158–75.

14 Karl Barth, *The Holy Spirit and the Christian Life: The Theological Basis of Ethics*, trans. R. Birch Hoyle (1938; reprinted in the Library of Theological Ethics,

Louisville: Westminster John Knox, 1993), 22. Cf. Barth's expression "the subtle works righteousness of infused love" (26).

15 *OC* VI, 250; my translation and emphasis. Cf. Calvin, *Bondage and Liberation*, 29.

16 Calvin, *Eternal Predestination*, 27–28, 45, 71.

17 Benjamin Breckinridge Warfield, *Calvin and Augustine*, ed. Samuel G. Craig (Philadelphia: Presbyterian and Reformed Publishing Co., 1956), 22.

18 Ibid., 322.

19 Lange van Ravenswaay, *Augustinus totus noster*, 181 (emphasis his; translation mine).

# 17  Calvin in ecumenical context

## JANE DEMPSEY DOUGLASS

John Calvin can be seen in an ecumenical context from the sixteenth century right into the twenty-first century. He had a broad and catholic understanding of the one church of Jesus Christ, an outreaching pastoral relationship to churches all over Europe that encouraged greater unity among them, and a passionate concern to make the worldwide reign of Christ visible. Many heirs to his thought have been active leaders and participants in the modern ecumenical movement, believing that Calvin's theology supported their work.

This chapter will identify elements of Calvin's own thought and work which laid a foundation for ecumenical work, selecting them from the broad outlines of Calvin's theology and its history surveyed in earlier chapters. Then it will suggest a few of the ways in which Calvin's influence remains visible in the modern ecumenical movement and in the worldwide church today.

First, however, a definition of "ecumenism" as it will be used here is in order. In a general sense, ecumenism has been understood as a movement in search of Christian unity, inspired by the Holy Spirit. Evidence of such a movement can be found in many periods of church history, including the sixteenth-century Reformation. Modern ecumenism, with its roots in the late nineteenth and early twentieth centuries, has grown out of the experience of Christians of many ecclesiastical traditions and many nations working together as individuals and as churches to witness to Christian unity in various ways: in the global mission of the church to bring the whole world under Christ's rule, in the attempt to reconcile different traditions' views of ministry and sacraments in order to bring about full communion, and in the effort to witness to God's justice in the world through daily work with a sense of Christian vocation and through the transformation of social institutions to protect the dignity of humanity and the health of the creation. Though ecumenism is described in different ways by different theologians in different contexts, certain elements are usually present: a sense of the Holy Spirit's renewing work in the church, enabling the church's unity to be more visible and its mission and service more faithful, so that Christ's reign of peace and justice can be made more visible in the world. This, then, is the lens through which we will attempt to see Calvin in ecumenical context.

Six elements of Calvin's life and thought seem particularly relevant to this task. (1) Calvin's catholic view of the church, together with his belief that the true church can be found under many forms of church order. (2) His struggle against the "idols." (3) His reaching out to and engagement with some churches of other traditions. (4) The multinational and multicultural community that Geneva became during Calvin's years as pastor. (5) Calvin's ministry to the diaspora of Calvinist churches all over Europe and to religious refugees. (6) Calvin's emphasis on the Christian life as stewardship, service to the neighbor, marked by obedience to God's command for justice. None of these elements is unique to Calvin in the sixteenth-century Reformation, except perhaps his sense of the scope of his ministry to the diaspora and to the religious refugees. Yet the way in which the elements come together has given a special character to Calvin's ministry and has had a profound influence on the following Reformed tradition, encouraging its engagement in the ecumenical movement. Let us take up these elements one by one for consideration.

## CALVIN'S FOUNDATIONS FOR ECUMENISM

### One church of Jesus Christ

There is only one church of Jesus Christ spread throughout the whole earth. The church is catholic or universal because all Christians are united in the one body of Christ, which cannot be sundered. Calvin followed Luther in noting as the marks of the true church, i.e., the identifying characteristics by which it can be recognized, only two: the Word of God purely preached and heard and the sacraments administered according to Christ's institution. Where these can be seen, there is surely a church of God. This formulation is, of course, a protest against the theology of the Roman Catholic Church which would identify the true church differently. It functions, however, to permit a Christian to find the church of Jesus Christ under many forms or structures. There is Christian freedom to exercise human governance in the realm of decorum and order in the church's life. In this realm the church can accommodate itself to many cultures and can change as circumstances and the needs of the church require. On the other hand, where one finds a church bearing these two marks, one should not forsake it or refuse to share in its worship.

Calvin understood the reforming movement in which he was engaged as evidence of the Holy Spirit's renewing work in his day, calling the church away from superstition and oppressive human laws to a new faithfulness to the Scriptures as God's word to the church, to a new way of understanding the church's tradition, to new and more just structures for church and society. He did not understand that he had left the church or created a new church but rather that he was helping to restore the one true church of Jesus Christ of all times and places.

Calvin emphasized the powerful bonds of love created by membership in the body of Christ. Especially in the context of the Lord's Supper, he taught that one cannot injure or offend any member of Christ's body without injuring and offending Christ himself. Nonetheless, Christian unity requires mutual accountability and mutual admonition.

Calvin frequently described the church as the church of the whole world, often using imagery from the Hebrew Bible of the reign of God where people of all nations will come to worship on the holy mountain. Calvin ended his sermons with a call to prayer drawn out of the particular concerns of the sermon. But then quite regularly the text of the sermon also refers to a set concluding prayer which said in part: "May he grant this grace not only to us, but also to all peoples and nations of the earth" . . .

### The struggle against idols

Calvin's struggle against the "idols" is grounded in his reading of the first two commandments of the Decalogue or Ten Commandments. The first is the command to have no other gods. Calvin believed that sinful humanity is constantly creating other gods than the God of Abraham and of Jesus Christ and giving them the worship due to God alone. The commandment not to make any graven images or worship them had for centuries in the west been subsumed under the first commandment, and Luther followed this practice. Calvin argued that some in the early church separated the prohibition of graven images as the second commandment, and he much preferred to do so. This, of course, gave it greater prominence.

Under the justification of "idol-smashing," church art was literally destroyed in some centers of the Reformation. What destruction was done in Geneva mostly preceded Calvin's arrival. Nonetheless, Calvin's emphasis on the spiritual nature of worship led him to encourage the simplicity of worship spaces without visual distraction, advice which most Calvinist churches, though not all, reflected till recent years.

What is more important for our purposes is Calvin's emphasis on undefiled loyalty to the one God, turning away from the superstitions which sinful minds create and from clinging to lesser goods than God. Worshiping God alone may require disobeying rulers who command what God forbids, even though obedience to rulers is normally seen as the will of God. This steely monotheism in the tradition of Calvin has led to many confrontations between church and state. We will see that the struggle against "the idols" has sometimes led Calvinists to separate from other Christians and sometimes brought them together with other Christians.

### Engagement with churches of other traditions

Calvin reached out to leaders of some rather different Protestant groups, searching for common ground. Perhaps he had been influenced during his years in Strasbourg by the enthusiasm of Martin Bucer for greater Christian unity. For example, Calvin corresponded with Heinrich Bullinger, leader of the church in Zurich, and even went to Zurich with his former colleague, William Farel, then pastor in Neuchâtel, to negotiate the Consensus of Zurich of 1549 on the Lord's Supper. This agreement, very close to Calvin's writing on the Lord's Supper, brought together the church of Geneva with the churches of French- and German-speaking Switzerland in an understanding of the Lord's Supper where they had previously been separated. It was important to Calvin that there be intercommunion among the Reformation churches, that differences in opinion should not break the fellowship.

Unfortunately this agreement probably worsened relationships with the Lutherans, whereas Calvin had hoped it might also further Lutheran–Reformed relationships. There had been earlier disappointments. Calvin had written Luther warmly in 1545, sending two treatises for his comment, along with a letter to Philip Melanchthon, with whom he was acquainted. But Melanchthon intercepted the letter for Luther as inopportune.

During Calvin's sojourn in Strasbourg, he was sent in 1541 among the city's representatives to the colloquy at Regensburg with representatives of the Roman Catholic Church. Whereas his more senior colleagues, Bucer and Melanchthon, drafted formulas in hopes of agreement with the Catholics, Calvin was more critical of their ambiguity. He also criticized Papal substitution of this colloquy for the free and universal council that had been so long anticipated.

Calvin's wide correspondence with church leaders included the Anglicans. He wrote to Cranmer, William Cecil, and Archbishop Matthew Parker. To Parker in 1561 he suggested renewing Cranmer's earlier proposal for a general meeting of all Protestant clergy to bring about greater unity among the Protestant churches. There was interest but no consequent action.

Ties also developed between Geneva and two reforming movements that had predated the Lutheran reformation. Relationships between the Reformed movement and the Waldensians had been initiated by emissaries to Farel in 1530, before Calvin came to Geneva. The Waldensians began as a twelfth-century reforming movement with some parallels to the early

Franciscans, but the Waldensians were declared heretics. Many fled to the mountains of Northern Italy to survive the persecution. Calvin supported the increasingly close relations with the Waldensians, sent pastors to them, and saw them increasingly identify themselves with Reformed faith and church order. He worked to muster political support for them when there was a massacre of Waldensians by Francis I in 1545. During the Strasbourg years, Calvin also became acquainted with leaders of the Czech Brethren, followers of Jan Hus.

### Multinational and multicultural Geneva

Before the Genevan reformation, the city had been rather poor, suffering from the decline of its trade fairs. With the Reformation, it became a remarkably international city. Refugees poured in, mostly from France, but also from many other countries in western, central, and northern Europe and from Italy. Merchants and craftspeople brought their skills, which enriched the life of the city and brought new prosperity. The influx of refugees, however, was a mixed blessing. The native Genevese often resented the foreigners. They were well aware that during Calvin's time in Geneva, nearly all the city's pastors were foreigners, including Calvin. He became a citizen only late in life. The city was regularly harassed by the neighboring Catholic Savoyards, who sometimes destroyed crops. Food was sometimes in short supply; and because everyone had to live within the walls, housing became scarce. But the city was resourceful in accommodating the refugees, and they later returned home to establish thriving Reformed churches.

Of great significance for this internationalized city was the establishment by Calvin in 1559 of the Academy, precursor of the University of Geneva. It supplemented the *collège*, primarily for basic education of the Genevese children, with an advanced program of study in theology (taught by Beza and Calvin), Greek, Hebrew, and philosophy. The Academy was intended to draw students from all over Christendom, and indeed nearly all the students at that time came from abroad. The largest group came from France to study for the ministry of the French Reformed Church, but many countries were represented. The Academy illustrates the strong international focus of Calvin's reforming program, not just for Geneva but for the church at large.

For Calvin and undoubtedly for others, the refugee experience had a theological impact. Calvin identified with the stories in the Hebrew Scriptures of the exile of the Jews and their persecution. He understood in the light of widespread Christian experience of exile and persecution that traditional claims that the suffering of the Jews through the ages was evidence of their guilt and punishment could no longer be accepted.

### Ministry to the Reformed churches of the "diaspora"

Calvin ministered from Geneva through his writings and correspondence to newly formed Reformed churches, for example in France, the Netherlands, and Germany. These were in addition to the Reformed churches in Switzerland that had become more closely linked with Geneva. Some new churches stemmed from refugee experience in Geneva. John Knox had served an English-speaking refugee congregation in Geneva, learning about Calvin's theology, worship, and church government. When he returned to Scotland in 1559, he organized a Presbyterian church much influenced by Geneva's experience.

What did these Reformed churches take from Geneva? Calvin's theology, the Genevan liturgy in some cases, often the Genevan Psalter – frequently translated into other languages while retaining the special Genevan psalm tunes, and corporate ministry by pastors, elders, and deacons. It was customary for each of the national Reformed churches to have its own confession of faith, a statement of a common faith, but set in the particular context of that church's life. As evidence of the conviction that they shared a common faith, Beza organized a project to create a *Harmony of the Confessions of Faith*, published in Geneva in 1581, well after Calvin's death. Here extracts from several confessions from Lutheran, Reformed, and Anglican churches were arranged topically to show their harmony.

In a preface to the catechism Calvin prepared for the church in Geneva in 1545, he wrote to the pastors in East Friesland, expressing the wish that there could be a common catechism for all churches. He accepted, however, that that is not likely to be the case. Nonetheless he urged that catechists take extreme care in their teaching that even with variety, people will all be directed to the one Christ whose truth will allow us to grow together into one body. To teach rashly and encourage dissension would be to profane baptism, which ought to direct us to a common faith. Calvin said he had written in Latin, still used then as a universal language, so that in a time of confusion and division of Christendom, there could be public testimonies of faith enabling churches to recognize one another and find mutual confirmation and holy fellowship. He believed catechisms are one of the best means of sharing common faith, so he published the catechism of Geneva for others also to use. We see here both Calvin's profound concern about common teaching of one faith and also his awareness that it will necessarily be expressed in different ways in different churches.

### The disciplined Christian life

Though Calvin was as committed as Luther to the doctrine of justification by the grace of Jesus Christ alone, nonetheless he emphasized the importance of a disciplined Christian life. One who has been saved by grace will, out of gratitude, desire to live in accordance with the will of God. How can one know that will? By turning to the law, no longer out of fear but as a free person, out of gratitude. The law teaches not only to worship God alone but also to respect and serve the neighbor. Calvin understood that every Christian is called to a vocation in the world where that person could serve the neighbor. Worldly possessions are a gift of God to be used in stewardship for the needs of one's own family but also of others in need. One can in Christian freedom enjoy the beauty of creation and the taste of good food and wine as gifts of God, but one must live in such a way that all God's people can also enjoy the goodness of creation. This means a simple lifestyle and sharing with the neighbor.

Calvin loved the Hebrew prophets, and he thundered down upon the congregation about those who exploit the poor, fail to pay a living wage, or perform shoddy work. He lived with a biblical vision of the reign of God as a reign of love, peace, and justice. The church's task is to make that reign of God increasingly more visible to the world. And so Christians must reform not only church institutions but also society so that justice will reign.

As much as Calvin stressed the solidarity of Christians within the body of Christ and their need to serve one another, he also stressed the solidarity of all humanity made in the image of God. Therefore any human being in need, however sinful or apparently unworthy of help, lays an ethical claim upon Christians to use whatever resources they have to meet that need, because they share the image of God and a common humanity.

## CALVIN IN ECUMENICAL CONTEXT

Having explored these six elements of Calvin's thought which help to create a foundation for ecumenism, we turn now to explore how those elements can be seen playing a role in the later ecumenical history of the church.

1. We should reflect on the coming together of the Reformed family in the nineteenth century. Despite all that has been said about the interconnection of the Reformed churches in the sixteenth century, by the mid-nineteenth century those churches had drifted apart, spread to European colonies in the New World and in the countries of the South, and they did not know one another well. Still, some Scottish and American church leaders realized that this separation was not normal for the Reformed family. Part of the motivation for change was that some of the churches were discovering each other on the mission field on the other side of the world.

So a process of outreach began, resulting in the formation in 1875 of the Alliance of the Reformed Churches throughout the World holding the Presbyterian System, the first of the world Protestant bodies. By the first meeting of the General Council in 1877 in Edinburgh, there were forty-nine member churches from Europe, the USA, South Africa, Australia, New Zealand, Ceylon, and the New Hebrides. Christian unity was a primary concern. They discussed whether there should be a new confession presenting a consensus of the Reformed confessions, but it was not produced. The new journal of the Alliance was called *The Catholic Presbyterian.*

The Alliance in its early years was also concerned about the relation between mission and unity. It urged that the new churches being planted, for example in Asia and Africa in areas where there had been no prior Christian society, should not perpetuate the divisions of Europe's churches, that new churches should be rooted in the indigenous cultures of the nations where they would live, and that they should be independent as quickly as possible and join the Alliance in their own right. These exhortations seem to reflect more the Reformed heritage we have been observing than the accepted missionary strategy of the day.

Work for justice, human rights, and religious freedom was also one of the themes of the early years of the Alliance. America was denounced for its treatment of its indigenous people, slavery was condemned, and the rights of workers in the newly industrialized countries were supported. Pastoral visits were made to "evangelical" groups in the Middle East and Russia that were experiencing persecution.

Early in the twentieth century, one of the powerful theologies that came to dominate the Protestant world was that of Karl Barth, a Reformed theologian. Barth was very conscious of his roots in the Reformation and his debt to Calvin and also to Luther. In this context it is appropriate to call attention to his role in the German Confessing Church movement, resisting the pressures of the government to transform the church and its teaching in accommodation to Nazi teaching. Participants came from Reformed, Lutheran, and United churches. The themes of the Theological Declaration of Barmen issuing from this movement are Reformation themes: that the Christ revealed in Scripture is the one Word of God to be trusted and obeyed; the insistence that Christ is Lord of every area of life, and there can be no other Lords; that Christ acts as Lord in the church, which belongs only to him, so the gospel cannot be accommodated to politics and ideology; that church offices are for service in the community, not for domination; that the state cannot become the "single and totalitarian order of human life," nor can the church become an organ of the state. We hear in this message the themes of Calvin's struggles against the "idols."

Reformed people, including the leadership of the Alliance, were deeply involved in the movements leading up to the formation of the World Council of Churches (WCC) just after World War II. The Princeton General Council of the Alliance in 1954 declared: "We believe that the deep stirring among the churches and Christian groups to surmount the barriers and to express the unity of the community of believers in accordance with the mind and will of Jesus Christ, the Head of the Church . . . is of God, not men, a sign of the Holy Spirit."[1]

Among the distinguished Reformed leaders in the new WCC were the first general secretary, Dr. Willem Visser 't Hooft; Prof. Hendrik Kraemer, first director of the Ecumenical Institute at the Château de Bossey; and Madeleine Barot, secretary general and long-term leader of the French Comité Inter-Mouvements auprès des Evacués (CIMADE) and first head of the WCC Department of Cooperation between Men and Women in Church and Society. Kraemer and Barot were laypeople.

The Alliance decided to continue its role in gathering the Reformed family and working for its greater unity with the understanding that it would do as many functions as possible through the WCC, such as emergency relief services and interfaith studies, and that it would bring to the WCC a Reformed theological witness in the further search for wider Christian unity.

In 1970 in Nairobi the Alliance merged with the International Congregational Council (meeting since 1891) to become the World Alliance of Reformed Churches. Today it has 218 Presbyterian, Reformed, Congregational, and united member churches in 107 countries on every inhabited continent. About three-fourths of these churches are located in the countries of the South: Asia, Africa, and Latin America. Among them are churches of the Czech Brethren and the Waldensians. About thirty churches are united churches coming mostly from North America, Germany, and Asia. The Asian united churches, such as the Church of North India, the Church of South India, the United Church of Christ in the Philippines, and the Church of Christ in Thailand, seem to be to some extent the fruit of the Reformed concern not to perpetuate the old divisions of Europe in new churches. They continue to honor their Reformed roots through membership in the Alliance. The Church of South India unites formerly Reformed congregations with others in a structure that possesses the historic episcopate. Another type of united church is the Evangelical Church of the River Plate in Argentina, now a member both of the Alliance and of the Lutheran World Federation. These united churches provide an ecumenical witness in the midst of the Reformed fellowship. Most member churches, except those too small, are also members of the WCC and other ecumenical bodies.

Though the member churches of the Alliance have consistently supported Calvin's catholic understanding of the church and a commitment to ecumenical work, it must be said that some heirs of Calvin's theology have placed more emphasis on rigorously pure doctrine and have often splintered and held back from ecumenical engagement. A recent handbook of Reformed churches worldwide resulting from an exhaustive search identifies many more Reformed churches than are members of the Alliance.

As part of its concern for justice, in the late twentieth century the Alliance was preoccupied with the struggle against apartheid in South Africa, declaring a *status confessionis* and suspending the membership of two white churches there that used theological justification for their support of apartheid. Shortly afterward, the Dutch Reformed Mission Church in South Africa, a church primarily of people of mixed race, adopted a remarkable statement in 1982 called the Belhar Confession. Here one finds powerful restatement in that painful situation of Calvin's teaching on the unity of the church, the lordship of Christ as the only head of the church, the solidarity of all humanity in one human nature, the reconciliation, love, and mutual responsibility that mark the true church's life, the freedom for varieties of gifts and languages and cultures to enrich the one visible people of God, and the call for justice to roll down like waters.

The confession is on the one hand a biblical and gracious statement of the heart of Reformed theology, and on the other hand a devastating indictment and repudiation of the situation in South Africa's racially segregated churches:

> ... the Church as the possession of God must stand where He stands, namely against injustice and with the wronged; that in following Christ the Church must witness against all the powerful and privileged who selfishly seek their own interests and thus control and harm others ... We believe that, in obedience to Jesus Christ, its only Head, the Church is called to confess and to do all these things, even though the authorities and human laws might forbid them and punishment and suffering be the consequence. Jesus is Lord.[2]

As in the Declaration of Barmen, we see the struggle against the "idols." We also see a passion for social justice.

Today the Dutch Reformed Mission Church has merged with the former black Dutch Reformed Church of Africa to form an interracial Uniting Reformed Church of Southern Africa, with the Belhar Confession among its confessional standards, and has invited the white Dutch Reformed Church to join them. Unification discussions continue.

Many Reformed people have come to believe that the severe problems of world economic injustice today as the result of economic globalization, where poor nations of the South are experiencing life-threatening suffering, constitute for this generation a confessional moment. The last General Council of the Alliance in Debrecen in 1997 called for a process of confession where the churches would study this issue to see what action they must take. Once again we hear the struggle against the "idols," an insistence that no realm is outside God's governance, and so one cannot argue simply for the autonomy of the markets. God's call for justice includes the economic realm, as Calvin certainly believed.

Finally we see an unexpected recognition of the significance of Calvin's theology in today's ecumenical movement coming from the Reformed–Catholic dialogue. Since the 1960s the Alliance has been engaged in bilateral dialogues with all the world Christian bodies and some traditions, like the Pentecostal one, which have no organized world bodies. Calvin would probably be pleased at the progress already made in Lutheran–Reformed dialogue, with full communion now established in Europe, North America, and some other localities. Another of the regular dialogue partners has been the Pontifical Council for Promoting Christian Unity, and new opportunities for joint Catholic–Reformed cooperation have emerged. At a special Catholic–Reformed conference held at Princeton Theological Seminary in 1996, Edward Idris Cardinal Cassidy, then responsible for that Council, spoke of challenges ahead, one of which is broadening the circle of the ecumenical movement to make it more comprehensive and inclusive. He suggested that "the dialogue between the World Alliance of Reformed Churches and the Catholic Church may have significance far beyond the constituencies they represent." He then pointed to statements that had been made by "evangelicals" outside the churches of the Alliance who are not now in the mainstream of the ecumenical movement who defend their distance on the grounds of their Calvinist theology: "The examples cited above suggest that if the dialogue between the World Alliance and the Roman Catholic Church is successful in helping to resolve long-standing theological differences between us, this may also be of service to other Christians not presently part of the usual ecumenical circles. This dialogue may serve as a bridge . . ."[3]

Cardinal Cassidy's suggestion reminds us that there are followers of Calvin who understand him differently, and it adds another dimension to the title, "Calvin in Ecumenical Context." It also underscores the serious need and relevance for ongoing study of the theology of John Calvin today both within the circle of those who claim his influence and with our ecumenical partners.

*Notes*

1 Lukas Vischer, "The Ecumenical Commitment of the World Alliance of Reformed Churches," *Reformed World* 38 (1985), 262.

2 "The Belhar Confession 1982," in *Preparatory Documents for the WARC Consultation in South Africa* (Geneva: World Alliance of Reformed Churches, 1993).

3 Edward Idris Cardinal Cassidy, "Ecumenical Challenges for the Future: A Catholic Perspective," *The Princeton Seminary Bulletin* n.s. 18 (1997), 26–27.

# 18  Calvin in context: current resources

KARIN MAAG AND PAUL FIELDS

Since the sixteenth century, the life and thought and works of John Calvin have provided a fertile field for scholars from a wide range of disciplines, including theology, history, linguistics, economics, and political science, to name but a few. Periodically, in order to guide interested researchers through the continually expanding mass of material on Calvin and sixteenth- and seventeenth-century Calvinism, various bibliographical survey articles have been prepared.[1] These articles have varied in their comprehensiveness, categories, and their chosen time period. In order not to go over previously charted territory, this contribution will focus on works published since 1990, and will focus on books rather than articles. Those wishing to keep abreast of literature, including articles, on Calvin and Calvinism on a yearly basis, are advised to consult the Calvin bibliography published annually in the November issue of the *Calvin Theological Journal*. The bibliography, together with other relevant material, are accessible through the Meeter Center's website www.calvin.edu/meeter. Another fine, though now slightly outdated, resource for finding information on Calvin resources is the second volume of *Reformation Europe: A Guide to Research*, edited by William S. Maltby.[2]

In order to provide the most coherent picture possible of recent scholarship, this contribution will begin with a wide lens, pointing out key reference works and tools for Calvin scholars, before moving on to primary and secondary sources. Throughout this chapter, it is our contention that Calvin scholars, from whatever discipline, need to take into account the context of the medieval and early modern world which shaped John Calvin and in which he made his mark. Thus, apart from the organizational advantages, the wider focus on the field of Calvin studies in this chapter reminds us that to divorce Calvin from his historical and intellectual context is to do him less than justice. A similarly broad approach should be used regarding the language of materials presented in this chapter. To restrict ourselves only to works published in English would leave aside major contributions to the field of Calvin studies. Indeed, one of the most observable characteristics of this field of research is its enduring international character.

## CALVIN'S WORKS — BASIC REFERENCE RESOURCES

Among the research tools that are most helpful for Calvin scholars are those which carry out the painstaking task of bibliographically describing Calvin's works. A particularly vital tool is the volumes of the *Bibliotheca Calviniana*, edited by Jean-François Gilmont and the late Rodolphe Peter.[3] A first volume, detailing all of Calvin's works published between 1532 and 1554, appeared in 1991. Volume two, covering Calvin's works from 1555 to 1564, appeared in 1994. Volume three, dealing with Calvin's works published posthumously from 1565 to 1600, appeared in 2000. This invaluable resource, done with a great attention to detail, is supported by similar bibliographies focusing on Calvin's works printed or published in a particular language, such as a Polish bibliography by Wieslaw Mincer and a Czech one by Michael Bihary.[4]

Another avenue open to those seeking guidance through the range and themes of Calvin's writings is to consult works such as *The Writings of John Calvin: An Introductory Guide*, by Wulfert de Greef, published in 1993 in its English translation.[5] This work, together with *Major Themes in the Reformed Tradition* and the *Encyclopedia of the Reformed Faith*, both edited by Donald K. McKim, enable scholars to build their analyses on a firm contextual foundation.[6] Another valuable general resource, both for its articles and the accompanying bibliographies, is *The Oxford Encyclopedia of the Reformation*, edited by Hans Hillerbrand.[7]

## CALVIN'S WORKS

As well as the bibliographical studies and guides to Calvin's works, several scholars or groups of scholars have been working since 1990 on new editions of many of Calvin's writings, whether in the *Supplementa Calviniana* or in the *Opera omnia*.[8] The *Supplementa Calviniana* is a long-term project dedicated to publishing previously unpublished sermons in their original languages. To date, the volumes containing sermons are: Volume I: 2 Samuel; Volume II: Isaiah chapters 13–29; Volume V: Micah; Volume VI: Jeremiah and Lamentations; Volume VII: Psalms; Volume VIII: Acts; and Volume XI in 2 parts: Genesis. For its part, the *Opera omnia* provides modern critical editions of the texts previously published in the *Calvini Opera*. To date the following works are available as part of its Series II – *Opera Exegetica*: Volume XVII: the commentary on Galatians, Ephesians, Philippians and Colossians; Volume XV: 2 Corinthians; Volume XIX:

Hebrews; Volume XIII: Romans; Volume XI in 2 parts: 2 John. The Series III – *Scripta Ecclesiastica* section of the *Opera* has published only Volume I – *De Aeterna dei Praedestinatione*. For those interested in Calvin's sermons in their original language, Max Engammare has edited two previously unpublished individual sermons preached by Calvin, one on Genesis (*La servante chassée*) and one from Isaiah (*La famine spirituelle*).[9] Such works enable scholars not only to deepen their knowledge of Calvin's theology, but also to study his methods of scriptural exegesis and homiletics. Similarly, Old Paths Publications from New Jersey has produced updated facsimiles of six sixteenth-century English works by Calvin.[10] To broaden the range of readers encountering Calvin's writings, Eberhard Busch and others have edited a two-volume compendium of Calvin's writings in French and Latin, with German translations.[11] Finally, recent translations of Calvin's 1559 *Institutes* have been produced in Korean and Russian.[12]

For those who wish to research Calvin's works in other formats, IDC Publishers produced in 1996 in microfiche a set called *The Works of John Calvin*. The set provides an affordable way to own seventy-six sixteenth-century works by Calvin, including commentaries, treatises, and various editions of the *Institutes*.[13] Those who wish to have all of Calvin's works in English on a CD may use the AGES Digital Library. Most of the works on the CD are those done by the nineteenth-century Calvin Translation Society.[14] A growing number of Calvin's English works are also available on the web through *Christian Classics Ethereal Books*, www.ccel.org.

Once again, however, concentrating on Calvin's writings alone limits the range of primary sources used to construct an analysis of the impact of Calvin's works in the sixteenth century. Thus several ambitious projects, either new or ongoing, have sought to provide modern critical editions of relevant church and government documents, complete with scholarly apparatus. One ongoing project, for instance, is the *Registres de la Compagnie des Pasteurs de Genève*, currently published up to 1616.[15] A second vista on Genevan church life comes through the first volume of the Genevan Consistory Registers, published in the French original by Droz in Geneva in 1996, and in English by Wm. B. Eerdmans Publishing Co. in 2000.[16]

Thanks to these new editions of crucial primary texts, and to the contextual work on Calvinism and the Reformation carried out by a number of scholars, Calvin specialists have access to a range of sources for their studies of John Calvin and his influence.

## CALVIN'S BIOGRAPHY

Among the recent biographical studies, one should highlight the work of two French scholars, Bernard Cottret and Denis Crouzet. Cottret's biography, entitled *Calvin: A Biography*, was published in an English translation in the fall of 2000, and provides an extensive yet readable study of Calvin's life and impact.[17] Crouzet's monograph, *Jean Calvin: vies parallèles*, focuses more on the psychology of Calvin, and is thus of particular interest to intellectual historians.[18]

## CALVIN'S THOUGHT – ITS ROOTS

Current research on Calvin's thought and influence continues to flourish, so much so that establishing organizational principles and highlighting trends is a complex undertaking. Yet beginning with works studying the roots of Calvin's thought, A. N. S. Lane's monograph, *John Calvin: Student of the Church Fathers* is the most comprehensive study to date on this subject.[19] Others have investigated Calvin's debt to his more immediate predecessors; see for instance Richard A. Muller's *The Unaccommodated Calvin: Studies in the Foundation of a Theological Tradition.*[20] A further possible source of influence on Calvin was the work of fellow theologians and writers of the sixteenth century. Their impact on Calvin is studied in *Calvin et ses contemporains* edited by Olivier Millet, and in the influential *Calvin in Context* by David Steinmetz.[21]

After establishing what were the foundations of Calvin's thought, we can turn to works that lay out the main themes of his intellectual production. These include T. H. L. Parker's *Calvin: An Introduction to His Thought*, Wilhelm Schwendemann's *Leib und Seele bei Calvin*, *The Theater of His Glory: Nature and the Natural Order in the Thought of John Calvin* by Susan Schreiner, and Olivier Millet's study, *Calvin et la dynamique de la parole: étude de rhétorique réformée.*[22] Another important work in this area, published in 1996, is a collected volume of Ford Lewis Battles' studies, entitled *Interpreting John Calvin*, edited by Robert Benedetto.[23] An interesting study of Calvin's theological perspective based on one of his lesser-known works, the *Psychopannychia*, is George Tavard's *The Starting Point of Calvin's Theology.*[24] Meanwhile, a more wide-ranging approach to the study of Calvin's thought appears in *The Legacy of John Calvin*, edited by David Foxgrover, a volume that contains the contributions of speakers at the 1999 Calvin Studies Society meeting.[25]

## CALVIN'S INFLUENCE AND IMPACT

Because so much of Calvin's work was focused on Scripture and scriptural exegesis, a number of scholars in recent years have explored the theme of Calvin and the Bible, including David L. Puckett's *John Calvin's Exegesis* of the Old Testament and, with a wider scope, *Biblical Interpretation in the Era of the Reformation* edited by Richard Muller and John Thompson.[26] Another study of Calvin's use of Scripture in the light of a particular issue is John Thompson's *John Calvin and the Daughters of Sarah: Women in Regular and Exceptional Roles in the Exegesis of Calvin, His Predecessors and His Contemporaries.*[27]

Calvin used his knowledge of Scripture both in his written theological works and commentaries, and in his sermons. Thus, Calvin's sermons offer another avenue for current scholarship. Works on Calvin's sermons include Albrecht Thiel's *In der Schule Gottes: die Ethik Calvins im Spiegel seiner Predigten über das Deuteronomium*, T. H. L. Parker's *Calvin's Preaching*, and Wilhelmus Moehn's *God roept ons tot Zijn dienst: een homiletisch onderzoek naar de verhouding tussen God en Hoorder in Calvijns preken over Handelingen 4;1–6:7.*[28]

From the sermons, one can move to broader questions regarding Calvin's theology and spirituality. The former topic is addressed in *Calvinus Sincerioris Religionis Vindex, Calvin as Protector of the Purer Religion*, edited by Wilhelm Neuser and Brian Armstrong, and bringing together the contributions of the 1994 International Congress on Calvin Research.[29] On a more narrowly focused theological topic, namely predestination, one can cite Harald Rimbach's *Gnade und Erkenntnis in Calvins Prädestinationslehre: Calvin im Vergleich mit Pighius, Beza und Melanchthon.*[30] Issues of spirituality are dealt with in works such as Serene Jones' *Calvin and the Rhetoric of Piety*, Denis E. Tamburello's *Union with Christ: John Calvin and the Mysticism of St. Bernard*, and Randall Gleason's *John Calvin and John Owen on Mortification: A Comparative Study in Reformed Spirituality.*[31]

Other key theological studies include Barbara Pitkin's *What Pure Eyes Could See: Calvin's Doctrine of Faith in its Exegetical Context*, as well as Philip Butin's *Revelation, Redemption, and Response: Calvin's Trinitarian Understanding of the Divine-Human Relationship.*[32] Finally, on a comparative note, there is Randall Zachman's work, *The Assurance of Faith: Conscience in the Theology of Martin Luther and John Calvin.*[33]

While the theology of Calvin continues to offer scope for many different avenues of research, some scholars have sought to integrate aspects of it into their particular domain of research. This is the case for William Stevenson's work, *Sovereign Grace: The Place and Significance of Christian Freedom in John Calvin's Political Thought.*[34] Another work that links Calvin's thought to political, social, and economic developments is Rémi Teissier du Cros' monograph, *Jean Calvin: de la réforme à la révolution.*[35] Other scholars have concentrated on Calvin's contributions to specific areas of church life, such as liturgy, as in T. Briener's work, *Calvijn en de Kerkdienst.*[36]

Researchers looking for articles on a range of topics may use Richard Gamble's compilation of materials culled from the Meeter Center's Calvinism Resources Database (CaRD). Published by Garland, the 14-volume set covers Calvin's biography, work, ministry, theology, economic and social impact, as well as Calvinism's international development.[37]

## CALVINISM

Although much of the research on Calvin and Calvinism from 1990 onwards has focused primarily on Calvin and his thought, other works have examined Calvinism particularly in specific national contexts. Indeed, Calvinism, like other religious movements, had to make some accommodations to local practices and views, while still endeavoring to retain the essentials of doctrine and worship. Studies of Calvinism across Europe and up to the present day can thus help establish what have been the core characteristics of Calvinism.

Apart from the importance of guides to Calvin's corpus and its themes, scholars of Calvin and Calvinism have also increasingly devoted their works to incorporating the impact of Calvin and Calvinism within the wider Reformation context. Although many of these works are not specifically about Calvin, they do indicate the trend of current scholarship towards a more wide-ranging approach, both thematically and chronologically.

Works such as *The Reformation World*, edited by Andrew Pettegree, *The European Reformations* by Carter Lindberg, *The Early Reformation in Europe* edited by Andrew Pettegree, and *The Reformation in National Context*, edited by Bob Scribner, Roy Porter, and Mikuláš Teich all provide essays and chapters setting the development of Calvinism within the wider Reformation context.[38] *The Reformation World* in particular devotes a significant proportion of the overall text to Calvinism across Europe in its different forms. The same is true for Willem Balke's work, *Omgang met de reformatoren.*[39] The Europe-wide impact of Calvinism is also highlighted in the collection of essays edited by Andrew Pettegree, Alastair Duke, and Gillian Lewis, *Calvinism in Europe, 1540–1620*, and its companion volume of primary source documents: *Calvinism in Europe, 1540–1620: A Collection of Documents.*[40] The influence of Calvinism is also highlighted in Salvatore Caponetto's *The Protestant Reformation in Sixteenth-Century Italy.*[41] Finally, *The Reformation in Eastern and Central Europe*, edited by Karin Maag, underscores the significance of Calvinism and other Reformation movements in an area of Europe otherwise often ignored by modern English-speaking scholarship.[42]

Other scholars have concentrated on the history of Calvinism. For instance, Willem van 't Spijker's work, *Geest, woord en kerk: opstellen over de geschiedenis van het gereformeerd protestantisme*, provides a general overview of the history of Reformed Protestantism.[43] *Later Calvinism: International Perspectives*, edited by W. Fred Graham, seeks precisely to look at the ways in which the theology and practices of Calvinism were shaped by both the passage of time and different socio-political contexts.[44] Carl Trueman's and R. Scott Clark's edited volume, *Protestant Scholasticism: Essays in Reassessment*, carries out a similar task from a specifically theological/intellectual standpoint.[45] Other works have examined the impact of Calvinism on a particular field of human activity, be it art, as in Paul Finney's edited volume, *Seeing Beyond the Word: Visual Arts and the Calvinist Tradition*, or social discipline, as in *Sin and the Calvinists: Morals Control and the Consistory in the Reformed Tradition*, edited by Raymond Mentzer.[46] Other areas of investigation deal more specifically with church life, such as the 1994 conference volume on preaching and pastoral office, *Reformatie: prediking en ambt: congresbundel 1992–1993*, edited by M. van Campen, W. de Greef, and F. van der Pol.[47]

Scholars have also focused on particular topics where a strong link can be made with the growth of Calvinism. One such topic is printing. Works such as Francis Higman's collected essays, *Lire et découvrir: la circulation des idées au temps de la Réforme*, *The Reformation and the Book*, edited by Jean-François Gilmont and published in an English translation in 1998, Gilmont's own *Jean Calvin et le livre imprimé*, and Higman's survey of French religious books, *Piety and the People: Religious Printing in French, 1511–1551*, all point to the importance of the links between Calvinism and the written word.[48] Because printing became one of the main tools used to transmit the message of religious change, these works remind us that the mode of transmission of ideas is at times as important as the ideas themselves.

Works on Calvinism with a specifically national focus have continued to appear since 1990, especially with the continued emphasis in current historical research on more local studies. Scholars who have investigated the impact of Calvinism on Geneva in particular include William G. Naphy, in his monograph, *Calvin and the Consolidation of the Genevan Reformation*, and Karin Maag in her *Seminary or University? The Genevan Academy and Reformed Higher Education, 1560–1620*.[49] For England, these include R. T. Kendall's *Calvin and English Calvinism to 1649*, and Peter White's *Predestination, Policy and Polemic: Conflict and Consensus in the English Church from the Reformation to the Civil War*.[50] Studies of Calvinism in France have been overshadowed to some extent by the works produced to mark the anniversary of the proclamation of the Edict of Nantes in 1998, but some books specifically on Calvinism continue to appear, such as Christopher Elwood's *The Body Broken: The Calvinist Doctrine of the Eucharist and the Symbolization of Power in Sixteenth-Century France*.[51] Another work on the subject is

Jean-Marc Berthoud's study, *Calvin et la France: Genève et le déploiement de la réforme au xvie siècle*.[52] Studies of Calvinism in the urban world of north-western Europe have also flourished, as for instance Benjamin Kaplan's *Calvinists and Libertines: Confession and Community in Utrecht, 1578–1620* or Guido Marnef's *Antwerp in the Age of Reformation: Underground Protestantism in a Commercial Metropolis, 1550–1577*.[53] Finally, for the chronically under-studied areas of eastern Europe, there is now Graeme Murdock's study of Hungary, *Calvinism on the Frontier, 1600–1660: International Calvinism and the Reformed Church in Hungary and Transylvania*.[54]

Apart from national studies of the impact and influence of Calvinism, a number of scholars have also been interested in tracing its influence in our own time. These works include *The Calvinist Roots of the Modern Era*, edited by Aliki Barnstone, Michael Manson, and Carol Singley, as well as Hans Scholl's edited volume, *Karl Barth und Johannes Calvin: Karl Barths Gottinger Calvin-Vorlesung von 1922*.[55] Ilka Werner's *Calvin und Schleiermacher im Geschpräch mit der Weltweisheit* also underscores the continuing interest in current scholarship in assessing Calvin and his work in the light of later theological inquiry.[56]

## CONCLUSION

Any survey of current scholarship in as large and diverse a field as Calvin studies is bound to be incomplete, not least because works are regularly appearing. In many ways, the range of topics relating to Calvin and Calvinism, though chaotic at first sight, is in fact a sign of the ongoing vitality of this area of research. It is clear that there is no single approach to the study of Calvin and Calvinism, and that it is by keeping abreast of the different currents of research that today's Calvin scholars can integrate their own research most effectively into the broader context.

There are, however, some trends that can be noted. Some of the most illuminating research on Calvinism at the current time seems to be coming increasingly from those who study Calvinism from a historical rather than a theological perspective. In part, this trend is due to the development of Reformation research centers, led by historians such as Andrew Pettegree of the Reformation Studies Institute at the University of St Andrews, and the late Heiko Oberman at the Division for late Medieval and Reformation Studies at the University of Arizona, or Robert Kingdon of the Institute for Research in the Humanities at the University of Wisconsin/Madison.

Increasingly, those studying Calvin's theology and that of his successors are also emphasizing the need to be aware of context. Thus while older works may have been more prone to stress the ways in which Calvin's theological perspective was distinct from that of both Catholics and other Protestants of his day, the trend in current theological studies of Calvin seems to be to understand the roots of Calvin's theological insights. Thus, more recent studies such as those of Anthony Lane and Richard Muller set Calvin within the theological context of his time, rather than separating him from it.

Furthermore, as scholars from different countries continue to study the impact of Calvinism in their own areas, recent years have seen a flowering of works highlighting the role of Calvinism on a European scale. These local studies (and more are still needed) have helped Calvin scholars to begin to make some comparisons across national boundaries, examining how one confessional group adapted itself to such a wide range of political and social contexts. Thanks to these local studies, wider themes such as church discipline, issues of political resistance, and the aims of higher education can be studied comparatively, based on Calvinist examples in a wide variety of national contexts.

Overall, the future of Calvin studies looks strong. Among the most important factors in sustaining effective and in-depth research on Calvin and Calvinism is to continue to emphasize to graduate students in particular the central importance of the mastery of other languages apart from English. Language proficiency enables scholars not only to be able to read important primary sources, but also to take full advantage of the writings of other Calvin scholars published in other languages. Continued commitment to archival research also remains a necessity, in order to continue to bring fertile new sources to this field of research. Finally, the example of collaborative projects such as the modern critical editions of Calvin's writings, and the ongoing publication of the registers of the Genevan Company of Pastors and the Genevan Consistory, are a good sign of the sustained enthusiasm for the study of Calvin and Calvinism in the twenty-first century.

*Notes*

1 Doede Nauta, "The State of Calvin-Research" (Amsterdam: Lecture given at the Europaischer Kongress fur Calvinforsschung, 1974), 1–18; Wilhelm H. Neuser, "International Calvin Research," in *Calvinus Reformator: His Contribution to Theology, Church and Society* (Pretoria, South Africa: Potchefstroom University Press, 1982), 1–6; Pieter Coertzen, "Some Observations on Calvin Research with Special Reference to South Africa," *In Die Skriflig* 27/4 (1993), 537–61; Richard C. Gamble, "Current Trends in Calvin Research, 1982–1990," in *Calvinus Sacrae Scripturae Professor: Calvin as Confessor of Holy Scripture* (Grand Rapids: Eerdmans, 1994), 91–112; Wilhelm H. Neuser, "Future Tasks of the International Calvin Research," *Hervormde teologiese* 54/1–2 (1998), 153–60; Richard A. Muller, "Directions in Current Calvin Research," in *Calvin Studies IX*: Papers presented at the Ninth Colloquium on Calvin Studies, (Davidson, NC: Davidson College, 1998), 70–88.

2 William S. Maltby, ed., *Reformation Europe: A Guide to Research II* (St. Louis: Center for Reformation Research, 1992).

3 Rodolphe Peter and Jean-François Gilmont, eds., *Bibliotheca Calviniana: Les oeuvres de Jean Calvin publiées au XVI siècle*, 3 vols. (Geneva: Librairie Droz, 1991–2000).

4 Wieslaw Mincer, *Jan Kalwin w Polsce Bibliografia* (Torun: Wydawnictwo Uniwersytetu Mikolaja Kopernika, 2000). Michael Bihary, *Bibliographia Calviniana* (Prague: M. Bihary, 2000).

5 Wulfert de Greef, *The Writings of John Calvin: An Introductory Guide* (Grand Rapids: Baker, 1993). W. de Greef, *Johannes Calvijn: zijn werk en geschriften* (Kampen: Uitgeverij de Groot Goudriaan, 1989).

6 Donald K. McKim, ed., *Major Themes in the Reformed Tradition* (Grand Rapids: Eerdmans, 1992). Donald K. McKim, ed., *Encyclopedia of the Reformed Faith* (Louisville: Westminster John Knox Press, 1992).

7 Hans J. Hillerbrand, ed., *The Oxford Encyclopedia of the Reformation*, 4 vols. (New York: Oxford University Press, 1996).

8 Erwin Mülhaupt et al., eds., *Supplementa Calviniana; sermons inédits, Vols. 1–3, 5–8* (Neukirchen: Neukirchener Verlag, 1936–61). Brian G. Armstrong, et al., eds., *Ioannis Calvini opera omnia*, vols. I, XI, XIII, XV, XVI, XIX (Geneva: Librairie Droz, 1992– ).

9 John Calvin, *La servante chassée* (Geneva: Zoé, 1995); John Calvin, *La famine spirituelle* (Geneva: Librairie Droz, 2000).

10 John Calvin, *The Necessity of Reforming the Church* (Audubon, NJ: Old Paths Publications, 1994); *Sermons on Galatians* (Audubon, NJ: Old Paths Publications, 1995); *Sermons on Election & Reprobation* (Audubon, NJ: Old Paths Publications, 1996); *Sermons on Psalm 119* (Audubon, NJ: Old Paths Publications, 1996); *The Deity of Christ and Other Sermons* (Audubon, NJ: Old Paths Publications, 1997); *Sermons on Melchisedek & Abraham* (Audubon, NJ: Old Paths Publications, 2000). See www.oldpathspublications.com.

11 Eberhard Busch, et al., eds., *Calvin Studienausgabe*, vols. I–II (Neukirchen: Neukirchener Verlag, 1994).

12 John Calvin, *Institutio Christianae religionis*. Korean and English, vols. I–IV (Seoul: Sungmoon Publication, 1993). *Institutio Christianae religionis*. Russian, vols. I–III (Grand Rapids: CRC World Literature Ministries, 1997–99).

13 Francis Higman, ed., *The Works of John Calvin* on microfiche (Leiden: IDC Publishers, 1996).

14 John Calvin, *The Comprehensive John Calvin Collection* (computer file) / AGES Software (Albany, OR: Ages, 1998). See http://www.ageslibrary.com/.

15 Olivier Fatio, et al., eds., *Registres de la Compagnie des Pasteurs de Genève*, vols. I–XII (Geneva: Librairie Droz, 1962– ).

16 Robert M. Kingdon, et al., eds., *Registres du consistoire de Genève*, vol. I (Geneva: Librairie Droz, 1996). Robert M. Kingdon, ed., *The Registers of the Consistory of Geneva in the Time of Calvin* (Grand Rapids: Eerdmans, 2000).

17 Bernard Cottret, *Calvin: biographie* ([Paris]: J. C. Lattes, 1995). M. Wallace McDonald, trans., *Calvin: A Biography* (Grand Rapids, Eerdmans, 2000).

18 Denis Crouzet, *Jean Calvin: vies parallèles* ([Paris]: Fayard, 2000).

19 Anthony N. S. Lane, *John Calvin: Student of the Church Fathers* (Edinburgh: T.&T. Clark, 1999).

20 Richard A. Muller, *The Unaccommodated Calvin: Studies in the Foundation of a Theological Tradition* (New York: Oxford University Press, 2000).

21 Olivier Millet, ed., *Calvin et ses contemporains: actes du colloque de Paris 1995* (Geneva: Librairie Droz, 1998). David C. Steinmetz, *Calvin in Context* (New York: Oxford University Press, 1995).

22 Olivier Millet, *Calvin et la dynamique de la parole: étude de rhétorique réformée* (Paris: H. Champion, 1992). T. H. L. Parker, *Calvin: An Introduction to His Thought* (Louisville, Westminster John Knox Press, 1995). Susan E. Schreiner, *The Theater of His Glory: Nature and the Natural Order in the Thought of John Calvin* (Grand Rapids: Baker, 1995). Wilhelm Schwendemann, *Leib und Seele bei Calvin: die erkenntnistheoretische und anthropologische Funktion des platonischen Leib-Seele-Dualismus in Calvins Theologie* (Stuttgart: Calwar, 1996).

23 Ford Lewis Battles, *Interpreting John Calvin*, ed. Robert Benedetto (Grand Rapids: Baker, 1996).

24 George H. Tavard, *The Starting Point of Calvin's Theology* (Grand Rapids: Eerdmans, 2000).

25 David Foxgrover, ed., *The Legacy of John Calvin: Calvin Studies Society Papers, 1999* (Grand Rapids: CRC, 2000).

26 David L. Puckett, *John Calvin's Exegesis of the Old Testament* (Louisville: Westminster John Knox Press, 1995). Richard A. Muller and John Thompson, eds., *Biblical Interpretation in the Era of the Reformation: Essays Presented to David C. Steinmetz in Honor of His Sixtieth Birthday* (Grand Rapids: Eerdmans, 1996).

27 John L. Thompson, *John Calvin and the Daughters of Sarah: Women in Regular and Exceptional Roles in the Exegesis of Calvin, His Predecessors, and His Contemporaries* (Geneva: Librairie Droz, 1992).

28 Wilhelmus H. T. Moehn, *God roept ons tot Zijn dienst: een homiletisch onderzoek naar de verhouding tussen God en Hoorder in Calvijns preken over Handelingen 4:1–6:7 = God calls us to His service = Dieu nous appelle à son service* (Kampen: Kok, 1996). T. H. L. Parker, *Calvin's Preaching* (Louisville: Westminster John Knox Press, 1992). Albrecht Thiel, *In der Schule Gottes: die Ethik Calvins im Spiegel seiner Predigten über das Deuteronomium* (Neukirchen: Neukirchener Verlag, 1999).

29 Wilhelm H. Neuser and Brian G. Armstrong, eds., *Calvinus Sincerioris Religionis Vindex: Calvin as Protector of the Purer Religion* (Kirksville, MO: Sixteenth Century Journal, 1997).

30 Harald Rimbach, *Gnade und Erkenntnis in Calvins Prädestinationslehre: Calvin im Vergleich mit Pighius, Beza und Melanchthon* (New York: Peter Lang, 1996).

31 Randall C. Gleason, *John Calvin and John Owen on Mortification: A Comparative Study in Reformed Spirituality* (New York: Peter Lang, 1995). Serene Jones, *Calvin and the Rhetoric of Piety* (Louisville: Westminster John Knox Press, 1995). Dennis Tamburello, *Union with Christ: John Calvin and the Mysticism of St. Bernard* (Louisville: Westminster John Knox Press, 1994).

32 Philip W. Butin, *Revelation, Redemption, and Response: Calvin's Trinitarian Understanding of the Divine-Human Relationship* (New York: Oxford University Press, 1995). Barbara Pitkin, *What Pure Eyes Could See: Calvin's Doctrine of Faith in Its Exegetical Context* (New York: Oxford University Press, 1999).

33 Randall C. Zachman, *The Assurance of Faith: Conscience in the Theology of Martin Luther and John Calvin* (Minneapolis: Fortress Press, 1993).

34 William Stevenson, *Sovereign Grace: The Place and Significance of Christian Freedom in John Calvin's Political Thought* (New York: Oxford University Press, 1999).

35 Rémi Teissier du Cros, *Jean Calvin: de la réforme à la révolution* (Paris: L'Hermattan, 1999).

36 T. Briener, *Calvijn en de Kerkdienst* (Heerenveen: Groen, 1999).

37 Richard C. Gamble, ed., *Articles on Calvin and Calvinism – A Fourteen-volume Anthology of Scholarly Articles* (New York: Garland Publishing Co., 1992).

38 Andrew Pettegree, ed., *The Reformation World* (New York: Routledge, 2000). Carter Lindberg, *The European Reformations* (Oxford: Blackwell, 1996). Andrew Pettegree, ed., *The Early Reformation in Europe* (New York: Cambridge University Press, 1992). Bob Scribner, Roy Porter, and Mikuláš Teich, eds., *The Reformation in National Context* (New York: Cambridge University Press, 1994).

39 Willem Balker, *Omgang met de reformatoren* (Kampen: De Groot Groudriaan, 1992).

40 Andrew Pettegree, Alastair Duke, and Gillian Lewis, eds., *Calvinism in Europe, 1540–1620* (New York: Cambridge University Press, 1994). Also, *Calvinism in Europe, 1540–1610: A Collection of Documents* (New York: St. Martin's Press, 1992).

41 Salvatore Caponetto, *The Protestant Reformation in Sixteenth-Century Italy* (Kirksville, MO: Thomas Jefferson University Press, 1999).

42 Karin Maag, ed., *The Reformation in Eastern and Central Europe* (Brookfield, VT: Ashgate, 1997).

43 Willem van 't Spijker, *Geest, woord en kerk: opstellen over de geschiedenis van het gereformeerd protestantisme* (Kampen: Kok, 1991).

44 W. Fred Graham, ed., *Later Calvinism: International Perspectives* (Kirksville, MO: Sixteenth Century Journal, 1994).

45 Carl R. Trueman, and R. Scott Clark, eds., *Protestant Scholasticism: Essays in Reassessment* (Carlisle: Paternoster, 1999).

46 Paul C. Finney, ed., *Seeing Beyond the Word: Visual Arts and the Calvinist Tradition* (Grand Rapids: Eerdmans, 1999). Raymond A. Mentzer, ed., *Sin and the Calvinists: Moral Control and the Consistory in the Reformed Tradition* (Kirksville, MO: Sixteenth Century Journal, 1994).

47 M. van Campen, W. de Greef, and F. van der Pol, eds., *Reformatie: prediking en ambt: congresbundel 1992–1993* (Apeldoorn: Stichting ter Bevordering van de Kennis van de Reformatie Congres, 1994).

48 Francis M. Higman, *Lire et découvrir: la circulation des idées au temps de la Réforme* (Geneva: Librairie Droz, 1998). Jean-François Gilmont, ed., *The Reformation and the Book* (Aldersgate, VT: Ashgate, 1998). Jean-François Gilmont, *Jean Calvin et le livre imprimé* (Geneva: Librairie Droz, 1997). Francis M. Higman, *Piety and the People: Religious Printing in French, 1511–1551* (Brookfield, VT: Scolar Press, 1996).

49 William G. Naphy, *Calvin and the Consolidation of the Genevan Reformation* (New York: St. Martin's Press, 1994; rpt. Louisville: Westminster John Knox Press, 2003). Karin Maag, *Seminary or University? The Genevan Academy and Reformed Higher Education, 1560–1620* (Brookfield, VT: Ashgate, 1995).

50 R. T. Kendall, *Calvin and English Calvinism to 1649* (Carlisle: Paternoster, 1997). Peter White, *Predestination, Policy, and Polemic: Conflict and Consensus in the*

*English Church from the Reformation to the Civil War* (New York: Cambridge University Press, 1992).

51 Christopher Elwood, *The Body Broken: The Calvinist Doctrine of the Eucharist and the Symbolization of Power in Sixteenth-Century France* (New York: Oxford University Press, 1999).

52 Jean-Marc Berthoud, *Calvin et la France: Genève et le déploiement de la réforme au xvie siècle* (Lausanne: L'Age d'Homme, 1999).

53 Benjamin J. Kaplan, *Calvinists and Libertines: Confession and Community in Utrecht, 1578–1620* (Oxford: Clarendon Press, 1995). Guido Marnef, *Antwerp in the Age of Reformation: Underground Protestantism in a Commercial Metropolis, 1550–1577* (Baltimore: Johns Hopkins University Press, 1996).

54 Graeme Murdock, *Calvinism on the Frontier, 1600–1660: International Calvinism and the Reformed Church in Hungary and Transylvania* (New York: Oxford University Press, 2000).

55 Aliki Barnstone, Michael Manson, and Carol Singley, eds., *The Calvinist Roots of the Modern Era* (Hanover, NH: University Press of New England, 1997). Hans Scholl, ed., *Karl Barth und Johannes Calvin: Karl Barths Gottinger Calvin-Vorlesung von 1922* (Neukirchen: Neukirchener Verlag, 1995).

56 Ilka Werner, *Calvin und Schleiermacher im Geschpräch mit der Weltweisheit* (Neukirchen: Neukirchener Verlag, 1999).

# Select bibliography

*Calvin's life and context*

Balke, Willem. *Calvin and the Anabaptist Radicals.* Trans. William J. Heynen. Grand Rapids: Eerdmans, 1981.

Bouwsma, William J. *John Calvin: A Sixteenth-Century Portrait.* New York: Oxford University Press, 1988.

Breen, Quirinus. *John Calvin: A Study in French Humanism.* Rpt. Hamden: Shoe String Press, 1968.

Cottret, Bernard. *Calvin: A Biography.* Trans. M. Wallace McDonald. Grand Rapids: Eerdmans, 2000.

Doumergue, Émile. *Jean Calvin, les hommes et les choses de son temps.* 7 vols. Lausanne: G. Bridel, 1899–1927.

Gamble, Richard, ed. *Articles on Calvin and Calvinism – A Fourteen-volume Anthology of Scholarly Articles.* 14 vols. New York: Garland Publishing Co., 1992.

Ganoczy, Alexandre. *The Young Calvin.* Trans. David L. Foxgrover and Wade Provo. Philadelphia: Westminster Press, 1987.

Gautier, Jean-Antoine. *Histoire de Genève des origins à l'année 1691.* 9 vols. Geneva, 1896–1914.

Higman, Francis. *The Style of John Calvin in His French Polemical Treatises.* Oxford: Oxford University Press, 1957.

Höpfl, Harro. *The Christian Polity of John Calvin.* Cambridge: Cambridge University Press, 1982.

Hughes, Philip E., trans. *The Register of the Company of Pastors of Geneva in the Time of Calvin.* Grand Rapids: Eerdmans, 1964.

Hugo, André Malan. *Calvijn en Seneca.* Groningen: Wolters, 1957.

Innes, William C. *Social Concerns in Calvin's Geneva.* Allison Park, PA: Pickwick Press, 1983.

Kingdon, Robert M. *Geneva and the Coming of the Wars of Religion in France, 1555–1563.* Geneva: Librairie Droz, 1956.

Kingdon, Robert M., Thomas A. Lambert, and Isabella M. Watt, eds. *Registers of the Consistory of Geneva in the Time of Calvin.* Trans. M. Wallace McDonald. Vol. I (1542–1544). Grand Rapids: Eerdmans, 2000.

Kingdon, Robert M., and Robert D. Linder, eds. *Calvin and Calvinism: Sources of Democracy?* Lexington, MA: Heath, 1970.

McGrath, Alistair. *A Life of John Calvin.* Oxford: Blackwell's, 1990.

Monter, E. William. *Studies in Genevan Government.* Geneva: Librairie Droz, 1964.

*Calvin's Geneva.* New York: John Wiley and Sons, 1967.

Naef, Henri. *Les Origines de la Réforme à Genève.* 2 vols. Geneva: A. Jullien; Paris: E. Droz, 1936.

Naphy, William G. *Calvin and the Consolidation of the Genevan Reformation with a New Preface.* Rpt. Louisville: Westminster John Knox Press, 2003.

Olson, Jeannine. *Calvin and Social Welfare: Deacons and the Bourse Française.* Sellingsgrove, PA: Susquehanna University Press, 1989.

Parker, T. H. L. *John Calvin: A Biography.* Philadelphia: Westminster Press, 1975.

Stauffer, Richard. *L'humanité de Calvin.* Cahiers Théologiques. Neuchatel, Switzerland: Éditions Delacaux et Niestlé, 1964. In English as *The Humanness of John Calvin.* Trans. George Shriver. Nashville: Abingdon Press, 1971.

Walker, Williston. *John Calvin: the Organiser of Reformed Protestantism (1509–1564),* New York: G. P. Putnam's Sons, 1906.

Wallace, Ronald S. *Calvin, Geneva and the Reformation.* Edinburgh: Scottish Academic Press, 1988.

Wendel, François. *John Calvin: The Origins and Development of His Religious Thought.* Trans. Philip Mairet. New York: Harper & Row, 1963.

  *Calvin et l'humanisme.* Paris: Presses Universitaires de France, 1976.

### Calvin's writings

de Greef, W. *The Writings of John Calvin. An Introductory Guide.* Trans. L. D. Bierma. Grand Rapids: Baker, 1989.

### Calvin as a biblical interpreter

Engammare, Max. "*Johannes Calvinus trium linguarum peritus?* La question de l'Hébreu," *Bibliothèque d'Humanisme et Renaissance* 58 (1996), 35–60.

Ganoczy, Alexandre, and Klaus Müller. *Calvins handschriftliche Annotationen zu Chrysostomus: Ein Beitrag zur Hermeneutik Calvins.* Wiesbaden: Franz Steiner, 1981.

Ganoczy, Alexandre, and Stefan Scheld. *Die Hermeneutik Calvins: Geistesgeschichtliche Voraussetzungen und Grundzüge.* Wiesbaden: Franz Steiner, 1983.

Giradin, Benoît. *Rhetorique et théologique: Calvin, le commentaire de l'Epître aux Romains.* Paris: Beauschesne, 1979.

Hazlett, W. Ian P. "Calvin's Latin Preface to His Proposed French Edition of Chrysostom's Homilies: Translation and Commentary," in James Kirk, ed., *Humanism and Reform: The Church in Europe, England, and Scotland 1400–1643. Essays in Honour of James K. Cameron,* 129–50. Studies in Church History, Subsidia 8. Oxford: Blackwell, 1991.

Kraus, Hans-Joachim. "Calvin's Exegetical Principles," *Interpretation* 31 (1977): 8–18.

Lane, A. N. S. *John Calvin: Student of the Church Fathers.* London: T. & T. Clark; Grand Rapids: Baker, 1999.

Muller, Richard A. "The Hermeneutic of Promise and Fulfillment in Calvin's Exegesis of the Old Testament Promises of the Kingdom," in David C. Steinmetz, ed., *The Bible in the Sixteenth Century,* 68–82. Durham: Duke University Press, 1990.

  *The Unaccommodated Calvin: Studies in the Foundation of a Theological Tradition.* Oxford Studies in Historical Theology. New York: Oxford University Press, 2000.

Parker, T. H. L. *Calvin's Old Testament Commentaries.* Edinburgh: T. & T. Clark, 1986.

*Calvin's New Testament Commentaries*. 2nd edition. Louisville: Westminster John Knox, 1993.

Pitkin, Barbara, *What Pure Eyes Could See: Calvin's Doctrine of Faith in Its Exegetical Context*. Oxford Studies in Historical Theology. New York: Oxford University Press, 1999.

Puckett, David L. *John Calvin's Exegesis of the Old Testament*. Columbia Studies in Reformed Theology. Louisville: Westminster John Knox, 1995.

Schreiner, Susan E. *Where Shall Wisdom Be Found? Calvin's Exegesis of Job from Medieval and Modern Perspectives*. Chicago: University of Chicago Press, 1994.

Steinmetz, David C. *Calvin in Context*. New York: Oxford University Press, 1995.

"Calvin and the Irrepressible Spirit," *Ex Auditu* 12 (1996), 94–107.

Thompson, John L. "The Immoralities of the Patriarchs in the History of Exegesis: A Reassessment of Calvin's Position," *Calvin Theological Journal* 26 (1991): 9–46.

*John Calvin and the Daughters of Sarah: Women in Regular and Exceptional Roles in the Exegesis of Calvin, His Predecessors, and His Contemporaries*. Travaux d'Humanisme et Renaissance 259. Geneva: Librairie Droz, 1992.

"Calvin's Exegetical Legacy: His Reception and Transmission of Text and Tradition," in David L. Foxgrover, ed., *The Legacy of John Calvin: Calvin Studies Society Papers 1999*, 31–56. Grand Rapids: CRC, 2000.

Torrance, Thomas F. *The Hermeneutics of John Calvin*. Monograph Supplements to the *Scottish Journal of Theology*. Edinburgh: Scottish Academic Press, 1988.

Walchenbach, John Robert. "John Calvin as Biblical Commentator: An Investigation into Calvin's Use of John Chrysostom as an Exegetical Tutor." Diss., University of Pittsburgh, 1974.

Wright, David F. "Calvin's 'Accommodation' Revisited," in Peter De Klerk, ed., *Calvin as Exegete: Papers and Responses Presented at the Ninth Colloquium on Calvin and Calvin Studies, 1993*, 171–90. Grand Rapids: CRC, 1995.

### Calvin's theology

Barth, Karl. *The Theology of John Calvin*. Trans. Geoffrey W. Bromiley. Grand Rapids: Eerdmans, 1995.

Battles, Ford Lewis. *Interpreting John Calvin*. Ed. Robert Benedetto. Grand Rapids: Baker, 1996.

Butin, Philip Walker. *Revelation, Redemption, and Response: Calvin's Trinitarian Understanding of the Divine-Human Relationship*. New York: Oxford University Press, 1995.

Dowey, Edward A., Jr. *The Knowledge of God in Calvin's Theology*. Columbia University Press, 1952. 3rd edition. Grand Rapids: Eerdmans, 1994.

Engel, Mary Potter. *John Calvin's Perspectival Anthropology*. Atlanta: Scholars Press, 1988.

Gerrish, Brian. *Grace and Gratitude: The Eucharistic Theology of John Calvin*. Minneapolis: Fortress, 1993.

Hesselink, I. John. *Calvin's First Catechism: A Commentary*. Louisville: Westminster John Knox Press, 1997.

Jansen, John F. *Calvin's Doctrine of the Work of Christ*. London: James Clarke, 1956.

Krusche, Werner. *Das Wirken des Heiligen Geistes nach Calvin*. Göttingen: Vandenhoeck & Ruprecht, 1957.

McKim, Donald K., ed. *Readings in Calvin's Theology*. Rpt. Eugene, OR: Wipf and Stock Publishers, 1998.

Niesel, Wilhelm. *The Theology of Calvin*. Trans. Harold Knight. Philadelphia: Westminster Press, 1956. Rpt. 1980.

Parker, T. H. L. *The Doctrine of the Knowledge of God: A Study in the Theology of John Calvin*. Grand Rapids: Eerdmans, 1952. 2nd revd. edition published as *Calvin's Doctrine of the Knowledge of God*. Edinburgh: Oliver & Boyd, 1969.

  *Calvin: An Introduction to His Thought*. Louisville: Westminster John Knox Press, 1995.

Partee, Charles B. *Calvin and Classical Philosophy*. Leiden: E. J. Brill, 1977.

Schreiner, Susan E. *The Theater of His Glory. Nature and its Natural Order in the Thought of John Calvin*. Durham, NC: Labyrinth Press, 1991.

Tavard, George H. *The Starting Point of Calvin's Theology*. Grand Rapids: Eerdmans, 2000.

Torrance, T. F. *Kingdom and Church*. Edinburgh: Oliver & Boyd, 1956.

Willis, E. David. *Calvin's Catholic Christology*. Leiden: E. J. Brill, 1966.

### Calvin's ethics

Battles, Ford Lewis. "Notes on John Calvin, *Justitia*, and the Old Testament Law," in Dikran Y. Hadadian, ed., *Intergerini Parietis Septum (Eph. 2:14): Essays Presented to Markus Barth on his Sixty-fifth Birthday*, 23–34. Pittsburgh, PA: Pickwick Press, 1981.

Calvin, John. "Catechism of the Church of Geneva." *Calvin: Theological Treatises*, ed. and trans. J. K. S. Reid. Library of Christian Classics, vol. XXII. Philadelphia: Westminster Press, 1954.

  *John Calvin's Sermons on the Ten Commandments*. Ed. and trans. Benjamin W. Farley. Grand Rapids: Baker, 1980.

DeKlerk, Peter, ed. *Calvin and Christian Ethics: Papers and Response at the Fifth Colloquium on Calvin and Calvin Studies, May 8–9, 1985*. Grand Rapids: Calvin Studies Society, 1987.

Foxgrover, David L. *John Calvin's Understanding of Conscience*. Diss., Claremont Graduate School, California, 1978.

Haas, Guenther H. *The Concept of Equity in Calvin's Ethics*. Waterloo, Ontario: Wilfred Laurier University Press, 1997.

Hesselink, I. John. *Calvin's Concept of the Law*. Allison Park, PA: Pickwick Publications, 1992.

Johnson, Merwyn S. "Calvin's Ethical Legacy," in David Foxgrover, ed., *The Legacy of John Calvin*. Grand Rapids: CRC, 2000.

Klempa, William. "John Calvin on Natural Law," in Timothy George, ed., *John Calvin and the Church: A Prism of Reform*, 72–95. Louisville: Westminster John Knox Press, 1990.

Sauer, James B. *Faithful Ethics According to John Calvin: The Teachability of the Heart*. Toronto Series in Theology, vol. 74. Lewiston, NY: Edwin Mellen Press, 1997.

### Calvin's preaching

Armstrong, Brian G. "Exegetical and Theological Principles in Calvin's Preaching, with Special Attention to his Sermons on the Psalms," in W. H. Neuser and H. J.

Selderhuis, eds., *Ordentlich und Fruchtbar: Festschrift für Willem Van't Spijker anlässlich seiner Abschieds als Professor der Theologischen Universität Apeldorn*, 191–209. Leiden: J. J. Groen en Zoon, 1997.

Calvin, John. *Sermons From Job*. Trans. Arthur Golding. London, 1574. Selected and trans. Leroy Nixon, 1952. Rpt. Grand Rapids: Baker, 1980.

*Sermons on Galatians*. Trans. Arthur Golding. London, 1574. Rpt. Audubon, NJ: Old Paths Publications, 1995.

*Sermons on the Epistle to the Ephesians*. Trans. Arthur Golding. London, 1577. Rpt. Edinburgh: Banner of Truth Trust, 1973.

*Sermons of M. John Calvin, on the Epistles of S. Paule to Timothie and Titus*. Trans. L.T., 1579 rpt. facsimile, Edinburgh: Banner of Truth Trust, 1983.

*John Calvin's Sermons on the Ten Commandments*. Ed. and trans. Benjamin W. Farley. Grand Rapids: Baker, 1980.

*Sermons on Galatians*. Trans. Kathy Childress. Edinburgh: Banner of Truth Trust, 1997.

DeVries, Dawn. *Jesus Christ in the Preaching of Calvin and Schleiermacher*. Louisville: Westminster John Knox Press, 1996.

Leith, John H. "Calvin's Doctrine of the Proclamation of the Word and Its Significance for Today," in Timothy George, ed., *John Calvin and the Church: A Prism of Reform*, 206–29. Louisville: Westminster John Knox Press, 1990.

Millet, Olivier, *Calvin et la dynamique de la parole: étude de rhétorique réformée*. Bibliothèque littéraire de la renaissance, série 3, tome 28. Geneva: Editions Slatkine, 1992.

Moehn, Wilhelmus H. Th. *God Calls Us to His Service: The Relation Between God and His Audience in Calvin's Sermons on Acts*. Geneva: Librairie Droz, 2001.

Mülhaupt, Erwin. *Die Predigt Calvins: Ihre Geschichte, ihre Form und ihre religiösen Grundgedanken*. Arbeiten zur Kirchengeschichte, vol. 18. Berlin and Leipzig: Walter de Gruyter, 1931.

Old, Hughes Oliphant. *The Reading and Preaching of the Scriptures in the Worship of the Christian Church*. Vol. IV: *The Age of the Reformation*. Grand Rapids: Eerdmans, 2002.

Parker, T. H. L. *The Oracles of God: An Introduction to the Preaching of John Calvin*. London and Redhill: Lutterworth Press, 1947.

*Calvin's Preaching*. Louisville: Westminster John Knox Press, 1992.

Stauffer, Richard. *Dieu, la création et la Providence dans la prédication de Calvin*. Berne: Peter Lang, 1978.

Thayer, Anne T. *Penitence, Preaching and the Coming of the Reformation*. Aldershot, Hampshire, England: Ashgate Publishers, 2002.

Wallace, Ronald S. *Calvin's Doctrine of the Word and Sacrament*. Edinburgh: Oliver & Boyd, 1953.

## Calvin on piety

Armstrong, Brian. "The Nature and Structure of Calvin's Thought According to the *Institutes:* Another Look," in *John Calvin's Magnum Opus*, 55–82. Potchefstroom, South Africa: Institute for Reformational Studies, 1986.

"The Role of the Holy Spirit in Calvin's Teaching on the Ministry," in P. DeKlerk, ed., *Calvin and the Holy Spirit*, 99–111. Grand Rapids: Calvin Studies Society, 1989.

Battles, Ford Lewis. *The Piety of John Calvin. An Anthology Illustrative of the Spirituality of the Reformer.* Grand Rapids: Baker, 1978.

"True Piety According to Calvin," in R. Benedetto, ed., *Interpreting John Calvin*, 289–306. Grand Rapids: Baker, 1996.

Beeke, Joel R. "Making Sense of Calvin's Paradoxes on Assurance of Faith," in David Foxgrover, ed., *Calvin Studies Society Papers, 1995–1997*, 13–30. Grand Rapids: CRC, 1998.

*The Quest for Full Assurance: The Legacy of Calvin and His Successors.* Edinburgh: The Banner of Truth Trust, 1999.

Benoît, Jean-Daniel. "The Pastoral Care of the Prophet," in J. T. Hoogstra, ed., *John Calvin: Comtemporary Prophet*, 51–67. Grand Rapids: Baker, 1959.

Bouwsma, William. "The Spirituality of John Calvin," in Jill Raitt, ed., *Christian Spirituality: High Middle Ages and Reformation*, 318–33. New York: Crossroad, 1987.

DeJong, James A. "'An Anatomy of All Parts of the Soul': Insights into Calvin's Spirituality from His Psalms Commentary," in Wilhelm H. Neuser, ed., *Calvinus Sacrae Scripturae Professor*, 1–14. Grand Rapids: Eerdmans, 1994.

DeKlerk, Peter, ed. *Renaissance, Reformation, Resurgence.* Grand Rapids: Calvin Theological Seminary, 1976.

*Calvin and the Holy Spirit.* Grand Rapids: Calvin Studies Society, 1989.

DeKoster, Lester R. "Living Themes in the Thought of John Calvin: A Bibliographical Study." Diss., University of Michigan, 1964.

Evans, William Borden. "Imputation and Impartation: The Problem of Union with Christ in Nineteenth-Century American Reformed Theology." Diss., Vanderbilt University, 1996.

Foxgrover, David L., ed. *Calvin Studies Society Papers, 1995–1997.* Grand Rapids: CRC, 1998.

*The Legacy of John Calvin: Calvin Studies Society Papers, 1999.* Grand Rapids: CRC, 2000.

Gamble, Richard C. "Calvin and Sixteenth-Century Spirituality," in David Foxgrover, ed., *Calvin Studies Society Papers, 1995–1997*, 31–51. Grand Rapids: CRC, 1998.

Gamble, Richard C., ed. *Articles on Calvin and Calvinism, vol. 1, The Biography of Calvin.* New York: Garland, 1992.

*Articles on Calvin and Calvinism, vol. 4, Influences upon Calvin and Discussion of the 1559 Institutes.* New York: Garland, 1992.

Garside, Charles, Jr., *The Origins of Calvin's Theology of Music: 1536–1543.* Philadelphia: American Philosophical Society, 1979.

George, Timothy, ed. *John Calvin and the Church: A Prism of Reform.* Louisville: Westminster John Knox Press, 1990.

Gerrish, Brian A. "Calvin's Eucharistic Piety," in D. Foxgrover, ed., *Calvin Studies Society Papers, 1995–1997*, 52–65. Grand Rapids: CRC, 1998.

Gleason, Randall C. *John Calvin and John Owen on Mortification: A Comparative Study in Reformed Spirituality.* New York: Peter Lang, 1995.

Greve, Lionel. "Freedom and Discipline in the Theology of John Calvin, William Perkins and John Wesley: An Examination of the Origin and Nature of Pietism." Diss., Hartford Seminary Foundation. Photocopy from Ann Arbor: Xerox University Microfilms, 1976.

Gründler, Otto. "John Calvin: Ingrafting in Christ," in E. Rozanne Elder, ed., *The Spirituality of Western Christendom*, 172–87. Kalamazoo, MI: Cistercian, 1976.

Hageman, Howard G. "Reformed Spirituality," in F. C. Senn, ed., *Protestant Spiritual Traditions*, 55–79. New York: Paulist Press, 1986.

Hall, T. Hartley. "The Shape of Reformed Piety," in Robin Maas and Gabriel O'Donnell, eds., *Spiritual Traditions for the Contemporary Church*, Nashville: Abingdon Press, 1990.

Harman, Allan. "The Psalms and Reformed Spirituality," *The Reformed Theological Review* (Australia) 53/2 (1994), 53–62.

Hesselink, I. John. "Governed and Guided by the Spirit: A Key Issue in Calvin's Doctrine of the Holy Spirit," in Heiko A. Oberman et al., eds., *Das Reformierte Erbe: Festschrift für Gottfried W. Locher*, Part 2, 161–71. Zurich: TVZ, 1992.

Hoogstra, Jacob T., ed. *John Calvin, Contemporary Prophet*. Grand Rapids: Baker, 1959.

Hulse, Erroll. "The Preacher and Piety," in Samuel T. Logan, Jr., ed., *The Preacher and Preaching*, Philippsburg, NJ: Presbyterian and Reformed, 1986.

Jones, Serene. *Calvin and the Rhetoric of Piety*. Louisville: Westminster John Knox Press, 1995.

Kingdon, Robert M. "The Genevan Revolution in Public Worship," *Princeton Seminary Bulletin* 20/3 (1999), 264–80.

Kolfhaus, Wilhelm. *Christusgemeinschaft bei Johannes Calvin*. Neukirchen Kreis Moers: Buchhandlung der Erziehungsvereings, 1939.

Lambert, Thomas A. "Preaching, Praying, and Policing the Reform in Sixteenth Century Geneva." Diss., University of Wisconsin-Madison, 1998.

Lee, Sou-Young. "Calvin's Understanding of *Pietas*," in Wilhelm H. Neuser and Brian G. Armstrong, eds., *Calvinus Sincerioris Religionis Vindex*, 225–39. Kirksville, MO: Sixteenth Century Studies, 1997.

Leith, John. *John Calvin's Doctrine of the Christian Life*. Louisville: Westminster John Knox Press, 1989.

Leith, John, ed. *John Calvin: The Christian Life*. San Francisco: Harper & Row, 1984.

Loggie, R. D. "Chief Exercise of Faith: An Exposition of Calvin's Doctrine of Prayer." *Hartford Quarterly* 5 (1965), 65–81.

Maurer, H. W. "An Examination of Form and Content in John Calvin's Prayers." Diss., University of Edinburgh, 1960.

McKee, Elsie Anne. "Contexts, Contours, Contents: Towards a Description of Calvin's Understanding of Worship," in David Foxgrover, ed., *Calvin Studies Society Papers, 1995–1997*, 66–92. Grand Rapids: CRC, 1998.

  *John Calvin on the Diaconate and Liturgical Almsgiving*. Geneva: Droz, 1984.

McKee, Elsie Anne, ed. and trans. *John Calvin: Writings on Pastoral Piety*. The Classics of Western Spirituality. New York: Paulist Press, 2001.

Neuser, Wilhelm H., ed. *Calvinus Sacrae Scripturae Professor: Calvin as Confessor of Holy Scripture*. Grand Rapids: Eerdmans, 1994.

Neuser, Wilhelm H. and Armstrong, Brian G. *Calvinus Sincerioris Religionis Vindex: Calvin as Protector of the Purer Religion*. Kirksville, MO: Sixteenth Century Journal, 1997.

Oberman, Heiko A. "The Pursuit of Happiness: Calvin Between Humanism and Reformation," in J. W. O'Malley, T. Izbicki, and G. Christianson, eds., *Humanity and Divinity in Renaissance and Reformation*, 251–83. Leiden: E. J. Brill, 1993.

Old, Hughes Oliphant. *The Shaping of the Reformed Baptismal Rite in the Sixteenth Century*. Grand Rapids: Eerdmans, 1992.

"What is Reformed Spirituality? Played Over Again Lightly," in John H. Leith, ed., *Calvin Studies VII*, 61–68. Davidson, NC: n.p., 1994.

Partee, Charles. "Calvin's Central Dogma Again," *Sixteenth Century Journal* 18/2 (1987), 19–28.

"Prayer as the Practice of Predestination," in Wilhelm H. Neuser, ed., *Calvinus Servus Christi*, 241–56. Budapest: Pressabteilung des Raday-Kollegiums, 1988.

Pitkin, Barbara. "Imitation of David: David as a Paradigm for Faith in Calvin's Exegesis of the Psalms," *The Sixteenth Century Journal* 24/4 (1993), 843–63.

Raitt, Jill, ed. *Christian Spirituality: High Middle Ages and Reformation*. New York: Crossroad, 1988.

Reid, W. Stanford. "The Battle Hymns of the Lord: Calvinist Psalmody of the Sixteenth Century," in C. S. Meyer, ed., *Sixteenth Century Essays and Studies*, II, 36–54. St. Louis: Foundation for Reformation Research, 1971.

Richard, Lucien. *The Spirituality of John Calvin*. Atlanta: John Knox Press, 1974.

Senn, Frank, ed. *Protestant Spiritual Traditions*. New York: Paulist Press, 1986.

Simpson, H. W. "*Pietas* in the *Institutes* of Calvin," in *Reformational Tradition: A Rich Heritage and Lasting Vocation*, 179–91. Potchefstroom, South Africa: Potchefstroom University for Christian Higher Education, 1984.

Tamburello, Dennis. *Union with Christ: John Calvin and the Mysticism of St. Bernard*. Louisville: Westminster John Knox Press, 1994.

Tripp, Diane Karay. "Daily Prayer in the Reformed Tradition: An Initial Survey," *Studia Liturgica* 21 (1991), 76–107, 190–219.

VanderWilt, Jeffrey T. "John Calvin's Theology of Liturgical Song," *Christian Scholar's Review* 25 (1996), 63–82.

Walchenbach, John Robert. "The Influence of David and the Psalms on the Life and Thought of John Calvin." Th.M. thesis, Pittsburgh Theological Seminary, 1969.

Wallace, Ronald S. *Calvin's Doctrine of the Christian Life*. London: Oliver and Boyd, 1959.

Willis-Watkins, David. "The *Unio Mystica* and the Assurance of Faith According to Calvin," in Willem van 't Spijker, ed., *Calvin Erbe und Auftrag: Festschrift für Wilhelm Heinrich Neuser zum 65. Geburtstag*, 77–84. Kampen: Kok, 1991.

"Calvin's Theology of Pastoral Care," in John H. Leith, ed., *Calvin Studies VI*, 36–46. Davidson, NC, 1992.

"The Third Part of Christian Freedom Misplaced," in W. Fred Graham, ed., *Later Calvinism: International Perspectives*, 471–88. Kirksville, MO: Sixteenth Century Journal, 1994.

Witvliet, John. "The Spirituality of the Psalter: Metrical Psalms in Liturgy and Life in Calvin's Geneva," in David Foxgrover, ed., *Calvin Studies Society Papers, 1995–1997*, 93–117. Grand Rapids: CRC, 1998.

Zachman, Randall C. *The Assurance of Faith: Conscience in the Theology of Martin Luther and John Calvin*. Minneapolis: Fortress Press, 1993.

### Calvin and social-ethical issues

Archives d'État de Genève. Archives hospitalières and Registres du Conseil.

Biéler, André. *La pensée économique et sociale de Calvin*. Geneva: Librairies de l'Université, Georg & Cie, 1961.

Borgeaud, Charles. *Histoire de l'Université de Genève*, I, *l'Académie de Calvin, 1559–1798*. Geneva: Librairies de l'Université, Georg & Cie, 1900.

Bucer, Martin. *Common Places of Martin Bucer*. Trans. and ed. David F. Wright. The Courtenay Library of Reformation Classics, 4. Abingdon, England: Sutton Courtenay Press, 1972.

Chrisman, Miriam. *Strasbourg and the Reform: A Study in the Process of Change.* New Haven: Yale University Press, 1967.

De Bèze, Théodore and Nicolas Colladon. *Vie de Calvin*. 1–118 in *Ioannis Calvini Opera Quae Supersunt Omnia*, XXI. Ed. Guilielmus Baum, Eduardus Cunitz, and Eduardus Reuss. Brunswick: Schwetschke and Sons, 1879.

Douglass, Jane Dempsey. *Women, Freedom, and Calvin.* The 1983 Annie Kinkead Warfield Lectures. Philadelphia: Westminster Press, 1985.

Gilmont. Jean-François. "Les sermons de Calvin: de l'oral à l'imprimé," *Bulletin de la Société de l'Histoire du Protestantisme Français* 141 (1995): 157–60.

Graham, W. Fred. *The Constructive Revolutionary: John Calvin and His Socio-Economic Impact.* N.p.: Michigan State University Press, 1987.

Hall, Basil. *Humanists and Protestants, 1500–1900.* Edinburgh: T. & T. Clark, 1990.

Kingdon, Robert M. "Social Welfare in Calvin's Geneva," *American Historical Review* 76 (February 1971), 50–69.

　*Adultery and Divorce in Calvin's Geneva*. Cambridge, MA: Harvard University Press, 1995.

Lambert, Thomas. "Daily Religion in Early Reformed Geneva," 33–54 in *Université de Genève Institut d'Histoire de la Réformation Bulletin Annuel*, XXI, *1999–2000*. Geneva: University of Geneva, February 2001.

Lambert, Thomas A. and Isabella M. Watt, eds. *Registres du Consistoire de Genève au temps de Calvin*, I. Travaux d'Humanisme et Renaissance 305. Geneva: Librairie Droz, 1996.

Lindberg, Carter. "'There Should Be No Beggars Among Christians': Karlstadt, Luther, and the Origins of Protestant Poor Relief," *Church History* 46 (September 1977), 313–34.

　"Luther on Poverty," *Lutheran Quarterly* 15/1 (Spring 2001), 85–101.

Maag, Karin. *Seminary or University? The Genevan Academy and Reformed Higher Education, 1560–1620.* St. Andrews Studies in Reformation History. Aldershot, England: Scolar Press, 1995.

McKee, Elsie Anne. *John Calvin on the Diaconate and Liturgical Almsgiving.* Travaux d'Humanisme et Renaissance 197. Geneva: Librairie Droz, 1984.

　*Diakonia in the Classical Reformed Tradition and Today.* Grand Rapids: Eerdmans, 1989.

Meylan, Henri. *La haute école de Lausanne, 1537–1937: Esquisse historique publiée à l'occasion de son quatrième centenaire.* Lausanne: F. Rouge & Cie, Librairie de l'Université, 1937.

Moens, W. J. C. "The Relief of the Poor Members of the French Churches in England as Exemplified by the Practice of the Walloon or French Church in Sandwich (1568–72)," *Proceedings of the Huguenot Society of London* (January 10 and March 14, 1894), 321–38.

Mottu-Weber, Liliane. "Des vers à soie à l'Hôpital en 1610: Un bref épisode de l'histoire de la soierie à Genève," *Revue du Vieux Genève* 12 (1982), 44–9.

Olson, Jeannine. "Calvin as Pastor-Administrator during the Reformation in Geneva," *Pacific Theological Review* 14/4 (Fall 1982), 78–83, rpt. in Richard Gamble, ed.,

*Articles on Calvin and Calvinism*, III, *Calvin's Work in Geneva.* New York: Garland Publishing, 1992, 2–9.

*Calvin and Social Welfare: Deacons and the Bourse française* (Selingsgrove: Susquehanna University Press; London and Toronto: Associated University Presses, 1989).

*Deacons and Deaconesses through the Centuries: One Ministry/Many Roles.* St. Louis: Concordia Publishing House, 1992.

*Registres de la Compagnie des Pasteurs de Genève au temps de Calvin.* Published under the direction of the Archives of the State of Geneva. Geneva: Librairie Droz, 1962– .

Spitz, Lewis W. and Barbara Tinsley. *Johann Sturm on Education: The Reformation and Humanist Learning.* St. Louis: Concordia Publishing House, 1995.

Thurston, Bonnie. *The Widows: A Women's Ministry in the Early Church.* Minneapolis: Fortress Press, 1989.


## Calvin and political issues

Allen, J. W. *A History of Political Thought in the Sixteenth Century.* 2nd edition. London: Methuen, 1941.

Bavinck, Herman. "Calvin and Common Grace," *Princeton Theological Review* 7 (1909), 437–65.

Chenevière, Marc Édouard. *La Pensée politique de Calvin.* Paris: Editions Je Sers, 1937.

Hancock, Ralph C. *Calvin and the Foundations of Modern Politics.* Ithaca: Cornell, 1989.

Linder, Robert. "Was the Protestant Reformation a Revolution? The Case of Geneva," in D. Baker, ed., *Church, Society and Politics*, 203–22. Oxford: Basil Blackwell, 1975.

Little, David. *Religion, Order, and Law.* New York: Harper & Row, 1969.

Skinner, Quentin. *The Foundations of Modern Political Thought.* 2 vols. Cambridge: Cambridge University Press, 1978.

Stevenson, William R., Jr. *Sovereign Grace: The Place and Significance of Christian Freedom in the John Calvin's Political Thought.* New York: Oxford University Press, 1999.

Walzer, Michael. *The Revolution of the Saints.* Cambridge, MA: Harvard University Press, 1965.

Witte, John, Jr. "Moderate Religious Liberty in the Theology of John Calvin," *Calvin Theological Journal* 31 (1996), 359–403.

Wolin, Sheldon. *Politics and Vision.* Boston: Little, Brown, 1950.


## Calvin and Calvinism

Armstrong, Brian G. *Calvinism and the Amyraut Heresy.* Madison: University of Wisconsin Press, 1969.

Asselt, Willem J. van and Eef Dekker, eds. *Reformation and Scholasticism: An Ecumenical Enterprise.* Texts and Studies in Reformation and Post-Reformation Thought. Grand Rapids: Baker Academic, 2001.

Hall, Basil. "Calvin against the Calvinists," in G. E. Duffield, ed., *John Calvin.* Appleford: Sutton Courtenay Press, 1996.

Kendall, R. T. *Calvin and English Calvinism to 1649.* Oxford: Oxford University Press, 1979.

Muller, Richard A. *Post-Reformation Reformed Dogmatics I: Prolegomena to Theology.* Grand Rapids: Baker, 1987.

*Christ and the Decree: Christology and Predestination from Calvin to Perkins.* Grand Rapids: Baker, 1988.

"Calvin and the 'Calvinists': Assessing Continuities and Discontinuities Between the Reformation and Orthodoxy," *Calvin Theological Journal* 30 (1995), 345–75; 31 (1996), 125–60.

*After Calvin: Studies in the Development of a Theological Tradition.* Oxford Studies in Historical Theology. Oxford: Oxford University Press, 2003.

Trueman, Carl R. and R. S. Clark, eds. *Protestant Scholasticism: Essays in Reassessment.* Carlisle: Paternoster, 1998.

## Calvin's heritage
### Calvin's geographical heritage

Benedetto, Robert, Darrell L. Guder, and Donald K. McKim. *Historical Dictionary of Reformed Churches.* Lanham, MD: Scarecrow Press, 1999.

Benedict, Philip. *Christ's Churches Purely Reformed: A Social History of Calvinism.* New Haven: Yale University Press, 2002.

Duke, Alastair, Gillian Lewis, and Andrew Pettegree, eds. *Calvinism in Europe 1540–1610: A Collection of Documents.* New York: St. Martin's Press, 1992.

McNeill, John T. *The History and Character of Calvinism.* New York: Oxford University Press, 1954.

Pettegree, Andrew, Alastair Duke, and Gillian Lewis, eds. *Calvinism in Europe: 1540–1620.* New York: Cambridge University Press, 1994.

Prestwich, Menna, ed. *International Calvinism 1541–1715.* Oxford: Clarendon Press, 1985.

Reid, W. Stanford, ed. *John Calvin: His Influence in the Western World.* Grand Rapids: Zondervan Publishing House, 1982.

*World Christian Encyclopedia.* 2nd edition, ed. David B. Barrett, George T. Kurian, and Todd M. Johnson. 2 vols. Oxford: Oxford University Press, 2001.

### Calvin's theological heritage

Bratt, John H., ed. *The Heritage of John Calvin.* Grand Rapids: Eerdmans, 1973.

Frei, Hans. *The Eclipse of Biblical Narrative: A Study in Eighteenth and Nineteenth Century Hermeneutics.* New Haven, Yale University Press, 1974.

Graham, W. Fred, ed. *Later Calvinism: International Perspectives.* Kirksville, MO: Sixteenth Century Journal Publishers, 1994.

Holwerda, David E., ed. *Exploring the Heritage of John Calvin.* Grand Rapids: Baker, 1976.

Schnucker, Robert V. *Calviniana: Ideas and Influence of Jean Calvin.* Kirksville, MO: Sixteenth Century Journal Publishers, 1988.

### Calvin's economic heritage

Lüthy, Herbert. "Variations on a Theme by Max Weber," in Menna Prestwich, ed., *International Calvinism 1541–1715*, 369–90. Oxford: Oxford University Press, 1985.

Valeri, Mark. "Religion, Discipline, and the Economy in Calvin's Geneva," *Sixteenth Century Journal* 28 (1997), 123–42.
Weber, Max. *The Protestant Ethic and the Spirit of Capitalism.* Trans. Talcot Parsons. Rpt. New York: Scribner, 1958.

## Calvin's political heritage
Forrester, Duncan. "Martin Luther and John Calvin," in Leo Strauss and Joseph Cropsey, eds., *History of Political Philosophy*, 3rd edition, 318–65. Chicago: University of Chicago Press, 1987.
Kelly, Douglas F. *The Emergence of Liberty in the Modern World: The Influence of Calvin on Five Governments from the 16th through 18th Centuries.* Philipsburg, NJ: Presbyterian and Reformed Publishing Co., 1992.

## Calvin's cultural heritage
Higman, Francis. "The Reformation and the French Language," *Esprit Créateur* (Winter 1976), 20–36.
Knudsen, Robert D. "Calvinism as a Cultural Force," in W. Stanford Reid, ed., *John Calvin: His Influence in the Western World*, 13–32. Grand Rapids: Zondervan Publishing House, 1982.
Robinson, Marilynne. "McGuffey and the Abolitionists," and "Puritans and Prigs," and "Marguerite de Navarre," in *The Death of Adam: Essays on Modern Thought*, 126–49, 150–73, 174–206. Boston: Houghton Mifflin Company, 1998.

## *Calvin's role in church history*
Greef, W. de. *The Writings of John Calvin: An Introductory Guide.* Trans. Lyle D. Bierma. Grand Rapids: Baker, 1993.
Oberman, H. A. "*Europa afflicta*: The Reformation of the Refugees," *Archive for Reformation History* 83 (1992), 91–111.

## *The place of Calvin in Christian theology*
Gerrish, B[rian] A. "John Calvin on Luther" (1968), rpt. as "The Pathfinder: Calvin's Image of Luther" in Gerrish, *The Old Protestantism and the New: Essays on the Reformation Heritage*, 27–48. Edinburgh: T. & T. Clark, 1982.
"From Calvin to Schleiermacher: The Theme and the Shape of Christian Dogmatics" (1985), rpt. in Gerrish, *Continuing the Reformation: Essays on Modern Religious Thought*, 178–95. Chicago: University of Chicago Press, 1993.
Lane, Anthony N. S. *Calvin and Bernard of Clairvaux.* Studies in Reformed Theology and History, new series 1. Princeton: Princeton Theological Seminary, 1996.
Lange van Ravenswaay, J[an] Marius J. *Augustinus totus noster: Das Augustinverständnis bei Johannes Calvin.* Forschungen zur Kirchen- und Dogmengeschichte 45. Göttingen: Vandenhoeck & Ruprecht, 1990.
LaVallee, Armand Aime. "Calvin's Criticism of Scholastic Theology." Diss., Harvard University, 1967.
McGrath, Alister [E.], *The Intellectual Origins of the European Reformation.* Oxford: Blackwell, 1987.
Mooi, R. J. *Het kerk- en dogmahistorisch element in de werken van Johannes Calvijn.* Wageningen: H. Veenman & Zonen, 1965.

Oberman, Heiko. *"Initia Calvini:* The Matrix of Calvin's Reformation," in Wilhelm
H. Neuser, ed., *Calvinus sacrae scripturae professor: Calvin as Confessor of Holy
Scripture*, Papers from the International Congress on Calvin Research 1990,
113–54. Grand Rapids: Eerdmans, 1994.
Smits, Luchesius. *Saint Augustin dans l'œuvre de Jean Calvin.* 2 vols. Assen: Van
Gorcum, 1957–58.
Warfield, Benjamin Breckinridge. *Calvin and Augustine.* Ed. Samuel G. Craig.
Philadelphia: Presbyterian and Reformed Publishing Co., 1956.

*Calvin in ecumenical context*

Bauswein, Jean-Jacques and Lukas Vischer, eds. *The Reformed Family Worldwide.*
Grand Rapids: Eerdmans, 1999.
Benedetto, Robert, Darrell L. Guder, and Donald K. McKim. *Historical Dictionary of
Reformed Churches.* Lanham, MD: Scarecrow Press, 1999.
Cassidy, Edward Idris Cardinal. "Ecumenical Challenges for the Future: A Catholic
Perspective," *The Princeton Seminary Bulletin* n.s.18 (1997), 9–28.
Cochrane, Arthur C., ed. *Reformed Confessions of the Sixteenth Century.* New Intro-
duction by Jack Rogers. Louisville: Westminster John Knox Press, 2003.
Fey, Harold E., ed. *The Ecumenical Advance: A History of the Ecumenical Movement,
Volume II, 1948–1968.* 2nd edition. Geneva: World Council of Churches, 1986.
Finney, Paul Corby, ed. *Seeing Beyond the Word: Visual Arts and the Calvinist Tradi-
tion.* Grand Rapids: Eerdmans, 1999.
McNeill, John T. and James Hastings Nichols. *Ecumenical Testimony: The Concern for
Christian Unity Within the Reformed and Presbyterian Churches.* Philadelphia:
Westminster Press, 1974.
Oberman, Heiko A. *The Roots of Anti-Semitism in the Age of Renaissance and Refor-
mation.* Philadelphia: Fortress Press, 1984.
Pradervand, Marcel. *A Century of Service: A History of the World Alliance of Reformed
Churches 1875–1975.* Grand Rapids: Eerdmans, 1975.
Rohls, Jan. *Reformed Confessions: Theology from Zurich to Barmen.* Trans. John
Hoffmeyer. Columbia Series in Reformed Theology. Louisville: Westminster
John Knox Press, 1998.
Rouse, Ruth and Charles Neill, eds. *A History of the Ecumenical Movement 1517–
1948.* 3rd edition. Geneva: World Council of Churches, 1986.
Sell, Alan P. F. *A Reformed, Evangelical, Catholic Theology: The Contribution of the
World Alliance of Reformed Churches, 1875–1982.* Grand Rapids: Eerdmans,
1991.
Vischer, Lukas. "The Ecumenical Commitment of the World Alliance of Reformed
Churches," *Reformed World* 38 (1985), 261–81.
Vischer, Lukas, ed. *Reformed Witness Today: A Collection of Confessions and State-
ments of Faith Issued by Reformed Churches.* Berne: Evangelische Arbeitsstelle
Oekumene Schweiz, 1982.
*Rowing in One Boat: A Common Reflection on Lutheran–Reformed Relations World-
wide.* Geneva: John Knox Centre International Réformé, 1999.

# Index